LANGUAGE

An Introductory Reader

LANGUAGE
An Introductory Reader

J. Burl Hogins
Robert E. Yarber

San Diego Mesa College

Harper & Row, Publishers
New York, Evanston, and London

Contents

Preface

Although most students come to college with 17 or 18 years of language experience, they rarely arrive liking the study of their native tongue. We can account for this antipathy in several ways: impoverished backgrounds, poor texts, or even poor teaching. Despite the cause, however, we college English teachers must meet its challenge. We must demonstrate, even to the recalcitrant student, the truth of Wittgenstein's observation: "The limits of my language mean the limits of my world."

It is in response to this need that we have designed this book. As the table of contents indicates, 47 essays are organized around ten major concepts, ranging from "What Is Language?" to "Semantics" to "How Language Shapes Our Thoughts." Following each unit are discussion questions and writing suggestions, as well as a list of recommended readings. Of particular interest for both student and teacher is the inclusion in the text of an objective test for each essay. This test may be used by the student as a self-check of his understanding of the selection, or by the teacher as the basis for class discussion or as a comprehension quiz. Emphasis throughout the book is on student interest. The first unit, for example, acknowledges the racial crisis and its linguistic implications. Nor have classic readings been ignored. It should be emphasized, however, that only those essays that have been found to be teachable, relevant, and challenging to today's student are included. In short, we believe this text has a freshness and point of view with which the student can immediately identify.

In the preparation of this book we have profited immeasurably from the suggestions of Clay Stratton, of Harper & Row, Publishers.

San Diego, California   J. Burl Hogins
                                                                 Robert E. Yarber

LANGUAGE
An Introductory Reader

A Linguistic
Potpourri

I

Wallop Yon Horse with a Parachute

by LEO ROSTEN

Going abroad? The guidebooks all urge you to learn a few basic phrases in the natives' language—on the assumption that foreigners love to hear an American roll his tongue around theirs. Well, I hate to say this, but the advice is cockeyed, and if you fall for it, you'll end up up to your armpits in the treacherous quicksands of phonetics.

Suppose you're in Uzbek and utter a debonair "Hello, Charley," in Kurdish. Sure, that will flatter a Kurd, but it also makes him think you understand his nasty lingo, so his eyes light up, and he answers you in a burst of colloquial Kurdish, which can give any American the heebie-jeebies. No, dear voyager, follow my advice: *Never try to speak a foreign tongue.* Speak English. The natives, spotting you for the illiterate you are, will knock themselves out to help you—and their joyous little cries and signs and pigeon prattle will be a lot easier for you to understand than the gibberish they let fly if you suck them in with a breezy *"Où est la can, frère Jacques?"* or *"Haben Sie ein Autojack?"*

The slightest slip in pronouncing one little vowel, in any patois, can make bedlam pop all around you. Take our own English, which is sheer misery for a foreigner to pronounce. The difference between "Call me" and "Kill me," for instance, is only 1/64 of an inch of air space, so a greenhorn in a hurry can wind up dead. I once had a sinister Moroccan accost me in Chicago with "Hollow Sarah!" Only quick thinking kept me from defending both my solidity and my manhood: The poor wretch obviously thought he was producing the proper noises for *"Hello, sir."* Or take a simple, straightforward sentence like "I want my meat well-done." Unsteadily uttered by, say, a Sicilian, that sentence comes out, "I want my mate walled in." Very few restaurants in New York will brick up your wife on such short notice.

Now, exactly the same booby traps await the *americano* who is fool enough to wander into the jungle of an alien argot. This morning in Paris (pronounced "Paree"), my dear wife almost drove the hotel *concierge* into a squirrel cage when she complained about the feeble amount of heat (the Gauls call it *chauffage*) coming out of our radiator. What Madame Rosten actually *said,* in her revised, unstandard version of French, was: "Attention! Chauffeurs are missing from my radiant editor!" The *concierge* replied that Madame's radiant editor (me) had ordered a car and chauffeur for 11, and it was only 8:40. My wife wailed that she had been shivering with cold since 6:20 and wanted the chauffeur turned up at once. The *concierge* exclaimed that he would telephone the garage immediately. My irate wife cried: "Stop trying to save a buck by borrowing a heater from a garage! Just rouse your lazy janitor, who is probably napping, or your phony superintendent, and turn up the heat or I'll report you to the police!" So the *concierge* phoned a superintendent of the police and demanded he turn up a chauffeur who had been kidnapped by a lazy janitor.

Semantic snafus like that can just about unhinge you. In Tokyo, last April, I carefully read aloud, from *"You, Too, Can Speak Japanese,"* the phonetic syllables for "I—would—like—a—massage." To which the Oriental attendant replied, with ceremonial hisses of joy and abnegation: "I would be honored to carry you there on my *back,* exalted thimble, but the cat is already late for the wedding." I think I had misled him. Either that, or he was relying on his vest-pocket edition of *"You, Too, Can Spoke Engrish."*

Occidental places can be just as disorienting. I once entered a men's store in Madrid and, in admirable Spanish, told the clerk I wanted to buy an umbrella and a pair of gloves. The oaf turned white, whinnied and ran away, bleating for his superior, to whom I coolly repeated: "I want—one—umbrella—and—pair—of—man's—gloves." The superior Iberian flinched. "But, *señor,*" the man quavered, "why you wish to wallop yon horse with a parachute?" Oh, it was jolly.

(The Spanish for umbrella is *paraguas,* which I mangled into *paracas,* which they took to mean *paracaidas,* which means parachute. Gentleman is *caballero,* which I gulped into *caballo,* which means horse. It was a cinch to nose-dive from *guante* [glove] to *guantada* [wallop] because I have never laid a glove on a horse, much less walloped one with a parachute. I have never even chastised a Chihuahua. Not even with a feather, which is *pluma,* much less a *plancha,* which is flatiron.)

I don't care *how* easy the guidebooks tell you it is to toss off a few fruity phrases in Flemish or Romanian or Greek. The depressing truth is that any language simply bulges with laryngeal traps and idiomatic ambushes. *Regardez* what happened yesterday to a handsome, intelligent, upstanding young American who went to a railway station in Paris to get some information on trains running to Nice. I came armed with a charming

little guide to French I had picked up at a great bargain (so what if it was
published in 1860?) from a bookstall on the Left Bank. The charade that
followed with the cretin behind the bars took this form—and I reserve all
dramatic rights, including the Swahili:

I (*smiling*):   *Bonjour, M'sieur,* is not this day reliable?

TICKET AGENT (*saluting*):   You speak French! What joys! Let me wax your
   elbow.

I (*modestly*):   *Voilà!* To affairs?

TICKET AGENT (*beaming*):   Advance.

I (*chuckling*):   I demand you: When, dear Amy (*cher ami*), does gentleman
   train go toward lady Nice?

TICKETEER (*enthusiastic*):   They are *very* nice trains, wet knight. Clean.
   Metallic. Ferrous.

I (*clearing throat*):   I fear I have been soft. What I intended to choke you
   is: "Explain such trains' *schedule!*"

TICKETEER (*crying*):   Who can blame you? You think *I* understand those
   swearing schedules? They are a sponge on French honor! They rife!
   They glut! They snore—

I: Please—only what—*time*—does—the—train— ·

TICKETEER (*slapping forehead*):   The *time?!* Smite my neck for buttering
   your confusion. It takes 12 hours from Paris.

I: No, no, I do not want the interval between farewelling Paris and hello-
   ing Nice. What I chattered was: "When—*when*—"

TICKETEER (*excited*):   *Always* it occupies 12 hours! Saturdays, Sundays, wash-
   days, apricots—

I: Please, dear backache, speak *slower.*

TICKETEER: Slower marches our *local train.* Naturally, the wagons are of
   diminished luxury—

I: (*shouting*):   Who denies? Merely recite! When shrink trains from Paris
   to the south—the *sud*—

TICKETEER (*flinging hands heavenward*):   Ahhh, a thousand apologies for
   my porcupine! Let us banish error once and for alright: To reach the
   Sudan, you approximate Marseilles—

I: The *south*—

TICKETEER (*puzzled*):   The Sudan *is* south of dirty Marseilles!

I: Of—*France!*

TICKETEER: It is south of France also. From Marseilles, you eat the bark
   off a boat—

I (*hollering*):   No! Arrest! I do not gnaw vessels! I thirst but one small piece
   of *entirely different in-for-ma-tion!*

Fourteen hours later, safe and sound, I was in Innsbruck. Well, it does
begin with "in" and *is* a small piece of an entirely different nation.

Alors, then, my innocents, profit from my porcupine. Shun the natives' own locutions. Dodge the sly cedilla, the *accent grave,* the umbrageous umlaut. If you want to buy a drink in Portugal, just say: "Booze—on the rocks." To see a movie in Russia, hail a *muzhik*: "Sasha, which way to the RKO Lenin?" If you're lost in Mozambique, stop any yokel with a bright "Blessings from your patron saint, and how do I get to the flea market?" Five will get you twenty if the peon doesn't take you by the hand and lead you there himself. Why drive the locals *loco* by asking them to wallop yon horse with a parachute?

COMPREHENSION QUIZ

1. Guidebooks urge travelers going abroad to
    a. practice a few phrases.
    b. learn several key verbs.
    c. learn a few idioms.
    d. learn a few basic sentences and questions.
2. The author says that advice to learn part of a language before traveling is
    a. unwise.
    b. crazy.
    c. treacherous.
    d. cockeyed.
3. The advice of the author is
    a. never attend foreign films.
    b. never try to speak a foreign tongue.
    c. try to unlearn English.
    d. forget your past failures.
4. According to the author, the depressing truth is that every language bulges with laryngeal traps and
    a. fruity phrases.
    b. idomatic ambushes.
    c. charming swamps.
    d. battered bulwarks.

DISCUSSION QUESTIONS

1. If you were trying to write a phrase book in English for foreign language speakers, what would be your main headings?
2. Has travel outside this country given you uncommon problems with language? Explain.
3. Point out several puns of Rosten. For example, when he tells of a difficulty in Japan, he says he was dis*oriented.*

WRITING SUGGESTIONS

1. Pretend you are trying to explain to someone poorly acquainted with our language the simple matters of cooking a hamburger, or getting the gas and oil checked at a service station.
2. Explain the background of the language difficulties you have had in another country.

Language
and Myths
About Language

by JACOB ORNSTEIN and WILLIAM GAGE

The Importance of Speech

Probably one of the first things you did this morning was talk to some-body. What's so remarkable about that? Most of the other two and one-half billion people in the world did the same thing. But suppose a dog awoke one morning and started talking! It would make the front page of every newspaper in the world.

We are so used to talking and hearing other people talk that we forget what a marvelous accomplishment human speech is. Only when we consider the plight of *not* being able to talk may we fully appreciate its importance.

Consider a deaf-mute or an aphasia victim, a person, that is, who sud-denly loses the ability to talk. He may still understand what is said and even communicate in writing; but such a person is as badly handicapped as one with the most distressing physical impairment. He needs institutional care in the same way as any cripple, or special training, at least, to enable him to carry on in the outside world.

One of the authors communicated with an aphasia victim recently, who could say almost nothing, and even said the reverse of what he meant—an intended "No" coming out "Yes," and vice versa. The man was a wealthy Florida realtor, yet one day he wrote: "Believe me, I'd give all my property and savings if I could only talk again."

By contrast, reading and writing—marks on paper that stand for speech sounds—are much less important. In fact, half the people on earth, even in

From Jacob Ornstein and William Gage, *The ABC's of Languages and Linguistics,* Philadelphia: Chilton Book Company, 1964. Reprinted by permission of the publisher.

this modern and advanced day, are illiterate or unable to read and write. Many of the world's languages, probably a large majority, have no writing system at all.

So although literacy is a tremendous advantage in human society, it is by no means essential. That is, you can still get along without being able to read or write. "Readers and writers, I can buy by the yard," says a New York City garment district tycoon.

Of course, this does not change the fact that illiteracy is one of the world's great social and educational problems. The point is that illiteracy does not incapacitate humans in the same way that aphasia does. People who cannot read or write may still get along quite well in our society, and even become successful. The speechless man is a hospital case until he is cured or rehabilitated.

There is a well-known story in the Bible that reflects the importance of language in human society. According to the Old Testament mankind spoke only one language until Nimrod began to build a tower that was to reach heaven. "And the Lord said, 'Behold, they are one people, and they have all one language, and this is only the beginning of what they will do; and nothing that they propose to do will now be impossible for them. Come, let us go down, and there confuse their language, that they may not understand one another's speech.' "

Some scholars attribute the source of this legend to the many languages of the slaves who were gathered together to build the famous "hanging gardens" of Babylon. The name "Babel" is said to be a variation of the word "Babylon," rather than the Hebrew *balal,* meaning "to confuse."

Some people believe there is nothing men couldn't do if they really understood each other's speech. Utopia requires far more than that, no doubt, but it is true that a shared tongue tends to unite people, while different languages divide them. If you have ever lived in an environment where you didn't understand the language, you know from your personal experience how welcome a few words of your native speech can sound. Even in the strange accents of strangers, our native tongue seems lovely to us, and we have a fellow-feeling for those who speak as we do.

George Bernard Shaw said that England and America are two countries separated by the same language. The wit of this remark results, partly, from the way it clashes with our conviction that the same language really unites people. A New York psychiatrist's experience corroborates this. By learning the jargon of emotionally disturbed hotrodders, he was able to communicate with them by discussing drag racing and other "tribal customs."

The story of the Tower of Babel shows how using different languages divides people. An even sharper distinction is that between users and non-users of language. This very ability to use language is one of the chief differences between man and the lower animals. The difference between language and animal cries is truly basic. It is brought out by the traditional linguistic definition: A language is a structured system of vocal symbols by which a social group cooperates. Animals may have social groups, and may cooperate by a system of vocal sounds. A recent study of porpoises indicates that this may go much further than we ever imagined in complexity. But the key words are "structured" and "symbols." An animal's alarm call does not "stand for" the idea of danger in anything like the same way that the word "tree" symbolizes everything from a small dogwood to a towering sequoia. Even clearer is the structural nature of language. Human speech is "put together." Words are affected by the other words that surround them in speech. Some words have no separate meaning. "With" or "and," for instance, do not stand for any idea by themselves. They are just the mortar that unites other words into a structural unit. Animal communication shows nothing like this.

The Unexpected Intricacies of Other People's Languages

At a party recently a linguist was asked whether people like the Eskimos had a real language or whether they just communicated through gestures and grunts. The gentlemen who asked this question, a well-educated person with a master's degree, was truly amazed when he learned that the Eskimos not only have a real language but that it is very complex in structure from our point of view. Then the linguist completely overwhelmed the linguistically-naive guest by writing for him a single word in Eskimo which is equivalent to an entire sentence in English or any European tongue. It was *A:slisa-ut-issar-si-niarpu-ba,* which simply means "I am looking for something suitable for a fishline."

There is probably no subject about which there are so many errors and downright misinformation as that of language—even among persons of higher education. One of the most widespread of these is that the language of technologically underdeveloped or primitive peoples must be very simple and crude. The fact of the matter is that from the standpoint of the speaker of English or a European tongue the languages of such groups often contain difficulties and subtleties which do not exist in our own.

Although English speakers may think it is unusual that certain languages have gender for verbs, much stranger things may be found. In the Nahuatl (Modern Aztec) of northern Mexico, for example, it is necessary in certain verbal forms to express whether the purpose of the action affects an animate being or an inanimate object. In English we say "I *see* the women" and "I *see* the house" and the verb does not change. In Nahuatl, however, in using the verb "to eat" with the root *cua,* the Aztec speaker makes sure to prefix *tla* to indicate that he is not eating a human being. It has been pointed out that this distinction appears most clearly in such words as *tetlazohtlani*, "one who loves (people)," as contrasted with *tla-tlazohtlani*, "one who loves (things)."

In Hupa, an Indian language of northern California, nouns as well as verbs have tenses. Thus one finds the following distinctions:

xonta—house (now existing)
xontate—house which will exist in the future
xontaneen—house which formerly existed

Even the speakers of many so-called primitive languages are convinced that their native speech has no grammar but feel that the users just make it up as it comes into their heads. They do, of course, having been trained since infancy to all of its ins and outs. When one of us tries to learn such a tongue he is, however, usually confronted by a system with some bewildering intricacies. There may be the necessity for distinguishing between objects which are in sight and those which aren't, as in southern Paiute where *ma avaaniaak'a a* means "He will give something visible to someone in sight."

There is the possibility of having different verb forms not only to show whether the principal object involved is an agent or something acted on—as with active and passive voice in some familiar languages—but in addition, as in many Philippine languages, to show that it is the instrument or that it is the beneficiary of an action. Thus in Maranao

somombali so mama sa sapi ko gelat (Emphasis on *so mama*, "the man")	"The man slaughters the cow with a knife."
or	
isomabali o mama so gelat ko sapi (Emphasis on *so gelat*, "a knife")	"With a knife, the man slaughters the cow."
begen ian reka	"He'll give it to you." (give–something he to–you)
began ka ian	"You he'll give it to." (give–for someone you he)

Different verb forms may be used to indicate who does what when relating an incident. In English our use of *he, she, it,* and *they* is often ambiguous: "When Tom went hunting with Harry, he shot a moose." Who shot a moose? In Cree when the "party of the first part," "of the second part," and sometimes "of the third part" are indicated, one says:

wāpamēw	A saw B
wāpamik	B saw A
wāpamēyiwa	B saw C

Returning to Eskimo, which was thought to be so primitive by the aforementioned dinner guest, we ought to point out that indeed its structure appears formidable to one acquainted with only Indo-European patterns. It is what is known as a polysynthetic, which means that entire sentences are incorporated into a single word. Each element of the word carries meaning but does not have an independent existence. We see immediately that the traditional parts of speech of Latin or English grammar become inadequate or actually misleading in describing such a tongue. For example, "Do you think he really intends to go to look after it?" can be expressed in Eskimo by the word: *Takusar-iartor-uma-faluar-nerp-a.*

This brings us to the misconception that all languages can be analyzed as one would analyze a European tongue such as Latin, Greek, or French. The American school of scientific linguists has done a great deal to break down this fallacy, thanks to the field work it has done in such remote areas as Africa, the Marshall Islands, and North and South American reservations. Each language is in a way an island, an entity unto itself, and must be approached as such. Distinctions which are important in one language or group of languages may be insignificant or entirely lacking in another. For example, in Hungarian and the Uralic tongues for the most part, gender, which is so important in the Romance languages and German, does not matter. This is carried so far that no separate words exist for *he* and *she,* both of which are expressed by *Ő*. Within a sentence, however, it becomes clear that one is talking about a female, either of the human or animal species. While the Romance languages as well as English make subtle distinctions in past tenses, such as "I looked," "I was looking," "I did look," or "I had looked," Chinese has basically only one form for the verb, as *kan,* "look, looked, will look, is looking," etc. However, suffixes may be added to the verbs to indicate various aspects, as *kanle,* "had looked, have looked, will have looked." This parallels the English perfect, which may be found in past, present, or future, though the English speaker, including many who have written grammars of Chinese, is inclined to feel that *-le* equates with the English past tense. There are many other aspects in Chinese.

It is interesting, even fascinating, to observe the distinctions that some languages make, while in others they are non-existent. One of the commonest of these is between a "we" which includes "you" and a "we but not you," as in the Maranao tongue:

Inclusive	*Exclusive*
tano	kami

To give just another example of linguistic variety, the Turkish language makes a strict distinction between personally observed and hearsay or attested past. For instance, to express the sentence, "His daughter was very beautiful," one of the two following forms must be used:

Hearsay	*Attested*
Kiz çok güzel imiş	Kiz çok güzel idi

In the first example *imiş* is used because the speaker does not know the statement to be a fact since he has no personal knowledge of it; while in the second *idi* is employed because he has personally verified that the young lady in question was beautiful.

In Basque, a non-Indo-European language spoken in the Spanish and French Pyrenees, the verb "has" affixes to indicate the subject, object, recipient, and the sex of the person addressed. In Japanese the terms of Indo-European grammar do not work too well either. In that language, for instance, *shiro* by itself stands for "white." Add the ending *katta* and you get *shirokatta*—"it was white," or literally, "it whited."

While it is impossible to delve deeply into the formal linguistics in a work of this scope, let us note—just to satisfy the curiosity of those with special thirst for knowledge—what sort of terminology the modern scientific linguist uses. Instead of using the traditional parts of speech whether they fit or not, he arranges the grammatical elements into form classes. Thus the Japanese words like *shiroi* are classified not as adjectives but into a particular form class, with explanations of both their adjectival, verbal, and other uses.

Other Misconceptions

One reason why we often assume that other peoples must express their thoughts the way it is done in English, German, or other European languages is that for centuries we have been under the influence of the classical traditions. This means that it was the custom to regard Greek and Latin as ideal languages and to speak of other tongues in the same terms until this was changed by the advent in the twentieth century of the American school of scientific linguistics.

Another widespread misconception is that other peoples must necessarily express a given thought as we do. That this is far from the case is, of course, reflected in the very term *idiom* which comes from the Greek word *idios* meaning individual (and from which the word *idiot* is also derived). No two languages in the world express all concepts and thoughts in exactly the same way. We say in English "I am hungry," but in French it is *"J'ai faim"*—which is more literally "I have hunger." All European languages have some way of saying "How are you?" but Burmese has no such expression and one must employ instead one of five or six levels of politeness. We say "I feel sorry for you," but Japanese renders this thought by *O kinodoku desu* or literally "It's a poison for your soul."

Information about the real world is organized according to the linguistic patterns of a given speech community in ways which are to a great extent arbitrary and not according to the canons of logic. All grammars contain a great deal that goes contrary to what we would regard as the sensible way of organizing things, and it is a mistake to think that any language is particularly logical or that the more exotic languages are as a whole less logical than the more familiar ones.

This divergence in patterns of expression is the reason that so many feel that every tongue has its own soul or spirit which means something beyond mere vocabulary and grammar. This is why no matter how well-done a translation may be, something will always be lost from the original because every language is inextricably interwoven with the peculiar culture of its speakers. As Dr. W. R. Parker of Indiana University has remarked, when in Goethe's *Faust* Dr. Faustus stops addressing Margaret by the formal *Sie* (for "you") and uses the intimate *du,* there is nothing in English which can convey this subtle yet significant change in tone. Here again the individual who in learning a tongue goes beyond its basic everyday expressions and becomes acquainted with its nuances and fine distinctions is in the best position to analyze what makes its speakers tick linguistically—and to a large extent, psychologically.

Still another type of myth is the one regarding the superiority and inferiority of languages. There is in fact a tremendous body of folklore built up about most tongues. Regarding French there is the legend that it possesses special attributes which enable it to express thoughts more clearly than in any other language. There is even a saying in French, *Ce qui n'est pas clair, n'est pas français:* "What is not clear, is not French." Nationalistic Germans have attributed to their language mystic qualities which supposedly give it special powers of vigorous expression. About Italian there exist many beliefs regarding its sonority and musicality. Incidentally, in this vein the Spanish emperor Charles V once said that English was the language to speak with merchants, German with soldiers, French with women, Italian with friends, and Spanish with God!

These beliefs have no basis in scientific linguistic fact any more than the assertions that any given language is prettier than another. Like the beauty of a painting or that of a woman, the charm of any tongue lies solely in the eyes—or ears—of the beholder. One often hears that German is not as beautiful as Spanish or Italian because it is guttural, and in the aesthetic judgment of some people gutturalness sounds harsh. From the scientific linguistic viewpoint this judgment is meaningless and a linguist would merely say that German has more guttural sounds than English, French, or Italian, or in more technical phraseology, that German has a high number of sounds produced with the velum, the flap of flesh which hangs down at the back of the mouth and which cuts off the breath stream between the oral and nasal cavity. Yet to many speakers of Semitic languages, gutturalness is not only not a defect but is a positive virtue. In Israel to speak Hebrew with a markedly guttural pronunciation is considered very chic. Arabic has an unusually high number of guttural sounds but few persons who claim this as their mother tongue would consider it one iota less beautiful than, let's say, French or English.

It is equally false to believe that the sounds of a particular language are in themselves easy or difficult. The degree of difficulty is dependent on the language background with which we start, and there are probably no sounds that the speakers of some language would not have trouble with. Incidentally, children of, say, a year and a half old, who have not yet mastered their own language, often make use of many sounds that the adults of their speech communities would class as extremely difficult. Learning the sounds of a first language is in part a process of learning to avoid sounds that don't belong to it.

At the root of many linguistic misconceptions is the undeniable fact that many people regard language as static and inflexible rather than something dynamic and ever-changing. It is common to hear statements to the effect that a certain language is incapable of expressing the concepts of modern society. This is a fallacy, and from the evidence of linguistic science there does not appear to be any tongue which cannot be harnessed to serve any verbal communication need. The fact that languages may express concepts through different patterns does not alter this principle at all. When Wycliffe was told that English was too "rude" for the Scriptures to appear in, he retorted, "It is not so rude as they are false liars."

It is, however, undeniable that the Wichita language of the Oklahoma Indian tribe of 500 souls is not in its present state suitable for discussing nuclear physics or celestial navigation. But this is primarily because the speakers of Wichita have never had to cope with such problems using their native language. If, however, the roles of Wichita and English were reversed, it might be English which would lack specialized terminology and expressions.

We do not know the details of the origin of speech. But we do know that languages have an organic existence, and that they develop according to the needs of the community employing them. The more technologically advanced the speakers are, the more equipped the language will be to cope with science, technology, and the concepts of an industrialized society. Conversely, the languages of such advanced nations as America, Germany, and France may and often do lack numerous concepts and nuances referring to the phenomena of nature and to pursuits like herding, hunting, and fishing, which are elaborately present in many tongues of people of a more primitive culture. Berber has a far richer vocabulary for discussing camels and livestock and their care than has Danish or Italian. Hopi is apparently far better equipped to deal with descriptions of vibratory phenomena than is any European language.

There are languages in existence in which there is no way of saying *stereophonic playback recorder* or *atomic warhead*. But this does not mean that the speakers of these languages could not coin such expressions. The coining of new terms—and this important fact is often not realized—is part of the organic development of any living language in a dynamically growing society. For example, the reason why the ancient Greek Homer had no word for motorcar is simply because he did not have such a vehicle to convey him through the hills and dales of his homeland. The modern Greeks, however, have coined a word for this useful vehicle terming it *autokinito,* composed of *auto* (self) and *kinito* (moving thing). That, after all, is the way the term *automobile,* used in most European languages, was conceived and constructed. But tastes vary in languages and although Czech, for example, uses the word *automobil,* Polish has preferred to express the same concept by the word *samochod,* composed of the elements *samo* (self) and *chod* (moving).

The Thai language was not equipped until a few years ago with words for most modern innovations. There was a tradition in Thailand of using Sanskrit roots in technical vocabulary much as we make use of Greek (astronomy, epiglottis, etc.). With modernization the Thais have avidly set about the business of coining new words, even to the extent of having contests for the best word made up to express some new western-derived concept. Preferably the new words should include Sanskrit elements already used in Thai and, ideally, should have some resemblance in sound to the term used in European languages.

The growth and development of languages presents still other opportunities for myth-building. It has been difficult for people to realize that every language is in a constant state of flux and is at any period moving in new directions usually considered to be corrupt and decadent by the purists. The constant mutability of language is obscured because of the tendency to think in terms of the standardized written form of a language. People felt that Latin was still the same thing the whole of the time that spoken Latin was becoming transformed into French, Spanish, Italian, and the other modern Romance languages. Beliefs in immunity to change on the part of any living language are totally without foundation. To this class we must consign all allegations that any language known within the span of recorded history is not really at all close to the original language of the first days of human speech. . . . Another perennial favorite that crops up here is the story that somewhere—usually in the mountains of Kentucky— the natives still speak "pure Elizabethan English."

Many of the most persistent myths about language occur in the field of the relation of speech to writing. Commonly people feel that a language which has never been written is not really a language at all. In fact an unwritten language can have all the other attributes of any language and can even have a rich literature, although necessarily a literature limited to what is handed down by oral tradition. In the case of languages which have been written for centuries people often feel that the writing represents the real language and the spoken form only a pale and probably corrupted reflection of it. Scientific linguists, while understanding the great importance of the written form and recognizing the many ways in which writing and speech interact with each other, are nevertheless forced to maintain the view that speaking is the basic symbol-using activity of mankind and that writing is a superstructure built upon it.

Fact, fancy, and even prejudice exist about languages just as they do about individuals and nations. While some of these beliefs are romantic and many appeal to the imagination, it would seem to be far better to know more about the true nature of language as a branch of the behavioral sciences than to perpetuate old wives' tales about it. . . .

COMPREHENSION QUIZ

1. How many of the world's languages have no writing system at all?
    a.   None.
    b.   A few.
    c.   Approximately half.
    d.   A large majority.
2. A language is a series of vocal symbols in a system which is
    a.   arbitrary.
    b.   structured.
    c.   without design.
    d.   without recurrence.
3. Non-European languages usually
    a.   follow the English system of tense.
    b.   contain difficulties and subtleties not found in English.
    c.   follow the English sentence pattern and syntax.
    d.   are easier to learn than English.
4. The Eskimo language can be analyzed in terms of
    a.   Latin.
    b.   Greek.
    c.   French.
    d.   none of the above.
5. The scientific linguist arranges grammatical elements into
    a.   traditional parts of speech.
    b.   synonyms and antonyms.
    c.   form classes.
    d.   none of the above.

6. The belief that one language is inherently pleasanter than another
   a. has no basis in scientific linguistic fact.
   b. has been demonstrated by scientific linguistic fact.
   c. accounts for the popularity of Italian opera singers.
   d. has had few adherents.
7. Language is
   a. static.
   b. dynamic.
   c. governed solely by logic.
   d. inflexible.
8. Although recognizing that writing and speech interact, scientific linguists believe that
   a. a study of the spoken form is more important.
   b. a language which has never been written is not really a language at all.
   c. the written form represents the real language.
   d. all spoken languages have a tendency to decay.

DISCUSSION QUESTIONS

1. What myths about language did you hold that were "exploded" in this essay?
2. What is the real form of a language: the spoken, or the written? Why?
3. Why would it be difficult to conduct a scientific meeting in the Apache dialect?
4. The authors of this essay claim there is no basis to believing that any particular language is intrinsically pleasanter than another. Do you disagree? Do some languages sound more beautiful to you than others?
5. How do the vocal sounds of the lower animals differ from those of man?
6. How do you explain the fact that the languages of primitive peoples often contain complexities and subtleties which do not exist in English? Why are they designated "so-called" primitive languages?

WRITING SUGGESTIONS

1. What evidence can you cite from your own experience that language is ever-changing? Consider pronunciation, meaning, spelling, and the addition of new words to the language.
2. Use the following quotation as the basis of a composition: "England and America are two countries separated by the same language."
3. If you are familiar with another language, what important distinctions in English are either insignificant or entirely lacking in the other language? Write a theme contrasting the distinctions.
4. How is each nation or culture the "prisoner" of its language?
5. What are some of the changes in attitudes toward language brought about by the American school of scientific linguistics?

6. In what ways are the linguistic patterns of English arbitrary? In what ways do they follow the canons of logic? Write a theme in which you present several examples of each kind of pattern. What conclusions can you make about the "logic" of English?

The Future
of Anglo-American

by ANTHONY BURGESS

Those rational horses of Gulliver's Utopia affirmed, in High Dutch neighings, that the telling of lies was not just an immoral act; it was a subversion of the purpose of language. After all, men developed language in order to communicate, and yet they consistently use it to convey "the thing which is not"—in other words, they will as readily discommunicate as communicate. Such equine ingenuousness is perhaps appropriate to an age which believed in reason and was soon to produce Jean-Jacques Rousseau. Lying, we must all accept, is a device to avoid tears, fighting, the loss of face; without deliberate lying we would soon have anarchy—all right for Houyhnhnms but not for Yahoos. Deliberate lying is in order; what worries me more and more these days is lying of an undeliberate kind.

We are all subject to the need for undeliberate lies. Whenever I commit myself to a generalization I have to lie—boldly and with a sort of desperation. "Chinese women have exquisite legs." Do they? I've seen many who have not. "For the most part," then. How do I know? Have I actually made an examination of the millions of pairs of female Chinese legs available on both sides of the Bamboo Curtain? Very well, then. "Of all the Chinese women I have seen, a great many have exquisite legs." Suspect, suspect. Are they any different from other women? "Some women have exquisite legs." And some women have not. I have failed to lie, and in so doing I have failed to engage. I've said nothing.

The circle is very vicious. "An oak is a tree" is an acceptable statement, so long as we are sure what a tree is (and an oak, for that matter), but human intercourse cannot be conducted on the basis of Lesson I of a language primer. Philosophers like Bertrand Russell used to insist that the

From Anthony Burgess, "The Future of Anglo-American," *Harper's Magazine*, February, 1968. Copyright © 1968 by Harper's Magazine, Inc. Reprinted by permission of Ashley Famous Agency, Inc., New York.

only acceptable statements were tautologies like "An oak is an oak" or "A rose is a rose" (Gertrude Stein took it further and made even tautology suspect). But language, of its very nature, resists tautology; it wants to launch out, risk lies, say "the thing which is not." And so human society is committed to downright lying ("You're the most beautiful girl in the world") or to the conjuring trick of bogus meaningfulness which is very nearly a lie. Gobbledygook is a means of disguising lies, and also a device for rendering sheer portentousness of sound somehow superior to the covenants of meaning. Last night on television I heard a doctor of divinity speaking about the achievement of an "ecumenical dialogue." It would be mean to question the meaning. I heard somebody else in a current-affairs program (I hope he was not from the Pentagon, but I fear he was) talk of a "viable escalation."

Generalize and you lie; avoid lies and you are left with tautology and gobbledygook—which, since neither predicates anything about anything, come very close together or, if you like, tend ineluctably to escalate into a dialogue. As Western society has accepted the domination of the scientific and the technological, its language must increasingly generalize. Go to a country like Malaya, where there are still plenty of Rousseauesque children of nature, and you will find that language is still refreshingly close to *things*. You don't speak much unless you can predicate about something demonstrable—that *padi* in that field, that snake in that grass. In objects imported from the prototechnological Victorian age, it is possible to avoid abstraction: a railway train is a *kereta api* or "fire carriage," and an express train is a *kereta api sombong*—a "haughty fire carriage" (*i.e.*, one too proud to stop). But introduce the great abstract ideas of the contemporary world and you leave the simple fishermen and *padi*-planters behind. You have to draw on Sanskrit (as we draw on Latin and Greek) for notions like "federation"—*persekutuan*—or institutions like the United Nations—*bangsa-bangsa sharikat*. The local river is a very tangible reality; the supermarket and the Laundromat are abstractions. The abstractions are moving in everywhere.

You can see how easy it is for modern language to move away from its referents. I very nearly said that "the local river is concrete"—not absurd as we in the West use language, but perhaps crassly inappropriate in that child-of-nature, thing-that-is context. But abstractions are really disguised metaphors (most thoroughly disguised when they derive from the classical languages), and metaphors can only keep their sensuous content when poetry insists on reminding us of it. Take a scientific term like *parthenogenesis,* put it in a poem, and the poem will not be able to resist digging out the "virgin" image (with the help of the Parthenon and the New Testament) and showing, with reference to the Old Testament, precisely what *genesis* means. Not that etymology is necessarily much help in giving us an anchor for an abstraction; it just happens to be the only source available, with some words, for a concrete image, the sense of a real thing out there in the world of the senses. The vague term "lady" at least takes on an image when we refer it back to the Anglo-Saxon *hlaefdige,* which has something to do with making a loaf. Somebody's there supervising the bread-making, perhaps. Or, even if she's actually baking it herself, her hands are clean. Superiority, neatness, calm, authority—those will do for a beginning.

Poetry, which reminds us of both the limitations and potentialities of language, is not much read nowadays. The irony is that poetry is regarded, by the hard-eyed and hard-headed, as somehow remote from reality, reality being represented by computers. Beatniks and teen-agers desperately try to hurl their own pale substitute for poetry—slang—in the face of the growing corpus of abstract language. But slang is ephemeral and often vague. God knows what "fun-people" are. "With it," in England, is defined as "not square," and "square" as "not with it." "With it" had to yield to "switched-on," but "switched-on" is already dying. Laboriously learn the slang of French teen-agers, like *son et lumière* and *PPH* (*passera pas l'hiver*—"won't last the winter") as derisive terms for the old (those over thirty), and French teen-agers will look at you in pity. The young won't meet the old on this matter of language; they seem to doubt the possibility of genuine communication. And if their slang is ephemeral, at least it's healthier to discard words than to let them grow stale and venerable and riddled with ambiguities.

For no venerable word—like "justice" or "democracy"—can be trusted anymore. We in the West think we know what democracy is, but the so-called democratic republics of the Soviet bloc are quite sure that they know too. The Russian words *pravosudiye* and *spravyedlivost'* will both have to be translated "justice," but we feel pretty certain that it's not the kind of justice we ourselves prize. Even within a single language community such terms can be polarized; if not, there would be no opposed political parties. Any discussion group in England or America resolves itself into a semantic wrangle about "liberty" or "the state" or "beauty" or "religion"; women's cookery circles at least know what they mean (though sometimes one wonders) by a soufflé or an angel cake. Something concrete there.

Cleanup by Big Brother

Concerned about the state of the English language at present, one must be even more concerned about its future. George Orwell, in *Nineteen Eighty-Four,* presented the semantic nightmare of Newspeak. He conceived of the total control of language by a ruling oligarchy (symbolized by a mythical figure called Big Brother) which should cleanse words of vagueness and ambiguity and impose on them an exactness appropriate to a totalitarian orthodoxy. Thus, "ungood" and its intensive "doubleplus ungood" are better than "bad" and the limitless range of intensives in Oldspeak, since they are defined in terms of what they oppose. There is a limited context for the use of "ungood"; its main meaning is "opposed to the principles of Ingsoc" (*i.e.,* "English Socialism," the ruling ideology). Since Big Brother personifies this ideology, a statement like "Big Brother is doubleplus ungood" can have no meaning. Wherever a statement made by the party (or by Big Brother, which is the same thing) seems to conflict with a previous statement, the principle of "doublethink" must come into operation. $2 + 2 = 4$, but $2 + 2$ can also equal 5, according to the policy of the party. The aim is not merely conformity; it is the extirpation of the power to think freely. When language is controlled, thought and action are also controlled. No more chaos, no more arguments about meanings, no more verbal speculations. Freedom to wander through the wild woods of language, perpetually missing the way, is a kind of slavery to the mess of imprecision that language always is; slavery to fixed definitions and forms becomes a kind of freedom. This is one explanation of the State's motto "Freedom is Slavery."

Needless to say, such a nightmare is incapable of fulfillment. Language cannot be fixed forever; the creation of new forms—which is one of the processes which keep language moving—takes place at a subliminal level, unsubmissive to external rules. Sounds change, and they cannot be stopped from changing. No legislation, and no act of the conscious will, brought about the soundshift which stopped "road" rhyming with "laud" and "weak" sounding like "wake." However much we yearn now for an academy which shall tell us precisely in what contexts a word may be used and thus establish a definition of that word forever, language insists on retaining its own curious autonomy. Any visitor to London now will notice that the question-tag "didn't I?" or "wasn't I?" is appearing in new contexts. A stranger in a pub will say, "I won five quid on the horses last month, didn't I?" There's no answer to that; you're not in a position to know whether he did or not. But the question-tag doesn't expect an answer anymore; it's merely a new emphasizer. Nobody knows when the new usage first sprang into being. One suddenly wakes up to the existence of a change in language (perhaps temporary, perhaps not), as self-willed as a wart.

How English will change in, say, the next century is anybody's guess, but there are certain pointers which indicate directions we shall be unable to resist. In England, the hegemony of East Midland English in its spoken form is already—unconsciously—being questioned. This form of English has always derived its glamour and authority from the fact that it developed in that region which contains the capital, London, and the two oldest universities, Oxford and Cambridge. It is the Queen's English, though the Queen herself employs variations of vowel sound which may be regarded as a little archaic—suggesting the England of her grandmother rather than that of her children. Now it is clear that this brand of "upper-class" English is already becoming something of a joke. Students at Oxford and Cambridge assert their regional origin rather than attempt to flatten it out into a non-provincial *koine*. If public schools like Eton, Harrow, and Winchester are legislated out of existence, there will be no stronghold for a patrician accent. The accents of the North and Midlands are now respectable, whereas they used to be vaudeville jokes; pop groups like the Beatles have given authority to the accent of Liverpool. What we are now hearing more and more is the "flat a" in words like "bath" and "dance"; the final or medial "r" in "park" and "far" is being sounded. In other words, American English is providing a speech norm; it is the only national speech which can contain British provincial sound-systems as well as its own regional variants.

I think that by 2067 the so-called American accent will prevail wherever English is spoken. The former British colonies are no longer tied to the accents of their masters; they will as soon send their students to American schools as to British ones. The death of the old ruling class in England is bound to mean the death of the ruling-class accent.

But will American pronunciation itself change? If its past history is a trustworthy guide, it will not change rapidly; there will be nothing like the revolution that took place in British speech in the two centuries before Shakespeare's birth. It is the English spoken four years after Shakespeare's death—by the Pilgrim Fathers of 1620—that still provides the phonetic norm for these United States. Most varieties of American speech remain close to the Elizabethan of Southern England—the avoidance of a round "o" in words like "not" and "thought"; the front "a" in "dance"; the "r" pronounced in all positions. An American asked to say Hamlet's line "Oh that this too too solid flesh would melt" invariably conveys the ambiguity in the word "solid" that Shakespeare must have wanted—a mixture of "solid," "sallied," and "sullied." One thing that American English has not retained is the "Irish" sound in words like "tea" and "reason," but the rest is close enough to the London English of the first Elizabeth's day. America is a progressive country, but American speech is highly conservative. One cannot imagine its being very different a century—or even two centuries—from now.

For "Finch" Say "Bird"

The question of the vocabulary of the future is answered by the foreseeable pattern of technological trends and, for that matter, by the population trends that must become technology's main preoccupation. Man will be less in touch with the natural world as Wordsworth and Thoreau knew it. As more and more land comes under cultivation, the ability to distinguish between the forms of wild life is bound to diminish and eventually die. A great deal of the poetry of the past will become unintelligible. The general term "bird" will swallow the swallow, the finch, the green linnet. "Vegetation" will have to serve for most of the varieties of green life—plant and weed alike. A huge technical lexicon will replace the old country lexicon, and this technical lexicon will not be well understood by its users. Vocables made out of initials—like DDT and PVC and LSD—will disclose nothing of their origin to the non-technical mind; they will be flavorless, rootless, so much plastic. More mass production of more things will step up the race toward total abstraction; one rose can be different from another, but washing machines and refrigerators are not all that strong on individuality.

The growth of vocabulary may go along with a simplification of grammar. The discarding of unwanted verb endings and noun endings, the rationalization of gender—these have been resisted by German, but its sister English has shaken off a great deal of the old Teutonic luxuriance. It seems likely that more strong verbs will go weak (perhaps partly out of deference to Oriental and African learners of the language), so that "go" will become "goed" in the past tense, "ate" will change to "eated," and "swam" and "swum" to "swimmed." The only remaining vestige of personal inflection in the verb—the present-tense "s"-ending as in "drinks" and "sleeps"—is superfluous, since the person is always indicated by a governing noun or pronoun: "he swim" or "John drink" makes perfectly good sense. There are already small signs that pronoun inflection isn't being taken as seriously as it used to be. One hears, in carefully prepared radio talks, not only "between you and I" but also "What will entry into the Common Market mean to we English people?" Pedagogues and English language examiners ought to be permissive about these rationalizations. That popular usage must sooner or later be bowed to is shown, I think, by the fact that framers of a Vietnamese primer for American troops have yielded to the form "I lay" (for "I lie") since the majority of GIs use it. And, in England, as most people say "due to" where "owing to" is officially correct, the posters of British Rail announce without shame: "Due to fog on the line trains may be late." These are straws in the wind of change.

I think that the concept of a unified English—Anglo-American, if you like—is already being realized. Television has something to do with it. A series made by a British television company can often pay its way only if it can be sold to America. Hence the sight and sound of Cockneys hurrying along the sidewalk (not pavement) to buy suspenders (not braces). The popular music and lyrics favored by British teen-agers are American-derived, even where British-composed, and the American idiom as well as pronunciation is accepted without self-consciousness. Even the most patriotic of Englishmen must admit that the English of the future has to be mainly American—though flavored by British contributions as much as by those from expatriate Russian Jews.

This common language of ENSPUN (the English Speaking Union) will be rich in vocabulary but spare in grammar. The lexical richness will be derived from science but humanized by slang—a desperate attempt on the part of the emotions and imagination to warm the cold heart of a cerebral civilization. But it is the vocabulary of generalization that will prevail. The desert Arabs used to have innumerable terms for "camel." The Malays have no single word for "you" but, instead, a battery of honorifics whose usage is decreed by protocol. This is the old way of language, the way of particularization, what—in the middle ages—was termed the "nominalist" way. With the "realist" or generalizing way, language must, inevitably, tell more lies, perpetrate more unwilled inaccuracies. We shall have to cherish our poets in the future far more than we have ever done in the past. It is only they who will be able to bring back the flavor of the particular to words that—cut off from nature—will be gray neutral counters. They will have the job of reminding us that words relate to things, not to abstract ideas.

Dr. Johnson saw the danger of words taking off into the empyrean, losing contact with the world of actuality. "I am not so far gone in lexicography," he said, "as to forget that, though words are the daughters of men, things are the sons of heaven."

COMPREHENSION QUIZ

1. The author of this selection believes that we are all
   a. confident in our use of language.
   b. subject to the need for undeliberate lies.
   c. poets at heart.
   d. speakers of an identical language.
2. According to Burgess, beatniks and teen-agers substitute slang for
   a. profanity.
   b. earlier linguistic forms.
   c. poetry.
   d. references to the Old Testament.
3. Burgess alludes to a "semantic nightmare" as portrayed by
   a. George Orwell.
   b. Graham Greene.
   c. D. H. Lawrence.
   d. C. P. Snow.
4. Sound changes in language
   a. can be predicted.
   b. cannot be stopped.
   c. are a sign of internal decay.
   d. are cyclic and regular in nature.
5. The author predicts that by 2067 the speech norm which will likely prevail in England is
   a. East Midland English.
   b. the Queen's English.

   c. the accents of the North and Midlands.
   d. American English.
6. Most varieties of American speech remain close to
   a. that of contemporary London.
   b. the "Irish" sound in many of their words.
   c. the accents of graduates from Eton, Harrow, and Winchester.
   d. the Elizabethan of Southern England.
7. American speech is
   a. given to sudden and abrupt change.
   b. highly conservative.
   c. remarkably free from idiomatic usage.
   d. less precise than that of the English.
8. The author predicts for the English language
   a. a simplification of grammar.
   b. a levelling off of vocabulary.
   c. an increase of regional accents.
   d. a stress on verb and noun endings.

DISCUSSION QUESTIONS

1. Burgess claims that teen-agers' slang is a substitute for poetry. What are some slang expressions in current use that illustrate this observation?
2. Would the eventual development of one dialect spoken throughout the United States be desirable?
3. What are the technological and social forces at work in this country that are "levelling off" regional differences in pronunciation?
4. Do you agree with Burgess that "without deliberate lying we would soon have anarchy"? How is Burgess using the term "lying"? In this sense, how do we lie?
5. What examples of gobbledygook can you recall hearing within the last few days? Who are the chief users of it?
6. Burgess says that words like "justice" and "democracy" cannot be trusted anymore. Why not? Can you think of other words to add to his list?
7. Which dialects of American English do you admire? Which do you find distasteful? Does this tell you anything about your attitudes toward the speakers of those dialects?

WRITING SUGGESTIONS

1. Write a composition using as your central idea the quotation by Dr. Johnson in the last paragraph of Burgess' essay.
2. Analyze the slang terms of a particular group. Include in your study the possible origins, meanings, and users of words you cite.

3. Find several examples of gobbledygook in the newspaper and rewrite them in clear, direct English.
4. Account for the fact that although America is a progressive country, American speech is highly conservative.
5. Burgess cites some indications of a growing simplification of English grammar. What additional evidence or examples can you add to those he notes?

The English Language
Is My Enemy!

by OSSIE DAVIS

A superficial examination of Roget's Thesaurus Of The English Language reveals the following facts: the word WHITENESS has 134 synonyms; 44 of which are favorable and pleasing to contemplate, i.e. purity, cleanness, immaculateness, bright, shining, ivory, fair, blonde, stainless, clean, clear, chaste, unblemished, unsullied, innocent, honorable, upright, just, straight-forward, fair, genuine, trustworthy, (a white man-colloquialism). Only ten synonyms for WHITENESS appear to me have negative implications—and these only in the mildest sense: gloss over, whitewash, gray, wan, pale, ashen, etc.

The word BLACKNESS has 120 synonyms, 60 of which are distinctly unfavorable, and none of them even mildly positive. Among the offending 60 were such words as: blot, blotch, smut, smudge, sully, begrime, soot, becloud, obscure, dingy, murky, low-toned, threatening, frowning, foreboding, forbidden, sinister, baneful, dismal, thundery, evil, wicked, malignant, deadly, unclean, dirty, unwashed, foul, etc. . . . not to mention 20 synonyms directly related to race, such as: Negro, Negress, nigger, darky, blackamoor, etc.

When you consider the fact that *thinking* itself is sub-vocal speech—in other words, one must use *words* in order to think at all—you will appreciate the enormous heritage of racial prejudgement that lies in wait for any child born into the English Language. Any teacher good or bad, white or black, Jew or Gentile, who uses the English Language as a medium of communication is forced, willy-nilly, to teach the Negro child 60 ways to despise himself, and the white child 60 ways to aid and abet him in the crime.

From Ossie Davis, "The English Language Is My Enemy!," *Negro History Bulletin*, April, 1967. Reprinted by permission of The Association for the Study of Negro Life and History, Inc., Washington, D.C.

Who speaks to me in my Mother Tongue damns me indeed! . . . the English Language—in which I cannot conceive myself as a black man without, at the same time, debasing myself . . . my enemy, with which to survive at all I must continually be at war.

COMPREHENSION QUIZ

1. Davis' article is based on a study of
    a. Webster's Third New International Dictionary.
    b. Roget's International Thesaurus of the English Language.
    c. popular American and English novels.
    d. the speech of middle-class white Americans.
2. He found 44 synonyms for "whiteness"
    a. which are favorable and pleasing to contemplate.
    b. which have negative implications.
    c. which suggest the history of the word.
    d. which are rejected by most speakers of English.
3. Approximately half of the synonyms for "blackness"
    a. are taken from Shakespeare's plays.
    b. are pleasing and favorable in meaning.
    c. are no longer in use.
    d. are distinctly unfavorable.
4. According to Davis, any child born into the English language is granted
    a. an enormous heritage of racial prejudgment.
    b. an advantage over children from other cultures.
    c. a language remarkably free of racial connotations.
    d. linguistic superiority.
5. The author says that to conceive himself as a black man in the English language is to
    a. utilize the rich resources of the language.
    b. distort the meaning of "black."
    c. debase himself.
    d. bring dignity and distinction to himself.

DISCUSSION QUESTIONS

1. How do you explain the meanings attributed to "whiteness"? Why does "blackness" have the meanings listed by Davis in his essay?
2. What do "denotation" and "connotation" have to do with this essay?
3. *Must* you use words in order to think, as Davis claims? Do infants think?
4. What other racial slurs or insults are "built into" the English language?

WRITING SUGGESTIONS

1. Look up the words "yellow," "purple," and "green" in Roget's *International Thesaurus* and summarize your findings in a report.
2. How does the white child "aid and abet" the Negro child to despise himself, according to Davis? Are there other ways this process goes on, in addition to language? Describe such ways in a theme.
3. Is there any way out of Davis' dilemma posed at the end of the essay?

Who Flang That Ball?

by W. F. MIKSCH

My assignment was to interview Infield Ingersoll, one-time shortstop for the Wescosville Wombats and now a radio sports announcer. Dizzy Dean, Red Barber and other sportscasters had taken back seats since the colorful Ingersoll had gone on the air. The man had practically invented a new language.

"I know just what you're gonna ask," Infield began. "You wanna know how come I use all them ingrammatical expressions like 'He swang at a high one.' You think I'm illitrut."

"No, indeed," I said. Frankly, I *had* intended to ask him what effect he thought his extraordinary use of the King's English might have on future generations of radio listeners.

But a gleam in Infield's eyes when he said "illitrut" changed my mind. "What I'd really like to get," I said, "is the story of how you left baseball and became a sportscaster."

Infield looked pleased. "Well," he said, "it was the day us Wombats plew the Pink Sox . . ."

"Plew the Pink Sox?" I interrupted. "Don't you mean played?"

Infield's look changed to disappointment. "Slay, slew. Play, plew. What's the matter with that?"

No Thinking This Way

"Slay is an irregular verb," I pointed out.

"So who's to say what's regular or irregular? English teachers! Can an English teacher bat three hundred?"

He paused belligerently, and then went on. "What I'm tryin' to do is easify the languish. I make all regular verbs irregular. Once they're all irregular, then it's just the same like they're all regular. That way I don't gotta stop and think."

He had something there. "Go on with your story," I said.

"Well, it was the top of the fifth, when this Sox batter wang out a high pop fly. I raught for it."

"Raught?"

"Past tense of verb to Reach. Teach, taught. Reach,—"

"Sorry," I said. "Go ahead."

"Anyhow I raught for it, only the sun blound me."

"You mean blinded?"

"Look," Infield said patiently, "you wouldn't say a pitcher winded up, would you? So there I was, blound by the sun, and the ball just nuck the tip of my glove—that's nick, nuck; same congregation as stick, stuck. But luckily I caught it just as it skam the top of my shoe."

"Skam? Could that be the past tense of to skim?"

"Yeah, yeah, same as swim, swam. You want this to be a English lesson or you wanna hear my story?"

"Your story please, Mr. Ingersoll."

"Okay. Well, just then the umpire cell, 'Safe!' Naturally I was surprose. Because I caught that fly, only the ump cell the runner safe."

"Cell is to call as fell is to fall, I suppose?" I inquired.

"Right. Now you're beginning to catch on." Infield regarded me happily as if there was now some hope for me. "So I yold at him, 'Robber! That decision smold!' "

"Yell, yold. Smell, smold," I mumbled. "Same idea as tell, told."

Infield rumbled on, "I never luck that umpire anyway."

"Hold it!" I cried. I finally had tripped this backhand grammarian. "A moment ago, you used nuck as the past for nick, justifying it by the verb to stick. Now you use luck as a verb. Am I to assume by this that luck is the past tense of to lick?"

Nobody Luck Him

"Luck is past for like. To like is a regular irregular verb of which there are several such as strike, struck. Any farther questions or should I go on?"

"Excuse me," I said, "you were saying you never luck that umpire."

"And neither did the crowd. Everyone thrould at my courage. I guess I better explain thrould," Infield said thoughtfully. "Thrould comes from thrill just like would comes from will. Got that? Now to get back to my story: 'Get off the field, you bum, and no back talk!' the umpire whoze."

"Whoze?"

"He had asthma," Infield pointed out patiently.

I saw through it instantly. Wheeze, whoze. Freeze, froze.

"And with those words, that ump invote disaster. I swang at him and smeared him with a hard right that lood square on his jaw."

"Lood? Oh, I see—Stand, stood. Land, lood—it lood on his jaw."

"Sure. He just feld up and went down like a light. As he reclone on the field, he pept at me out of his good eye."

"So I Quat"

"Now wait. What's this pept?" I asked.

"After you sleep, you've did what?" Infield inquired.

"Why, slept—oh, he peeped at you, did he?"

"You bet he pept at me. And in that peep I saw it was curtains for me in the league henceforward. So I beat him to it and just up and quat."

"Sit, sat. Quit—well, that gets you out of baseball," I said. "Only you still haven't told me how you got to be on radio and television."

"I guess that'll have to wait," Infield said, "on account I gotta hurry now to do a broadcast."

As he shade my hand good-by, Infield grun and wank at me.

COMPREHENSION QUIZ

1. The narrator of this short story is
    a. an English teacher.
    b. a reporter.
    c. a radio sports announcer.
    d. a baseball pitcher.
2. Ingersoll tells the narrator
    a. his greatest sports thrill.
    b. his opinion of the younger baseball players.
    c. his predictions for the pennant race.
    d. how he left baseball and became a sportscaster.
3. In telling his story, Ingersoll
    a. makes the regular verbs irregular.
    b. demonstrates a mastery of the King's English.
    c. makes the irregular verbs regular.
    d. expresses admiration for English teachers.
4. Ingersoll left baseball because
    a. he had an unsuccessful year at the plate.
    b. he struck an umpire.
    c. the fans ridiculed his English.
    d. he was hit by a baseball.

5. The author of this selection is showing
    a. the benefits of a good vocabulary.
    b. his unfamiliarity with baseball.
    c. what might happen if logic were applied to English verbs.
    d. the consistency of the English language.

DISCUSSION QUESTIONS

1. What often confusing features of the English language are touched on in this story?
2. What other irregularities of the language provide difficulties for foreigners learning English?
3. How "logical" are Ingersoll's various constructions?
4. How does the author of this selection show that the narrator was finally "converted" to Ingersoll's linguistic point of view?

WRITING SUGGESTIONS

1. Prepare an answer to Ingersoll's question, "Can an English teacher bat three hundred?" What is really implied in the question?
2. The principal parts of the verb "drink" are "drink," "drank," and "drunk." What are the principal parts of "think"? By referring to a history of the English language, account for the difference in forms.

What Is Language?

by ARCHIBALD A. HILL

1. Some Basic Assumptions

The subject of linguistics presents an initial difficulty because the word which designates it is unfamiliar. The word can easily be defined as the scientific analysis of language, but it is doubtful if such a definition is meaningful to anyone who lacks familiarity with this kind of analytic activity. It is far better to begin by defining language, since language is closer to the reader's experience. Yet even the definition of language presents unsuspected difficulties and needs preliminary discussion before it is attempted directly.

If a group of educated speakers are asked to define the language they are using, the reply will probably be "All the words and sentences used to express our thoughts." The definition is satisfactory in everyday situations, since long practice has made plain what is meant, and consequently most hearers know how to respond accurately. But for all that, the definition is not sufficiently accurate to be the basis for analysis. Terms like "words and sentences," which seem transparent to a speaker of a Western language, would be more misleading than enlightening if applied to some languages. Moreover, there are phenomena similar to language which this definition does not identify. Most important, the definition identifies language activity by thought. Language activity can be observed, and is therefore subject to verification. Thought can be observed only by subjective introspection, and so is not subject to verification. Language activity is therefore more knowable, thought less knowable. Obviously a definition must define the less knowable by the more knowable if it is to cast light. In what follows, such a definition will be attempted. There must first be a warning, the need for which will be clearer as we advance. A definition is not a description. A definition gives only those characteristics which have diagnostic value for

From Archibald A. Hill, *Introduction to Linguistic Structure.* Copyright © 1958 by Harcourt, Brace & World, Inc., New York. Reprinted by permission of the publisher.

recognition. A description attempts to give all characteristics, preferably in the order of their importance. A definition necessarily leaves out much and may make use of relatively trivial characteristics, but it is not to be condemned for that reason.

Most professional students of language proceed from a few assumptions, one of which is that the fundamental forms of language activity are the sequences of sounds made by human lips, tongues, and vocal cords—the phenomena usually distinguished by the narrower name of "speech." Though this first assumption may seem like a truism, it is important, since many who accept it verbally still act as if they did not believe it. Some few even deny it. There are only two reasons for questioning the assumption. Writing has great permanence and great prestige. Further, the basis of our education is training in the manipulation of written symbols of ever-increasing complexity. Highly literate people, and those who would like to be literate, are therefore apt to think of writing as the real center of language and of speech as peripheral and derived—often badly—from the written forms.

There are a number of facts which should settle this question of priority. First, speech reaches back to the origins of human society; writing has a history of only about seven thousand years.[1] Also, no contemporary community of men is without language, even though it is probably still true that most of the world's several thousand language communities remain in the preliterate stage, without benefit of alphabet or even picture symbol. Individual members of literate communities, furthermore, learn their language some years before they learn to read or write it; and adults, even adults who are professional writers, carry on a good deal more speech activity in daily living than activity involving writing. The final fact is that all writing systems are essentially representations of the forms of speech, rather than representations of ideas or objects in the nonlinguistic world. There are exceptions to this statement, like the Arabic numbers which work independently of the words for numbers in the Western languages. The exceptions, however, are in a minority disproportionate to the majority of

[1] The great antiquity of language, as compared with writing, is a reasonable assumption, but it is often presented without evidence. To arrive at the conclusion that language is older than writing, linguists and anthropologists start from the observed fact that in modern communities, all organized cooperative activity rests firmly and necessarily on language as the means of controlling and directing interaction. This being so in all observed communities, it is assumed by archaeological anthropologists that when remains of past communities show material evidence of social organization, these remains are those of communities which possessed language. Communities which show such evidences of social organization also show artifacts or other evidences which are much older than the remains of any communities which show evidences of even primitive systems of writing. It is possible that early human communities possessed some other form of highly organized communication, such as the gesture language which has been occasionally proposed since the days of Locke (cf. Max Müller, *Lectures on the Science of Language*, London, 1862, p. 31). But though possible, such a nonvocal symbol system is unlikely. Language is now a universal activity; it is an extra and unnecessary hypothesis to suppose something else.

symbols which always indicate the forms of language. The point can be driven home by a pair of simple examples. The symbol for *one* in Japanese writing is a single stroke, that for *two* two strokes, and so on. It might be thought that such a symbol has no relation to the Japanese word for *one* (*ichi*) but represents instead the nonlinguistic idea of "oneness." Actually the occurrence of the single stroke is correlated with the occurrence of the word. It occurs not only in the number but also in such forms as *ichiji, primary*. The Japanese symbol, therefore, has a quite different range from the letter sequence *one* of English, which is not used in the dissimilar word *primary*. The one-stroke symbol corresponds with the occurrence of the Japanese word *ichi,* proving that the one-stroke symbol is a representation of the word (though an understandably pictorial one), and not a direct representation of the idea of oneness.

Written symbols can be understood, furthermore, insofar as they fit into a linguistic structure, even when they refer to nothing in the non-linguistic world. Thus, if an English text should have the sentence "He *sprashes* it," the second word could immediately be recognized as a verb in the third person singular and as a sequence of sounds quite in accord with English structural habits, though it represents nothing in the outside world at all. For the purposes of this book, therefore, the linguist's assumption that language is a set of sounds will be adopted. It is no contradiction of this assumption that the sounds can be secondarily translated into visual marks, grooves on a wax disk, electrical impulses, or finger movements.

Linguists assume that the description and analysis of language must begin with description of the sounds and their patterning and that description of meaning must be put off until the first task is done. Such an attitude is often misunderstood to be a denial of meaning, but this is not true. The linguist's desire to put off analysis of meaning is no more than an application of the principle of working from the more knowable to the less knowable, and though linguistics has not as yet had very striking results in semantic analysis, it can be hoped that the next few decades will see results of real value in semantics.

2.   The Defining Characteristics of Language

Working with the assumptions given above, linguists can offer a set of five defining characteristics which serve to set off language from other forms of symbolic behavior and to establish language as a purely human activity. Often animal communication will have one or more of these five characteristics, but never all of them.

First, language, as has been said, is a set of sounds. This is perhaps the least important characteristic, since the communication of mammals and birds is also a set of sounds. On the other hand, the system of communication which is in some ways most strikingly like language, that of bees, is a set of body movements, not sounds. It would be easy, further, to imagine a language based on something else than sound, but no human language is so constructed. Even the manual language of the deaf is derived from the pre-existent spoken language of the community.

Second, the connection between the sounds, or sequences of sounds, and objects of the outside world is arbitrary and unpredictable. That is to say, a visitor from Mars would be unable to predict that in London a given animal is connected with the sound sequence written *dog,* in Paris with the sequence *chien,* in Madrid with *perro.* The arbitrary quality of language symbols is not infrequently denied, for a number of reasons. Sometimes the denial is based on nothing more than the notion that the forms of one's native language are so inevitably right that they must be instinctive for all proper men. Sometimes the denial is more subtle. It is often maintained that all language, even though now largely arbitrary, must once have been a systematic imitation of objects by means of sound. It is true that there are some imitative words in all languages, but they are at best a limited part of the vocabulary. It is easy to imitate the noise of a barking dog, for instance, but difficult if not impossible to imitate a noiseless object, such as a rainbow. Though imitative words show similarity in many languages, absolute identity is rare. A dog goes "bow-wow" in English, but in related languages he often goes "wow-wow" or "bow-bow." The imitative words do not, after all, entirely escape from the general arbitrariness of language. The imitative origin of language appears, therefore, at worst unlikely and at best unprovable. The same injunction holds for theories of language origin which speculate that it is an imitation of facial or other gestures.

If it is assumed that language is arbitrary, what is meant by the statement? Just that the sounds of speech and their connection with entities of experience are passed on to all members of any community by older members of that community. Therefore, a human being cut off from contact with a speech community can never learn to talk as that community does, and cut off from all speech communities never learns to talk at all. In essence, to say that language is arbitrary is merely to say that it is social. This is perhaps the most important statement that can be made about language.

In contrast, much of animal communication is instinctive rather than social. That is to say, all cats mew and purr, and would do so even if they were cut off from all communication with other cats. On the other hand, some animal communication seems to share the social nature of human speech and is therefore learned activity. A striking example is the barking of dogs, which is characteristic only of the domesticated animal, not of dogs in the wild state. Similarly, the honey dances of bees may not be altogether without an arbitrary element. It is also likely that when more is known of the cries and chatterings of the great apes in the wild state, a considerable social element in their communication may be found. Nor should it be thought that all human communication is social. A part of our communication consists of instinctive reactions which accompany language, like the trembling of fear or the suffusion of blood which accompanies anger. Yet even in the nonlinguistic accompaniments of speech, the tones of voice and the gestures, it is now clear that there is more of arbitrary and socially learned behavior than had at one time been supposed.

Third, language is systematic. I cannot hope to make this statement completely clear. . . . However, some observations may now be made about the system of language. As in any system, language entities are arranged in recurrent designs, so that if a part of the design is seen, predictions can be made about the whole of it, as a triangle can be drawn if one side and two angles are given. Suppose there is an incomplete sentence like "John _____s Mary an _____." A good deal about what must fill the two blanks is obvious. The first must be a verb, the second a noun. Furthermore, not all verbs will go in the first blank, since it requires a verb whose third person singular is spelled with -s and which can take two objects (that is, not such a verb as *look* or *sees*). Nor will all nouns fit in the second place, since an initial vowel is required, and the noun must be one which takes an article. There is no difficulty in deciding that the sentence could be either "John gives Mary an apple" or "John hands Mary an aspirin," but not "John *gaves* Mary an *book*."[2]

Another observation that can be made about language systems is that every occurrence of language is a substitution frame. Any sentence is a series of entities, for each of which a whole group of other entities can be substituted without changing the frame. Thus the sentence "John gives Mary an apple" is such a substitution frame. For *John* there can be replacements like *he, Jack, William, the man, her husband,* or many others. For the verb, entities like *buys, takes, offers,* as well as the alternatives *hands* or *gives,* may be used. This characteristic of extensive substitutability for all parts of any language utterance is of some importance in that it enables us to say that parrots, no matter how startlingly human their utterances may be, are not carrying on language activity. A parakeet may produce the sentence "Birds can't talk!" with human pitch, voice tones, and nearly perfect sounds. But the bird never says "Dogs can't talk!" or "Birds can't write!" His utterance is a unit, not a multiple substitution frame.

Still another characteristic of language systems is that the entities of language are grouped into classes, always simpler, more predictable, and

2 [An] asterisk placed before a form means that it is believed to be impossible. In historical treatments of language, on the other hand, an asterisk before a form indicates that it has been reconstructed by comparison but is not actually recorded. These two uses of the asterisk should not be confused.

more sharply separated than the infinite variety of objects in the world.
For instance, a whole series of objects is grouped under the single word
chair, and *chair* is put into the large class of nouns. In dealing with objects
in the outside world it may be difficult to decide whether something is a
chair, a stool, or merely a rock. In language, we think of nouns and verbs
as quite separate and are apt to say that the one class represents things, the
other events. But in the outside world, as the physicists tell us, it is often
hard to decide whether an object is best described as thing or as event.

To return once more to the defining characteristics of language, the
fourth characteristic is that it is a set of symbols. That is to say, language
has meaning. In this form the statement is a platitude and does not distinguish language from other activities which are also symbolic. The nature
of language symbols turns out to be rather different from the symbols of
other types of communication. The simplest nonlinguistic symbol can be
defined as a substitute stimulus. Pavlov's famous dogs, fed at the sound of a
bell, eventually began to drool at the sound of the bell even when no food
was present. The dogs were responding to a substitute stimulus. Nonlinguistic symbols can also be substitute responses, and these can also be taught
to animals. A dog who learns to "speak" at the sight of food has learned
such a substitute response. In human speech, however, one of the most
striking facts is that we can talk about things which are not present, and we
can talk about things which ordinarily produce a strong physical reaction
without experiencing that reaction. For instance, I can talk about apples
even though there are none in the room, and I can talk about them without always making my mouth water, even when I am hungry. This type
of language, which occurs without an immediately present stimulus or
response, is called "displaced speech," and it is obviously of great importance. It is what enables man to know something of the past and of the
world beyond the limited range of his vision and hearing at a given moment.

The crucial fact in producing this almost miraculous and purely human
effect seems to be that a given language entity can be both substitute stimulus and substitute response, and can also be a stimulus for further language
responses or a response to other language stimuli. I can talk about apples
when they are absent because "something reminds me of them." That is,
I can make language responses to what is before me, and these language
responses can stimulate the further response *apple* without any direct
physical stimulus to my vision, touch or smell. *Apple* can call forth still
further language entities, like *pear* or *banana,* in an endless chain; these
entities are both stimuli and responses. When human speakers do this, they
are setting up what philosophers call a "universe of discourse." The ability
to make connected discourse within the symbol system is what enables men
to talk at length, and profitably, about things they have never seen. By
means of language men make elaborate models of distant experience and

eventually test their accuracy by acting upon them. All that is known of animal communication leads to the supposition that precisely what is absent from it is the kind of symbolic activity here described, symbolic activity connected not merely with experience but with all parts of the symbol system itself. We believe, in short, that animals are incapable of displaced speech.

The paragraphs above are rather general, so that a concrete example may be helpful. Let us suppose that two speakers of English are together in a room. One of them is cold. A direct response for him would be to close the window.

Instead of this he can use the substitute response, which is also substitute stimulus: "John, please close the window for me." John can either close the window or reply with a further substitute: "Just a minute. Wait until I finish this page." Such a reply may produce acceptance or may lead to a discussion of John's procrastinating character, of the fact that his parents did not discipline him properly in youth and that modern young people are generally rebellious and unmannerly. To all of this John may reply that modern times are marked by progress and the disappearance of old taboos. In the meantime the window may have been quietly closed, or completely forgotten in the warmth of discussion. What is important is that each speaker has begun reacting, not to the immediate situation, but to the other speaker's language and to his own. And in so doing, each has been building a model of general social conditions, of wide scope and ultimately of some value, even in a random and unchecked conversation of the sort described.

We are now ready to turn to the last defining characteristic of language, the fact that it is complete. By this is meant that whenever a human language has been accurately observed, it has been found to be so elaborated that its speakers can make a linguistic response to any experience they may undergo. This complex elaboration is such a regular characteristic of all languages, even those of the simplest societies, that linguists have long ago accepted it as a universal characteristic. Nevertheless, in early books about language, and in the descriptions by linguistically untrained travelers today, there are statements that tribe X has a language with only two or three hundred words in it, forcing the tribe to eke out its vocabulary by gesture.[3] Linguists maintain that all such statements are the product of lack of knowledge, and are false. Skepticism about such statements is borne out by

[3] A typical recent statement of this sort was reported by Leonard Bloomfield in "Secondary and Tertiary Responses to Language," *Language*, XX, 1944, p. 49n.

"A physician of good general background and education, who had been hunting in the north woods, told me that the Chippewa language contains only a few hundred words. Upon question, he said that he got this information from his guide, a Chippewa Indian. When I tried to state the diagnostic setting, the physician, our host, briefly and with signs of displeasure repeated his statement and then turned his back to me. A third

the fact that in all instances where it was possible to check on tribe X, its language proved to be complete as usual, whereupon the statement was transferred to tribe Y, whose language was as yet unknown. The statement that human language is complete once again serves to distinguish it from animal activity. In the communication of bees, for instance, the subjects of systematic discourse are severely limited. Bees cannot, apparently, make an utterance equivalent to "The beekeeper is coming."

The statement that human language is always complete should not be interpreted to mean that every language has a word for everything. Obviously the ancient Greeks had no words for automobiles or atom bombs, and probably the modern Yahgan of Tierra del Fuego lack them as well. The completeness of language lies rather in the fact that a speaker of ancient Greek would have been perfectly capable of describing an automobile had he seen one, and further that had automobiles become important in ancient Greece, the speakers of Greek would have been perfectly capable of coining a word for them. It is a characteristic of vocabulary that, except in languages which have gone out of use, it is always expansible, in spite of the fact that resistance to new forms may frequently appear. Since language enables the user to make appropriate responses to all things and since vocabulary is thus characteristically "open," differences in vocabulary between two languages are not an accurate measure of the difference in efficiency or excellence of the two tongues. The fact that Eskimo does not have as highly developed a vocabulary of philosophy as does German merely indicates that the Eskimos are less interested in philosophy; on the other hand, Eskimo has a highly developed vocabulary for various kinds of snow, indicating that snow is important in Eskimo society. The completeness of human language and the openness of vocabulary make a groundless chimera of the occasionally expressed fear that a language might so degenerate as to become useless.

We can now attempt a definition of language, though the definition will be cumbersome. Language is the primary and most highly elaborated form of human symbolic activity. Its symbols are made up of sounds produced by the vocal apparatus, and they are arranged in classes and patterns which make up a complex and symmetrical structure. The entities of language are symbols, that is, they have meaning, but the connection between symbol and thing is arbitrary and socially controlled. The symbols of language are simultaneously substitute stimuli and substitute responses and can call forth further stimuli and responses, so that discourse becomes independent of an immediate physical stimulus. The entities and structure of

---

person, observing this discourtesy, explained that I had some experience of the language in question. This information had no effect."

For a good general account of the completeness of primitive languages and the use of gesture as a substitute among mutually unintelligible language groups, consult Ralph L. Beals and Harry Hoijer, *An Introduction to Anthropology*, Macmillan, New York, 1965.

language are always so elaborated as to give the speaker the possibility of making a linguistic response to any experience. Most of the above can be paraphrased by saying that every language is a model of a culture and its adjustment to the world.

3. Language and the Study of its Nature

Since language is something that we habitually take for granted, it may not be clear, even after this discussion, why language and, even more, the study of language are important. Primarily they are important because language is a solely human activity, which separates man from other living beings. But though this may be readily granted, it is not always realized how fundamentally language is a defining characteristic of man. Even among students of man it is probably more common to define him as "the tool-making animal" than as "the talking animal." But it is quite possible that tool making is less crucially human than talking is. For one thing, it is natural that an archaeologist's attention should turn toward tools, which can be dug up, rather than toward language, which cannot. For another, it is not always easy to recognize how fundamental language is, even in our own society. There are individuals who lead nearly normal lives in spite of being deprived of speech, so that it may be argued that speech—admittedly the fundamental form of language—is a dispensable form of activity. Yet such speechless individuals always develop some form of substitute language, and all such substitutes presuppose the individual's membership in a society fully provided with speech. There are many things, such as wearing neckties, making movies, or cooking, which only human beings do. But many of these are not universal among men, and all of them are secondary. As for tool making, this activity is universally human, but it is in some sense shared with the higher primates. When, however, it is argued that tool making involves more than the use of a convenient stick or stone and is the purposeful molding of an object for future use, it would seem that the tool maker is an individual capable of displaced speech and of shaping his activity in accord with a symbolic model. In other words, as soon as man is defined as a maker of tools whose use lies in the future, we presuppose the existence of language. Therefore linguists, and many anthropologists, believe that language is the phenomenon most basic in human society. Historical anthropologists assume that when humanoid remains are found in a situation indicating an organized community, they are necessarily remains of a group possessed of language. If, then, it is language more than anything else we can observe which makes us men, it is ultimately the study of language which is most likely to throw light on the essential humanness of human beings. I wish at this point, however, to make a specific disclaimer. There are characteristics inaccessible to science which also distinguish man;

the science of language is not concerned with these and should under no circumstances be understood as denying them. On the other hand, the existence of spiritual qualities ought equally to be understood as not being a bar to the study of those things which can be investigated by science.

If scientific study of language can throw light on human qualities and activities, there is no direction in which there is greater likelihood of illumination than in the investigation of thought, whether that investigation be understood as a part of psychology of a part of logic. It was said earlier that linguists do not deny the existence or importance of mind. The American linguist insists that language entities cannot be profitably investigated in terms of the mental concepts or thoughts back of them, but this insistence ought always to be understood as carrying with it the corollary that mental concepts can be profitably investigated in terms of the language entities which are so largely instrumental in their formation. It has also been said that language is basic to society. It is therefore probable that increased knowledge of language will mean increased knowledge of society. The promise is already recognized and has already borne fruit, since anthropologists have made brilliant use of linguistic insights. Less broad than thought and society, another area in which linguistic knowledge is beginning to prove useful is in the study of literature, if for no other reason than that literature is an art constructed in language. Similarly, the practical activity of language instruction, whether that of a foreign or the native tongue, can profit by knowledge of the nature of the material which is to be imparted.

I have up to now spoken of the importance of language study from the broad aspect of human knowledge; for the individual student the impact of language study is different. The native language provides its speakers an ever-present and deeply habituated instrument by which they measure and control experience. All adults have had a long indoctrination in the attitude that language is both a transparent glass through which we see the world and a tool by which we mold it. Therefore the first stages of study of language for the sake of knowledge rather than with a practical aim are apt to be disquieting, or even to seem useless. A somewhat parallel case can be drawn from optics. We think of our eyes as instruments which transmit the "real" appearance of objects directly to our minds. It is often disturbing to realize that our eyes necessarily influence the appearance of objects and that a surface which appears flat to us can scarcely appear so to the nearly spherical eye of a fly. Yet to say that language study is apt to be difficult or disquieting is not the same thing as to say that it is of no value to the individual. An important aim of education is the adjustment of the individual to the world in which he has to live, and linguistic knowledge is a help toward that end. The individual's understanding of reality is increased if he can learn to distinguish the ways in which the structure of his language may influence his perception of reality. Study of language is one of the best ways in which a narrow belief in the rightness of one's own ways of doing things, and the wrongness of every other way, can be broken down. It is instructive to find that some languages, even among the European group, are not felt to be inadequate because they do not distinguish between fingers and toes by separate vocabulary items. The knowledge that there are languages which have no tenses at all and others which attach tenses to their nouns is a good introduction to the myriad activities which indeed remain much the same throughout the world. A student trained in language is aware, on the practical level, of language pitfalls. A very little training may prepare him for failure of communication when an Englishman and an American talk about *corn*. More sophistication is needed for dealing with the situation reported by Bloomfield in which an Englishman misunderstood his American pronunciation of *Comedy Theatre* as a request for a nonexistent *Carmody Theatre*.[4] In all such instances, the student trained in language will deal with the inevitable failure of understanding in realistic terms, without wasting time in denouncing one group or the other for not knowing its own language. And similarly, he is prepared to deal with the difficulties of a foreign language on a more realistic level than by supposing that there is a one-to-one correspondence between its forms and those of English.

By now, I hope that some meaning has been given to the definition of linguistics as the scientific study of language. Linguistics has for its goal the understanding of language, and it is secure in the belief that such understanding will increase human knowledge. It strives to present a picture of language as complete as possible, as consistent as possible, and as simple as possible, again secure in the belief that if these conditions are fulfilled it will be as truly and revealingly a science as is chemistry or astronomy. . . .

COMPREHENSION QUIZ

1. No contemporary community of men is without
   a. an alphabet.
   b. at least a crude form of picture symbols.
   c. a language.
   d. a form of literature.
2. The results linguistics has had on semantic analysis thus far can be described as
   a. slight.
   b. remarkable.
   c. absolutely none.
   d. moderate.
3. The idea that language is a set of sounds is perhaps the
   a. least important characteristic.

4 *Language*, New York: Holt, 1933, p. 81.

   b.   most common characteristic.
   c.   least common characteristic.
   d.   most important characteristic when defining language.
4.   No human language is based on
   a.   body movements.
   b.   anything other than sound.
   c.   sound and body movements.
   d.   all of these.
5.   Language which occurs without an immediately present stimulus or response is called
   a.   symbolic replacement.
   b.   language entity recognition.
   c.   displaced speech.
   d.   substitution framing.
6.   All of the following are characteristics of language except
   a.   it is a set of sounds.
   b.   it is systematic.
   c.   it is incomplete.
   d.   it is a set of symbols.
7.   The fact that Eskimo does not have as highly developed a vocabulary of philosophy as does German indicates
   a.   nothing.
   b.   Eskimos are not as advanced as Germans.
   c.   Eskimos are less interested in philosophy.
   d.   Eskimos lack the opportunity for experiences that would increase their philosophic vocabulary level.
8.   Linguistic knowledge is beginning to prove useful in all of the following except
   a.   art.
   b.   thought.
   c.   society.
   d.   literature.

DISCUSSION QUESTIONS

1.   What is the difference between a definition and a description, according to Hill? Apply his distinction to the common definitions for an adjective, an adverb, and a pronoun.
2.   What do you understand to be the difference between an utterance and a multiple substitution frame as used in this essay?
3.   Using Hill's terms, what would the word *meteorite* be, an event or a thing? The Chinese would consider this phenomenon a verb. What linguistic implications does this have?
4.   How would you demonstrate the striking aspect of human language called "displaced speech"?
5.   What is a "universe of discourse"? Why is it valuable to men?

6. What does Hill mean when he says, "To say that language is arbitrary is merely to say that it is social"?
7. Comment upon the statement, "Every language has a word for everything."
8. Why does the vocabulary of a language which has gone out of use no longer exist?
9. What examples can you cite to support Hill's statement that "Anthropologists have made brilliant use of linguistic insights"?
10. Is linguistics a science? Explain your answer.

WRITING SUGGESTIONS

1. Support or refute the idea that speech, the fundamental form of language, is a dispensable form of activity.
2. Write a convincing paper affirming the proposition that "It is language more than anything else we can observe which makes us men." Be sure that your arguments would not be refuted on a scientific basis. The paragraph beginning "Since language is something . . ." of Hill's essay may be useful as you prepare to write.
3. Locate and report on an example of anthropological use of linguistic insights.
4. Write a short essay explaining how linguistics is an aid to the education of an individual.

One World–
But Which Language?

by MARGARET MEAD

How shall we begin to talk with one another all around the globe? What language shall we use? Must we forever be dependent on interpreters? Will the speakers of a few major languages—Chinese, English, Russian, Spanish and French—dominate the earth? Must we lose the "little" languages? Or can we make a choice that will include all the world's peoples?

We are in the process of creating a new civilization in which, for the first time, people everywhere are beginning to take part in the events that are shaping our common future. The realization of the dream of world-wide communication and the growing belief that men *can* plan for change are opening new potentialities for human relationships. But there is a paradox. For although our ability to see and hear has been vastly expanded, we still cannot talk with one another easily or on an equal basis. With every door of communication opening wide, we are held back by the barrier of language.

It has been estimated that there are some 3,000 "known" languages. But this does not include a very large number of living languages spoken by people whose voices are just beginning to be heard in the modern world. And looking ahead, we must think in terms of all the languages there are, not only of the few we are familiar with—even if we do not speak any but our own and perhaps one more. But we must also ask whether the idea of protecting the dignity of all languages is compatible with the hope of giving all men the chance to talk with one another.

In the past, when only a few travelers made their way to far-off places, they translated their experiences of new landscapes and new peoples, strange sights and sounds and smells, as best they could into their own tongue. Often,

From Margaret Mead, "One World—But Which Language?," *Redbook Magazine*, April, 1966. Copyright © 1966 by McCall Corporation, New York. Reprinted by permission of the publisher.

of course, they introduced new words along with the exotic things they brought back home. Commonplace English words like *coffee, tea, chocolate, tomato, tapioca, tobacco* and *cola* all carry distant echoes of adventurous travel, modified to fit the sound patterns of English. And when people went abroad as conquerors, traders or colonists, two things were very likely to happen. Those who were dominant imposed their own language as the high-level mode of communication; and very often they made use of a trade language or "pidgin" as a low-level mode of communication. Both practices accentuated the differences of those who came into contact with one another.

Today all this is changing, and perhaps the necessity of making a new choice presents to us a unique opportunity. We can, if we will, do away with the inevitable inequalities existing between native and foreign speakers of the major languages. It is not enough to have a few people who can converse comfortably or even many people who can address one another formally and correctly. The very rapid movement of jokes and slang, fashions and fads and slogans from one continent to another suggests that even now people, especially young people, are struggling to create a kind of common idiom in spite of language barriers. This may well be the moment, while world-wide communication is a new phenomenon, to establish a secondary world language that all the world's peoples will learn, in addition to their own, for use around the whole earth.

There are those who believe that the choice is already being made. They point to the number of people everywhere who are using one or another of the major languages for business, science and international politics. If they are right, sooner or later the languages of the most populous and powerful advanced nations will swamp the smaller languages and the world will be more strongly than ever divided into blocs. But I believe the choice is still open. If we can move fast enough, we may arrive at a decision that will bring people everywhere into more meaningful contact.

It is possible that Americans may play a decisive role in what happens. We have had a very special relationship to foreign languages ever since English won out over all the languages of other colonists and, later, of immigrants who came to this country. However, the kind of choice we make will depend on our contemporary interpretation of our historic linguistic tradition.

From one point of view, the more obvious one, we have rejected every language other than our own in our developing of American English. Our insistence that every child in school must be taught in English and that adults, for the most part, must use English in their work has meant two things. Native speakers of English were freed from the necessity of ever having to learn another language and all others broke their ties to the past by giving up their native tongue. Adequate English became a symbol of full citizenship. Those who did not learn it were cut off from freedom of movement out of their own language group, and even from some kinds of intimacy with their American-educated, English-speaking children. Foreign languages became something you might study—but seldom learned to speak —in school.

Only in World War II, when we discovered that it was very inconvenient to be engaged on a world scale and ignorant on a world scale, did we recognize the wastefulness of this. Then suddenly we found that we could teach—and thousands of young men could learn—the most "difficult" languages fast and well. Fortunately, the spark of interest and the curiosity about languages is still alive.

From another point of view, the less obvious one, our insistence on the primacy of English has had as its basis the deep belief that a common language is crucial for social unity. As one result, even in the period of our greatest linguistic isolationism, a few Americans began to campaign for a world language. Out of the tradition that you could be fully American only if you spoke American English they drew the idea that the beginning of world community depended on the invention of a new, artificial language for world-wide use. Since this would be the language of no nation, it could, without offending anyone, become everyone's language.

What these pioneers did not notice, however, was that each of these invented languages, because it was basically a simplification of existing European languages, would still give tremendous advantages to those who spoke any one of them. Conversely, these artificial languages offered little to all those with a different linguistic tradition. So the various candidate languages were tried out—in vain. This, of course, did a great deal of harm, for with each failure the danger increased that more people would treat the idea and the advocates of an auxiliary universal language as silly, boring and cranky.

Why, then, are we coming back to the idea? In fact, we have not "come back" but have moved in a new direction. Recently students of the relationship between language and culture, working together with the new scientists of the cybernetic revolution, have learned a great deal about natural languages—all languages that have been molded by the speech of many people over many generations. Especially important has been the concept of redundancy that has been developed by electronic engineers.

This concept has to do with the patterning of the different aspects of speech and with what happens when the patterning is broken or distorted by some kind of interference or "noise." For example, how much can be left out and how much must be expressed in more than one way for someone to understand what is being said to him in a transatlantic telephone call? Using the concept of redundancy, linguists began to think afresh about the usefulness of all the elements, the different kinds of patterning, that give complexity and richness to natural languages. This in turn gave them the essential clue to the unworkability of artificial languages, except for very special purposes. These languages lack the resources of redundancy that make natural languages such good instruments for the most diverse users.

In the abstract, redundancy is a complicated concept, partly because it involves all the levels of speech. But every child, learning to speak, masters its uses in practice, and all of us are aware of some of the elements. Listening to a United Nations debate without seeing the speakers, anyone can tell when there is a language switch. Though we may not understand a word, our ear informs us that we are now listening to a different combination of sound patterns as well as different patterns of intonation, pitch and rhythm.

In the same way, listening to a group of English speakers whose words we do understand, we can—with a little practice—identify one as an Australian, another as a Scot and a third as a South African by consistent variations not only in sound, intonation and rhythm patterns but also in grammatical usage and the meanings given to words and expressions. As we listen, any one or all of these sets of variations may be (from our point of view) "noise"—something that interferes with our understanding of what is said—and yet, because we share what is basic to the language, usually we do get the message.

We can think of speech (spoken language) as consisting of interrelated sets of patterns, each of which, as it is used, gives us specific information. In English, for example, intonation informs us as to whether a speaker is asking a question, making a statement or issuing a command. As spoken, "Go!" sounds very different from "Go?" or "Go." Even if we do not catch the word itself, we do grasp part of the speaker's intended meaning. And when a German or a Frenchman speaks grammatically correct English but uses the intonations of his own language, we may miss a part of the message but still get the part that is communicated, in this case, by words and grammar. Redundancy refers to the fact that the same or related or confirming information is given by different means—at different levels, through different sets of patterns and by different elements within the same set—all interlocking in speech.

A single sentence can illustrate how redundancy works. If someone said to you, "Mary had her new hat on yesterday," you would recognize this as English from the sound pattern itself. A drop in the speaker's voice at the end would tell you that this was a statement, not a question; the position of the first two words ("Mary had," not "Had Mary") would suggest the same thing. "Mary" would tell you that this was a girl; "her" would confirm your expectation. The form of the verb would tell you the event was in the past; "yesterday" would confirm this and pinpoint the time. This is, of course, a simplification and only a beginning. And if one adds that gesture and posture play a part in communication, the range within which redundancy operates is widened even further.

The important thing is that each language has its own range and regularities of patterning at all levels—on which the poet and the tone-deaf person and the little child will draw, although with a very different appreciation of the resources of the same language. Yet each can make himself understood. We are learning today that deaf children who can "hear" language rhythms only when they are magnified in special earphones can still in this way get a firm grasp of how their language operates in speech.

A language that works has been shaped by men and women, old people and little children, intelligent people and dunces, people with good memories, and people with poor memories, those who pay attention to form and those who pay attention to sound, and people with all the diversity of interests present in their culture over generations. This very multiplicity of speakers creates the redundancy that makes a language flexible and intelligible to all the different kinds of people who are its speakers at any time. A natural language allows for the whole range of human intelligence and responsiveness, and it is far richer and more expressive than are any individual's capacities for using it. This is why the invented languages failed—each in its form presented only a very limited set of possibilities worked out by a few people in only one period.

And this is why, if we are to have a universal language, it must be a natural language. It must have the complex resources on which all the world's people can draw. But it cannot be one of the present-day major languages now in competition. For we need to protect all the languages there are. Soon diversity of language will be the principal remaining evidence of man's extraordinary inventiveness in creating different ways of living, and language will have to carry the sense of intimacy within a way of life and the continuity of long generations. As American English expresses our deepest values and other languages give us insight into the values of other peoples, so also every language carries that which is most significant for its native speakers.

In time, this is also what a universal secondary language must carry for the peoples of the whole world—the significance of world-wide talking with one another within a shared civilization. If we chose as a secondary language the natural language of a small, politically unimportant, non-European literate people, we could accomplish our several purposes.

It can be done now. It may be very difficult to do later.

COMPREHENSION QUIZ

1. Dr. Mead asserts that we are in the process of creating a new civilization in which
    a. no one really shares.
    b. everyone is cognizant of his responsibilities.
    c. people everywhere are beginning to help shape our common future.
    d. no one is fully aware of what will be in the future.

2. The paradox of our time is that
    a. we talk to each other, but we cannot fully understand one another.
    b. our ability to talk to one another has not kept pace with our ability to see and hear each other.
    c. everyone talks, but few have wisdom.
    d. all of the above.
3. What is the estimate of the number of "known" languages?
    a. 3,000
    b. 2,500
    c. 30,000
    d. 4,850
4. The insistence that every child learn English and that every job be carried on in English, has resulted in the notion that adequate English is a symbol of full
    a. acceptance.
    b. rejection.
    c. citizenship.
    d. communication.
5. From one point of view, the primacy of English has had as its basis the belief that a common language is crucial for
    a. survival.
    b. social unity.
    c. good relations.
    d. a good education.
6. Just by listening to a different combination of sound patterns as well as different patterns of intonation, pitch and rhythm, we know that
    a. we are listening to a different language.
    b. we are hearing an educated speaker.
    c. either a Scot or an American is speaking.
    d. (a) and (c) above.
7. One of the main requirements of a universal language is that it be
    a. natural.
    b. neutral.
    c. new.
    d. redundant.
8. The author recommends, as a universal language, the language of
    a. a new African nation.
    b. English.
    c. Chinese.
    d. a non-European people.

DISCUSSION QUESTIONS

1. What advantages can you cite for a universal language?
2. Will our world ever be "one" in practical terms?
3. What do you see as the requirements of a universal language before you would give up your own present one?

WRITING SUGGESTIONS

1. Write an address to a group of college students attempting to persuade them of the necessity of a universal language.
2. Why everyone should (or should not) speak English.
3. Must everyone speak in order to be a good citizen?

Recommended Readings to Part 1

Black, Max (ed.). *The Importance of Language*. Englewood Cliffs, N.J.: Prentice-Hall, 1962.

Chase, Stuart. *The Tyranny of Words*. New York: Harcourt, Brace and World, 1938.

Hall, Robert A. *Linguistics and Your Language*. New York: Anchor Books, 1950.

Hayakawa, S. I. *The Use and Misuse of Language*. New York: Fawcett, 1962.

Pedersen, Holger. *The Discovery of Language*. Bloomington: Indiana University Press, 1962.

Pei, Mario. *Language for Everybody*. New York: Pocket Books, 1956.

Potter, Simeon. *Our Language*. Baltimore: Penguin, 1962.

What Is Language?

II

The Miracle
of the Desart

by CHARLTON LAIRD

The Lonesome Land

To most of us a desert is a place with too little water and too much sand, but to our ancestors a "desart" was any wild place where no one lived. Imagine that you live in such a place. No other human being is near, and you have never seen anything human except the reflection of yourself in a pool. You suppose you are as unique as the sun and the moon.

You live in a world of sight and sound, but sounds of a limited sort. You know the rushing wind, the pattering sleet. You know the lonesome and terrifying howls of the wolves, the insane laughter of the loons, the chattering of chipmunks and squirrels. You can extract meaning from these sounds. You know that after the wind may come rain or snow or hail to beat upon you. You know that with the wolves abroad you want a good fire at night, and that with the loons crying a certain season of the year has come. You can guess that if the chipmunk chatters and jerks his tail with uncommon violence he is probably either hungry or angry. But to none of these sound makers, wind or wolf or chipmunk, can you say anything. Nor do they mean to say anything to you; not even the loon, in whose voice there is a human note, means to discuss the weather. You are living in a world almost devoid of communication.

And so one evening you are lonely and empty because the moon is shining and there is a strange beauty over the land. Being sad, you imagine the nicest thing that could happen to you—that there might be another creature such as you, such as you are though a little different, for there seem to be two chipmunks and numerous loons. Except that this creature, since it would be like you, would not scurry off to hide in a hole, nor disappear

From Charlton Laird, *The Miracle of Language*, New York: The World Publishing Company. Copyright © 1953 by Charlton Laird. Reprinted by permission of the publisher.

with a whirring of wings. It would come and want to live with you, and the two of you could do everything together. And if you happened to like each other very much—well, you could look at each other in the moonlight and feel good inside. You might even touch each other, very intimately. Beyond that you could not go, for how can any creature, you would assume, let another know how he is feeling or what he is thinking?

Oh, you could rub your belly if you were hungry, smile and nod your head if you wanted to agree, and bellow if you were angry or got burned. But if you looked at another creature and felt very loving, how could you let the other creature know it? Or how could you find out if the other creature felt the same way? Or maybe a little bit different?

Since you have already imagined the impossible, and in the moonlight with the strange shapes and shadows everywhere it is very pleasant and strangely comforting to imagine nice and impossible things, you imagine something more. You imagine that by some sort of magic, whenever you want the other creature to know what you are thinking, your thoughts will appear in the other person. This creature, too, can give you thoughts just by wanting you to have them. Then, if you love each other, you can tell each other all about it, only by wanting the other one to know.

But that could not happen. That would be a miracle; being practical and taking little stock in miracles, you go off and try to drown your lonely feeling in fermented goat's milk.

Far from being fantastic, this miracle is occurring at the moment. Anyone reading this page knows essentially what I was thinking when I wrote it. Wherever this page goes, to Denver or Dublin, people will know what I was thinking. . . . Similarly if any of these people were here in this room, and instead of writing I were to start creating, with my tongue and my teeth and the holes in my head, the intermittent sounds which we call speech, they would know immediately what I am thinking. Furthermore, for all or any of this to occur, neither you nor I need be conscious of the way it occurs. I need only want you to know, and you need only refrain from leaving the room or throwing down the book.

In short "the miracle of the desart" can and does occur; it occurs so commonly that most of us never give it a thought. The very babes learn to take advantage of it, just as they learn to walk or to hold a spoon. The miracle is . . . language.

The Mechanics of a Miracle

The miracle of speech does not grow less if we examine it. Let us consider what happens. At first let us take the simplest sort of instance, in which one person speaks a word and another hears it. Any word would do, but let us use the word *wrist*.

What has the speaker done when he utters this word? By gentle pressure of the diaphragm and contraction of the intercostal muscles he has emitted a little air, scrupulously controlled, although the muscles which expelled the air are so strong they could shake his whole body if they were used vigorously. He has slightly tightened some membranes in his throat so that the column of air has forced the membranes to vibrate. Meanwhile a number of minute movements, especially of the tongue, have caused the center of vibration to spread sideways across the tongue, move suddenly forward, concentrate just back of the upper teeth, and then cease. With the cessation of this voiced sound, the column of air hisses against the upper teeth and gums, and is suddenly and momentarily stopped by a flip of the tongue. The tongue strikes the roof of the mouth with the portion just back from the tip, and spreads so that the whole column of air is suddenly damned up and then released. All this must be done with the muscles of the throat relatively relaxed, and when the little explosion has taken place, everything must stop at once.

Now the word *wrist* has been spoken, only a word, but the whole operation is so complex and delicately timed that nobody could do this by thinking about it. It can be done successfully, in the main, only when it is done unconsciously. In part it can be learned, and people having speech defects sometimes learn part of the practice by laborious study, but good speech is always mainly unconscious speech. Any tennis player, even if he could not explain this enigma, could provide an analogy for it. When he sees a rapidly flying tennis ball coming toward him, he knows what he must do. He must maneuver himself into the proper position, be poised with his weight properly distributed, meet the ball with the proper sweep of his arm and with his racket held at just the right pitch, and all this must be timed to stop the flying ball at a precise point. But if the tennis player pauses to think of all these actions and how he will perform them, he is lost. The ball will not skim back over the net, building air pressure as it goes until it buzzes down into the opponent's corner. If the tennis player thinks about anything except where he wants the ball to go and what he plans for the next stroke, he will probably become so awkward that he will be lucky to hit the ball at all. Rapid, precise muscular actions can be successfully carried out only by the unconscious part of the brain. And so with the speaker. He cannot speak well unless he speaks unconsciously, for his movements are as precise, as complicated, and as exactly timed as those of the tennis player. Anyone who doubts it, need only observe the distress of a speaker who has not learned English as a child, trying to say the word *clothes.*

So much for the speaker. Now for the hearer. Sound waves which are set in motion by humming, purring, and hissing in the speaker's throat and head penetrate to the listener's inner ear, and there set up kindred vibrations. At once that marvelous agglomeration of nerves, nuclei, and whatnot which we call the brain makes the hearer aware that a familiar sound has been produced, and presents him with various concepts associated with the sound. And here we are in the presence of meaning.

The End and Means of Meaning

How is it possible that two people who may never have seen each other before, or who may not even live on the same continent, or be alive in the same century have immediate, similar, and complicated ideas in the presence of a sound? Especially is this even amazing when we consider that there are hundreds of thousands of these sounds with millions of meanings and still more millions of implications so delicate that they cannot be defined. Somehow millions of people have agreed, at least roughly, as to the meaning of the word *wrist* and the other countless words in the language, and this in spite of the fact that the human animal is so varied and contentious that seldom will two human beings agree about anything, whether the subject be religion, politics, or what will "go" with that hat.

Of course when the word *wrist* is spoken by one person and heard by another, little communication has as yet taken place. The single word raises almost as many questions as it answers. Is the speaker thinking that his wrist is arthritic, or that certain brush strokes can best be made with the wrist? These questions can be partially answered by adding a few more words, but in spite of anything he can do the speaker is likely to remain to a degree ambiguous. He cannot be precise because the syllable he is uttering has no precise meaning.

Thus "the miracle of the desart" is far enough from the divine to exhibit a human flaw. Exact communication is impossible among men. Gertrude Stein may have felt that "a rose is a rose is a rose," but our speaker, if he considers the matter carefully, must know that a wrist is not necessarily a wrist. It may be some bones hung together by ligaments. It may be the skin outside these bones. It may be the point which marks the end of the sleeve. If the speaker is a tailor, *wrist* may be a command to hem a glove. But even granted that both speaker and hearer agree that *wrist* is here associated with the bones, flesh, and skin at the juncture of the human hand and arm, they may still associate highly varied feelings with this part of the body. The speaker may have big, bony wrists, and have hated them all her life. The hearer may have been forced out of an Olympic skiing contest when he fell and broke a wrist. There is no one thing which *wrist* calls up in exactly the same form to everyone; there are not even areas of meaning which are the same for everybody. Meanings exist only in minds, and minds result from beings and experiences; no two of them are alike, nor are the meanings they contain. Still, granted that meaning is not and never can be exact, there remains a body of agreement as to the association to be connected with certain sounds which is staggering to contemplate.

But we have only begun, for we started with the simplest sort of example of spoken language. A word like *no* can mean *no, damn it,* or *yes,* or dozens of things between and among these meanings, depending upon the way in which the word is pronounced and the sounds modulated. The uttering and grasping of words, furthermore, become immeasurably complicated as soon as a speaker starts running them together into sentences. But for the moment let us complicate the situation only slightly by making the speaker also a writer, and let him make a few marks on any sort of object. These marks can now take the place of sound and can call up the concepts associated with *wrist* wherever they go. They can continue calling up these concepts long after the man who made them is dead; they can do so for hundreds, even thousands, of years. Clay cones and slabs of stone, scratched with marks which were long undecipherable, could still produce something like their original meaning when their language was rediscovered, although no living man had known how to speak or write or think the language for thousands of years.

Man, then, can be defined, if one wishes, as a languagized mammal. A cow can communicate in a cowlike way by bawling and dogs can express themselves to a degree by looking soulfully from one end while wagging the other, but man is probably more significantly distinguished from his fellow creatures by his complicated means of communication than by any other difference. In short, man as we know him could not exist without language and until there was language. Civilization could not exist until there was written language, because without written language no generation could bequeath to succeeding generations anything but its simpler findings. Culture could not be widespread until there was printed language.

In the beginning was the word. Or, if in the beginning was the arboreal ape, with the word and an opposable thumb he scrambled down from the trees and found his way out of the woods.

The Miracle and the Nature of Man

Now having said so much, we have implied a great deal more. If language is intimately related to being human, then when we study language we are, to a remarkable degree, studying human nature. Similarly we may expect language to be what it is because human beings are what they are. But we should not expect to study language by making inferences from other fields of study. That way madness lies—or at least, monumental blunders. For instance, in the nineteenth century, students of society assumed that since the theory of evolution revealed new truths about human anatomy the same theory working in the same way should reveal new truths about human society. It did not. It led folklorists and anthropologists into one misbegotten generalization after another, and scattered the pages of a monumental work like *The Golden Bough* with errors which must now be patiently corrected. Any field of study which does not have principles of its own is a poor study, and surely no one can accuse language of paucity. We must expect language, however it is rooted in mankind and civilization, to have principles of its own, and if we want the truth we must respect them.

Men have not always done so. There was, for instance, a serious group of enthusiasts for language who hoped to reform national conduct and international manners, to harden sloppy thinking and to clear muddy expression by reforming our vocabulary. These people were well intentioned, and certainly their ends were desirable. If we could stop an international gangster with a few well-chosen words, that would be an admirable stroke. But it does seem a good bit to achieve with nothing more tangible than a refurbished vocabulary, particularly since a large number of learned and eloquent people have been laboring for a long time, using the excellent disciplines of grammar, rhetoric, and lexicography, to encourage the precise use of language, and in spite of them national and international hoodlums are still with us. But let us see what these people proposed by way of method.

They recognized, first, that words have many usages, and that unless we are sure in what sense a word is being used we are likely to misunderstand one another. Furthermore, they recognized that many serious arguments, even fights and wars, grow out of misunderstandings, and that these misunderstandings may rest on various usages of words. Our language is so lacking in precision, they felt, that communication with any exactitude is impossible. Could exact communication be achieved, they trusted, we should find ourselves in complete harmony.

To follow their reasoning we might take a simple sentence like the following: *Civilized man cannot live without religion.* Obviously this sentence means many things depending upon the definition of the words. When is a man *civilized*? When can he be said to live? What degree of withoutness is *without*? By religion do you mean belief in a supernatural and omnipotent being, adherence to a recognized church, the practice of an abiding faith, a conviction that there is order and purpose in the universe, or what? A word like *religion* can have a score of meanings, or more, and even seemingly unequivocal words like *can* and *not* have various uses. Accordingly, some of the reformers decided to make American diction so precise that words could be used with mathematical exactness, and to do this they planned a dictionary. In this work all words would be defined in all uses and each would be given a label. To be clear, one need only affix the label.

According to the New Dictionary, the sentence above would read something like the following: $Civilized_{10}$ man_8 can_2 not_1 $live_{14}$ $without_3$ $religion_9$.

Now the statement has become clear and precise. As soon as the reader has looked up each of these words in the New Dictionary and learned that *religion* here means "conviction of the existence of a supreme being," and that *live* means "enjoy one's powers to the fullest," he will be approaching some certainty as to the meaning of the sentence, and be the readier either to agree with it or to dispute it more violently than before.

The Miracle Will Have No Nostrums

Undoubtedly if this method were feasible it would promote the precise use of language. But the procedure has faults and they are pretty obvious. Not the least of them are these: nobody would be willing to use this method, and nobody could use it if he wanted to, because it ignores human nature and because it defies fundamental principles of human language.

It ignores, for instance, the fundamental principle that language constantly changes. So far as we know, it always has changed; it is changing now, and we have good reason to suppose it will continue to change in spite of handbooks on usage and the grade-school teacher. A dictator like Hitler can influence language considerably; if he wishes to jail everybody caught using the Greek roots in the word *telephone* and let them out only if they will use the equivalent German roots in *Fernsprecher,* most of them will say *Fernsprecher.* But not even a dictator with a concentration camp can keep language from changing, because it changes in more ways than any dictator could detect. The guards in the concentration camp themselves would be changing it unconsciously. So would the dictator. Before we could decide which was $religion_{21}$ and which $religion_{22}$ and print a dictionary with those decisions, the language would have changed.

No writer would use this language and no speaker could speak it. Would Mr. Hemingway consent to write about an old man and the sea, looking up in his dictionary every time he used the word *sea* to discover whether this was sea_{15} or sea_{18}? Would the president of the National City Bank require all his letters to be written with it? I doubt it. Bankers, as far as I have observed them, are even more conservative with their language than with their loans.

In short, this system could not be used for many reasons, but mainly because it ignores the nature of the human mind, as the mind expresses itself in language. We have no difficulty distinguishing between the words *religion* and *theology* because we have differences in form and sound with which to associate differences in meaning, but if *theology* were $religion_{21}$, we never could remember whether it was religion-sub-twenty-one, religion-sub-twenty-two, or religion-sub-twelve.

If a language like this is unusable in writing, it is worse than unusable in speaking. The new language might reduce gossip, but ordinary conversation would cease altogether and that would be a pity. To speak at all in the new language, all of us would have to wheel monumental dictionaries about with us, using something like a self-service grocery cart. Talk would however die in a good cause, for it would carry this artificial language along with it. No language has ever been able to survive unless rooted in common speech. Language is a product of the human mind and the human vocal organs; it follows the ways of the human mind and the human larynx. For the moment, let us postpone consideration of larynxes and speculate a little about brains and language.

Dialect: The Miracle in the Making

We have already agreed that every speaker or writer uses words as they exist for him; figuratively, he picks them out of his own brains. The Anglo-Saxons had a fine phrase for speaking, "to unlock the word-hoard," just as though each person about to speak his mind would first go to his great safe-deposit box of words, and pick out those he wanted to present to you. Many of these jewels and pieces of old linguistic treasure would be similar to other word-jewels in other people's word-hoards, but each is an individual piece with its own background and character, made anew though on a familiar model. Quite literally each of us has his own word-hoard, be it large or small, and every word in that treasury is a little different from any word owned by anyone else, different in meaning, in pronunciation, and in the manner in which its owner uses it.

Now, since each of us owns his own words and uses them in his own way, it follows that each of us speaks a dialect. More properly, each of us participates in a number of ways of speaking and has what is sometimes called an *idiolect*. Each of us shares family speech habits, shares also a neighborhood dialect or several neighborhood dialects, and has occupational speech peculiarities, perhaps of several sorts. For instance, an old lady of my acquaintance was fond of the word *pesky* and unconsciously bequeathed it to all her children. These children grew up with their family peculiarities, but added to them the community speech common in Iowa. They say *goin'* and *doin'*. One left home early and his speech is tinged with pronunciations from San Antonio, Texas. One became an engineer and his language is spattered with *pylons* and *safety factors*. Another became a labor leader and the jargon of his job is all over his talk. That is, each of these children of the old lady now speaks a dialect which reflects his home, his family and acquaintances, his occupation, and many other things.

Some people, of course, suppose that dialects are shameful, or at least unfortunately conspicuous like a large Adam's apple, and they try to "correct" their dialectal peculiarities. But how can we decide which is the "correct" dialect? It used to be easy. We used to assume that the New England dialects were better than the others, because most of the lexicographers came from New England, and they put their own pronunciations into the dictionaries. Noah Webster, in prescribing a pronunciation, remarked that he knew the word was pronounced differently in the South. "But in Connecticut," he added, "we pronounce it this way." Apparently he assumed that in matters of speech, a New Havenite could do no wrong; a Yankee was born a linguistic standard. But lexicographers are no longer so provincial—besides, a considerable number of them come from the Middle West and the South. They are inclined to ask why is it better to pronounce *idea* with the sound of an *r* at the end and *mother* without it, than to change one nasal for another at the end of *going*? Students of language now tend to find all dialects equally interesting, and to write those into dictionaries which incline to be central.

When people try to "correct" their speech, they often succeed only in mixing up their dialects more than they were mixed before, or they develop a stilted pronunciation. A friend of mine was born in a little community of Latter Day Saints, and acquired the dialect peculiar to that group, in which the sounds customarily heard in *harm* and *warm* are transposed. My friend discovered to his horror that he was saying *form* where other people said *farm*. This was a serious matter, for he had to work with agricultural people, and he carefully taught himself to say *farm* with a fine, broad *a*. But he did not learn the related words; he still says *farmer formers* when he means *former farmers,* and he talks about the *business of forming* on farms. Personally, I preferred the speech of another of my Mormon friends, who was more forthright. She was a dean of women and, feeling responsible for the conduct of the students, was outraged when they stormed, shouting, into the college dining hall. "Why," she said, "they act as if they were barn in a born." We all liked her, more so because her speech was redolent of her background and character.

Basically all speech is dialectal. It exists as dialects, and if it is to be understood, it must be studied as dialects. This is one reason that there are, at this writing, at least two zealous efforts to study local American speech. One program is dedicated to preparing a linguistic atlas of the country, tracing dialects and their movements by careful study of a relatively small number of locutions. Dialect maps have already been prepared for New England, and are in process elsewhere; they are modeled upon some excellent European dialect maps. A second project envisages a monumental dialect dictionary. Both works will be fascinating, if and when they can be finished. Meanwhile anyone interested in language can have fun with two excellent albums of dialect records; one for the United States, *The Linguaphone Language Records,* and one for the British Isles, *British Drama League Dialect Records,* both readily available.

Miracle with Dual Controls

We may now observe a paradox embodied in the apparently diametric statements in the earlier and later parts of this chapter. First we noticed that language relies upon a body of human agreements bewildering in its complexity. Human beings can speak, and can be understood, only because they have at their call millions of meanings and countless ways of putting these meanings together to produce larger and more exact meanings. These meanings and means of meaning, although they may later become codified, rest upon an agreement unconsciously entered into, signed, and sealed by all of us. Language is language only because it has currency; the giving of currency is an act of social faith, the utilizing of the common by-product of many minds busy with their own affairs. Thus looked at from one point of view, language is a common product made by all of us, in process of being remade by all of us, existing in any real sense because it is made by all of us, and understandable only if studied as the commonality of many minds over many generations.

On the other hand we have seen that language as it exists is always the possession of individuals. Vocabularies are individual vocabularies, and ways of speaking are always the ways of individuals. A man's speech is as peculiar to him, as inseparable from him, as is his own shadow. It has grown with him, and most of it will die with him; like his shadow, it is to a degree made anew every day. He inevitably speaks a dialect, his own dialect, which is in turn a compact of many regionalisms, a linguistic goulash which every man brews after his own recipe. Looked at from this point of view, language becomes a pattern of infinitely blending dialects.

Philosophically, here is a dualism strange indeed. Like the higher forms of life, language results from engendering by opposites. But unlike mammalian life, it never becomes either male or female; it carries always with it the impress of this curious duality, and it must always be studied as at once general and particular, common and individual. This is not the least of the curiosities of language. Nor is it the only one.

COMPREHENSION QUIZ

1. In the imaginary episode about the man alone in a wilderness, the author says that we would be in a world almost devoid of
   a. communication.
   b. speech.
   c. language.
   d. discussion.
2. Calling language a "miracle" is based on the notion that

a. we need to communicate.
b. we often take language for granted.
c. that men and women communicate infrequently.
d. that people on a desert are rarely alone.
3. Speaking the word *wrist* can be done successfully, in the main, only when it is done
a. deliberately.
b. unconsciously.
c. spontaneously.
d. discreetly.
4. Exact communication among men is
a. rare.
b. impossible.
c. convenient.
d. disturbing.
5. Man as we know him could not exist without language and until there was
a. hope.
b. "miracles."
c. language.
d. communication.
6. Every speaker or writer uses words as they exist for
a. his listener.
b. himself.
c. the society.
d. posterity.

DISCUSSION QUESTIONS

1. Discuss the Biblical account of the Tower of Babel.
2. In your judgment, why do men need to know the nature of language?

WRITING SUGGESTIONS

1. Construct a mythical island and describe some of the linguistic problems a group of four persons might have if they each had differing languages.
2. Examine some of the different meanings a common word like "run" has.
3. Report on some of the theories of language, such as the "bow-wow" or "ding-dong" theories.

What Language Is

by ERNEST W. GRAY

. . . Language [is] a group of sounds distinguishable from one another and arranged in a system by means of which thoughts and feelings (neural events) can be communicated from one person to another. Note that this definition does not include writing. The omission follows the practice of most modern students of language (linguists) in considering speech as the real language, writing simply a substitute for speech. (Hastily we should add that our intent is not to depreciate the importance of writing . . . it is simply to point out historical relation of speech and writing.) When it was realized that wisdom and knowledge could be passed from generation to generation only in limited amounts by speech, the human race was able to invent a substitute for the human voice, not equal in versatility it is true, but enormously valuable in preserving much knowledge that would otherwise have been lost. Our libraries are the monuments to this invention. Writing has thus developed from speaking; it was, in its origin at least, dependent on speech, and even now speech seems to have a greater effect on writing than writing does on speech (except for the speech of very highly educated people·whose contact with written language is much more frequent than is most people's).

The definition of language as a system of sounds applies to all of the nearly three thousand languages in the world—to English as much as to Japanese, to Turkish as much as to Ojibway. A single language, however, may be defined as a system of sounds familiar and usable to a limited number of people and unfamiliar to all others in the world. This means that the system has features that belong to it alone and that these features prevent the use of the system by anyone who has not learned it. Thus English has two sounds usually represented in writing by *th,* as in *this* or *thin,* which are not regularly present in the German or French language systems. This does not mean that German-speaking or French-speaking people cannot make these sounds. The physical apparatus used in making speech sounds is so similar in all human beings that everyone born without a physical defect can quite adequately make the sounds required by any language in the world. If a child of English-speaking parents had been kidnapped at birth and brought up by Turkish-speaking foster parents he would learn Turkish with the same ease as a child born of Turkish-speaking parents. In other words, language is a learned activity; there is nothing inherent about it. The great difficulty most of us have in learning a foreign language when we are grown is that through almost unlimited practice we have accustomed our muscles and nerves to make various sounds and to avoid others that have no place in our language system and would in fact simply be impediments to communication. Then when we try to make our muscles and nerves create unaccustomed sounds we encounter the resistance of habit. Any non-Britisher who has driven an automobile in the British Isles, where the rule is to keep to the left, will testify to the difficulty of responding properly to the necessities of such a traffic system. Even after weeks of practice a moment of relaxed attention will find one drifting toward the right. And in speech, so much more deep-seated in habit, the difficulty of learning unaccustomed sounds for many people is almost insuperable. Many Germans who learned their English as adults still, after thirty years of speaking English, say *zis* for *this,* and many Americans never quite learn to say the *r* in a French word so as not to make a native French-speaker grin.

A language then is a sound system known to and used by a limited number of people. It is obvious that some sound systems have many more resemblances than others. If we heard German spoken or Italian we are continually hearing what seem like English words rather badly mispronounced but still recognizable. When this occurs there are two possibilities. One is that the languages in question are related, that is, that they have a common ancestor or that one has developed from the other. The other possibility is that the people using the two languages have such similar cultures that they have borrowed sounds and other speech devices from each other. Though the first possibility is more likely, the second also exists, especially when a particular cultural activity has been developed in one country and then has been adopted by another. German and English sometimes sound alike because they are quite closely related. But sometimes Italian, too, which is far more distantly related to English, sounds familiar. This is because certain cultural activities, music, for example, developed in Italian a vocabulary that has been taken over by English with little change. English is related to French, Swedish, Gaelic, Russian, as well as to German, though there is a closer relationship to German than to Russian or Gaelic. These languages and others are related because they have a common ancestor and they are said to belong to the same language family. English belongs to the language family generally called Indo-European.

Another word that must be defined is the word *dialect*. Everyone is aware that people who live in different parts of the United States speak a little differently. Eating lunch once in Ireland at the same table with four strangers, I thought I recognized the sound of one man's speech as that of someone from the southwest part of the United States, probably Texas. But the other three people didn't sound like Americans at all. And they didn't sound like Irish or English either. This was a bit puzzling. Later on I found that the first man was a Texan who had married a woman born in Ireland but who had lived most of her life in England. The other two were her relatives, whose history had been similar to hers. All of them spoke in a way that I could easily understand but in a way quite perceptibly different from my own way of speech. In other words they spoke different dialects from mine. *A dialect, then, is a version of a language having minor differences in the sound system which are clearly noticeable to a person speaking a different dialect of the same language, but which do not seriously interfere with communication.*

Dialects are not always connected with geography. Sometimes they are due to social differences. A man who has worked all his life as a laborer is not likely to speak very much like a minister or a judge even though each may have been born and lived all his life in the same city. Not only will the laborer's choice of words be different and more limited in range but the items in his sound system will not be quite the same. However, these men are not likely to have much difficulty in understanding each other, provided that they talk about subjects with which both are familiar. Many expert users of the language have at their command more than one social dialect, just as people trained for the stage often have these plus various regional dialects.

The written version of English is a sort of dialect, different from any speech dialect, yet an efficient means of communication among the users of widely varying speech dialects. It is of course not a dialect, strictly speaking, since it is not a sound system, but it has many resemblances to a dialect. Most speakers of English are thoroughly familiar with the "dialect" of written English.

And finally it is important to define a less familiar term, the term *idiolect. An idiolect is an individual way of speaking.* Each person has his own idiolect. It is because of this phenomenon that we can recognize the voice of an acquaintance even when we cannot see him—when talking on the telephone or from different rooms in the same building, for example. Nothing is more miraculous about language than the existence of idiolects. Every individual speaks in a recognizably different fashion from everyone else, yet this same individual with his unique way of speaking can (in the case of English at any rate) communicate successfully with literally millions of other people. No one speaks just exactly like anyone else, but over thousands of miles of the earth we speak enough alike to transfer our particular thoughts and feelings to one another. . . .

COMPREHENSION QUIZ

1. Which of the following statements is true?
    a. Writing, rather than speech, is regarded as the real language by most linguists.
    b. Writing is equal to speech in versatility.
    c. Speech has a greater effect on writing than writing has on speech.
    d. Writing has a greater effect on speech than speech has on writing.
2. Gray's definition of language applies
    a. only to Indo-European languages.
    b. only to those languages that have an alphabet.
    c. to all languages except Turkish, Japanese, and Ojibway.
    d. to all of the languages in the world.
3. Which of the following statements is false?
    a. Speaking developed from writing, according to most scientific linguists.
    b. Everyone born without a physical defect can make the sounds required by any language in the world.
    c. Language is a learned activity.
    d. The physical apparatus used in making speech sounds is similar in all human beings.
4. Languages are related when
    a. they have a common ancestor.
    b. they borrow vocabulary terms from each other.
    c. their alphabets are similar.
    d. they are spoken by neighboring countries.
5. Which of the following statements is false?
    a. A language is a sound system known to and used by a limited number of people.
    b. English belongs to the language family generally called Indo-European.
    c. A dialect is characterized by sound differences which seriously interfere with communication.
    d. Dialects are not always connected with geography.
6. An idiolect is
    a. the dialect of a particular cultural level.
    b. an individual way of speaking.
    c. a slang term adopted by the young.
    d. an impediment of speech related to aphasia.

DISCUSSION QUESTIONS

1. What are the distinctions Gray makes between *language* and *a language*?
2. Why do most definitions of language exclude writing? Is writing regarded as less important?

3. In connection with the second paragraph of Gray's essay, look up the term "phoneme." How do phonemes differ from the letters of the alphabet?
4. Gray says that expert users of the language have at their command more than one social dialect. Describe the situations that would require such mastery.

WRITING SUGGESTIONS

1. Gray refers to borrowings that English has made from other languages. Consider a particular subject area such as music, fashion, or food, and investigate its use of foreign terminology.
2. How does a dialect differ from a language? How does the dialect of native speakers in your city differ from that of speakers in other parts of the country?
3. What social values are attached to dialects? Consider, for example, the "snob appeal" of certain dialects.

The Origin
of Speech

by ASHLEY MONTAGU

Speech is the expression or communication of thoughts and feelings by uttered or spoken words, vocal sounds, or gestures. When and in what manner did speech come into being? It is a question that has often been asked. Today we are in a better position to attempt an answer to that question than at any previous time. Hunting requires the cooperative endeavors of several men. Where an animal could evade a single hunter it would be less likely to do so when two or more hunters were stalking it. The selective value of cooperation in hunting would have been very high, and such hunting undoubtedly made its contribution to the development of man's cooperative nature, for a high premium would have been put upon the cooperators, and an unequivocally negative one upon the noncooperators. In every hunting society of which we have knowledge, this remains so to the present day.

Speech comes into being when two or more individuals agree to attach the same meaning to the same sounds, and thereafter use those sounds consistently with the meanings that have been bestowed upon them. The meanings are symbols which stand for things which are not present to one's senses in physical form. Speech, then, is behavior made artificially clear. It is a tool. It is the expression of intelligence, and therefore, man's most useful tool. To this day, the way a man speaks is a good indication of the quality of his intelligence.

The great apes are all capable of vocalization, varying from whines, cries, and squeaks, to screams, growls, and roars. The orang-utan and the gorilla tend to be comparatively silent and taciturn. In the natural state and in captivity the chimpanzee tends to be noisy. Anatomically the great apes *appear* to be endowed with all the vocal arrangements necessary for speech, but they do not speak. In spite of their ability to make a large range of sounds it has not been possible to teach them to speak. Possibly silence has its adaptive value under forest conditions, for life in the forest is not altogether without its hazards from predators, especially for the young ones. The apes do not speak because there were never any selective pressures upon them to adapt to their environment in such a manner.

It has been suggested that the erect posture may have had something to do with those anatomical rearrangements in nose, lips, throat, and adjacent structures which, together with the necessary changes in the brain, made human speech possible. It has also been stated by some writers on the subject that in the great apes, the front of the vocal cords is covered by the epiglottis. This is said to hamper free vibration of the cords. But I do not believe this is, in fact, the case. In the apes the epiglottis is shorter and situated nearer the vocal cords and less crowded by the tongue than in man. It is difficult to see how this could prevent the use of those organs for speech, were these creatures otherwise capable of it. In the evolution of man, while the top of the skull has ballooned, the base of the skull has been squeezed and crowded. The oral cavity is short, wide, and deep, with a thick bulbous tongue. The back of the tongue is positioned nearer the epiglottis, and the larynx extends somewhat farther down the neck. The soft palate moves more freely than in the apes, and is capable of closing off the oralpharynx from the nasopharynx. Man is believed to be the only animal capable of doing this. The soft palate may be controlled as a valve, at will, shunting noisy air away from the nasal passages and into the oral cavity where long drawn-out expiratory sounds can be chopped into meaningful speech units.

Communication may be defined as any process of transmitting and receiving information, signals, or messages, whether by gesture, voice, or other means. It is the unit of the social situation. Language may be defined as any *system* of communication between animals. Speech may be defined as a verbal form of language which conveys information by chopping vocal tones into pulsations of discrete vibrating segments. Man alone can articulate such speech segments, and by means of his speech organs transmit symbols to others. Language is the formal code, the institution, the abstraction; speech is the message, the act. We *speak* a language according to the agreed, the formal, rules. The languages of man are mutually translatable, but the languages of animals are not—they are at most only interpretable.

Every muscle involved in speech is steered and controlled by spoken sounds. Because speech has to be learned by hearing the spoken sounds, those who are born deaf are unable to speak properly, if at all. They are deaf-mute. Intelligible speech requires the correlated activities of the larynx, pharynx, cheeks, mouth, tongue, and lips, activities which it takes years to learn. It used to be thought that there were special areas in the brain for speech, such as Broca's and Wernicke's, in the left frontal and temporal lobes respectively. It is now known that this is highly unlikely to be the case on theoretical, anatomical, and physiological grounds. Conrad has resumed the evidence showing that damage to almost any part of the cortex of the brain can produce a loss of the ability to use language (aphasia). It has also been shown that Broca's area can sometimes be damaged without causing any such impairment.

Under hunting conditions in cooperation with one's fellow-hunters the highest premium, as we have already said, would have been placed upon behavior calculated to achieve the desired end—the securing of the quarry. Such successful cooperative hunting would have been greatly facilitated were the hunters able to communicate by sound with their fellow-hunters. It would be highly desirable to transmit instantly information regarding changing intentions and strategies paralleling the changing conditions during the hunt. Different individuals, from their various angles of vision, would see and foresee behavior likely to yield the most favorable result, and would want to communicate this to their fellow-hunters, particularly over distances where gestures would be ineffective. The only way in which this could be satisfactorily achieved while running, and the running itself would facilitate such expiratory sounds, would be by meaningful vocalizations which conveyed to everyone what was required in order to meet the changing conditions which were either being observed or foreseen.

It has been repeatedly pointed out that during man's early evolution problem-solving abilities would have been at the highest premium. This would be especially so during the hunt. With the ability to interpret and imitate the meaningful cries of one's companions, such a combination of abilities would have had a high survival value. Thus, the development of tools, of intelligence, and of speech would have gone hand in hand. Those individuals having the ability to solve problems quickly and to interpret the expressions of others would be more likely to leave a progeny than those wanting in such a combination of abilities. Thus, speech, as well as tool-making and intelligence, would have had the highest adaptive value.

In stalking and in chasing prey, speech would constitute an invaluable aid. It would, however, appear unlikely that speech first developed during the stalking phase of man's economic activities, for in stalking prey it is essential to be quiet, and under such conditions speech would not have developed, unless in the form of gestural or sign language. Gestural and sign language almost certainly accompanied rather than preceded spoken language, and has always remained an essential part of speech. Pantomime and the mimicking of sounds would often go together, as they do to this day. Most verbalized communication consists of a combination of articulate sound, voice, and gesture. Communication is often effective by the use of one or the other of these alone.

It is more likely that the stage of evolution during which speech developed corresponded with that phase of man's economic activities in which he moved on from a small-game collector to become an active hunter. *Zinjanthropus,* therefore, may not yet have developed speech, though it is possible that he developed the rudiments of speech at least, for toolmaking implies a degree of mental development which suggests the existence of a capacity for speech—however rudimentary that capacity and that speech may have been. It is more likely that the early hunters would attempt to make meaningful cries during the chase than during their collecting or simple stalking of small game. But even in the securing of small game a good deal of running was often necessary, although not as much as in hunting. In running, and in the excitement of the chase, there would be a strong tendency toward the violent expiration of sounds, which could readily be converted into a meaningful cry or yell. All that is necessary is the repetition and imitation of such sounds in similar contextual situations for them to become established as words. In this manner a simple vocabulary would come into being, which could then serve as a basis for further elaboration and development.

Speech was among the early tools originated by man during the early hunting phase of his evolution. Because of its high adaptive value as the medium through which cooperation is secured, speech has played a seminal role in man's evolution. That it originated under the pressure of necessity, and was preserved by natural selection, is in conformity with all that we know concerning the evolution of many of man's other traits. As Sophocles wrote:

> Of all the wonders, none is more wonderful than man,
> Who has learned the art of speech, of wind-swift thought,
> And of living in neighborliness.

If we would seek for the one trait which separates man from all other animals, it is speech. Until a child can speak it acts like a young ape. When it is able to speak it acts like a human being. The difference in conduct is not due to any difference in age of any kind, but is intimately associated with the presence or absence of the ability to talk. A one-year-old child can solve most of the problems with which a chimpanzee is normally faced, and it is therefore said to be of "chimpanzee-age." But as soon as the child learns to talk, it makes rapid progress, and is soon way ahead of the ape. Speech bridges interhuman space. Words, their meanings, and interconnections, rapidly serve to organize the human world for the child in a manner impossible to the ape. Words, as symbols, serve as the repositories and transmitter mechanisms of the ideas, the wisdom, the traditions, and the culture of the group, for what cannot be directly perceived or tangibly felt, the child, through the stimulus of the word-symbols, can imagine, with a resulting expansion of his mental horizons. Speech is the means by which the raw material *Homo* is transformed into the finished article *sapiens.*

Speech is the most instrumental of the tools of intelligence. It is intelligence made explicit in the use of symbols largely for the attainment of practical ends. The meaning of a word is always the action it produces, the changes it effects. Speech is the organization of thought through symbols. Hence, the best way to the study of the thought of any people is through their language, for their language is the expression of their thought. We know nothing of the language of early man, but it was at first undoubtedly very simple, and largely limited to the achievement of practical ends. Probably in the course of later development *speculative* or *rational intelligence* gradually developed, a speculative or rational intelligence involving the organization of complex abstractions and systems of symbols, incorporated into and reflected by the character of the language. From its very origins the natural function of speech has always been to keep man in touch with his fellow man.

COMPREHENSION QUIZ

1. According to Montagu, speech comes into being when
   a. a hunting society evolves into a tool-making culture.
   b. two or more individuals agree to attach the same meaning to the same sounds.
   c. rivalry occurs between hunters.
   d. outsiders cause a society to band together for its protection.
2. Every muscle involved in speech is steered and controlled by
   a. the soft palate.
   b. the oralpharynx.
   c. spoken sounds.
   d. the nasopharynx.
3. The theory that there are special areas in the brain for speech is
   a. highly unlikely.
   b. supported by the studies of Conrad.
   c. proven by studies of the left frontal and temporal lobes.
   d. demonstrated by experiments with deaf-mutes.
4. Speech is the one trait which
   a. links man with the anthropoids.
   b. is regarded as hereditary by geneticists.
   c. separates man from all other animals.
   d. is free of symbols.
5. Which of the following statements is false?
   a. Speech is the most instrumental of the tools of intelligence.
   b. The meaning of a word is always the action it produces, the changes it effects.
   c. Speech is the organization of thought through symbols.
   d. From its early beginning, speech involved the organization of complex abstractions and systems of symbols.

DISCUSSION QUESTIONS

1. Imagine a child growing up in an environment in which no one speaks. What kinds of sounds would he produce? What does this suggest about the nature of speech?
2. In what ways is speech a tool?
3. Montagu says that the great apes are all capable of vocalization. Why has it not been possible to teach them to speak?
4. How does Montagu distinguish between *speech* and *language*? Does he agree in his definition with Gray?

WRITING SUGGESTIONS

1. How convincing is Montagu's theory of the origin of speech? Contrast it with other theories of the origin of speech. Which is most convincing?
2. Write a paper in which you demonstrate the seminal role that speech has played in man's evolution.

Something About English

by PAUL ROBERTS

Historical Backgrounds

No understanding of the English language can be very satisfactory without a notion of the history of the language. But we shall have to make do with just a notion. The history of English is long and complicated, and we can only hit the high spots.

The history of our language begins a little after A.D. 600. Everything before that is pre-history, which means that we can guess at it but can't prove much. For a thousand years or so before the birth of Christ our linguistic ancestors were savages wandering through the forests of northern Europe. Their language was a part of the Germanic branch of the Indo-European Family.

At the time of the Roman Empire—say, from the beginning of the Christian Era to around A.D. 400—the speakers of what was to become English were scattered along the northern coast of Europe. They spoke a dialect of Low German. More exactly, they spoke several different dialects, since they were several different tribes. The names given to the tribes who got to England are *Angles, Saxons,* and *Jutes.* For convenience, we can refer to them as Anglo-Saxons.

Their first contact with civilization was a rather thin acquaintance with the Roman Empire on whose borders they lived. Probably some of the Anglo-Saxons wandered into the Empire occasionally, and certainly Roman merchants and traders traveled among the tribes. At any rate, this period saw the first of our many borrowings from Latin. Such words as *kettle, wine, cheese, butter, cheap, plum, gem, bishop, church* were borrowed at this time. They show something of the relationship of the Anglo-Saxons with the Romans. The Anglo-Saxons were learning, getting their first taste of civilization.

They still had a long way to go, however, and their first step was to help smash the civilization they were learning from. In the fourth century the Roman power weakened badly. While the Goths were pounding away at the Romans in the Mediterranean countries, their relatives, the Anglo-Saxons, began to attack Britain.

The Roman had been the ruling power in Britain since A.D. 43. They had subjugated the Celts whom they found living there and had succeeded in setting up a Roman administration. The Roman influence did not extend to the outlying parts of the British Isles. In Scotland, Wales, and Ireland the Celts remained free and wild, and they made periodic forays against the Romans in England. Among other defense measures, the Romans built the famous Roman Wall to ward off the tribes in the north.

Even in England the Roman power was thin. Latin did not become the language of the country as it did in Gaul and Spain. The mass of people continued to speak Celtic, with Latin and the Roman civilization it contained in use as a top dressing.

In the fourth century, troubles multiplied for the Romans in Britain. Not only did the untamed tribes of Scotland and Wales grow more and more restive, but the Anglo-Saxons began to make pirate raids on the eastern coast. Furthermore, there was growing difficulty everywhere in the Empire, and the legions in Britain were siphoned off to fight elsewhere. Finally, in A.D. 410, the last Roman ruler in England, bent on becoming emperor, left the islands and took the last of the legions with him. The Celts were left in possession of Britain but almost defenseless against the impending Anglo-Saxon attack.

Not much is surely known about the arrival of the Anglo-Saxons in England. According to the best early source, the eighth-century historian Bede, the Jutes came in 449 in response to a plea from the Celtic king, Vortigern, who wanted their help against the Picts attacking from the north. The Jutes subdued the Picts but then quarreled and fought with Vortigern, and, with reinforcements from the Continent, settled permanently in Kent. Somewhat later the Angles established themselves in eastern England and the Saxons in the south and west. Bede's account is plausible enough, and these were probably the main lines of the invasion.

We do know, however, that the Angles, Saxons, and Jutes were a long time securing themselves in England. Fighting went on for as long as a hundred years before the Celts in England were all killed, driven into Wales, or reduced to slavery. This is the period of King Arthur, who was not entirely mythological. He was a Romanized Celt, a general, though probably not a king. He had some success against the Anglo-Saxons, but it was only temporary. By 550 or so the Anglo-Saxons were firmly established. English was in England.

Old English

All this is pre-history, so far as the language is concerned. We have no record of the English language until after 600, when the Anglo-Saxons were converted to Christianity and learned the Latin alphabet. The conversion began, to be precise, in the year 597 and was accomplished within thirty or forty years. The conversion was a great advance for the Anglo-Saxons, not only because of the spiritual benefits but because it reestablished contact with what remained of Roman civilization. This civilization didn't amount to much in the year 600, but it was certainly superior to anything in England up to that time.

It is customary to divide the history of the English language into three periods: Old English, Middle English, and Modern English. Old English runs from the earliest records—i.e., seventh century—to about 1100; Middle English from 1100 to 1450 or 1500; Modern English from 1500 to the present day. Sometimes Modern English is further divided into Early Modern, 1500–1700, and Late Modern, 1700 to the present.

When England came into history, it was divided into several more or less autonomous kingdoms, some of which at times exercised a certain amount of control over the others. In the century after the conversion the most advanced kingdom was Northumbria, the area between the Humber River and the Scottish border. By A.D. 700 the Northumbrians had developed a respectable civilization, the finest in Europe. It is sometimes called the Northumbrian Renaissance, and it was the first of the several renaissances through which Europe struggled upward out of the ruins of the Roman Empire. It was in this period that the best of the Old English literature was written, including the epic poem *Beowulf*.

In the eighth century, Northumbrian power declined, and the center of influence moved southward to Mercia, the kingdom of the Midlands. A century later the center shifted again, and Wessex, the country of the West Saxons, became the leading power. The most famous king of the West Saxons was Alfred the Great, who reigned in the second half of the ninth century, dying in 901. He was famous not only as a military man and administrator but also as a champion of learning. He founded and supported schools and translated or caused to be translated many books from Latin into English. At this time also much of the Northumbrian literature of two centuries earlier was copied in West Saxon. Indeed, the great bulk of Old English writing which has come down to us is in the West Saxon dialect of 900 or later.

In the military sphere, Alfred's great accomplishment was his successful opposition to the viking invasions. In the ninth and tenth centuries, the Norsemen emerged in their ships from their homelands in Denmark and the Scandinavian peninsula. They traveled far and attacked and plundered at will and almost with impunity. They ravaged Italy and Greece, settled in France, Russia, and Ireland, colonized Iceland and Greenland, and discovered America several centuries before Columbus. Nor did they overlook England.

After many years of hit-and-run raids, the Norsemen landed an army on the east coast of England in the year 866. There was nothing much to oppose them except the Wessex power led by Alfred. The long struggle ended in 877 with a treaty by which a line was drawn roughly from the northwest of England to the southeast. On the eastern side of the line Norse rule was to prevail. This was called the Danelaw. The western side was to be governed by Wessex.

The linguistic result of all this was a considerable injection of Norse into the English language. Norse was at this time not so different from English as Norwegian or Danish is now. Probably speakers of English could understand, more or less, the language of the newcomers who had moved into eastern England. At any rate, there was considerable interchange and word borrowing. Examples of Norse words in the English language are *sky, give, law, egg, outlaw, leg, ugly, scant, sly, crawl, scowl, take, thrust*. There are hundreds more. We have even borrowed some pronouns from Norse— *they, their,* and *them*. These words were borrowed first by the eastern and northern dialects and then in the course of hundreds of years made their way into English generally.

It is supposed also—indeed, it must be true—that the Norsemen influenced the sound structure and the grammar of English. But this is hard to demonstrate in detail.

A Specimen of Old English

We may now have an example of Old English. The favorite illustration is the Lord's Prayer, since it needs no translation. This has come to us in several different versions. Here is one:

> Fæder ure þu ðe eart on heofonum si þin nama gehalgod. Tobecume þin rice. Gewurðe þin willa on eorðan swa swa on hoefonum. Urne gedæghwamlican hlaf syle us to dæg. And forgyf us ure gyltas swa swa we forgyfaþ urum gyltendum. And ne gelæd þu us on costnunge ac alys us of yfele. Soðlice.

Some of the differences between this and Modern English are merely differences in orthography. For instance, the sign *æ* is what Old English writers used for a vowel sound like that in modern *hat* or *and*. The *th* sounds of modern *thin* or *then* are represented in Old English by þ or ð. But of course there are many differences in sound too. *Ure* is the ancestor of modern *our*, but the first vowel was like that in *too* or *ooze*. *Hlaf* is modern *loaf*; we have dropped the *h* sound and changed the vowel, which in *hlaf* was pronounced something like the vowel in *father*. Old English had some sounds which we do not have. The sound represented by *y* does not occur in Modern English. If you pronounce the vowel in *bit* with your lips rounded, you may approach it.

In grammar, Old English was much more highly inflected than Modern English is. That is, there were more case endings for nouns, more person and number endings for verbs, a more complicated pronoun system, various endings for adjectives, and so on. Old English nouns had four cases—nominative, genitive, dative, accusative. Adjectives had five—all these and an instrumental case besides. Present-day English has only two cases for nouns —common case and possessive case. Adjectives now have no case system at all. On the other hand, we now use a more rigid word order and more structure words (prepositions, auxiliaries, and the like) to express relationships than Old English did.

Some of this grammar we can see in the Lord's Prayer. *Heofonum,* for instance, is a dative plural; the nominative singular was *heofon. Urne* is an accusative singular; the nominative is *ure.* In *urum gyltendum* both words are dative plural. *Forgyfaþ* is the first person plural form of the verb. Word order is different: "urne gedæghwamlican hlaf syle us" in place of "Give us our daily bread." And so on.

In vocabulary Old English is quite different from Modern English. Most of the Old English words are what we may call native English: that is, words which have not been borrowed from other languages but which have been a part of English ever since English was a part of Indo-European. Old English did certainly contain borrowed words. We have seen that many borrowings were coming in from Norse. Rather large numbers had been borrowed from Latin, too. Some of these were taken while the Anglo-Saxons were still on the Continent (*cheese, butter, bishop, kettle,* etc.); a larger number came into English after the Conversion (*angel, candle, priest, martyr, radish, oyster, purple, school, spend,* etc.). But the great majority of Old English words were native English.

Now, on the contrary, the majority of words in English are borrowed, taken mostly from Latin and French. Of the words in *The American College Dictionary* only about 14 percent are native. Most of these, to be sure, are common, high-frequency words—*the, of, I, and, because, man, mother, road,* etc.; of the thousand most common words in English, some 62 percent are native English. Even so, the modern vocabulary is very much Latinized and Frenchified. The Old English vocabulary was not.

Middle English

Sometime between the years 1000 and 1200 various important changes took place in the structure of English, and Old English became Middle English. The political event which facilitated these changes was the Norman

Conquest. The Normans, as the name shows, came originally from Scandinavia. In the early tenth century they established themselves in northern France, adopted the French language, and developed a vigorous kingdom and a very passable civilization. In the year 1066, led by Duke William, they crossed the Channel and made themselves masters of England. For the next several hundred years, England was ruled by Kings whose first language was French.

One might wonder why, after the Norman Conquest, French did not become the national language, replacing English entirely. The reason is that the Conquest was not a national migration, as the earlier Anglo-Saxon invasion had been. Great numbers of Normans came to England, but they came as rulers and landlords. French became the language of the court, the language of the nobility, the language of polite society, the language of literature. But it did not replace English as the language of the people. There must always have been hundreds of towns and villages in which French was never heard except when visitors of high station passed through.

But English, though it survived as the national language, was profoundly changed after the Norman Conquest. Some of the changes—in sound structure and grammar—would no doubt have taken place whether there had been a Conquest or not. Even before 1066 the case system of English nouns and adjectives was becoming simplified; people came to rely more on word order and prepositions than on inflectional endings to communicate their meanings. The process was speeded up by sound changes which caused many of the endings to sound alike. But no doubt the Conquest facilitated the change. German, which didn't experience a Norman Conquest, is today rather highly inflected compared to its cousin English.

But it is in vocabulary that the effects of the Conquest are most obvious. French ceased, after a hundred years or so, to be the native language of very many people in England, but it continued—and continues still—to be a zealously cultivated second language, the mirror of elegance and civilization. When one spoke English, one introduced not only French ideas and French things but also their French names. This was not only easy but socially useful. To pepper one's conversation with French expressions was to show that one was well-bred, elegant, *au courant*. The last sentence shows that the process is not yet dead. By using *au courant* instead of, say, *abreast of things,* the writer indicates that he is no dull clod who knows only English but an elegant person aware of how things are done in *le haut monde.*

Thus French words came into English, all sorts of them. There were words to do with government: *parliament, majesty, treaty, alliance, tax, government;* church words: *parson, sermon, baptism, incense, crucifix, religion;* words for foods: *veal, beef, mutton, bacon, jelly, peach, lemon, cream, biscuit;* colors: *blue, scarlet, vermilion;* household words: *curtain, chair, lamp, towel, blanket, parlor;* play words: *dance, chess, music, leisure, con-*

versation; literary words: *story, romance, poet, literary;* learned words: *study,* *logic, grammar, noun, surgeon, anatomy, stomach;* just ordinary words of all sorts: *nice, second, very, age, bucket, gentle, final, fault, flower, cry, count, sure, move, surprise, plain.*

All these and thousands more poured into the English vocabulary between 1100 and 1500 until at the end of that time many people must have had more French words than English at their command. This is not to say that English became French. English remained English in sound structure and in grammar, though these also felt the ripples of French influence. The very heart of the vocabulary, too, remained English. Most of the high-frequency words—the pronouns, the prepositions, the conjunctions, the auxiliaries, as well as a great many ordinary nouns and verbs and adjectives —were not replaced by borrowings.

Middle English, then, was still a Germanic language, but it differed from Old English in many ways. The sound system and the grammar changed a good deal. Speakers made less use of case systems and other inflectional devices and relied more on word order and structure words to express their meanings. This is often said to be a simplification, but it isn't really. Languages don't become simpler; they merely exchange one kind of complexity for another. Modern English is not a simple language, as any foreign speaker who tries to learn it will hasten to tell you.

For us Middle English is simpler than Old English just because it is closer to Modern English. It takes three or four months at least to learn to read Old English prose and more than that for poetry. But a week of good study should put one in touch with the Middle English poet Chaucer. Indeed, you may be able to make some sense of Chaucer straight off, though you would need instruction in pronunciation to make it sound like poetry. Here is a famous passage from the *General Prologue to the Canterbury Tales,* fourteenth century:

> Ther was also a nonne, a Prioresse,
> That of hir smyling was ful symple and coy,
> Hir gretteste oath was but by Seinte Loy,
> And she was cleped Madame Eglentyne.
> Ful wel she song the service dyvyne,
> Entuned in hir nose ful semely.
> And Frenshe she spak ful faire and fetisly,
> After the scole of Stratford-atte-Bowe,
> For Frenshe of Parys was to hir unknowe.

Early Modern English

Sometime between 1400 and 1600 English underwent a couple of sound changes which made the language of Shakespeare quite different from that of Chaucer. Incidentally, these changes contributed much to the chaos in which English spelling now finds itself.

One change was the elimination of a vowel sound in certain unstressed positions at the end of words. For instance, the words *name, stone, wine, dance* were pronounced as two syllables by Chaucer but as just one by Shakespeare. The *e* in these words became, as we say, "silent." But it wasn't silent for Chaucer; it represented a vowel sound. So also the words *laughed, seemed, stored* would have been pronounced by Chaucer as two-syllable words. The change was an important one because it affected thousands of words and gave a different aspect to the whole language.

The other change is what is called the Great Vowel Shift. This was a systematic shifting of half a dozen vowels and diphthongs in stressed syllables. For instance, the word *name* had in Middle English a vowel something like that in the modern word *father*; *wine* had the vowel of modern *mean*; *he* was pronounced something like modern *hey*; *mouse* sounded like *moose*; *moon* had the vowel of *moan*. Again the shift was thoroughgoing and affected all the words in which these vowel sounds occurred. Since we still keep the Middle English system of spelling these words, the differences between Modern English and Middle English are often more real than apparent.

The vowel shift has meant also that we have come to use an entirely different set of symbols for representing vowel sounds than is used by writers of such languages as French, Italian, or Spanish, in which no such vowel shift occurred. If you come across a strange word—say, *bine*—in an English book, you will pronounce it according to the English system, with the vowel of *wine* or *dine*. But if you read *bine* in a French, Italian, or Spanish book, you will pronounce it with the vowel of *mean* or *seen*.

These two changes, then, produced the basic differences between Middle English and Modern English. But there were several other developments that had an effect upon the language. One was the invention of printing, an invention introduced into England by William Caxton in the year 1475. Where before books had been rare and costly, they suddenly became cheap and common. More and more people learned to read and write. This was the first of many advances in communication which have worked to unify languages and to arrest the development of dialect differences, though of course printing affects writing principally rather than speech. Among other things it hastened the standardization of spelling.

The period of Early Modern English—that is, the sixteenth and seventeenth centuries—was also the period of the English Renaissance, when people developed, on the one hand, a keen interest in the past and, on the other, a more daring and imaginative view of the future. New ideas multiplied, and new ideas meant new language. Englishmen had grown accustomed to borrowing words from French as a result of the Norman

Conquest; now they borrowed from Latin and Greek. As we have seen, English had been raiding Latin from Old English times and before, but now the floodgates really opened, and thousands of words from the classical languages poured in. *Pedestrian, bonus, anatomy, contradict, climax, dictionary, benefit, multiply, exist, paragraph, initiate, scene, inspire* are random examples. Probably the average educated American today has more words from French in his vocabulary than from native English sources, and more from Latin than from French.

The greatest writer of the Early Modern English period is of course Shakespeare, and the best-known book is the King James Version of the Bible, published in 1611. The Bible (if not Shakespeare) has made many features of Early Modern English perfectly familiar to many people down to present time, even though we do not use these features in present-day speech and writing. For instance, the old pronouns *thou* and *thee* have dropped out of use now, together with their verb forms, but they are still familiar to us in prayer and in Biblical quotation: "Whither thou goest, I will go." Such forms as *hath* and *doth* have been replaced by *has* and *does*; "Goes he hence tonight?" would now be "Is he going away tonight?"; Shakespeare's "Fie, on't, sirrah" would be "Nuts to that, Mac." Still, all these expressions linger with us because of the power of the works in which they occur.

It is not always realized, however, that considerable sound changes have taken place between Early Modern English and the English of the present day. Shakespearian actors putting on a play speak the words, properly enough, in their modern pronunciation. But it is very doubtful that this pronunciation would be understood at all by Shakespeare. In Shakespeare's time, the word *reason* was pronounced like modern *raisin*; *face* had the sound of modern *glass*; the *l* in *would, should, palm* was pronounced. In these points and a great many others the English language has moved a long way from what it was in 1600.

Recent Developments

The history of English since 1700 is filled with many movements and countermovements, of which we can notice only a couple. One of these is the vigorous attempt made in the eighteenth century, and the rather half-hearted attempts made since, to regulate and control the English language. Many people of the eighteenth century, not understanding very well the forces which govern language, proposed to polish and prune and restrict English, which they felt was proliferating too wildly. There was much talk of an academy which would rule on what people could and could not say and write. The academy never came into being, but the eighteenth century did succeed in establishing certain attitudes which, though they haven't had much effect on the development of the language itself, have certainly changed the native speaker's feeling about the language.

In part a product of the wish to fix and establish the language was the development of the dictionary. The first English dictionary was published in 1603; it was a list of 2500 words briefly defined. Many others were published with gradual improvements until Samuel Johnson published his *English Dictionary* in 1755. This, steadily revised, dominated the field in England for nearly a hundred years. Meanwhile in America, Noah Webster published his dictionary in 1828, and before long dictionary publishing was a big business in this country. The last century has seen the publication of one great dictionary: the twelve-volume *Oxford English Dictionary*, compiled in the course of seventy-five years through the labors of many scholars. We have also, of course, numerous commercial dictionaries which are as good as the public wants them to be if not, indeed, rather better.

Another product of the eighteenth century was the invention of "English grammar." As English came to replace Latin as the language of scholarship it was felt that one should also be able to control and dissect it, parse and analyze it, as one could Latin. What happened in practice was that the grammatical description that applied to Latin was removed and superimposed on English. This was silly, because English is an entirely different kind of language, with its own forms and signals and ways of producing meaning. Nevertheless, English grammars on the Latin model were worked out and taught in the schools. In many schools they are still being taught. This activity is not often popular with school children, but it is sometimes an interesting and instructive exercise in logic. The principal harm in it is that it has tended to keep people from being interested in English and has obscured the real features of English structure.

But probably the most important force on the development of English in the modern period has been the tremendous expansion of English-speaking peoples. In 1500 English was a minor language, spoken by a few people on a small island. Now it is perhaps the greatest language of the world, spoken natively by over a quarter of a billion people and as a second language by many millions more. When we speak of English now, we must specify whether we mean American English, British English, Australian English, Indian English, or what, since the differences are considerable. The American cannot go to England or the Englishman to America confident that he will always understand and be understood. The Alabaman in Iowa or the Iowan in Alabama shows himself a foreigner every time he speaks. It is only because communication has become fast and easy that English in this period of its expansion has not broken into a dozen mutually unintelligible languages.

COMPREHENSION QUIZ

1. According to Roberts, the history of our language begins a little after
   a. A.D. 400.
   b. A.D. 600.
   c. A.D. 1066.
   d. A.D. 1485.
2. Such borrowings as "kettle," "wine," "cheese," "bishop," and "church" show something of the relationship of the
   a. Romans with the Jutes.
   b. Danes with the Celts.
   c. Celts with the Anglo-Saxons.
   d. Anglo-Saxons with the Romans.
3. From A.D. 43 to A.D. 410 Britain was ruled by
   a. the Romans.
   b. the Celts.
   c. the Anglo-Saxons.
   d. the Danes.
4. In the ninth and tenth centuries England was attacked and plundered by
   a. the Picts.
   b. Goths and Vandals.
   c. the Danes.
   d. the Celts.
5. The English words "sky," "give," "law," "scant," "take," "they," and "them" are borrowed from the
   a. Norse.
   b. Celts.
   c. Northumbrians.
   d. Midland dialect.
6. Which of the following statements is false?
   a. Old English was much more highly inflected than Modern English is.
   b. Modern English uses a more rigid word order than Old English did.
   c. In vocabulary, Old English is quite different from Modern English.
   d. The majority of words in Modern English are borrowed.
7. The linguistic effects of the Norman Conquest are most obvious
   a. in spelling changes.
   b. in sentence structure.
   c. in sound changes.
   d. in vocabulary.
8. Roberts laments the study and teaching of Modern English according to the rules of
   a. Anglo-Saxon.
   b. Latin.
   c. Middle English.
   d. French.

DISCUSSION QUESTIONS

1. What generalizations can you make about the Old English words Roberts cites as having survived? How do they compare or differ from words of Latin derivation? Does the difference imply something about the respective cultures of the Romans and the Anglo-Saxons?
2. Why does the "silent" *e* survive in modern English? How were the following words pronounced in Middle English: "hoped"; "seemed"; "rained."
3. According to Roberts, what are the basic differences between Middle English and Modern English?
4. What is the importance of the Great Vowel Shift? How has it affected the pronunciation of Modern English?
5. If you are familiar with another language, explain why word order is less important in that language than in English.

WRITING SUGGESTIONS

1. In a theme, explain why it is unwise to teach English grammar using the terminology and concepts of Latin and Greek.
2. What changes in the English language have you observed in the last five years? Restrict your observations to a particular field, such as new words, grammar, pronunciation, spelling, or slang.
3. Write a paper summarizing the contributions of France or Scandinavia to the formation of the English language.
4. What are some of the practical effects of the printing press on the English language?
5. What are the effects of technology—apart from the printing press—on the English language? Consider particularly the impact of radio and television.

Recommended Readings to Part II

Baugh, Albert C. *A History of the English Language*. 2nd ed. New York: Appleton-Century-Crofts, 1957.

Bloomfield, Leonard. *Language*. New York: Holt, Rinehart and Winston, 1933.

Bloomfield, Morton, and Leonard Newmark. *A Linguistic Introduction to the History of English*. New York: Alfred A. Knopf, 1963.

Carroll, John B. *The Study of Language*. Cambridge: Harvard University Press, 1953.

Dinneen, Francis P. *An Introduction to General Linguistics*. New York: Holt, Rinehart and Winston, 1967.

Laird, Charlton. *The Miracle of Language*. New York: Fawcett, 1953.

Marckwardt, Albert H. *Introduction to the English Language*. New York: Oxford University Press, 1942.

Roberts, Paul. *English Syntax*. New York: Harcourt, Brace & World, 1964.

Sapir, Edward. *Language*. New York: Harcourt, Brace & World, 1949.

Wilson, Graham (ed.). *A Linguistic Reader*. New York: Harper & Row, 1967.

How Language Shards Our Thoughts

III

How Language
Shapes
Our Thoughts

by STUART CHASE

In the current mass of talk about talk, communication about communication, the emphasis is generally on the talker's power over his language, and thus over people who hear his words. Students are coached to increase their vocabulary, improve their delivery, and so control their audience. Commentators view with alarm the propaganda victories of Hitler, McCarthy, the Moscow radio.

The reverse of the process is seldom mentioned—the power which language exerts over the talker. The talker (or writer) never feels this power. He is as unconscious of it as of the circulation of his blood. He assumes that he is in command of his thoughts and of the words in which they are clothed.

The idea that the structure of the language we use affects our thought, may even be prior to thought, is beyond the purview of most of us. The first serious modern student to realize the power of a language over its speakers was probably Benjamin Lee Whorf. He was a linguist with imagination.

There are at least a dozen disciplines now contributing to the scientific study of communication—semantics, cybernetics, the mathematical theory of Claude Shannon, the perception theory of Ames and Cantril, and so on. Central in the whole complex is linguistics, probably the most exact of all the social sciences. Developed by Bloomfield, Sapir, Jesperson, and others, both here and abroad, linguistics begins by analyzing the sounds we make, of which the simplest unit is called a *phoneme*. It finds the actual patterns of spoken sounds in a given language, follows their combinations into words,

From Stuart Chase, "How Language Shapes Our Thoughts," *Harper's Magazine*, April, 1954. Copyright © 1954 by Stuart Chase. Reprinted by permission of A. Watkins, Inc., New York.

and so to sentences and to syntax—the basic grammatical structure that carries meaning.

To collect a new language, the exploring linguist goes into the field like an anthropologist, settles in a native community, establishes a working relationship with the head man, and proceeds to record the sounds the villagers make. He often begins with numbers. "How do you say *one, two, three* in this village?" If he can get these wild flowers of speech upon a sound track, his delight knows no bounds. Many native languages, like the trumpeter swan, are in grave danger of extinction.

The linguist recognizes, as the classical grammarian did not, that people talked long before they wrote. "Noises made with the face" antedated "scratches made with the fist" by a hundred thousand years or more. He begins his researches, accordingly, at the more rewarding end—with live speech. In analyzing the sounds made by speakers of English, for instance, the linguist develops a formula—in a special code looking like algebra—which sums up every combination that one-syllable words, or word-like forms, may have, and bars out every combination they do not, and *cannot*, have. MPST, for example, can be pronounced as in "glimpsed"; KSTHS, as in "sixth." On the other hand, the formula for English speakers rejects sound combinations readily pronounceable in other languages, such as LITK, FPAT, NWENG, DZOGB.

An advertising man in his cubicle on Madison Avenue, after a week of dreaming, may christen a new breakfast food "crunchy, vitamin-packed THRUB," but he cannot call it DLUB, not in English he can't. If he tried to name it NFPK, a common sound in other tongues, he would undoubtedly be fired. Again English permits no words to begin with NG, but Eskimo is full of them.

Some linguists, having mastered their phonemes and field work, go on to a new dimension in communication. They call it *meta*linguistics, or superlinguistics. After syntax, said Whorf, "then on to further planes still, the full import of which may some day stagger us." I will not deny that, as a student of semantics, their import staggers me. Metalinguistics is the top rung of communication study; it throws the longest shadow. It may be doing for language what relativity did for physics. Furthermore, it is based on linguistic relativity. Metalinguists ask: How does a given language shape the thought of the speaker and his view of nature and the world? How does the structure of English, say, differ from that of Maya, and what are the comparative effects on speakers of the two?

Whorf, had he lived, might have become another William James or Franz Boas, so brilliant were his powers of projecting scientific observations into fruitful generalizations.

Actually, thinking [he says] is most mysterious, and by far the greatest light upon it that we have, is thrown by the study of language. This study shows that the forms of a person's thoughts are controlled by inexorable laws of pattern, of which he is unconscious. These patterns are the unperceived intricate systematizations of his own language—shown readily enough by a candid comparison and contrast with other languages, especially those of a different linguistic family. His thinking itself is in a language—in English, in Sanskrit, in Chinese. And every language is a vast pattern-system, different from others, in which are culturally ordained the forms and categories by which the personality not only communicates, but analyzes nature, notices or neglects types of relationship, channels his reasoning, and builds the house of his consciousness. This doctrine is new to Western science, but it stands on unimpeachable evidence.

Whorf was born in Boston in 1897, and graduated from M.I.T. as a chemical engineer in 1918. He took a job with a large insurance company in Hartford as a specialist on fire prevention in chemical industries, and remained with the company until his death in 1941. While still in school he developed an interest in language and how it was put together. At Hartford he spent long hours in the Watkinson Library, which specializes in Amerindian languages, and his intensive program of independent study won him scientific recognition by 1928. He deciphered certain Aztec inscriptions for the first time. In 1930 he took a leave of absence to go to Mexico under a grant from the Social Science Research Council, to study Aztec and Maya inscriptions at first hand. Later he published a brilliant paper on the deciphering of Maya codices.

He spent the best part of two years on the Hopi language, and as we shall see, based some of his most daring speculations upon its remarkable structure. His only book, unfinished and, alas, unpublished, now in the possession of Clyde Kluckhohn, is a Hopi-English dictionary. All this work, remember, was done as an avocation; daytimes he was a chemical engineer.

He often visited Yale, where he became a firm friend of Edward Sapir, the great Amerindian scholar. Sapir encouraged him to carry linguistics into broader fields. At Yale he did his only formal academic work, giving a course of lectures on his consuming interest.

After mastering, through library and field work, the accumulated knowledge in linguistics, he wrote a famous essay in the *Technology Review,* entitled "Linguistics as an Exact Science." In it the reader will find ample justification for the view that prediction fares better here than in the other social sciences. The power to predict, of course, is the test of any science. But linguistics was a foundation stone on which he stood to lift his eyes. Only a unique combination of the scientific method and an imagination almost poetic could have produced his great contribution to the study of communication.

In addition to the dictionary, Whorf left a score of papers, upon which I am principally basing this essay. The core of his thinking can be found in "Four Articles on Metalinguistics," issued in reprint form by the Foreign

Service Institute in Washington in 1950. The Institute, a kind of university in the State Department, prepares young career men for government service overseas with courses in languages, comparative cultures, economic geography, and so on. In addition, it operates an active research center in linguistics, directed by George Trager and Henry Lee Smith, Jr. (You remember Dr. Smith, the man on the radio who could tell by your accent exactly in what corner of the country you were reared.)

Language, more than any other trait, makes us human, distinguishes us from all other creatures. The opposed thumb we share with the great apes. We are born with a relatively large area in the brain for manipulating tongue, larynx, and the speech apparatus. We are also endowed with a drive to talk: but the words and the language structure have to be learned. Curiously enough, the first word normally learned in English, "mamma," is a sound heard around the world. Many other languages have similar phonemes for mother.

Of all the tens of thousands of behavior patterns and belief systems we learn from the culture, language is far and away the most important. It has long been recognized that every man alive—or who ever lived for that matter—is culture-bound. It remained for Whorf and his group to demonstrate that every one of us is language-bound.

Speech, says Whorf, is the best show man puts on. "It is his own particular act on the stage of evolution, in which he comes before the cosmic backdrop" to play his part. Julian Huxley hazards the guess that culture and language may be displacing evolution in the case of man.

The metalinguists demonstrate that the forms of a person's thoughts are controlled by patterns learned early, of which he is mostly unconscious. Thinking is a language process, whether in English, Russian, or Hopi. Every language is a complex system, with three main functions:

1. To communicate with other persons.
2. To communicate with oneself, or, as we say, think.
3. To mold one's whole outlook on life.

Thinking follows the tracks laid down in one's own language; these tracks will converge on certain phases of "reality," and completely bypass phases which may be explored in other languages. In English, for instance, we say "Look at that wave." But a wave in nature never occurs as a single phenomenon. In the Hopi language they say, "Look at that slosh." The Hopi word, whose nearest equivalent in English is "slosh," gives a closer fit to the actual physics of wave motion, connoting movements in a mass.

Most of us were brought up to believe that talking is merely a tool which something deeper called "thinking" puts to work. Thinking, we have assumed, depends on laws of reason and logic common to all mankind. These laws are said to be implicit in the mental machinery of human beings, whether they speak English or Choctaw. Languages, it follows, are simply parallel methods for expressing this universal logic. On this assumption it also follows that any logical idea can be translated unbroken, or even unbent, into any language. A few minutes in the glass palace of the United Nations in New York will quickly disabuse one of this quaint notion. Even such a common concept as "democracy" may not survive translation.

Another set of assumptions underlying Western culture, says Whorf, imposes upon the universe two grand cosmic forms: *space* and *time*. Space in our thinking is static, three-dimensional, and infinite; beyond the last area is always another area. *Time* is kinetic and one-dimensional, flowing perpetually and smoothly from the past to the present and into the future. It took the genius of Einstein to correct these cosmic assumptions, and most of us are still firmly wedded to them.

Linguistic relativity makes it clear that Newton took his concepts of Absolute Space and Absolute Time, not so much out of profound cogitation, as out of the language he spoke. They had been lying there for thousands of years. Both "time" and "space" affect the behavior of everyone in Western culture. "Time," especially, causes us to be oriented towards calendars, dates, "the course of history," time tables, clocks, time wages, races against time, accounting, compound interest, actuarial statistics, annals, diaries, the age of the rocks, of the earth, of the solar system, of the universe. The book of Genesis gets the cosmos launched in 4004 B.C. It is difficult for Westerners to conceive of what Fred Hoyle, the astronomer, calls "continuous creation," for we want to start things moving at a definite date, and build up from there. Time impels us to look ahead in planning programs, schedules, appropriations, balanced budgets. Our love affair with time causes other cultures whose languages permit a less hurried outlook, say the Chinese, to regard us as somewhat mad.

The assumptions underlying the culture of the Hopi also impose two grand cosmic forms upon the universe: the *objective* and the *subjective*; the manifest and the unmanifest. The first is everything accessible to the human senses, without distinction between past and present. The second is "the realm of expectancy, of desire and purpose, of vitalizing life, of efficient causes, of thought thinking itself out . . . into manifestation." It exists in the hearts and minds of animals, plants, mountains, as well as men. This subjective realm is intensely real to a Hopi, "quivering with life, power, and potency."

All languages contain terms of cosmic grandeur. English includes "reality," "matter," "substance," "causation," as well as "space" and "time." Hopi includes the cosmic term *tunátya*, meaning a special and exalted kind of "hope." It is a verb, not a noun—the action of hoping, the stirring toward hope—and is bound up with communal ceremonies, like prayers for the harvest, and for the forming of rain clouds.

The ancient Greeks, with their belief in a universal rule of reason, nevertheless did their thinking in Greek, which, like all Indo-European tongues, followed what is called the "subject-predicate" form. If there is a verb there must be a noun to make it work; it could not often exist in its own right as pure action. The ancient Greeks, as well as all Western peoples today, say, "The light flashed." Something has to be there to make the flash; "light" is the subject; "flash" is the predicate. The whole trend of modern physics, however, with its emphasis on the *field,* or the whole process, is away from subject-predicate propositions. A Hopi Indian, accordingly, is the better physicist when he says, *"Rehpi"*—"flash!"—one word for the whole performance, no subject, no predicate, and no time element. (Children tend to do this too.) In Western languages we are constantly reading into nature ghostly entities which flash and perform other acts. Do we supply them because our verbs require substantives in front of them?

Again, the Hopi language does not raise the tough question whether things in a distant village exist at the same present moment as things in one's own village. Thus it avoids the idea of *simultaneity,* which has plagued Western scientists for generations, and was only banished by relativity. The thoughts of a Hopi about events always include *both* space and time, for neither is found alone in his world view. Thus his language gets along adequately without tenses for its verbs, and permits him to think habitually in terms of space-time. For you or me really to understand relativity, we must abandon our spoken tongue altogether and take to the special language of calculus. But a Hopi, Whorf implies, has a sort of calculus built into him.

No human being is free to describe nature with strict objectivity, for he is a prisoner of his language. A trained linguist can do better because he, at least, is aware of the bondage, and can look at nature through a variety of frames. A physicist can do better by using the language of mathematics. Semanticists are now painfully learning how to do better. It is not easy for anybody. Says Whorf:

> We are thus introduced to a new principle of relativity, which holds that all observers are not led by the same physical evidence to the same picture of the universe, unless their linguistic backgrounds are similar, or can in some way be calibrated.

Indo-European languages can be calibrated with each other: English, Italian, Spanish, French, Russian, German, Latin, Greek, and the rest, back to Indo-Hittite all use the subject-predicate form. All speakers of these languages are capable of observing the world in a roughly similar way, at least on the high levels of "time," "space," and "matter." Hopi cannot be calibrated with them; neither can Chinese, nor thousands of other languages, living and dead.

Speakers of Chinese dissect nature and the universe very differently than Western speakers, with a profound effect upon their systems of belief.

A Chinese writer, Chang Tung-Sun, vigorously supports the thesis of linguistic relativity in a monograph reprinted in the semantic quarterly ETC.

Kant imagined that he was dealing in universal categories in *The Critique of Pure Reason,* but actually, says Chang, he was only discussing standard forms of Western thought, a very limited approach. Kant's logic was one of the subject-predicate variety, which is not normal in Chinese. An intelligent Chinese gentleman does not know what Kant is talking about—unless he learns some Western tongue in which to read Kant's words.

Our Western verb "to be," observes Chang, used with an adjective predicate, implies the existence of the adjective as an independent quality. When we say, "This is yellow and hard," we tend to assume the existence of two qualities, "yellowness" and "hardness," which suggests to a Chinese something Chang calls a "cosmic substance." "The substance is characterized by its attributes, and the attributes are attributed to the substance," observes Chang, in considerable astonishment at such a circular performance. The verb "to be" creates great congeries of identities, and blossoms in Aristotle's laws of logic, of which the first is the law of identity, "A is A." This "law" is causing a lot of trouble today in charges of guilt by association.

No such law is possible in the Chinese language, where logic follows a quite different path. In Chinese, one does not attribute existence to "yellowness" and "hardness," or to polar words like "longness" and "shortness." Rather one says: "the long and the short are mutually related"; "the difficult and easy are mutually complementary"; "the front and the rear are mutually accompanying."

In the West we say, "This is the front of the car, and that is the rear, and let's have no more nonsense about it!" But in the Chinese view, Westerners are guilty of considerable nonsense in creating "frontness" and "rearness" as entities. Even a Westerner can see that if a car is torn in two in a crash, the part with the radiator grille becomes the "front," and the part toward the now severed windshield becomes the "rear"—*of that segment.* We can see, if we work hard enough, that there are no such entities as "frontness" or "rearness," "difficulty" or "easiness," "longness" or "shortness," by themselves out there. The Chinese language has this useful correction built in; we Westerners have to sweat it out with the help of linguistics, semantics, and mathematics.

Linguists have also emphasized that Chinese is a "multi-valued" language, not primarily two-valued like English and Western languages generally. We say that things must be "good" or "bad," "right" or "wrong," "clean" or "dirty," "black" or "white"—ignoring shades of gray. When an economist talks about a middle road between "socialism" and "capitalism," both camps vie in their ferocity to tear him apart. (I have been that unhappy economist.)

Speakers of Chinese set up no such grim dichotomies; they see most situations in shades of gray, and have no difficulty in grasping the significance of a variety of middle roads. As a result, Chinese thought has been traditionally tolerant, not given to the fanatical ideologies of the West. Racial, religious, and doctrinal conflicts have been hard to maintain in China, because a Chinese speaker does not possess an unshakable confidence that he is totally right and that his opponent is totally wrong. Observe that this is not a moral judgment, but structural in the language.

This happy lack of two-valued thinking raises an interesting question. Communism, as formulated by Marx and developed by Lenin, is rigidly two-valued. The heroic worker stands against the wicked capitalist and one or the other must go down. There is no place for shades of gray or for innocent bystanders. Those who are not with us are against us. Which side are you on?

Russian is an Indo-European language, and the two-sided choice is readily accepted by its speakers. The choice is accepted, too, by top leaders of the Chinese Communists today, for they went to Moscow to be indoctrinated, and to learn the Russian language. But four hundred million Chinese have not been to Moscow or learned Russian, or any other Indo-European language, and there is small prospect of their doing so. How, then, can the Chinese people become good ideological Communists, since it is difficult if not impossible for them to take seriously the central dialectic of Marxism? The structure of their language seems to forbid the idea.

The Wintu Indians of North America are even more shy of the law of identity than the Chinese, says D. D. Lee, writing in the *International Journal of American Linguistics*. We say, "This *is* bread," but in Wintu they say, "We call this bread." They avoid the "is of identity," and so are less likely to confuse words with things. When a Wintu speaks of an event not within his own experience, he never affirms it but only suggests, "Perhaps it is so." When Mrs. Lee asked her informant the word for "body," she was given a term signifying "the whole person." Thus the Wintus seem to have antedated the psychosomatic school.

The Coeur d'Alene Indians of Idaho have long antedated other modern scientists. They do not speak in terms of simple cause-and-effect relations as we do, but rather in terms of *process,* as Western scientists are now painfully learning to do. Their language requires speakers to discriminate between three causal processes, denoted by three verb forms: growth, addition, secondary addition. "If, given a more sophisticated culture," says Whorf, "their thinkers erected these now unconscious discriminations into a theory of triadic causality, fitted to scientific observations, they might thereby produce a valuable intellectual tool for science." Our specialists can do this by taking thought fortified with mathematics, but the Coeur d'Alenes seem to do it automatically.

Eskimo breaks our single term "snow" into many words for different kinds of snow—a procedure which all skiers can applaud. Aztec, however, goes in the opposite direction; here we find one word for "snow," "ice," and "cold." In Hopi, "wave," "flame," "meteor," and "lightning" are all verbs, suiting their dynamic quality. Looking into the August sky, a Hopi says: "*Reh-pi!* It meteors." (Observe how in English we need a djin called "it" to power the meteor.)

It is easier and clearer to recite the story of William Tell in the Algonquin language than in English or French, because it is equipped with enough possessive pronouns to distinguish easily between "his" as applied to Tell, and as applied to his son. Writing in English I must continually watch my step with pronouns, lest I attach them to the wrong person or thing.

Chichewa, spoken by a tribe of unlettered Negroes in East Africa, has two past tenses, one for events which continue to influence the present, and one for events which do not. With this structure, says Whorf, "a new view of time opens before us. . . . It may be that these primitive folks are equipped with a language which, if they were to become philosophers or mathematicians, could make them our foremost thinkers upon *time.*"

The metalinguists cause us to realize that language is not a tool with which to uncover a deeper vein of reason, universal to all thinkers, but a shaper of thought itself. Shaping the thought, it helps to shape the culture, as in the Western cult of the Adoration of Time. They are making us realize that we get our view of the world, our *Weltanschauung,* as much from words inside our heads as from independent observation. When, as scientists, we try to become independent observers, the words may distort the readings, unless we take special precautions. Einstein could not accurately talk about relativity in German or English, he had to talk about it in the calculus of tensors. There is no reason to suppose that English, German, Russian, or any Indo-European language, with its two-valued logic, its monster-making subject-predicate form, is the ultimate in communication.

The structure, or grammar, of each language, says Whorf, "is not merely a reproducing instrument for voicing ideas but rather is itself the shaper of ideas, the program and guide for the individual's mental activity, for his analysis of impressions." The world is presented to us in a kaleidoscopic flux of impressions which must be organized by our minds, which means by the linguistic system built into our minds. We cut up the seamless web of nature, gather the pieces into concepts, because, within our speech community, we are parties to an agreement to organize things that way, an agreement codified in the patterns of language. This agreement is, of course, an unstated one, but "its terms are absolutely obligatory"; we cannot talk at all except by subscribing to the rules. People who try to avoid them land in mental hospitals.

"A sort of Copernican revolution in communication" is implied by metalinguistics, according to John B. Carroll in his book *The Study of Language.* Sober scientists are shy of revolutions and we find considerable skepticism among contemporary linguists and social scientists for the *Wel-*

tanschauung view. They may note a trend in that direction, but they want more research—say, the time concept isolated and compared in a hundred different languages. Whorf, one suspects, would be the first to welcome such a project.

Criticism comes too from the intellectuals and the literati. It is directed not only at metalinguistics, but at all serious attempts to analyze language, and linguistic relativity, except those inaugurated by classical grammarians. As a student of semantics, and author of *The Tyranny of Words,* I have felt the sting of this criticism. Some men show a strong disposition, says Whorf, to make a virtue of ignorance and denounce any effort to understand the machinery of the mind. To them language is given, and one no more pries into it than into the financial affairs of one's friends.

I doubt whether language makes people of different cultures perceive the space-time world very differently. An Eskimo, I suspect, sees an iceberg about the way I do—though in more detail, with all its food signals clear. Rather, as Carroll suggests, the particular language we learn causes us to pay attention to some things more than to others; it shifts the emphasis of our perception. Also it certainly influences large, high-order concepts like "time," and gives an illiterate Hopi Indian a better aptitude for grasping the fourth dimension than, say, your author. A multivalued language like Chinese helps maintain ideological tolerance, and it may be that Chinese speakers will be unable to absorb Marxism in consequence. But we shall have to wait for a while for proof of that.

Metalinguistics may or may not produce a Copernican revolution, but it will be an important consideration in any workable plan for One World; in the engineering of an acceptable international language; in an understanding of people living in cultures other than our own. (The linguists find serious difficulties with Basic English, Esperanto, and other preliminary attempts.)

There are no languages properly to be termed "primitive." The living standards of Australian bushfellows may leave something to be desired, but the structure of their language is more complicated than English. Though systems differ widely, yet in their order, harmony, and subtle powers of apprehending reality, they demonstrate the link which binds all men together. "The crudest savage," says Whorf, "may unconsciously manipulate with effortless ease a linguistic system so intricate, manifoldly systematized, and intellectually difficult, that it requires the lifetime study of our greatest scholars to describe its workings."

A Papuan head-hunter, similarly conditioned, could mathematize as well as physicists from Princeton, and, conversely, scientist and yokel, scholar and tribesman, may all fall into similar kinds of logical impasse. "They are as unaware of the beautiful and inexorable systems that control them, as a cowherd is of cosmic rays."

Metalinguistics has gone far enough to build a fire under anyone interested in communication. One hopes that other students in many cultures will take up the torch which Whorf laid down.

COMPREHENSION QUIZ

1. The first to realize the power of language over its speakers was
    a. Whorf.
    b. Bloomfield.
    c. Shannon.
    d. Ames.
2. Which of the following sound combinations would be rejected by English speakers?
    a. KSTHS
    b. MPST
    c. THRUB
    d. DZOGB
3. The discipline which asks how a given language shapes the thought of the speaker and his view of nature and the world is
    a. cybernetics.
    b. linguistics.
    c. metalinguistics.
    d. semantics.
4. Whorf and his followers demonstrated that every one of us is
    a. culture bound.
    b. group oriented.
    c. language bound.
    d. ethnocentric.
5. The three main functions of language include all except
    a. to communicate with other persons.
    b. to communicate with oneself.
    c. to relate introspective impulses outwardly.
    d. to mold one's whole outlook on life.
6. Analogous to the Western Culture's two grand cosmic forms of time and space, the Hopi Indian has
    a. time and motion.
    b. energy and mass.
    c. the manifest and the unmanifest.
    d. the present and the future.
7. None of the following languages uses the subject-predicate form except
    a. Hopi.
    b. Indo-Hittite.
    c. Chinese.
    d. all of these.

8. Unlike Chinese, the English language is
    a. multi-valued.
    b. two-valued.
    c. mono-valued.
    d. none of these.

DISCUSSION QUESTIONS

1. In the opening paragraph of "How Language Shapes Our Thoughts," Stuart
    Chase implies that the users of a language exercise considerable influence over
    their language. What kind of power do you exercise over your language? Can
    you classify your influence, e.g., choice of words and choice of subject?
2. What are some of the social forces that might make a language become extinct?
3. Discuss the proposition that language molds one's whole outlook on life.
4. Choose a word like "diamond" and determine how a jeweler, a mine worker,
    and a socialite might view it.
5. What is the difference between a shack and a cottage? Between a home and a
    house? Between being stubborn and possessing self-assurance?

WRITING SUGGESTIONS

1. Construct a hypothetical island on which dwell an American, a Frenchman,
    and an Eskimo. Then deal with some of the linguistic difficulties involved in
    their attempt to cook a meal together.
2. Write a paper based on the following sentence: "Language makes us human,
    and distinguishes us from all other creatures."
3. Write a paper on the notion that the concept of "time" affects our behavior by
    orienting us towards calendars, dates, clocks, races against time, etc.
4. Write a precis of the Chase essay.

Language,
Logic,
and Grammar

by L. M. MYERS

A language may be defined roughly as consisting of a set of words and some habitual ways of putting them together. Dictionaries deal primarily with the individual words; grammars with characteristic forms and with ways of arranging words in coherent communications. There is inevitably some overlapping between the two.

Word-form and Word-order

In some languages the connections between words are shown largely by changes in form. Thus in Latin, "Marcus vidit Quintum" and "Marcum vidit Quintus" mean quite different things, although the same three words are used in the same order. The first means that Marcus saw Quintus; the second, that Quintus saw Marcus. The endings in -us and -um show which is the subject and which is the object of the action, regardless of the order.

In some other languages, like Chinese, words never change their form. The meaning of a group of words therefore depends on the choice of words and the order in which they are arranged.

Originally, English was very much like Latin in this respect. Most words were *inflected*; that is, they had a number of forms that showed variations in their basic meanings, and indicated their relations to each other. Now most of these inflections have been lost, and the structure of the language has become more like that of Chinese. Even the endings that remain

From L. M. Myers, *American English: A Twentieth-Century Grammar*, Englewood Cliffs: Prentice-Hall, Inc., 1952. Reprinted by permission of the author.

have lost most of their power to show distinctions. Look at the following
sentences:

> He and I saw it yesterday.
> Him and me seen it yesterday.

There are good reasons . . . for avoiding the second. But we understand it
as readily as the first, and take it to mean the same thing. Our usual way
of showing differences in meaning is by varying the *order* of words, as in
the following sentences.

> John hit Tom.
> Tom hit John.

On the other hand, there are times when changes in the forms of words
make a considerable difference in the meaning:

> The man helps the boys.
> The men helped the boy.

A study of English grammar therefore involves both the forms and the order
of words.

The Problem of Meaning

If we want to keep our feet on the ground while we are making such
a study, we had better begin by trying to understand something about how
words came to "mean" anything at all. If we simply take it for granted that
they do and go on from there, we will never have any real understanding
of the language, no matter how many grammatical rules we memorize.

Let us suppose that on an uninhabited island a freak rock-formation
has resulted in the white streaks on a cliff forming the letters P A I N. This
would mean absolutely nothing to the animals, the trees, or the rocks themselves. It would still mean nothing if an illiterate savage landed on the
island and looked at it. But if an American landed, the letters would look
to him like a familiar word, and would call up the reactions connected with
earlier acquaintance with that word. For the first time the letters would
suggest a meaning—"pain." This meaning would occur in the man's mind.
The cliffs and the letters would be no more intelligent than before.

If a Frenchman landed on the island and noticed the same letters, an
entirely different meaning would be suggested, since it happens that in
French the letters P A I N also form a word—but the word means "bread,"
and not an uncomfortable sensation.

Most of us probably have a feeling that the letters must somehow mean something all by themselves, even if there is nobody there to appreciate them; but it is hard to see how they could mean two such different things as "pain" and "bread." If we think the matter over, we are forced to agree that meaning is the product of human nervous systems, and does not reside in the letters on the cliff.

The next question that comes up is, would the letters on the cliff have a meaning of their own if they had been deliberately written to form a word? Suppose the American had written down the sentence, "I have a *pain* in my back," and had then torn up the paper so that one piece contained just the word "pain." If the Frenchman happened to pick that piece up, it would suggest to him the idea "bread." Would the word "really" mean what the American intended to convey, or what it happened to suggest to the Frenchman?

Three Kinds of Meaning

We could argue this point forever without getting anywhere, for the fact is that we use the words *mean* and *meaning* in a number of different ways; and if we don't keep at least three of these carefully separated in our minds, we can become badly confused.

Meaning (1)   What the speaker intends to indicate.
Meaning (2)   What is suggested to a particular listener.
Meaning (3)   A more or less general habit of using a given word to indicate a given thing.

A good many writers on the language neglect the first two of these and treat the third far too rigidly, as if the connection between the word and the thing were absolute, instead of a never-quite-uniform habit. You have probably heard such statements as: "*Buffalo* does not mean the American bison, but an entirely different animal"; or: "*Penny* really means an English coin—the American coin is a *cent*."

This is putting the cart before the horse. We can discover meaning (3) —often referred to as the "real" meaning—only by observing the occurrences of meanings (1) and (2). To deny that these meanings are real is as unreasonable as it would be to deny the reality of a family of two or eleven on the grounds that the "average" family consists of five. It is quite true that the English used the word *penny* for one kind of a coin before we used it for another. But it is equally true that the newer meaning is very common in America; and it is *not* true (in spite of what some dictionaries say) that this meaning is merely "colloquial." Even our most formal writers might say, "He had a dime, two nickels, and three *pennies*," though they probably express the total by saying "twenty-three *cents*."

Of course we could not communicate at all without some sort of agreement that certain words are to be used to stand for certain things. Therefore meaning (3)—"a more or less general habit of using a given word to indicate a given thing"—is also perfectly legitimate. But we should not pretend that this more or less general habit is absolutely uniform, or that any number of books or teachers can ever make it so.

We can only guess how the habit started, and a number of very different guesses have been made. A linguist can trace the connection between English *father* and Latin *pater,* or between English *fish* and Latin *piscis*; but he cannot give a satisfactory reason why one of these pairs of words should be applied to male parents and the other to animals that live in the water. They would work exactly as well if their meanings were reversed. This last point is important. The "agreement" to use certain words for certain things is basically arbitrary. It is also, in the main, informal, habitual, and unenforceable.

Why Communication is Never Perfect

We cannot understand each other unless we approximate the habits of those with whom we communicate; but we can only approximate. Until we find two people with identical physical equipment, nervous systems, and backgrounds of past experience, we cannot expect to find even two people who use a language in exactly the same way. Schools and other forces tend to keep our language habits somewhat similar, but perfect uniformity is not even theoretically possible. This is true of both individual words and of ways of putting them together. Moreover, it is true of the ways we react to language as well as of the ways we express it.

Let us look at a single short sentence:

John hurt Mary.

Most of us would say offhand that we understand this perfectly. Yet it conveys, by itself, very little definite information, as we can see by trying to answer the following questions: Are John and Mary people, pigs, or one of each? Are they real or imaginary? Was the hurting mental, physical, or what?

Suppose that as I wrote the sentence I was thinking of one pig biting another; that Jim Smith, as he reads it, gets the impression of one child scratching and kicking another; and that Sally Jones builds up the picture of a love affair marked by deep spiritual suffering. Each of these "meanings" is perfectly legitimate; but unless we can somehow get closer together, our communication will not be very successful. From the *words themselves* we get only the following information:

1. *John* is presumably male and animate, and there is some probability that he is human. He may be either real or imaginary.
2. *Mary* is presumably female. Her other possibilities are parallel to John's.
3. *Hurt* indicates some sort of action with an unpleasant effect that has already occurred.
4. The position of the words indicates that the direction of the action was from John to Mary.

Thus each word, by itself, *limits the possibilities* a good deal; and the relative position of the words limits them still further. The question is, can we limit them enough to communicate our ideas accurately and effectively?

We can make some progress in this direction by using additional words. Suppose I expand the sentence to read: "My little black pig, John, hurt my little white pig, Mary, by biting her in the left ear." This answers two of the questions listed above—John and Mary are pigs rather than people, and the hurting was physical. The reader may even accept that fact that the pigs are real rather than imaginary, although this cannot be proved by words alone. But other questions remain—how big is *little*, how much it hurt, and so forth. No matter how many words we use, or how carefully we arrange them, we can never directly transfer an idea from one mind to another. We can only hope to stimulate in the second mind an idea *similar* to that in the first. The words pass through our minds. The pigs, we hope, stay in their pens. And the exact nature of the connection between the words, the minds, and the pigs is not the easiest thing in the world to explain. At the very least we have to consider:

1. The relation between the words and the minds of the people who use them.
2. The relations between the words and the things and activities they stand for.
3. The relations of the words to each other.

Words and the Human Nervous System

The human brain operates something like an electronic computing machine. It contains millions of short nerve-lengths comparable to wires, and millions of nerve-connections comparable to switches. The workings of this complex system are not fully understood, but we do know that electrical impulses pass through it at a very regular speed of about four hundred feet per second. It is the passage of these impulses that constitutes our thinking.

Even the simplest thought requires the passage of a current over a complicated circuit containing innumerable switches. When an impulse starts, it might follow any one of an enormous number of routes, depending on how the switches click. But once a route has been selected, there is some tendency for the switches to set, so that a second impulse starting from the same point as the first can more easily duplicate the route than pick out a new one of its own. It is by this setting of the switches that memory and habits develop. It may take a number of repetitions to have a significant effect.

A switch may be set so firmly that a possible connection is blocked out temporarily, or even permanently. For instance, most of us have had the experience of doing a complicated problem of arithmetic, in the midst of which we have made a very obvious mistake, such as multiplying two by two and getting two as the result. We have then checked it over several times without finding the error—two times two still seems to give us two. One of our switches has temporarily been jammed in the wrong position. Fortunately, not every passage of a nerve impulse jams a switch; it merely makes it easier for it to turn one way than another.

There are always a number of impulses passing through different circuits, and these affect each other. The way we think at a given time is therefore determined largely by our previous experiences—not only the things we have encountered, but the particular paths that our nerve impulses have followed as a result of encountering them. No two of us started out with exactly the same wiring system, and the original differences have been increased by later activity.

The explanation just given is greatly oversimplified, but perhaps it will help us to understand something about the way we use words. Early in life we learn to associate words with people, things, events, and relations. Words as such as not permanently stored in the brain like cards in a filing cabinet. When a man hears or sees a word he receives an impulse which must pass along some circuit, determined by his previous experience with both words and things. When he hears it again, the new impulse tends to follow the same circuit, unless some intervening experience modifies it. On the other hand, when some other stimulus sends an impulse along part of the same circuit, he "remembers" the word. Meanwhile it, as a word, has completely disappeared from his mind. But the effect it has had on his nervous system, by operating some of the switches, persists. Consequently, if he has associated the word with a given situation, the recurrence of some aspect of that situation, either in physical fact or in mental review, is likely to reactivate the circuit, and he is again conscious of the word.

For instance, I look into a pen and see one animal bite another, and hear the second one squeal. I would not say anything, even to myself, unless I was to some extent interested in the activity. But if I was interested enough to notice it, part of the reaction of noticing would probably be the passing of words through my mind. The particular words that passed would be determined by my previous experiences. If I had seen similar animals before, I might say "One pig bit the other," or "One pig hurt the other," depending on whether I was more impressed by the action or its effect. If they were my own animals, I would probably think of them as individuals rather than simply as pigs, and might therefore say, "John hurt Mary."

Simple as this sentence is, I could not possibly have said it without having had a number of past experiences—enough to guess at the probable effect of John's teeth on Mary's ear and nervous system, and the significance of her squeal. Not being, myself, a small female pig, I must base my guess on a whole chain of assumptions; but I can be reasonably confident of its accuracy.

Certain events in the outside world have made impressions on my nervous system. I have associated words with these *impressions,* and not directly with the events themselves. If I attempt to communicate by the use of words, I must try to arouse *similar impressions in the nervous system* of the man I am talking to. Similar, not identical. His own past experiences, which cannot possibly be exactly the same as mine, are bound to affect his reactions. Even if he realizes that I am talking about my two pigs, his internal response may be quite surprising. I am expecting him to feel something like "Isn't that too bad?" but his actual sentiments may be "So what?" or even "Three cheers for John!"

We may be tempted to say: "Oh, he understands, all right. He just reacts differently." But what we call his understanding is merely a part of his total reaction, and cannot be separated, except verbally, from the rest of it. If you don't believe this, try telling a mother some time: "Oh, your boy is all right; he just broke a leg and a couple of ribs." The only thing she will understand from the word *just* is that you are an inhuman brute. As for the rest of the sentence, you have sent out a message saying "The damage to your son is temporary, so there is nothing to worry about." She has received one saying: "My darling is suffering, and there is no justice, and how do I know that one of his ribs hasn't punctured a lung?" And if you try to tell her that that is not a reasonable interpretation of your words, she will simply say (if she is still bothering to speak to you), "You have never been a mother." Her past experiences and her set of values are different from yours, especially where her son is concerned. Even if you had been more tactful in your report, your words could not possibly "mean" to her what they "mean" to you.

Words and Things

The second relation—between words and the things they stand for— also needs some attention. We have already seen that the connection between a word and a thing is neither necessary nor direct. It is also important to realize that it is never quite the same twice, because the thing itself is always changing. If you buy a quart of milk, drink half of it, leave the rest in a warm kitchen for a couple of days, and then drink *that,* are you drinking the *same* milk?

The question cannot be answered intelligently without realizing that two quite different ideas are indicated by the word *same.* In the sense of continuity, it *is* the same milk you left there. In the sense of identity of structure, it is *not.* Important changes have taken place, and your tongue recognizes the effect of some of these changes at the first sip. Moreover, these changes have been taking place every instant that the milk has been there, and other changes have been taking place in the bottle. Such changes are not always perceptible, and we can often afford to disregard them, but they are inevitably taking place *all the time*; and the fact that we don't notice them does not prevent them from being real. It does no good to say that for "all practical purposes" a thing remains the same, unless we are quite sure that we can predict in advance what "all practical purposes" will be. If the bottle crystallizes and breaks at a tiny jar, or the milk picks up and multiplies germs that kill us, we cannot dispose of the unfortunate results by insisting that the "same" things were perfectly all right a while ago.

To go one step further into the matter, we may bring up the question of whether anything is the same, even at a given instant, to two different observers. Again the answer seems to be no. Since our senses, nervous systems, and backgrounds of past experience vary, no two people can get identical impressions of the "same" thing. The actual thing (unless it is something like a bullet or an axe) does not get into our heads. What does get in—what we are conscious of and what we talk about—is merely the impression made on our nervous system. Therefore when two people look at a Pekingese dog, and she says, "Oh, the cute little darling!" while he says "What a disgusting little slug," they are not applying different words to the *same* thing. Each of them is describing, not the physical dog, but the impression created in his own mind by a combination of his present sense-perceptions and his past experiences. Even if they agree verbally that it is a Pekingese, the meeting of their minds is not complete; because the word Pekingese still "means" something different to each of them.

It follows that "using the same words for the same things" is not even theoretically possible, because there simply aren't any "same things." The best we can hope for is a reasonable approximation. Our remote ancestors, when they developed the language, did not know this. A few of them had imaginative glimpses of the truth, but on the whole they believed very firmly that many things were identical, permanent, and alike to all observers; and the structure of the language, like the structure of their physical theories, reflected this belief. Until the development of modern physics and neurology there was no definite proof that they were wrong.

A good many men, for a good many centuries, have been trying to devise and encourage the use of a language suitable for perfect communication—a language in which every word has a fixed meaning, which any properly trained person can recognize; and in which the arrangement of words is completely systematic and "logical." We can now see that such a language would be possible only if words operated in a vacuum, or at least in a perfectly uniform medium, of which each human skull somehow contained a part. We must therefore lower our sights.

Of course an approximate agreement as to the significance of words and word-arrangements is possible, or we could not communicate at all; and among people of similar backgrounds and training, communication over a limited range of subjects may reach a high degree of reliability. Dictionaries and grammars, if they are well made and sensibly used, may increase the uniformity of our language habits and thus improve the quality of our communication. But they may do us more harm than good if we let them blind us to the fact that language is not, and never can be, an independent, objective structure governed by its own laws. At its theoretical best, language can also stimulate similar (never identical) reactions in necessarily different nervous systems. Aside from its effect on these nervous systems, it has no importance at all.

The man who goes through life complaining that his friends (a) don't say what they mean, and (b) don't understand him when he speaks plain English, deserves pity rather than blame. He suffers from a delusion that makes it hard for him to look through the words and find out what the man behind them means; and equally hard for him to select and arrange his own words with some attention to the response that they probably will arouse, rather than the one they "should" arouse. If his delusion makes him haughty and ill-tempered, it is probably because of continual frustration rather than natural viciousness.

COMPREHENSION QUIZ

1. A study of English grammar involves
    a. word form.
    b. word order.
    c. semantic variations.
    d. both (a) and (b).
2. The agreement to use certain words for certain things is
    a. arbitrary.
    b. habitual.
    c. unenforceable.
    d. all of these.
3. Myers likens the operation of the human brain to
    a. a radio circuit.

    b.   a computer.

    c.   a pinball machine.

    d.   a combination tape recorder and radio transmitter.

4. In order for man to develop a perfect language, where the arrangements of words would be completely systematic and "logical,"

    a.   words would need to operate in a vacuum.

    b.   the language would need to be a highly inflected one.

    c.   illiteracy would need to be eliminated.

    d.   every one would have to see all words the same way.

5. To find two people who use language in exactly the same way, they would need to have all except which of the following?

    a.   Identical physical equipment.

    b.   Identical understanding of each other.

    c.   Identical nervous systems.

    d.   Identical backgrounds of past experience.

6. Early in life we learn to associate words with all except

    a.   people.

    b.   things.

    c.   relations.

    d.   all of the above.

7. The connection between a word and a thing is neither necessary nor

    a.   unnecessary.

    b.   similar.

    c.   direct.

    d.   indirect.

8. When two people describe the same object with different words, they are

    a.   applying different words to the same object.

    b.   describing the impression created in their own minds by present sense perceptions.

    c.   describing the impression created by past experiences.

    d.   describing the impression created by both the past experiences and present sense perceptions.

DISCUSSION QUESTIONS

1. Why can we never directly transfer an idea from one mind to another?

2. How do we form habits? How do we break them?

3. Why is it impossible to "use the same words for the same things"?

4. Why does Myers say that the word "penny" is not merely a colloquialism?

5. Can anyone give a satisfactory reason why a bird is called a bird and not an apple?

6. Explain the differences between the words in each of the following pairs: officer, cop; curious, nosey; cheap, inexpensive; daring, foolhardy.

7. Will the increased uniformity of our language habits improve the quality of our communication? Why or why not?

8. What does Myers mean when he says that we cannot use the same words for the same things because "there simply aren't any 'same things' "?

WRITING SUGGESTIONS

1. Construct four sentences in which you use four different contextual meanings of the same word.
2. Write a simple declarative sentence and then list as many different meanings this sentence may have as you can.
3. Not only do words have different meanings for the people using them, but so do the inflections of words in sentences. See how many different meanings you can get for the sentence, "She feeds her dog biscuits."
4. Write a paper on the new proposed international language known as Interlingua.
5. Write a short account of a personal experience you have had in which a misunderstanding occurred because you and another person understood a word in a different sense.

Recommended Readings to Part III

Hayakawa, S. I. (ed.). *Our Language and Our World.* New York: Harper & Row, 1959.

Lee, Irving J. *Language Habits in Human Affairs.* New York: Harper & Row, 1941.

Nesbit, F. F. *Language, Meaning, and Reality.* New York: Exposition, 1955.

Whorf, B. L. *Language, Thought, and Reality.* Cambridge: Massachusetts Institute of Technology Press, 1956.

IV

Regional,
Cultural,
and Social
Varieties
of English

Cultural Levels
and Functional Varieties
of English

by JOHN S. KENYON

The word *level,* when used to indicate different styles of language, is a metaphor, suggesting higher or lower position and, like the terms *higher* and *lower,* figuratively implies "better" or "worse," "more desirable" or "less desirable," and similar comparative degrees of excellence or inferiority in language.

The application of the term *level* to those different styles of language that are not properly distinguished as better or worse, desirable or undesirable, creates a false impression. I confess myself guilty of this error along with some other writers. What are frequently grouped together in one class as different levels of language are often in reality false combinations of two distinct and incommensurable categories, namely, *cultural levels* and *functional varieties.*

Among *cultural levels* may be included, on the lower levels, illiterate speech, narrowly local dialect, ungrammatical speech and writing, excessive and unskillful slang, slovenly and careless vocabulary and construction, exceptional pronunciation, and, on the higher level, language used generally by the cultivated, clear, grammatical writing, and pronunciations used by the cultivated over wide areas. The different cultural levels may be summarized in the two general classes *substandard* and *standard.*

Among *functional varieties* not depending on cultural levels may be mentioned colloquial language, itself existing in different degrees of familiarity or formality, as, for example, familiar conversation, private correspondence, formal conversation, familiar public address; formal platform

From John S. Kenyon, "Cultural Levels and Functional Varieties of English," *College English,* October, 1948. Reprinted by permission of the National Council of Teachers of English.

or pulpit speech, public reading, public worship; legal, scientific, and other expository writing; prose and poetic belles-lettres. The different functional varieties may roughly be grouped together in the two classes *familiar* and *formal* writing or speaking.

The term *level*, then, does not properly belong at all to functional varieties of speech—colloquial, familiar, formal, scientific, literary language. They are equally "good" for their respective functions, and as classifications do not depend on the cultural status of the users.

The two groupings *cultural levels* and *functional varieties* are not mutually exclusive categories. They are based on entirely separate principles of classification: *culture* and *function*. Although we are here principally concerned with the functional varieties of standard English (the highest cultural level), yet substandard English likewise has its functional varieties for its different occasions and purposes. Thus the functional variety colloquial English may occur on a substandard cultural level, but the term *colloquial* does not itself designate a cultural level. So the functional variety formal writing or speaking may occur on a lower or on a higher cultural level according to the social status of writer or speaker, and sometimes of reader or audience. It follows, for instance, that the colloquial language of cultivated people is on a higher cultural level than the formal speech of the semiliterate or than some inept literary writing.

Semiliterate formal speech is sometimes heard from radio speakers. I recently heard one such speaker solemnly announce, "Sun day will be Mother's Day." Because the speaker, in his ignorance of good English, thought he was making himself plainer by using the distorted pronunciation *sun day* instead of *the* standard pronunciation *sundy,* he was actually misunderstood by some listeners to be saying, "Some day will be Mother's Day." About forty years ago the great English phonetician Henry Sweet used this very example to show that "we cannot make words more distinct by disguising them."[1] He was referring to the use, as in this instance, of the full sound of vowels in unaccented syllables where standard English has obscure vowels. On the same page Sweet gives another example of the same blunder: "Thus in the sentence *I shall be at home from one to three* the substitution of tuw for tə [ə = the last sound in *sofa*] at once suggests a confusion between the preposition and the numeral." This was also verified on the radio. Not long ago I heard a radio speaker announce carefully, "This program will be heard again tomorrow from one two three." I have also recorded (among many others) the following such substandard forms from the radio: *presidEnt* for the standard form *presidənt,* the days of the week ending in the full word *day* instead of the standard English syllable *-dy, ay man* for the correct ə *man, cahnsider* for *cənsider, tooday* for *təday, too go* for *tə go, Coalumbia* for *Cəlumbia,* etc. This is merely one sort

[1] Henry Sweet, *The Sounds of English* (Oxford, 1910), p. 78.

among many of substandard features in the formal speech of the semi-literate.[2]

To begin my strictures at home, in *American Pronunciation* (9th ed., 4th printing, p. 17), I use the page heading "Levels of Speech." This should be "Functional Varieties of Standard Speech," for the reference is solely to the different uses of speech on the one cultivated level. Similarly, in the Kenyon-Knott *Pronouncing Dictionary of American English* (p. xvi, § 2), I carelessly speak of "levels of the colloquial" where I mean "styles of the colloquial," as three lines above. For though there are different cultural levels of colloquial English, the reference here is only to standard colloquial.

S. A. Leonard and H. Y. Moffett, in their study, "Current Definition of Levels in English Usage,"[3] say (p. 348): "The levels of English usage have been most clearly described in Dr. Murray's Preface ["General Explanations," p. xvii] to the *New English Dictionary*. I have varied his diagram a little in order to illustrate better the overlapping between the categories." It appears to me that Leonard and Moffett have so varied the diagram as to obscure Murray's intention. For he is not here primarily exhibiting levels of speech but is showing the "Anglicity," or limits of the English vocabulary for the purposes of his dictionary.[4] The only topical divisions of his diagram that imply a cultural level are "slang" and "dialectal," and the only statement in his explanation of the diagram that could imply it is, "Slang words ascend through colloquial use." This may imply that slang is on a lower cultural level than "colloquial, literary, technical, scientific, foreign." We may also safely infer that Murray would place "Dialectal" on a lower level than colloquial and literary if he were here concerned with cultural levels. Murray's diagram rests consistently on the same basis of classification throughout ("Anglicity"), and he emphasizes that "there is absolutely no defining line in any direction [from the central nucleus of colloquial and literary]." Moreover, Murray's exposition here concerns only vocabulary, with no consideration of the other features that enter so largely into "levels" of language—grammatical form and structure, pronunciation, spelling, and meaning—of styles, in short, only so far as they are affected by vocabulary. These he treats of elsewhere but without reference to levels.

It is not quite clear just how far Leonard and Moffett intend their grouping "literary English," "standard, cultivated, colloquial English," and "naïf, popular, or uncultivated English" to be identical with what they call Murray's "levels," his description of which they commend. But it is clear that they call their own grouping "three levels of usage" (p. 357) and classify them together as a single descending scale (cf. "the low end of the

---

[2] See further *American Speech*, VI, No. 5 (June, 1931), 368–72.

[3] *English Journal*, XVI, No. 5 (May, 1927), 345–59.

[4] The word *Anglicity* is a coinage of the *Oxford Dictionary*. They define it as "English quality, as of speech or style; English idiom."

scale," p. 358). The inevitable impression that the average reader receives from such an arrangement of the scale is: Highest level, literary English; next lower level, colloquial English; lowest level, illiterate English; whereas, in fact, the first two "levels" are functional varieties of the one cultural level standard English, while the third ("illiterate or uncultivated," p. 358) is a cultural level.

Krapp has a chapter on "The Levels of English Speech,"[5] in which he reveals some awareness of the confusion of cultural levels with functional varieties. He says:

> Among those who pay any heed at all to convention in social relationships, a difference of degree is implicit in all use of English. This difference of degree is usually thought of in terms of higher and lower, of upper levels of speech appropriate to certain occasions of more formal character, of lower levels existing, if not necessarily appropriate, among less elevated circumstances. These popular distinctions of level may be accepted without weighting them too heavily with significance in respect of good, better, and best in speech. A disputatious person might very well raise the question whether literary English, ordinarily regarded as being on a high level, is really any better than the spoken word, is really as good as the spoken word, warm with the breath of the living moment.

At the risk of having to own the hard impeachment of being disputatious, I must express the fear that the logical fallacy in treating of levels, which Krapp rather lightly waves aside, is having a serious effect on general ideas of speech levels, and especially of the significance of colloquial English in good usage. Krapp's grouping, frankly on a scale of "levels" throughout, constitutes a descending scale from the highest, "Literary English," through "Formal Colloquial," "General Colloquial," "Popular English," to the lowest, "Vulgar English." Here the fallacy is obvious: Literary English, Formal Colloquial, and General Colloquial are not cultural levels but only functional varieties of English all on the one cultural level of standard English. The last two, Popular English and Vulgar English, belong in a different order of classification, cultural levels, without regard to function.

So in his succeeding discussion *level* sometimes means the one, sometimes the other; now a functional variety of standard English, and now a cultural level of substandard or of standard English. It is functional on page 58 ("a choice between two levels") and on page 60 ("level of general colloquial"), cultural on page 62 ("popular level" and "cultivated level") and on pages 63–64 ("popular level," "level of popular speech"), functional on page 64 ("general colloquial level"), cultural again on the same page ("popular level," "still lower level"), cultural on page 67 ("vulgar . . . level of speech," "applying the term 'vulgar' to it at certain levels"), cultural on

5 George Philip Krapp, *The Knowledge of English* (New York, 1927), pp. 55–76.

page 68 ("its own [popular] level"), cultural and functional in the same phrase on page 68 ("speakers from the popular and the general colloquial level meet and mix"), and so on most confusingly to page 75.

The same kind of mixture of cultural levels and functional varieties is thrown into one apparently continuous scale by Kennedy: "There is the formal and dignified language of the scholarly or scientific address or paper. . . . The precision and stateliness of this uppermost level . . . is a necessary accompaniment of thinking on a high plane."[6] Next in order he mentions colloquial speech, which he refers to as "the second level, . . . generally acceptable to people of education and refinement." Clearly this is not a cultural level but a functional variety of standard English, like the "uppermost level." The third level is, however, a cultural one: "the latest slang," workmen's "technical slang and colloquialisms which other persons cannot comprehend," "grammatical solecisms." "The speech of this third level can fairly be ranked as lower in the social scale." His fourth level is also cultural: "At the bottom of the scale is the lingo, or cant, of criminals, hobos, and others of the lowest social levels."

Finally, Kennedy fixes the false mental image of a continuous and logically consistent descent from "the cold and lonely heights of formal and highly specialized scientific and scholarly language" to "the stupid and slovenly level of grammatical abuses and inane slang." In reality there is no cultural descent until we reach his third "level," since "formal and dignified language" and "colloquial speech" are only functional varieties of English on the one cultural level of standard English.

In Perrin's excellent and useful *Index*,[7] under the heading "Levels of Usage," he names "three principal levels": "Formal English" (likened to formal dress), "Informal English" (described as "the typical language of an educated person going about his everyday affairs"), and "Vulgate English." From his descriptions it appears clearly that Formal and Informal English are functional varieties of standard English, while Vulgate is a substandard cultural level. A similar classification appears in his table on page 365.

On page 19 Perrin uses *level* apparently in the sense of functional variety, not of cultural level: "Fundamentally, good English is speaking or writing in the level of English that is appropriate to the particular situation that faces the speaker or writer. It means making a right choice among the levels of usage." His advice, however, involves two choices: (1) choice of a standard cultural level and (2) choice of the appropriate functional variety of that level.

A clear instance of the inconsistent use of the term *level* is found in Robert C. Pooley's *Teaching English Usage* (New York, 1946), chapter iii, "Levels in English Usage." He names five levels: (1) the illiterate level; (2) the homely level; (3) standard English, informal level; (4) standard English,

---

6 Arthur G. Kennedy, *Current English* (Boston, 1935), pp. 15–17: "Speech Levels."
7 Porter G. Perrin, *An Index to English* (Chicago, 1939), pp. 364–65.

formal level; and (5) the literary level. In (1) and (2) *level* has an altogether different meaning from that in (3), (4), and (5). In the first two *level* plainly means "cultural level"; in the last three it just as plainly means "functional variety of standard English," all three varieties being therefore on the one cultural level of standard English. So *level* in the two groups belongs to different orders of classification. All misunderstanding and wrong implication would be removed from this otherwise excellent treatment of levels if the last three groups were labeled "Standard English Level, Informal Variety"; "Standard English Level, Formal Variety"; and "Standard English Level, Literary Variety." Pooley's groups contain three cultural levels (illiterate, homely, standard) and three functional varieties of the standard cultural level (information, formal, literary).

The misapplication to colloquial English of the term *level*, metaphorically appropriate only to cultural gradations, is especially misleading. We often read of English that is "on the colloquial level." For example, Krapp writes: "*Who do you mean?* . . . has passed into current spoken use and may be accepted on the colloquial level."[8] This implies that colloquial English is on a different cultural level from formal English (literary, scientific, etc.), and a too frequent assumption, owing to this and other misuses of the term *colloquial,* is that its cultural level is below that of formal English. This supposition, tacit or explicit, that colloquial style is inferior to formal or literary style, leads inescapably to the absurd conclusion that, whenever scientists or literary artists turn from their formal writing to familiar conversation with their friends, they thereby degrade themselves to a lower social status.

This misuse of *level* encourages the fallacy frequently met with of contrasting colloquial with standard English, logically as fallacious as contrasting white men with tall men. For instance, Mencken writes: "'I have no doubt *but* that' . . . seems to be very firmly lodged in colloquial American, and even to have respectable standing in the standard speech."[9] This contrast, not always specifically stated, is often implied. For example, Kennedy writes: "Colloquial English is, properly defined, the language of conversation, and especially of familiar conversation. As such it may approximate the standard speech of the better class of English speakers, or it may drop to the level of the illiterate and careless speaker."[10] *May approximate* should be replaced by *may be on the level of.*

Similarly, on page 440: "Some measure words [are] still used colloquially without any ending in the plural . . . ; but most of these are given the *s* ending in standard English usage." Here *standard* is confused with *formal.*

Kennedy (pp. 534, 616) several times contrasts colloquial English with

[8] *A Comprehensive Guide to Good English* (New York, 1927), p. 641.
[9] H. L. Mencken, *The American Language* (4th ed.; New York, 1936), p. 203.
[10] *Op. cit.,* p. 26.

"standard literary English." This implies that colloquial English is not standard, while literary English is. If he means to contrast standard colloquial with standard literary, well and good; but I fear that most readers would understand the contrast to be of colloquial with standard.[11]

The term *colloquial* cannot properly designate a substandard cultural level of English. It designates a functional variety—that used chiefly in conversation—and in itself says nothing as to its cultural level, though this discussion, and the dictionary definitions, are chiefly concerned with cultivated colloquial, a functional variety of standard English. When writers of such standing as those I have mentioned slip into expressions that imply lower cultural status of colloquial English, it is not surprising that some teachers fall into the error. One teacher expressed the conviction that colloquialisms should not be represented as standard American speech. But the context of the statement indicated that its author was using *colloquialism* in the sense of "localism." I could hardly believe how frequent this gross error is, until I heard it from a well-known American broadcaster.[12]

The best dictionaries, at least in their definitions, give no warrant for the various misuses of *colloquial, colloquially, colloquialism, colloquiality*. I urge the reader to study carefully the definitions in the *Oxford English Dictionary*, with its many apt examples from standard writers, and in *Webster's New International Dictionary, Second Edition*, with its quotations from George Lyman Kittredge. Kittredge's views on the standing of colloquial English are well known. It is said that somebody once asked him about the meaning of the label "Colloq." in dictionaries. He is reported to have replied, "I myself speak 'colloke' and often write it." I cannot verify the story, but it sounds authentic.

It seems to me inevitable that the frequent groupings of so-called "levels" such as "Literary, Colloquial, Illiterate," and the like, will lead the reader to suppose that just as Illiterate is culturally below Colloquial, so Colloquial is culturally below Literary. While I can scarcely hope that my humble remonstrance will reform all future writing on "levels of Engish," I believe that writers who confuse the meaning of the term *level* must accept some part of the responsibility for the popular misunderstanding of the true status of colloquial English; for I cannot avoid the belief that the popular idea of colloquial English as something to be looked down

[11] Greenough and Kittredge in *Words and Their Ways in English Speech* (New York, 1909), chap. vii, only apparently treat literary English as the sole standard form: "What is the origin of standard or literary English?" (p. 80). They use *standard* in a special sense for their particular purpose, calling it "the common property of all but the absolutely illiterate," "the language which all educated users of English speak and write" (therefore including colloquial). For the usual current meaning, see the definitions of *standard* quoted in *American Pronunciation* (6th and subsequent eds.), pp. 14–15.

[12] Leonard and Moffett also mention the frequency of this blunder (*op. cit.*, p. 351, n. 5).

upon with disfavor is due in part to the failure of writers on the subject to distinguish between *cultural levels of English* and *functional varieties of standard English.*

COMPREHENSION QUIZ

1. In unaccented syllables, standard English has
    a. stressed vowels.
    b. unstressed vowels.
    c. blended vowels.
    d. the full sound of vowels.
    e. obscured vowels.
2. According to Kenyon, which of the following would not be classified as a functional variety of English?
    a. Literary English.
    b. Formal platform or pulpit speech.
    c. Clear grammatical writing.
    d. Familiar conversation.
3. Before the term "level" can be metaphorically appropriate, when used to indicate different styles of language, it
    a. must suggest higher or lower position.
    b. must not suggest higher or lower position.
    c. must not refer to the cultural gradations.
    d. must refer to functional varieties.
    e. necessarily implies a comparison.
4. If we accept the use of the word "level" to apply to functional varieties of English,
    a. it would require a change in our basic thinking.
    b. it would be confusing to academicians only.
    c. it would lead to the conclusion that a shift from formal writing to familiar conversation would be degrading the speaker to a lower social status.
    d. it would not lead to the conclusion that a shift from formal writing to familiar conversation would be degrading the speaker to a lower social status.
    e. we would destroy the concept of cultural and functional English.
5. The term "colloquial"
    a. is properly designated as a substandard level of English.
    b. designates a cultural level.
    c. contains within itself the implication that it is a functional level.
    d. cannot properly designate a functional variety of English.
    e. cannot properly designate a substandard cultural level of English.

DISCUSSION QUESTIONS

1. This essay was written to correct a false impression of which language scholars themselves are, at times, guilty. What is this false impression?

2. Technically, what is the difference between the words "level" and "variety"?
3. The author says "We may also safely infer that Murray would place 'dialectal' on a lower level than 'colloquial' and 'literary' if he were here concerned with cultural levels." Why may he "safely infer" this? What logical reasoning leads to this inference?
4. Would Kenyon say this statement is correct: "Fundamentally, good English is speaking or writing in the level of English that is appropriate to the particular situation that faces the speaker or writer"?
5. To what problems can the misuse of the term "level" lead?
6. This essay discusses "colloquial" as a usage term. What do you understand to be the difference between cultivated colloquial, general colloquial, and literary English?
7. Comment on this sentence from the essay: ". . . colloquialisms should not be represented as standard American speech." Explain your position on this issue.
8. According to Kenyon, the confusion with the meaning of the term "level" has fostered the idea that colloquial English is something to be looked down upon with disfavor. What other possible effects has this confusion had?

WRITING SUGGESTIONS

1. Defend the position that colloquial language is a variety of speech and not a level of speech.
2. Examine the misuse of the terms "functional varieties" and "cultural levels," indicating the effects of this misuse.
3. Analyze your different "functional varieties" of language and explain the conditions under which you use each of these varieties.

Social

and Educational Varieties

of Speech

by W. NELSON FRANCIS

We have already noted that there are social varieties of English, differ-ing in pronunciation, grammar, and vocabulary. These are the natural modes of speech of people who differ in education and in the positions they occupy in the social system. It is here, even more than in regional variation, that value judgments are most likely to be made. Specifically, the dialect of educated people who occupy positions of influence and responsibility is commonly called "good English" and that of people lower on the educa-tional and social scale "bad English." Let us briefly investigate the implica-tions of these terms.

Applied to language, the adjective *good* can have two meanings: (1) "effective, adequate for the purpose to which it is put" and (2) "acceptable, conforming to approved usage." The first of these is truly a value judgment of the language itself. In this sense the language of Shakespeare, for exam-ple, is "good English" because it serves as a highly effective vehicle for his material. On the other hand, the language of a poorer writer, which does not meet adequately the demands put upon it, might be called "bad Eng-lish." The second meaning of *good* is not really a judgment of the language itself but a social appraisal of the persons who use it. An expression like *I ain't got no time for youse* may be most effective in the situation in which it is used, and hence "good English" in the first sense. But most people, including those who naturally speak this way, will call it "bad English" because grammatical features like *ain't, youse,* and the double negative construction belong to a variety of English commonly used by people with little education and low social and economic status.

This second meaning of the terms *good English* and *bad English* is much more common than the first. It is easier, no doubt, to identify a dialect by certain overt items of grammar and vocabulary than it is to estimate the effectiveness of a specific sample of language. Furthermore, the notion that the language of social and educational inferiors is "bad" has been extensively taught in schools, so that even those who speak it naturally often get the idea that there is something intrinsically wrong with their language, usually without clearly understanding why. Others, of course, alter their language to make it conform more nearly to what they have been taught to consider "good." In effect, they adopt a social dialect appropriate to a higher position on the educational and social scale.

It is unfortunate that these two notions—effectiveness and social prestige—have both come to be expressed in the same terms, as value judgments of the language itself. They are not necessarily connected. What is called "bad English" in the usual sense may be highly effective in the appropriate context. Conversely, language which is socially and educationally impeccable may be most ineffective, as anyone who has listened to a dull speech can testify. It is true that on the whole the language of the more educated is likely to be more effective, since it has a larger vocabulary and somewhat more complex grammar and hence is capable of finer and more subtle shades of meaning as well as finer effects of rhythm and tone. But unless these resources are used skillfully they do not necessarily produce better language from the point of view of effectiveness. On the other hand, writers like Mark Twain, Ring Lardner, and William Faulkner have shown that vernacular or uneducated English can be used with great effectiveness in literature.

As with other kinds of variation, social levels of English shade gradually into one another. But we can recognize three main levels. At the top is **educated or standard English;** at the bottom is **uneducated English,** and between them comes what H. L. Mencken called the **vernacular.**[1] These have in common the larger part of their grammar, pronunciation, and basic vocabulary but are marked by significant differences in all three areas.

Educated or **Standard English** is that naturally used by most college-educated people who fill positions of social, financial, and professional influence in the community. Some people learn it as their native speech, if they come from families that already belong to this social class. Others acquire it in the course of their schooling and later by conscious or unconscious imitation of their associates. Control of standard English does not,

[1] H. L. Mencken, *The American Language,* 4th ed. (New York: Alfred A. Knopf, 1937), p. 417.

of course, guarantee professional, social, or financial success. But it is an almost indispensable attribute of those who attain such success.

In addition to its social importance, educated English is on the whole a more flexible and versatile instrument than the other social varieties. As the language of the professions and the learned disciplines, it is called on to express more complex ideas, for which it has developed an extensive vocabulary. Its grammar, too, is more complex, and it uses longer sentences with more levels of subordination. This does not mean that it presents greater difficulties to the listener or reader, provided he is familiar with its vocabulary and grammar. But the fact that it is often used to express complicated and difficult material means that, unskillfully used, it can be vague or obscure. When its resources of vocabulary and grammar are over-exploited in the expression of simple ideas, it may become the inflated jargon sometimes called "gobbledygook":

> With regard to personnel utilizing the premises after normal working hours, it is requested that precautions be observed to insure that all windows and doors are firmly secured and all illumination extinguished before vacating the building.

This is obviously only a much elaborated expression of the request that can be more simply and effectively stated:

> If you work late, be sure to lock the doors and windows and turn off the lights when you leave.

In the first sense of the phrase "good English," this translation is good and the gobbledygook which it translates, though it contains no errors of grammar or usage, is incredibly bad.

The British version of standard English, RP, is the same for all speakers regardless of their place of origin. In America, however, there is no such thing as a single standard form of American English, especially in pronunciation. The nearest thing to it is the speech of anonymous radio and television announcers, which one linguist has aptly called "network English."[2] In contrast to the well known individual commentators, who are allowed to use their native regional pronunciation, the network announcers all use a common version of English which is in most features that of the Inland Northern area. The contrast between a routine sports announcer and Dizzy Dean is the contrast between "network English," faultless but rather dull, and a picturesque use of South Midland vernacular.

Because of its nationwide use, network English is an acceptable standard form everywhere. But it is not a prestige dialect. Educated speakers in Boston, New York, Philadelphia, Richmond, Charleston, Atlanta, or New

---

[2] William A. Stewart, in a discussion of the problem of teaching standard English to nonstandard speakers, Bloomington, Indiana, August 1964.

Orleans use the dialects of their own regions in educated form. The last
five Presidents of the United States are a good example of the diversity of
pronunciation to be found in standard English. President Johnson speaks
the educated South Midland speech of Texas. President Kennedy's Boston
speech with its lack of postvocalic /r/ and its intrusive /r/ at the end of
words like *Cuba,* was very distinctive. President Eisenhower's speech was
a good illustration of the Middle Western variety sometimes called General
American. It betrayed his Kansas origin in spite of a military career that
took him to many parts of the English-speaking world. President Truman
retained many of the South Midland features of his native Missouri, and
President Roosevelt spoke the educated version of New York City speech,
somewhat modified by his Harvard education and New England connections. Although most of these men had long careers in politics and frequently addressed nationwide audiences, each of them used the educated
version of his native regional dialect.

   Vernacular English is the variety naturally used by the middle group of
the population, who constitute the vast majority. Their schooling extends
into or through high school, with perhaps a year of college or technical
school. They occupy the lesser white-collar jobs, staff the service trades,
and fill the ranks of skilled labor. Many of these jobs require considerable
verbal skill and have extensive occupational vocabularies. Vernacular speakers, when "talking shop," characteristically show considerable control of
technical vocabulary and relatively complex grammar.

   Just as jargon and gobbledygook are the result of overpretentious style
in standard English, so the **hyperurbanism or hyperform** is in the vernacular.
A hyperurbanism is a usage which results from the overcorrection of one
of the supposedly "bad" (*i.e.* nonstandard) features of the vernacular. For
example, the usage of pronoun case in the vernacular differs from that of
standard English in several respects, one being that a pronoun subject when
coordinated with another pronoun or with a noun may be the objective
case:

vernacular:	Him and Joe went.
standard:	Joe and he went.
vernacular:	You and me can do it.
standard:	You and I can do it.

The native speaker of the vernacular who aspires to speak standard learns
to change this use of the objective case to the standard subjective. But this
change often leads to uncertainty about pronoun case in coordination constructions elsewhere than as subject. The vernacular speaker who has learned
that *you and me* is incorrect as subject is likely to be suspicious of it anywhere, so he says *between you and I,* which is just as much a violation of
standard grammar as *you and me can do it.*

This is not the place for an extended discussion of the features which distinguish the vernacular from standard educated English. Many of them are identified and discussed in the standard handbooks and dictionaries of usage. . . . Since the vernacular shades gradually into educated standard, many of these items characterize only the varieties of vernacular nearest to uneducated English. Many points of usage which are condemned as non-standard by handbooks actually represent **divided usage;** that is, they are accepted and used by some standard English speakers but rejected by others. Sometimes the division is regional: a form or construction which is vernacular or uneducated in one region may be standard in another. An example is the use of *like* in such sentences as *It looks like it might rain* and *He acts like he's hungry.* This usage, condemned as nonstandard by most hand-books, is certainly standard in England and in the American South in all but the most formal style. In the American North and Midland it is prob-ably to be classed as vernacular. At least, a recent advertising slogan that used *like* in this way stirred up considerable discussion and condemnation among those who feel responsible for protecting standard English from ver-nacular encroachments. In fact, some aspirants to standard "correctness" avoid the use of *like* as a subordinator entirely, replacing it with *as* in sen-tences like *He drove as a crazy man.* This hyperurbanism throws away the nice semantic distinction between the prepositions *like* and *as,* as in the following:

He is acting *like* a lawyer in this affair.
He is acting *as* a lawyer in this affair.

The implication of the first is either that he is not a lawyer at all or that his lawyerlike behavior is inappropriate or unwelcome. In the second, no such judgment is implied; the sentence merely states that in the affair in question his participation is limited to the role of lawyer. It is frequently the effect of a hyperurbanism to gain a supposed (but spurious) "correctness" at the expense of precision. It thus becomes an example of "bad English" in the first sense discussed above. If preciseness in communication is an important quality of language, which certainly few will deny, the hyperurbanism that blurs preciseness in the interest of a fancied correctness is a greater linguistic offense than the nonstandard vernacular usage which is accurate and clear.

The vernacular is very much with us and presumably always will be. It is the stratum of English where there develop many new features of gram-mar, pronunciation, and vocabulary which are ultimately accepted into standard usage. In a democratic society like that of America, it is an essen-tial medium of communication even for the educated, who must at least understand and accept its usage, though they do not necessarily have to speak it. In fact, if they can speak it only with conscious and obvious effort, educated speakers should avoid it, for people are quick to take offense at what they consider patronizing. But those native speakers of the vernacular who have also acquired a command of educated standard English should not lose control of the vernacular, since a native command of it can be of great value on many occasions.

A practical illustration is the case of the college professor of English, a native speaker of educated English, who needed a rare part for his car. He consulted a colleague who had at one time been a garage mechanic and spoke the appropriate form of the vernacular. The colleague told him where to telephone to inquire for the part, but added "You'd better let me do the phoning; it'll cost you twice as much if you do it."[3]

Uneducated English is that naturally used by people whose schooling is limited and who perform the unskilled labor in country and city. Certain grammatical features, such as the double or multiple negative (which was standard in Chaucer's English) and the use of *them* as a plural demonstrative, are common to most regional varieties. But in other respects uneducated English shows much regional variety in all its features. An uneducated speaker may find that he has difficulty making himself understood outside his home region. Such features as past-tense *holp* for *helped* and *drug* for *dragged* have clear-cut regional distribution.[4] Likewise regional differences of pronunciation, which, as we have seen, exist on all levels, are much greater in uneducated speech. The same is true of vocabulary; the local words and expressions which more educated speakers avoid (though they may consider them picturesque and use them occasionally for special effect) persistently survive in uneducated speech. For this reason dialectological investigations like the Linguistic Survey of England often confine themselves almost wholly to uneducated, preferably illiterate, informants.[5]

Uneducated English doesn't often get into writing, since its users have little occasion to write and may be semiliterate or even wholly illiterate.[6] In literary writing, uneducated speakers are often marked as such by attempts to represent their pronunciation by distorted spelling, including a liberal use of eye dialect. But a truly skillful use of uneducated English in literature suggests the level of the speaker without resorting to the rather cheap device of eye dialect. Notice in the following passage from William

[3] This anecdote is told of himself by Professor J. J. Lamberts of Arizona State University.

[4] Atwood, *Survey*, pp. 9f., 16f. [E. Bagby Atwood, *A Survey of Verb Forms in the Eastern United States* (University of Michigan Press, 1953)]

[5] Harold Orton and Eugen Dieth, *Survey of English Dialects* (Leeds: E. J. Arnold & Son, Ltd., 1962), pp. 14–17, 44. In the Linguistic Atlas of the United States and Canada, however, three types of informants—representing roughly what we have called uneducated, vernacular, and educated English—are used. See Hans Kurath, *Handbook of the Linguistic Geography of New England* (Washington: American Council of Learned Societies, 1939), pp. 41–44.

[6] C. C. Fries, in preparing his *American English Grammar* (New York: Appleton-Century-Crofts, 1940), found a plentiful source of uneducated written English in letters written to a government bureau whose constituents included many uneducated speakers.

Faulkner's great novel *As I Lay Dying* how the nature of the speaker—an uneducated Mississippi farmer—is indicated by grammar and vocabulary, without any attempt to illustrate pronunciation at all.

> It was nigh toward daybreak when we drove the last nail and toted it into the house, where she was laying on the bed with the window open and the rain blowing on her again. Twice he did it, and him so dead for sleep that Cora says his face looked like one of these here Christmas masts that had done been buried a while and then dug up, until at last they put her into it and nailed it down so he couldn't open the window on her no more. And the next morning they found him in his shirt tail, laying asleep on the floor like a felled steer, and the top of the box bored clean full of holes and Cash's new auger broke off in the last one. When they taken the lid off they found that two of them had bored on into her face.
>
> If it's a judgment, it aint right. Because the Lord's got more to do than that. He's bound to have. Because the only burden Anse Bundren's ever had is himself. And when folks talks him low, I think to myself he aint that less of a man or he couldn't a bore himself this long (p. 68).[7]

Here the markers of uneducated regional dialect are such grammatical items as the verb phrase *had done been buried* and the double negative in *couldn't open the window on her no more,* the lexical item *toted,* and idioms like *talks him low* and *he aint that less of a man.*

The uneducated English of this sample contrasts with the following passage from the same novel, representing the English of a country doctor from the same region:

> When Anse finally sent for me of his own accord, I said "He has wore her out at last." And I said a damn good thing, and at first I would not go because there might be something I could do and I would have to haul her back, by God. I thought maybe they have the same sort of fool ethics in heaven they have in the Medical College and that it was maybe Vernon Tull sending for me again, getting me there in the nick of time, as Vernon always does things, getting the most for Anse's money like he does for his own. But when it got far enough into the day for me to read weather sign I knew it couldn't have been anybody but Anse that sent. I knew that nobody but a luckless man could ever need a doctor in the face of a cyclone. And I knew that if it had finally occurred to Anse himself that he needed one, it was already too late (p. 37).[8]

There are items here which are not educated standard—*wore* as past participle, for example. But the general level of the English is educated colloquial, quite different from that of the previous passage. Note especially the grammatical complexity of the last sentence.

[7] From William Faulkner, *As I Lay Dying,* New York: Random House, Inc. Copyright 1930, 1957 by William Faulkner. Reprinted by permission of the publisher.
[8] *Ibid.*

The speaker who is confined to uneducated English finds himself under a great handicap if he wishes to improve his position in society. This is true even in his own region; it is doubly so when he moves to another dialect area, where he may find not only that his speech is a liability when it comes to getting a good job, but even that he can't make himself understood at all. Furthermore, in an age when more and more of the unskilled tasks are being done by machines, the number of jobs available to persons unable to use any but uneducated English gets smaller every year. The geographical and social mobility of our people presents a great problem to the schools, one of whose tasks is to help students acquire a kind of language which will be an asset to them rather than a handicap. The problem is especially acute in the Northern cities which have had a large influx of uneducated people from the South. It is encouraging to observe that linguists, especially dialectologists, are being called on to help with this problem. The idea is getting about that the speaker of uneducated English is better served if an attempt is made not to "correct" his language and eradicate his "bad language habits," but to extend his linguistic range and versatility by helping him acquire a new dialect that is socially more acceptable. Some educators are even experimenting with the techniques developed for teaching foreign languages, in order to emphasize that the task is the positive one of learning something new rather than the negative one of eliminating something bad. Already the results of tentative efforts of this sort are showing promise.

Helping speakers of uneducated English to a command of the vernacular or of standard English is only part of the problem, of course. There must be other kinds of training, and above all there must be tangible evidence that the effort will be worthwhile; otherwise motivation will be lacking, and without motivation learning is impossible. But in this area the informed student and teacher of language can certainly be of great social usefulness.

COMPREHENSION QUIZ

1. The English used by most people who are college educated and who fill positions of social, financial, and professional influence in the community is known as
    a. vernacular English.
    b. educated English.
    c. common English.
    d. colloquial English.
    e. mature English.
2. The term "vernacular" was coined by which of these critics of English usage?
    a. H. L. Mencken.
    b. William B. Stewart.
    c. E. Bagby Atwood.

    d.   J. J. Lambert.

    e.   Harold Orton.

3. According to Francis, which group of the following writers have shown that uneducated English can be used with great effectiveness in literature?

    a.   Mark Twain, Ring Lardner, and James Thurber.

    b.   Ring Lardner, James Thurber, and Ernest Hemingway.

    c.   James Thurber, Ernest Hemingway, and William Faulkner.

    d.   Ernest Hemingway, William Faulkner, and Mark Twain.

    e.   William Faulkner, Mark Twain, and Ring Lardner.

4. If you say, "Indicate the route to my habitual abode" when you more simply and effectively could have said, "Show me the way to go home," you are using what is sometimes called

    a.   vague description.

    b.   vernacular.

    c.   a hyperurbanism.

    d.   gobbledygook.

    e.   bad English.

5. The nearest thing America has to the British version of standard English, RP, is

    a.   Inland Northern or "network English."

    b.   South Midland English.

    c.   Middle Western English.

    d.   theatrical English.

    e.   idiomatic English.

6. An overcorrection of one of the supposedly nonstandard features of vernacular English results in a usage known as

    a.   jargon.

    b.   postvocalic omission.

    c.   an hyperurbanism.

    d.   a divided usage.

    e.   a dialectological omission.

7. One idea that is meant to help the speaker of uneducated English is to

    a.   gradually correct his language and eradicate his "bad habits."

    b.   make no attempt to correct his language, but concentrate on eradicating future bad habits.

    c.   attempt actually to teach him the basic structure of the language using symbols rather than words.

    d.   make no attempt to correct his language but extend his linguistic range by helping him acquire a new dialect that is socially more acceptable.

    e.   use group clinic techniques to bring about a change of attitudes toward language.

DISCUSSION QUESTIONS

1. Francis says that the nearest thing we have to a national standard English is "network English." How might America develop a standard national English? Is such a thing desirable?

2. The illustration of the use of the word "like" when "as" is more precise, explains the term "hyperurbanism." Cite other examples of hyperurbanism.
3. What is a dialectologicist? Why do dialectological surveys often confine themselves to uneducated, often illiterate informants?
4. In the paragraph beginning, "Uneducated English doesn't often get into writing . . . ," what is the "cheap device of eye dialect" mentioned in this essay?
5. Compare the use of the term "level" with the definition of the term "cultural level" as advanced by Kenyon in the article preceding this one. Would Kenyon agree with Francis' usage?
6. Can you call to mind any specific examples of "language which is socially and educationally impeccable," but which can qualify as " 'bad' English because of its dullness"?
7. Are there distinct advantages in using educated English compared to vernacular, or uneducated English?

WRITING SUGGESTIONS

1. The essay defines the three social levels of English. Write three letters of application for a position, using each of the levels.
2. Write the directions from your classroom to your living quarters, first using the inflated jargon called "gobbledygook." Next, re-write the directions more simply and effectively.
3. Write a theme on the subject, "It is Worthwhile to Improve Your Language," which would be addressed to a group of people who spoke uneducated English. Remember to use their language!

Regional Variations

by ALBERT H. MARCKWARDT

Early travelers to America and native commentators on the language agree on the existence of regional differences at an early period in our national history. Mrs. Anne Royal called attention to various Southernisms in the works which she wrote during the second quarter of the nineteenth century, and as early as 1829, Dr. Robley Dunglison had identified many of the Americanisms, in the glossary he compiled, with particular portions of the country. Charles Dickens recognized regional differences in the English he encountered in his first tour of the United States, and William Howard Russell, reporting on Abraham Lincoln's first state banquet, at which he was a guest, mentions his astonishment at finding "a diversity of accent almost as great as if a number of foreigners had been speaking English."

A number of other observers, however, were sufficiently impressed by the uniformity of the language throughout the country to make this a matter of comment. De Tocqueville, in a rather extended treatment of the language of the young republic, flatly declared, "There is no patois in the New World," and John Pickering, along with Noah Webster easily the most distinguished of our early philologists, also remarked on the great uniformity of dialect through the United States, "in consequence," as he said, "of the frequent removals of people from one part of our country to another."

There is truth in both types of comment. People in various parts of the United States do not all speak alike, but there is greater uniformity here than in England or in the countries of Western Europe, and this makes the collection of a trustworthy body of information upon the regional variations in American English a somewhat difficult and delicate matter.

The gathering of authentic data on the dialects of many of the countries of Western Europe began in the latter decades of the nineteenth century. The *Atlas linguistique de la France* followed closely upon the heels of the

Sprachatlas des deutschen Reichs, and the activities of the English Dialect Society were initiated about the same time. In 1889 a group of American scholars organized the American Dialect Society, hoping that the activities of this organization might result in a body of material from which either a dialect dictionary or a series of linguistic maps, or both, might be compiled. The society remained relatively small, however, and although some valuable information appeared in its journal *Dialect Notes,* a systematic survey of the regional varieties of American English has not yet resulted from its activities.

The past quarter of a century, however, has seen the development of such a survey. Beginning in 1928, a group of researchers under the direction of Professor Hans Kurath, now of the University of Michigan, undertook the compilation of a *Linguistic Atlas of New England* as the first unit of a projected *Linguistic Atlas of the United States and Canada.* The New England atlas, comprising a collection of some 600 maps, each showing the distribution of a single language feature throughout the area, was published over the period from 1939 to 1943. Since that time, field work for comparable atlases of the Middle Atlantic and of the South Atlantic states has been completed, and the materials are awaiting editing and publication. Field records for atlases of the North Central states and the Upper Middle West are virtually complete, and significant beginnings have been made in the Rocky Mountain and the Pacific Coast areas. Surveys in Louisiana, in Texas, and in Ontario are also under way. It is perhaps not too optimistic to predict that within the next twenty-five years all of the United States and Canada as well will have been covered in at least an initial survey.

For a number of reasons it is not easy to collect a body of valid and reliable information on American dialects. The wide spread of education, the virtual extinction of illiteracy, the extreme mobility of the population —both geographically and from one social class to another—and the tremendous development of a number of media of mass communication have all contributed to the recession of local speech forms. Moreover, the cultural insecurity of a large portion of the American people has caused them to feel apologetic about their language. Consequently, they seldom display the same degree of pride or affection that many an English or a European speaker has for his particular patois. Since all dialect research is essentially a sampling process, this means that the investigator must take particular pains to secure representative and comparable samples from the areas which are studied. Happily, the very care which this demands has had the result of developing the methodology of linguistic geography in this country to a very high level.

In general, the material for a linguistic atlas is based upon the natural responses of a number of carefully selected individuals representing certain carefully chosen communities, which in themselves reflect the principal strains of settlement and facets of cultural development in the area as a whole. Since the spread of education generally results in the disappearance of local or regional speech forms, and since the extension of schooling to virtually all of the population has been an achievement of the past seventy-five years, it became necessary for the American investigator to differentiate between the oldest generation, for whom schooling beyond the elementary level is not usual, and a middle-aged group who is likely to have had some experience with secondary schools. In addition, it is highly desirable to include some representatives of the standard or cultivated speech in each region, that their language may serve as a basis of comparison with the folk speech. Accordingly, in the American atlases, from each community represented, the field worker will choose at least two, and sometimes three representatives, in contrast to the usual practice of European researchers, who may safely content themselves with one. Moreover, it is equally necessary to make certain that the persons chosen in any community have not been subject to alien linguistic influences; consequently, only those who have lived there all of their lives, and preferably those who represent families who have long been identified with the area in question, are interviewed, although as one moves westward into the more recently settled areas this is not always possible.

Since complete materials are available only for the eastern seaboard and for the area north of the Ohio River as far west as the Mississippi, tentative conclusions relative to the regional variations in American English can be presented only for the eastern half of the country. The principal dialect areas presented in Kurath's *Word Geography of the Eastern United States,* are indicated on the page opposite.

The three major dialect boundaries, it will be noted, cut the country into lateral strips and are labeled by Professor Kurath *Northern, Midland,* and *Southern* respectively. The line which separates the Northern and Midland areas begins in New Jersey a little below Sandy Hook, proceeds northwest to the east branch of the Susquehanna near Scranton, Pennsylvania, then goes westward through Pennsylvania just below the northern tier of counties. In Ohio the boundary dips below the Western Reserve, then turns northwest again, passing above Fort Wayne, Indiana. When it approaches South Bend it dips slightly to the southwest and cuts through Illinois, reaching the Mississippi at a point slightly above Quincy. The other principal boundary, that separating the Southern and Midland areas, begins at a point somewhat below Dover in Delaware, sweeps through Baltimore in something of an arc, turns sharply southwest north of the Potomac, follows the crest of the Blue Ridge in Virginia, and south of the James River swerves out into the North Carolina Piedmont. As we approach the lower part of South Carolina and Georgia the boundary is as yet unknown.

Even these necessarily incomplete results of the survey carried on under Professor Kurath and his associates have modified considerably our previous

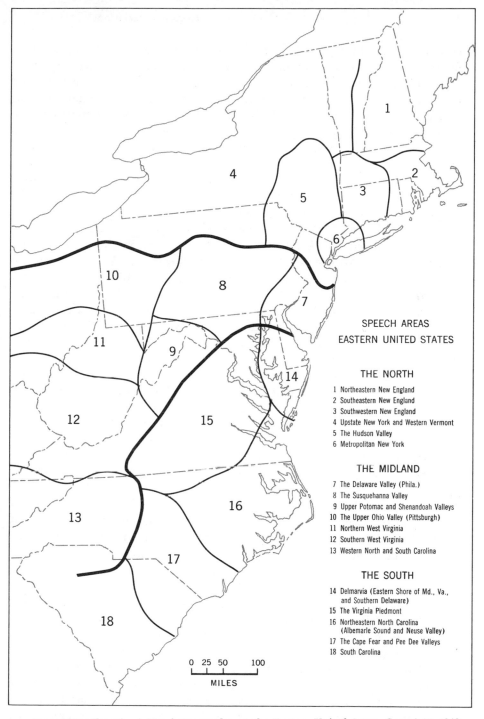

SPEECH AREAS
EASTERN UNITED STATES

THE NORTH

1 Northeastern New England
2 Southeastern New England
3 Southwestern New England
4 Upstate New York and Western Vermont
5 The Hudson Valley
6 Metropolitan New York

THE MIDLAND

7 The Delaware Valley (Phila.)
8 The Susquehanna Valley
9 Upper Potomac and Shenandoah Valleys
10 The Upper Ohio Valley (Pittsburgh)
11 Northern West Virginia
12 Southern West Virginia
13 Western North and South Carolina

THE SOUTH

14 Delmarvia (Eastern Shore of Md., Va.,
   and Southern Delaware)
15 The Virginia Piedmont
16 Northeastern North Carolina
   (Albemarle Sound and Neuse Valley)
17 The Cape Fear and Pee Dee Valleys
18 South Carolina

```
  0  25 50      100
  |——|——|————————|
      MILES
```

From Hans Kurath, *A Word Geography of the Eastern United States.* Copyright 1949 by The University of Michigan Press, Ann Arbor. Reprinted by permission of the publisher.

conceptions of the regional distribution of American speech forms. This modification is brought about principally by adding one concept and eliminating another. The concept thus eliminated has been variously known as Middle Western, Western, or General American. The older view of American dialects, reduced to its simplest terms, recognized the existence of a New England type of speech, a Southern type, and the remainder was generally blanketed by some such term as General American.

It seems clear now that what is neither New England nor Southern—which includes, of course, something between three-quarters and nine-tenths of the continental United States—is far too diverse and lacking in homogeneity to be considered a single major dialect. We know, for example, that there are a significant number of differences, both in vocabulary and in verb inflections, between the folk speech of most of Pennsylvania and that of New York state, and between Michigan and Wisconsin on the one hand, and most of Indiana and large portions of Illinois and Ohio on the other. As our information for the rest of the country becomes available, there can be little doubt that this conclusion will be strengthened.

The concept which has been added is the recognition of a Midland type of speech as distinct from both North and South. An examination of the evidence which Professor Kurath presents in his *Word Geography* leaves no doubt that the speech of this area, though it is by no means uniform, is sufficiently differentiated from both North and South to justify its classification as a major dialect area. This conclusion is supported not only by Atwood's study of the verb forms in the eastern portion of the country but by the available materials from the North Central States.

The map shown on page 145 includes also a few, but not all, of the sub-dialect areas which merit recognition. In the North the principal area is that which separates coastal New England from western New England, New York state, and the territory to the west. In general, this boundary follows the line of the Green Mountains, the Berkshire Hills, and the Connecticut River. The Metropolitan New York area consists of a broad circle with the city itself at the center; the Hudson Valley area encompasses the original Dutch settlements in New York and northern New Jersey, spreading into northeastern Pennsylvania. The Midland area is divided into northern and southern sub-areas, the line of demarcation being just a little south of the Old National Road in Ohio, Indiana, and Illinois. Within the Southern dialect region, the Virginia Piedmont and the Delmarva peninsula constitute distinct sub-areas.

Thus far it is the lexical materials gathered in connection with the various atlas projects which have been analyzed most extensively, and as the title of Professor Kurath's work indicates, his plotting of the major dialect areas is based upon vocabulary evidence. For example, characteristic Northern expressions that are current throughout the area include *pail, swill, whiffletree* or *whippletree, comforter* or *comfortable* for a thick quilt, *brook, co-boss* or *come-boss* as a cow call, *johnnycake, salt pork,* and *darning needle* for a dragonfly. In the Midland area we find *blinds* for roller shades, *skillet, spouting* or *spouts* for eaves, a *piece* for food taken between meals, *snake feeder* for a dragonfly, *sook* as the call to calves, *armload* for an armful of wood; and one *hulls* beans when he takes off the shells. A quarter *till* the hour is a typical Midland expression, as is the elliptical *to want off,* or *out,* or *in.* The South has *lightwood* as the term for kindling, a *turn* of wood for an armful; stringbeans are generally *snap beans; hasslet* is the term for the edible inner organs of a pig, *chittlins* for the small intestine; and in this area cows are said to *low* at feeding time.

The sub-dialect areas also have their characteristic forms. In coastal New England, for instance, *pigsty* is the normal term for pig-pen, *bonny clapper* for curdled sour milk, *buttonwood* for a sycamore, and *pandowdy* for a cobbler type of dessert. Eastern Virginia has *cuppin* for a cowpen, *corn house* for a crib. *Lumber room* survives as the term for a storeroom. A grasshopper is known as a *hopper grass,* and *batter bread* is used for a soft cornbread containing egg.

As far as the sectors of the American lexicon which reflect regional differences are concerned, the matter is trenchantly summarized in Kurath's *Word Geography,* where the author points out first of all that the vocabularies of the arts and sciences, of industries, commercial enterprises, social and political institutions, and even many of the crafts, are national in scope because the activities they reflect are organized on a national basis. He then goes on to say:

> Enterprises and activities that are regionally restricted have, on the other hand, a considerable body of regional vocabulary which, to be sure, may be known in other parts of the country, even if it is not in active use. The cotton planter of the South, the tobacco grower, the dairy farmer, the wheat grower, the miner, the lumberman, and the rancher of the West have many words and expressions that are strictly regional and sometimes local in their currency.

> Regional and local expressions are most common in the vocabulary of the intimate everyday life of the home and the farm—not only among the simple folk and the middle class but also among the cultured . . . Food, clothing, shelter, health, the day's work, play, mating, social gatherings, the land, the farm buildings, implements, the farm stocks and crops, the weather, the fauna and flora—these are the intimate concern of the common folk in the countryside, and for these things expressions are handed down in the family and the neighborhood that schooling and reading and a familiarity with regional or national usage do not blot out.[1]

It is not only in the vocabulary that one finds regional differences in American speech. There are pronunciation features as well. Throughout

[1] Hans Kurath, *A Word Geography of the Eastern United States.* Copyright 1949 by The University of Michigan Press.

the Northern area, for example, the distinction between [o] and [ɔ] in such word pairs as *hoarse* and *horse, mourning* and *morning* is generally maintained; [s] regularly occurs in *grease* (verb) and *greasy,* and *root* is pronounced by many with the vowel of *wood.* Within the Northern area such sub-dialects as coastal New England and Metropolitan New York also show many characteristic forms; the treatment of the vowel of *bird* is only one of these, and words of the *calf, pass, path, dance* group constitute another. In the Midland area speakers fail to distinguish between *hoarse* and *horse.* Rounding is characteristic of the vowels of *hog, frog, log, wasp* and *wash,* and in the last of these words an *r* often intrudes in the speech of the not too highly educated. The vowels of *due* and *new* will resemble that of *food* rather than *feud.* In the South, *r* is "lost" except before vowels, as it is in eastern New England and New York City but not in the Northern area generally. Words like *Tuesday, due,* and *new* have a y-like glide preceding the vowel, and final [z] in *Mrs.* is the normal form.

Among the older, relatively uneducated group and even to some extent among the middle-aged informants who have had some secondary schooling there are also regional differences in inflectional forms and syntax. For example, *hadn't ought* for "oughtn't," *see* as a past tense form, *clim* for "climbed" among the oldest sector of the population, *wan't* for "wasn't," *be* in such expressions as *How be you?,* and the choice of the preposition *to* in *sick to his stomach* are all characteristic of the Northern area. *Clum* for "climbed," *seen* for "saw," *all the further* and *I'll wait on you* are to be found in the Midlands, whereas *belongs to be, heern* for "heard," *seed* as the past tense of "to see," *holp* for "helped," *might could* and *mought have* are characteristic of the South.

All of this raises the question as to how the regional forms of American English developed in our three and one-half centuries of linguistic history. The first factor which must be taken into account is settlement history. Where did our earliest settlers come from, and what dialects did they speak? . . . [At] the time of the earliest settlements, English local and regional dialects were in a stronger position than they are today in that they constituted the natural speech of a greater portion of the English-speaking population and were in customary use farther up the social scale.

Moreover, it is quite unlikely that any single local settlement, even at the outset, ever consisted entirely of speakers of the same dialect. Of ten families of settlers gathered in any one place, two might well have spoken London English, three or four others one of the southern or southeastern county dialects. There would be in addition a couple of families speaking northern English and another two or three employing a western dialect. In the course of their being in constant contact with each other, compromises for the everyday terms in which their dialects differed would normally have developed, and one could reasonably expect to find a southern English term

for a water receptacle, a northern word for earthworm, and a western designation for sour milk. Matters of pronunciation would eventually, perhaps
after a slightly longer time, be compromised in much the same manner.
Moreover, the resultant compromises for various localities would be different. In the first place, no two localities would have had exactly the
same proportions of speakers of the various English dialects, and even if
they had, the two localities would not have arrived at precisely the same
set of compromises. Thus, early in our history we developed, at various
points on the Atlantic seaboard, a number of local cultures, each with distinctive social characteristics of its own—including a dialect which was
basically a unique blend of British types of speech, supplemented in its
vocabulary by borrowings from the Indians and from Dutch and German
neighbors.

With the beginning of the nineteenth century, three changes occurred
which were to have a profound effect upon the language situation in America. First, the industrial revolution resulted in the growth of a number of
industrial centers, uprooting a considerable proportion of the farm population and concentrating it in the cities. The development of the railroad
and other mechanical means of travel increased greatly the mobility of
the average person. The large-scale migrations westward also resulted in
some resettlement and shifting, even among those who did not set out on
the long trek. All of this resulted in a general abandonment of narrowly
local speech forms in favor of fewer, more or less general, regional types.
Some local speech forms have remained even to the present day. These
are usually known as relics, particularly when they are distributed in isolated spots over an area rather than in concentration. *Open stone peach,*
for example, is a relic for freestone peach, occurring in Maryland. *Smurring
up,* "getting foggy," survives as a relic in eastern Maine and more rarely on
Cape Cod and Martha's Vineyard.

Even prior to the shifts in population and changes in the culture pattern, certain colonial cities such as Boston, Philadelphia, and Charleston
had acquired prestige by developing as centers of trade and foci of immigration. They became socially and culturally outstanding, as well as economically powerful, thus dominating the areas surrounding them. As a
consequence, local expressions and pronunciations peculiar to the country-
side came to be replaced by new forms of speech emanating from these centers. A fairly recent instance of this is to be found in the New England
term *tonic* for soda water, practically co-extensive with the area served by
Boston wholesalers. Professor Kurath considers the influence of these centers as second only to the influence of the original settlement in shaping
the regional types of speech on the Atlantic seaboard and in determining
their geographic boundaries.

Nor was the general process of dialect formation by any means com-

pleted with the settlement of the Atlantic seaboard. As the land to the
west came to be taken up in successive stages (for example, western New
York, Michigan, Wisconsin in the North; southern Ohio, Indiana, and
southern Illinois in the Midland area) the same mixtures of speech forms
among the settlers were present at first, and the same linguistic compromises had to be worked out. The same processes occurred in the interior
South, in Texas, and later on in the Far West. Consequently, the complete
linguistic history, particularly with respect to regional forms, of the United
States will not be known until all of the facts concerning the present regional distribution of speech forms have been collected, and until these
facts have been collated with the settlement history of the various areas
and the speech types employed by the settlers at the time they moved in.
In its entirety this would necessitate a greater knowledge of the local
dialects of seventeenth-century England than we have at present.

Moreover, such environmental factors as topography, climate, and plant
and animal life also play their parts in influencing the dialect of an area,
just as they did in the general transplanting of the English language to
America. The complexity and size of the network of fresh-water streams
will affect the distribution and meaning of such terms as *brook, creek,
branch,* and *river.* In parts of Ohio and Pennsylvania, for example, the
term *creek* is applied to a much larger body of water than in Michigan. It
is even more obvious that in those parts of the country where snow is a
rarity or does not fall at all, there will be no necessity for a battery of terms
to indicate coasting face down on a sled. It is not surprising that those
areas of the country where cows can be milked outside, for at least part
of the year, will develop a specific term for the place where this is done:
witness *milk gap* or *milking gap* current in the Appalachians south of the
James River. The wealth of terms for various types of fences throughout
the country is again dependent, in part at least, on the material which is
available for building them, be it stones, stumps, or wooden rails.

Different types of institutions and practices which developed in various
parts of the country also had their effect upon regional vocabulary. Those
settlements which did not follow the practice of setting aside a parcel of
land for common grazing purposes had little use for such terms as *green*
or *common.* The meaning of *town* will vary according to the place and
importance of township and county respectively in the organization of local
government. The same principle applies equally well to foods of various
kinds, which reflect not only materials which are readily available, but
folk practices as well. The German custom of preparing raised doughnuts
as Lenten fare survives in the Pennsylvania term *fossnocks,* shortened from
Fastnachtskuchen.

Finally, a new invention or development introduced into several parts
of the country at the same time will acquire different names in various

places. The baby carriage, for example, seems to have been a development of the 1830's and '40's, and this is the term which developed in New England. Within the Philadelphia trade area, however, the article became known as a *baby coach,* whereas *baby buggy* was adopted west of the Alleghenies and *baby cab* in other regions throughout the country. Nor have we necessarily seen an end to this process. Within the last two decades the building of large, double-lane limited-access automobile highways has been undertaken in various parts of the country, yet the terminology for them differs considerably. In eastern New York, Connecticut, and Rhode Island these are *parkways,* but *turnpikes* in Pennsylvania, New Jersey, New Hampshire, Maine, Massachusetts, Ohio, and Indiana. In New York *thruway* is used, and they are *expressways* in Michigan and *freeways* in California. These would seem to be regionalisms in the making.

It is of interest also to look at the dialect situation from the point of view of various words which are employed in various parts of the country for the same concept. One of the most interesting and instructive distributions is to be found in connection with the terms used for *earthworm.* This word is used by cultivated speakers in the metropolitan centers. *Angleworm* is the regional term in the North, *fishworm* in the Midland area, and *fishing worm* in the coastal South. *Fish bait* and *bait worm* occupy smaller areas within the extensive *fishworm* region, but are also distributed over a wide territory.

In addition, there is a large number of local terms, many of which are used principally by the older and less-educated inhabitants. The Merrimack Valley, in New Hampshire, and Essex County, Massachusetts, have *mud worm. Eace worm* is used in Rhode Island. *Angle dog* appears in upper Connecticut, and *ground worm* on the Eastern Shore of Virginia. *Red worm* is used in the mountains of North Carolina, and an area around Toledo, Ohio, uses *dew worm.* Scattered instances of *rainworm* appear on Buzzards Bay in Massachusetts, throughout the Pennsylvania German area, and in German settlements in North Carolina, Maine, and Wisconsin. We have, thus, a wealth of older local terms, three distinct regional words, and the cultivated *earthworm* appearing in addition as a folk word in South Carolina and along the North Carolina and Virginia coast. Where and how did the various terms originate, and what can be determined about their subsequent history?

Earthworm itself is not an old word; it appears to have been compounded only shortly before the earliest English migrations to America. The earliest *Oxford English Dictionary* citation of the word in its present form is 1591; it appears also as *yearth worm* some thirty years earlier. The various regional terms all seem to have been coined in America; the dictionaries either record no British citations or fail to include the words at all.

The local terms have a varied and interesting history. *Mud worm* seems to occur in standard British English from the beginning of the nineteenth century on. *Eace worm,* as a combined form, goes back at least to Middle English; the first element was a term for "bait" as early as Aelfric; it is used today in a number of southern counties in England from Kent to Gloucester. *Angle dog* is used currently in Devonshire. *Ground worm,* though coined in England, was transferred to North Carolina and Maryland in the eighteenth century. *Red worm* appears first in England in 1450 and continues through to the mid-nineteenth century, though chiefly in books on fishing, as does *dew worm,* which goes back even farther, to the late Old English period. *Rainworm,* though it appears in Aelfric as *renwyrm,* may be a reformation, even in British English, on the pattern of *Regenwurm* in German, for there is a gap of seven centuries in the citations in the *Oxford English Dictionary* and there is reason to believe that its revival in 1731 was influenced by the German form. Moreover, with but one exception, it has been cited for the United States only in areas settled by Germans.

Thus we have in the standard cultivated term one of relatively recent British formation. Apparently the regional terms were compounded in America, whereas the local terms represent survivals either of dialect usage or anglers' jargon and one loan translation. It is worth noting that the common Old English term, *angle twicce,* surviving as *angle twitch* in Cornwall and Devon, seems not to have found its way to America, and there are, furthermore, such other English formations as *tag worm, marsh worm,* and *garden worm* which have not been recorded in America.

At times, too, changes in meaning seem to have entered into the dialect situation, as is illustrated by the development of the regional terms *skillet* and *spider,* the former current in the Midland and the Virginia Piedmont, the latter in the North and in the Southern tidewater area. *Frying pan* is the urban term and is slowly supplanting the others. *Spider* was originally applied to the cast-iron pan with short legs, from which the name was presumably derived, but it was ultimately transferred to the flat-bottomed pan as well. This would seem also to explain the local term *creeper,* used in Marblehead, Massachusetts. *Skillet,* a term of doubtful etymology, first appears in English in 1403, when it was applied to a long-handled brass or copper vessel used for boiling liquids or stewing meat. It is still so used in dialects throughout England. The shift in meaning to a frying pan took place only in America, but an advertisement of 1790, offering for sale "bakepans, spiders, skillets," would suggest that even as late as this a distinction between the two was recognized. The examples above have been offered only as a suggestion of the various languages processes which have played a part in the distribution and meaning of some of our dialect terms. It is quite obvious that no definitive conclusions about these matters can be reached until the actual facts of dialect distribution are better known than they are at present. . . .

COMPREHENSION QUIZ

1. All of the following have increased the difficulty of collecting a body of valid and reliable information on American dialects except
   a. the wide spread of education.
   b. the virtual extinction of illiteracy.
   c. the extreme mobility of the population.
   d. the relatively large area to be covered, coupled with the relatively small size of the American Dialect Society.
   e. the tremendous development of a number of media of mass communications.
2. In searching for suitable subjects when gathering material for a linguistic atlas, all of the following are sought, except
   a. representatives of the cultivated speech of the area.
   b. natives of the area, who have lived there all of their lives.
   c. persons subject to alien linguistic influences.
   d. carefully selected individuals representing certain carefully chosen communities.
2. In searching for suitable subjects when gaehering material for a linguistic atlas,
3. The conclusion that there exists a Midland type of speech as distinct from both North and South is supported by Professor Kurath's evidence and
   a. Atwood's study of verb forms in the eastern portion of the country.
   b. Atwood's study of dialects in the Midwest.
   c. the interpretations applied to the map of speech areas in *Word Geography of the Eastern United States.*
   d. the emergence of available materials from the Eastern states.
   e. none of these.
4. According to Professor Kurath's *Word Geography*, a typical Midland expression used when telling the time is
   a. a quarter to.
   b. a quarter of.
   c. a quarter 'till.
   d. a quarter before.
   e. nigh onto.
5. Early in our history we developed on the Atlantic Seaboard a dialect which was basically a unique blend of all of the following types of speech except
   a. British.
   b. Dutch.
   c. French.
   d. German.
   e. Indian.
6. All of the following changes which began in the early nineteenth century had profound effects on the language situation in America except
   a. the Industrial Revolution.
   b. the population shift to the cities.
   c. the development of mechanical means of travel, bringing increased mobility to the average person.

    d.   the large-scale migration westward.

    e.   the abandonment of narrowly local speech forms in favor of fewer, more or less general, regional types.

7. The baby carriage, introduced into several parts of the country at the same time, acquired all of the following names except

    a.   baby coach.

    b.   baby van.

    c.   baby buggy.

    d.   baby cab.

    e.   all of these.

8. Kurath considers the two most influential factors in the shaping of regional types of speech as

    a.   growth of centers of influence and the influence of original settlement.

    b.   growth of centers of influence and mobility of population.

    c.   influence of original settlement and various environmental factors.

    d.   mobility of population and various environmental factors.

    e.   growth of centers of influence and various environmental factors.

DISCUSSION QUESTIONS

1. What experiences have you had where you were in rather close contact with someone of a different dialect and some of his or her expressions were unconsciously "picked up" by you?

2. What are some of the ways topography, climate, and plant and animal life influence the dialect of an area?

3. Of what value is the knowledge of dialect origins? Do the methods of identification listed in this essay seem to be valid? Explain.

4. What kinds of questions would you ask in the preparation of a linguistic atlas?

5. Exactly what do you understand to be the difference between the term "dialect" and the term "sub-dialect"?

6. Cite influences upon dialect that environmental factors have had, in addition to those mentioned by Marckwardt.

7. In what ways do different types of institutions and practices which develop in various parts of the country have their effect upon regional vocabulary?

8. If ten astronauts and their families from widely separated locations in the U.S. settled another planet, what compromises for everyday terms would you see develop?

WRITING SUGGESTIONS

1. Write a short (500 words) evaluation of the methods employed to obtain information on dialects in the U.S.

2. Defend or attack Marckwardt's assertion that "the cultural insecurity of a large

portion of the American people has caused them to feel apologetic about their language."

3. If funds to carry on the linguistic atlas were dependent upon your ability to persuade those in control, show how you would write a convincing request for those funds.

Digging
"The Man's"
Language

by FRANK RIESSMAN and FRANK ALBERTS

Every reader of *Saturday Review* has at least one second language he or she didn't learn at school. It may be the *lingua franca* of executive committees ("Let's finalize this."), of cocktail party analysts ("His trouble is, he's a latent heterosexual."), perhaps of *belles lettres* ("It was a Hemingway meal.").

Whatever its derivations, the second language is clearly understood by its educated middle-class users to function as an additive to their primary language. And that primary language—the customary English of our schools, more or less standardized in pronunciation—is one of the principal distinguishing marks by which the user is recognized and accepted into the middle class.

What happens, however, when one of those languages that the middle class regards as secondary—in this case, the dialect of the school-age child from one of our nation's disadvantaged urban areas—is discovered to be functioning as a primary language? More pertinent, how is a teacher charged with instructing these children in standard English to perform her task with any degree of meaningfulness?

The answers to these questions, both of pivotal importance in any educational attempt to work with the poor, are exemplified in the following story about a teacher in a grade school in a disadvantaged area.

One day after class, as she was putting on her hat to leave for the day, one of her students approached her with the compliment, "That's sure a tough hat you got on."

The teacher, who had heard enough Hip spoken among her charges to be with it, tried the time-honored approach to correcting the boy: "Don't say 'tough.' Say 'pretty' or 'nice.' "

The boy thought about that a moment, then concluded: "Okay, but that pretty hat sure is tough."

That might have been the end of this particular story except that this particular teacher also gave some thought to the exchange.

First, she realized that she had come up against a case of linguistic inversion—a social situation in which a dialect was the primary language.

Second, and most important, the teacher recognized that by attempting to correct her student's speech in the conventional way, she had confused him about the nature of the avowed teaching objective. Worse, she had antagonized him. To the student's mind, the teacher had been asking him, not so much to learn something, but to reject something—his primary language, the slang, the non-standard Hip spoken in his home, on his street, among his friends and neighbors. The result was hostility—a determination by the student to *not* learn—expressed, with just the necessary touch of humor, in the put-down phrase, ". . . that pretty hat sure is tough."

In short, this teacher had hit on a truth fundamental to the fact of language: One's primary language, because it is primary, is not to be denied lightly, for it is, in very basic ways, one's own self. Asking the disadvantaged child to suppress the language he brings to the learning situation is equivalent to demanding that he suppress his identity, and all the defenses that go with it—in Hip parlance, to require that the child "blow his own cool."

Cognizant of this truth, the teacher assayed a new approach to the business of teaching her students standard English. She made a game of it, the Dialect Game. Taking a term she had often heard her students use among themselves—the word "cool"—she asked them to explain its meaning in *their* language. After some understandable hesitation, she got the following examples:

"Well, you know—like, you dig this cool sound."

"You play it cool."

"The fuzz falls by—you cool it." (Laughter)

Then the teacher asked her class how the same thing might be said in the language the students heard on TV or radio.

"Calm," "casual," "collected" were some of the answers she got, to which she added the more formal "nonchalant."

As the lesson proceeded, the students—who usually all but fell asleep during formal English classes—relaxed, their interest increased. They became aware that they were playing a game, digging the teacher's jive. They were picking up new words, new ways of expression in a context which did not demand that their reject their own language. In short, they were learning standard English as they might learn a foreign language, a second language.

They were also learning about language itself, its forms and the social roles it plays. In their discussion of the word "cool," for example, they learned not only the denotative synonyms for the word in "The Man's" language, but also that standard English really possesses no perfect equivalent of "cool," no term with its rich connotative content.

The same is true, the students began to realize, of many of the Hip words and phrases that make up their primary language—"far out," "hung up," "cop out," to cite a few. The students were becoming familiar with a basic fact of language—the concept of nuances, the age-old bane of translators. By being asked to approach standard English as if it were a foreign language, the students became aware of the essential untranslatability of much of language *per se.*

This, in turn, led to their understanding why words and phrases foreign to every primary language are incorporated in that language intact, without translation—for example, *coup d'etat* and *leitmotiv.* In much the same way—and with far more psychological impact—the students learned that many of the Hip words and phrases that make up their primary language have been accepted for usage in standard English conversation. Knowing this, they were in the position to equip themselves with a basic sense of linguistic style, which can be simply defined as the ability to choose among words and phrases according to their social appropriateness.

The key ground rule of the Dialect Game—for both teacher and teaching situation—is acceptance of the students' nonstandard primary language. The instructor who makes clear to his pupils that their primary language is not something to be denied or suppressed, but is in fact a linguistic entree to that other language which, in more formal circumstances, can produce more effective results, is building firmly on positive grounds. The importance of this teaching method in assisting the disadvantaged to gain entrance to our nation's Greater Society has nowhere been more dramatically stated than by Negro author Ralph Ellison, when he wrote:

> If you can show me how I can cling to that which is real to me, while teaching me a way into the larger society, then I will not only drop my defenses and my hostility, but I will sing your praises and I will help you to make the desert bear fruit.

There are a number of simple adaptations of the Dialect Game that fit a variety of special teaching situations. For example, one of the authors recently employed a "Hiptionary" in a completely systematic and formal way in tutoring a disadvantaged high school student in standard English. The "Hiptionary," or "Hip workbook" to be more accurate, was based in large part on the unpublished *The Other Language* developed by Anthony Romeo at Mobilization for Youth. Among the Hip words and phrases employed were:

bug   to disturb, bother, annoy
ace   best friend
fuzz   police

The rather immediate result of this approach was that the student—in this case, a teen-age girl—learned a great many standard English words for the Hip words with which she had long been familiar. She derived genuine pleasure and pride in her growing facility to use "big words."

The important point about teaching standard English to disadvantaged students equipped linguistically with Hip or nonstandard dialects is that the process is additive—the teacher *builds on* what the pupil brings to the teaching situation; he does not *take away from* the pupil. In this way, the students' sense of language—all language—grows, and with that growth can come a love of language and its literary forms.

The implications of this positive, additive approach to the teaching of standard English is strikingly exemplified in the case of another disadvantaged group, the Puerto Ricans. The usual classroom approach in the United States is to require that these children speak only English, not their native Spanish, usually on the grounds that this is the best (with the implication that this is the *only*) way to learn standard English.

This may be a perfectly acceptable way of teaching a new language to an adult, but it plays psychological havoc with a child from a minority culture. In his mind, the teacher's insistence on "English only" is equated with "no Spanish here," an outright rejection of the culture associated with his home, family, and friends. One more rejection has been added to the many he has experienced in the society to which he has been transplanted.

The result is resentment, a dragging of the feet in matters linguistic—in no way alleviated by the fact that, while the other children in the class already know a good deal of standard English, the Puerto Rican is automatically in the inferior position of having to acquire that language.

The Dialect Game can be varied for this situation, too. Instead of emphasizing the need for Spanish-speaking children to learn English, the teacher can reverse the situation so that the Spanish-speakers teach their language to the English-speakers. The advantages are:

First—and perhaps, psychologically, foremost—the Puerto Rican children are placed temporarily in a position of some superiority, for they are helping their classmates. Second, both Spanish and English become important in the classroom—both are recognized as languages, and *as languages* both are acceptable. Third, the English-speaking students get an opportunity to learn a foreign language. And fourth, the Spanish-speaking children, in order to teach their language to an English-speaker, must acquire an increasing knowledge of English in order to communicate with their classmates.

Of course, the process is not that simple and requires additional techniques. But in the broader societal context, this variation of the Dialect Game, because it employs the child's primary language as the basic element of his culture, eliminates the gratuitous condescension inherent in classroom concentration on superficials such as "colorful" native costumes and customs or "songs from many lands." The primary objective is to teach language, and this approach does. But one of its principal benefits is that it also teaches culture, and, more importantly, a respect for culture.

Once again, the process is additive and positive—and these qualities are essential if we of the middle-class are to be taken seriously when we assert that we want to bring the strengths and interests of the deprived into the mainstream of American life today.

COMPREHENSION QUIZ

1. One of the distinguishing marks of the educated middle class is
   a. its use of "school" English as its primary language.
   b. its consistent reliance upon "hip" language.
   c. its awareness and constant use of socially inappropriate language.
   d. its use of dialect and jargon for formal occasions.
2. A social situation in which a dialect serves as the primary language is known as
   a. linguistic adaptability.
   b. the Dialect Game.
   c. verbal osmosis.
   d. linguistic inversion.
3. According to the authors, one's primary language
   a. should be abandoned in the early school years.
   b. is not to be denied lightly.
   c. has little social significance.
   d. always conforms to the customary English of our schools.
4. This article relates a story about a grade school teacher who discussed with her class the word
   a. "tough."
   b. "fuzz."
   c. "dig."
   d. "cool."
5. The important point about teaching standard English to disadvantaged students is that the teacher
   a. urge the student to abandon his former language habits.
   b. use humor to indicate the shortcomings of their dialect.
   c. build on what the pupil brings to the teaching situation.
   d. point out the superiority of his own dialect.
6. Which of the following is *not* an advantage of the Dialect Game for Puerto Rican children:
   a. The game provides an opportunity for the Puerto Rican children to learn "big words."

b. The Puerto Rican children are placed temporarily in a position of some superiority.

c. Both Spanish and English become important in the classroom.

d. The English-speaking students get an opportunity to learn a foreign language.

DISCUSSION QUESTIONS

1. What is a "primary language," as referred to in this article?
2. What is a *lingua franca*? How is it learned? How does it differ from one's primary language?
3. Did the teacher in this article respond appropriately to the compliment given her by one of her students?

WRITING SUGGESTIONS

1. The authors of this article claim that the study of customs or "songs from many lands" and "colorful" native costumes are merely superficials and in reality imply "gratuitous condescension." Do you agree? Do such activities really teach culture and, more importantly, a respect for culture?
2. How does the English class often contribute to the rejection experienced by children from the disadvantaged urban areas? What improvements or suggestions can you suggest to avoid such rejection?

American Slang

by STUART BERG FLEXNER

American slang, as used in the title of this dictionary, is the body of
words and expressions frequently used by or intelligible to a rather large
portion of the general American public, but not accepted as good, formal
usage by the majority. No word can be called slang simply because of its
etymological history; its source, its spelling, and its meaning in a larger
sense do *not* make it slang. Slang is best defined by a dictionary that points
out who uses slang and what "flavor" it conveys.

I have called all slang used in the United States "American," regardless
of its country of origin or use in other countries.

In this preface I shall discuss the human element in the formation of
slang (what American slang is, and how and why slang is created and
used). . . .

The English language has several levels of vocabulary:

Standard usage comprises those words and expressions used, understood,
and accepted by a majority of our citizens under any circumstances or
degree of formality. Such words are well defined and their most accepted
spellings and pronunciations are given in our standard dictionaries. In
standard speech one might say: *Sir, you speak English well.*

Colloquialisms are familiar words and idioms used in informal speech
and writing, but not considered explicit or formal enough for polite conversation or business correspondence. Unlike slang, however, colloquialisms
are used and understood by nearly everyone in the United States. The use
of slang conveys the suggestion that the speaker and the listener enjoy a
special "fraternity," but the use of colloquialisms emphasizes only the informality and familiarity of a general social situation. Almost all idiomatic
expressions, for example, could be labeled colloquial. Colloquially, one
might say: *Friend, you talk plain and hit the nail right on the head.*

Dialects are the words, idioms, pronunciations, and speech habits peculiar to specific geographical locations. A dialecticism is a regionalism or localism. In popular use "dialect" has come to mean the words, foreign accents, or speech patterns associated with any ethnic group. In Southern dialect one might say: *Cousin, y'all talk mighty fine.* In ethnic-immigrant "dialects" one might say: *Paisano, you speak good the English,* or *Landsman, your English is plenty all right already.*

Cant, jargon, and *argot* are the words and expressions peculiar to special segments of the population. *Cant* is the conversational, familiar idiom used and generally understood only by members of a specific occupation, trade, profession, sect, class, age group, interest group, or other sub-group of our culture. *Jargon* is the technical or even secret vocabulary of such a sub-group; jargon is "shop talk." *Argot* is both the cant and the jargon of any professional criminal group. In such usages one might say, respectively: CQ-CQ-CQ . . . *the tone of your transmission is good; You are free of anxieties related to interpersonal communication;* or *Duchess, let's have a bowl of chalk.*

Slang[1] is generally defined above. In slang one might say: *Buster, your line is the cat's pajamas,* or *Doll, you come on with the straight jazz, real cool like.*

Each of these levels of language, save standard usage, is more common in speech than in writing, and slang as a whole is no exception. Thus, very few slang words and expressions (hence very few of the entries in this dictionary) appear in standard dictionaries.

American slang tries for a quick, easy, personal mode of speech. It comes mostly from cant, jargon, and argot words and expressions whose popularity has increased until a large number of the general public uses or understands them. Much of this slang retains a basic characteristic of its origin: it is *fully* intelligible only to initiates.

Slang may be represented pictorially as the more popular portion of the cant, jargon, and argot from many sub-groups (only a few of the sub-groups are shown below). The shaded areas represent only general overlapping between groups.

Eventually, some slang passes into standard speech; other slang flourishes for a time with varying popularity and then is forgotten; finally, some slang is never fully accepted nor completely forgotten. *O.K., jazz* (music), and *A-bomb* were recently considered slang, but they are now standard usages. *Bluebelly, Lucifer,* and *the bee's knees* have faded from popular use. *Bones* (dice) and *beat it* seem destined to remain slang forever: Chaucer used the first and Shakespeare used the second.

It is impossible for any living vocabulary to be static. Most new slang words and usages evolve quite naturally: they result from specific situations. New objects, ideas, or happenings, for example, require new words to de-

[1] For the evolution of the word "slang," see F. Klaeber, "Concerning the Etymology of Slang," *American Speech,* April, 1926.

scribe them. Each generation also seems to need some new words to describe the same old things.

Railroaders (who were probably the first American sub-group to have a nationwide cant and jargon) thought *jerk water town was* ideally descriptive of a community that others called a *one-horse town.* The changes from *one-horse town* and *don't spare the horses* to *a wide place in the road* and *step on it* were natural and necessary when the automobile replaced the horse. The automobile also produced such new words and new meanings (some of them highly specialized) as *gas buggy, jalopy, bent eight, Chevvie, convertible,* and *lube.* Like most major innovations, the automobile affected our social history and introduced or encouraged *dusters, hitch hikers, road hogs, joint hopping, necking, chicken* (the game), *car coats,* and *suburbia.*

The automobile is only one obvious example. Language always responds to new concepts and developments with new words.

Consider the following:

wars: *redcoats, minutemen, bluebelly, over there, doughboy, gold brick, jeep.*
mass immigrations: *Bohunk, greenhorn, shillalagh, voodoo, pizzeria.*
science and technology: *'gin, side-wheeler, wash-and-wear, fringe area, fall-out.*

turbulent eras: *Redskin, maverick, speak, Chicago pineapple, free love, fink, breadline.*

evolution in the styles of eating: *applesauce, clambake, luncheonette, hot dog, coffee and.*

dress: *Mother Hubbard, bustle, shimmy, sailor, Long Johns, zoot suit, Ivy League.*

housing: *lean-to, bundling board, chuck house, W.C., railroad flat, split-level, sectional.*

music: *cakewalk, bandwagon, fish music, long hair, rock.*

personality: *Yankee, alligator, flapper, sheik, hepcat, B.M.O.C., beetle, beat.*

new modes of transportation: *stage, pinto, jitney, kayducer, hot shot, jet jockey.*

new modes of entertainment: *barnstormer, two-a-day, clown alley, talkies, d.j., Spectacular.*

changing attitudes toward sex: *painted woman, fast, broad, wolf, jailbait, sixty-nine.*

human motivations: *boy crazy, gold-digger, money-mad, Momism, Oedipus complex, do-gooder, sick.*

personal relationships: *bunky, kids, old lady, steady, ex, gruesome two-some, John.*

work and workers: *clod buster, scab, pencil pusher, white collar, graveyard shift, company man.*

politics: *Tory, do-nothing, mug-wump, third party, brain trust, fellow traveler, Veep.*

and even hair styles: *bun, rat, peroxide blonde, Italian cut, pony tail, D.A.*

Those social groups that first confront a new object, cope with a new situation, or work with a new concept devise and use new words long before the population at large does. The larger, more imaginative, and useful a group's vocabulary, the more likely it is to contribute slang. To generate slang, a group must either be very large and in constant contact with the dominant culture or be small, closely knit, and removed enough from the dominant culture to evolve an extensive, highly personal, and vivid vocabulary. Teen-agers are an example of a large sub-group contributing many words. Criminals, carnival workers, and hoboes are examples of the smaller groups. The smaller groups, because their vocabulary is personal and vivid, contribute to our general slang out of proportion to their size.

Whether the United States has more slang words than any other country (in proportion to number of people, area, or the number of words in the standard vocabulary) I do not know. Certainly the French and the Spanish enjoy extremely large slang vocabularies. Americans, however, do use their general slang more than any other people.

American slang reflects the kind of people who create and use it. Its diversity and popularity are in part due to the imagination, self-confidence, and optimism of our people. Its vitality is in further part due to our guarantee of free speech and to our lack of a national academy of language or of any "official" attempt to purify our speech. Americans are restless and frequently move from region to region and from job to job. This hopeful wanderlust, from the time of the pioneers through our westward expansion to modern mobility, has helped spread regional and group terms until they have become general slang. Such restlessness has created constantly new situations which provoke new words. Except for a few Eastern industrial areas and some rural regions in the South and West, America just doesn't look or sound "lived in." We often act and speak as if we were simply visiting and observing. What should be an ordinary experience seems new, unique, or colorful to us, worthy of words and forceful speech. People do not "settle down" in their jobs, towns, or vocabularies.

Nor do we "settle down" intellectually, spiritually, or emotionally. We have few religious, regional, family, class, psychological, or philosophical roots. We don't believe in roots, we believe in teamwork. Our strong loyalties, then, are directed to those social groups—or sub-groups as they are often called—with which we are momentarily identified. This ever-changing "membership" helps to promote and spread slang.

But even within each sub-group only a few new words are generally accepted. Most cant and jargon are local and temporary. What persists are the exceptionally apt and useful cant and jargon terms. These become part of the permanent, personal vocabulary of the group members, giving prestige to the users by proving their acceptance and status in the group. Group members then spread some of this more honored cant and jargon in the dominant culture. If the word is also useful to non-group members, it is on its way to becoming slang. Once new words are introduced into the dominant culture, via television, radio, movies, or newspapers, the rapid movement of individuals and rapid communication between individuals and groups spread the new word very quickly.

For example, consider the son of an Italian immigrant living in New York City. He speaks Italian at home. Among neighborhood youths of similar background he uses many Italian expressions because he finds them always on the tip of his tongue and because they give him a sense of solidarity with his group. He may join a street gang, and after school and during vacations work in a factory. After leaving high school, he joins the navy; then he works for a year seeing the country as a carnival worker. He returns to New York, becomes a longshoreman, marries a girl with a German background, and becomes a boxing fan. He uses Italian and German borrowings, some teen-age street-gang terms, a few factory terms, slang with a navy origin, and carnival, dockworker's, and boxing words. He spreads words from each group to all other groups he belongs to. His Italian parents will learn and use a few street-gang, factory, navy, carnival, dock-worker's, and boxing terms; his German in-laws will learn some Italian words from his parents; his navy friends will begin to use some of his Italian expressions; his carnival friends a few navy words; his co-workers on the docks some carnival terms, in addition to all the rest; and his social friends, with whom he may usually talk boxing and dock work, will be interested in and learn some of his Italian and carnival terms. His speech may be considered very "slangy" and picturesque because he has belonged to un-usual, colorful sub-groups.

On the other hand, a man born into a Midwestern, middle-class, Protes-tant family whose ancestors came to the United States in the eighteenth century might carry with him popular high-school terms. At high school he had an interest in hot rods and rock-and-roll. He may have served two years in the army, then gone to an Ivy League college where he became an adept bridge player and an enthusiast of cool music. He may then have become a sales executive and developed a liking for golf. This second man, no more usual or unusual than the first, will know cant and jargon terms of teen-age high-school use, hot-rods, rock-and-roll, Ivy League schools, cool jazz, army life, and some golf player's and bridge player's terms. He knows further a few slang expressions from his parents (members of the Jazz Age of the 1920's), from listening to television programs, seeing both American and British movies, reading popular literature, and from fre-quent meetings with people having completely different backgrounds. When he uses cool terms on the golf course, college expressions at home, business words at the bridge table, when he refers to whiskey or drunkenness by a few words he learned from his parents, curses his next-door neighbor in a few choice army terms—then he too is popularizing slang.

It is, then, clear that three cultural conditions especially contribute to the creation of a large slang vocabulary: (1) hospitality to or acceptance of new objects, situations, and concepts; (2) existence of a large number of diversified sub-groups; (3) democratic mingling between these sub-groups and the dominant culture. Primitive people have little if any slang because their life is restricted by ritual; they develop few new concepts; and there are no sub-groups that mingle with the dominant culture. (Primitive sub-groups, such as medicine men or magic men, have their own vocabularies; but such groups do not mix with the dominant culture and their jargon can never become slang because it is secret or sacred.)

But what, after all, are the advantages that slang possesses which make it useful? Though our choice of any specific word may usually be made from habit, we sometimes consciously select a slang word because we be-lieve that it communicates more quickly and easily, and more personally, than does a standard word. Sometimes we resort to slang because there is no one standard word to use. In the 1940's, *WAC, cold war,* and *cool* (music) could not be expressed quickly by any standard synonyms. Such words often become standard quickly, as have the first two. We also use slang because it often it more forceful, vivid, and expressive than are standard usages. Slang usually avoids the sentimentality and formality that older words often assume. Taking a girl to a *dance* may seem sentimental, may convey a degree of formal, emotional interest in the girl, and has overtones of fancy balls, fox trots, best suits, and corsages. At times it is more fun to go to a *hop*. To be *busted* or without a *hog* in one's *jeans* is not only more vivid and forceful than being penniless or without funds, it is also a more optimistic state. A *mouthpiece* (or *legal beagle*), *pencil pusher, sawbones, boneyard, bottle washer* or a course in *biochem* is more vivid and forceful than a lawyer, clerk, doctor, cemetery, laboratory assistant, or a course in biochemistry—and is much more real and less formidable than a legal counsel, junior executive, surgeon, necropolis (or memorial park), laboratory technician, or a course in biological chemistry.

Although standard English is exceedingly hospitable to polysyllabicity and even sesquipedalianism, slang is not. Slang is sometimes used not only because it is concise but just because its brevity makes it forceful. As this dictionary demonstrates, slang seems to prefer short words, especially monosyllables, and, best of all, words beginning with an explosive or an aspirate.[2]

We often use slang *fad* words as a bad habit because they are close to the tip of our tongue. Most of us apply several favorite but vague words to any of several somewhat similar situations; this saves us the time and effort of thinking and speaking precisely. At other times we purposely choose a word because it is vague, because it does not commit us too strongly to what we are saying. For example, if a friend has been praising a woman, we can reply "she's *the bee's knees*" or "she's a real *chick*," which can mean that we consider her very modern, intelligent, pert, and understanding— or can mean that we think she is one of many nondescript, somewhat confused, followers of popular fads. We can also tell our friend that a book we both have recently read is *the cat's pajamas* or *the greatest*. These expressions imply that we liked the book for exactly the same reasons that our friend did, without having to state what these reasons were and thus taking the chance of ruining our rapport.

In our language we are constantly recreating our image in our own minds and in the minds of others. Part of this image, as mentioned above,

---

[2] Many such formations are among our most frequently used slang words. As listed in this dictionary, *bug* has 30 noun meanings, *shot* 14 noun and 4 adjective meanings, *can* 11 noun and 6 verb, *bust* 9 verb and 6 noun, *hook* 8 noun and 5 verb, *fish* 14 noun, and *sack* 8 noun, 1 adjective, and 1 verb meaning. Monosyllabic words also had by far the most citations found in our source reading of popular literature. Of the 40 words for which we found the most quotations, 29 were monosyllabic. Before condensing, *fink* had citations from 70 different sources, *hot* 67, *bug* 62, *blow* and *dog* 60 each, *joint* 59, *stiff* 56, *punk* 53, *bum* and *egg* 50 each, *guy* 43, *make* 41, *bull* and *mug* 37 each, *bird* 34, *fish* and *hit* 30 each, *ham* 25, *yak* 23, *sharp* 14, and *cinch* 10. (Many of these words, of course, have several slang meanings; many of the words also appeared scores of times in the same book or article.)

is created by using sub-group cant and jargon in the dominant society; part of it is created by our choice of both standard and slang words. A sub-group vocabulary shows that we have a group to which we "belong" and in which we are "somebody"—outsiders had better respect us. Slang is used to show others (and to remind ourselves of) our biographical, mental, and psychological background; to show our social, economic, geographical, national, racial, religious, educational, occupational, and group interests, memberships, and patriotisms. One of the easiest and quickest ways to do this is by using counter-words. These are automatic, often one-word responses of like or dislike, of acceptance or rejection. They are used to counter the remarks, or even the presence, of others. Many of our fad words and many student and quasi-intellectual slang words are counter-words. For liking: *beat, the cat's pajamas, drooly, gas, George, the greatest, keen, nice, reet, smooth, super, way out,* etc. For rejection of an outsider (implying incompetence to belong to our group): *boob, creep, dope, drip, droop, goof, jerk, kookie, sap, simp, square, weird,* etc. Such automatic counters are overused, almost meaningless, and are a substitute for thought. But they achieve one of the main purposes of speech: quickly and automatically they express our own sub-group and personal criteria. Counter-words are often fad words creating a common bond of self-defense. All the rejecting counters listed above could refer to a moron, an extreme introvert, a bird-watcher, or a genius. The counters merely say that the person is rejected—he does not belong to the group. In uttering the counter we don't care what the person is; we are pledging our own group loyalty, affirming our identity, and expressing our satisfaction at being accepted.

In like manner, at various periods in history, our slang has abounded in words reflecting the fear, distrust, and dislike of people unlike ourselves. This intolerance is shown by the many derogatory slang words for different immigrant, religious, and racial groups: *Chink, greaser, Heinie, hunkie, mick, mockie, nigger, spik.* Many counters and derogatory words try to identify our own group status, to dare others to question our group's, and therefore our own, superiority.

Sometimes slang is used to escape the dull familiarity of standard words, to suggest an escape from the established routine of everyday life. When slang is used, our life seems a little fresher and a little more personal. Also, as at all levels of speech, slang is sometimes used for the pure joy of making sounds, or even for a need to attract attention by making noise. The sheer newness and informality of certain slang words produces a pleasure.

But more important than this expression of a more or less hidden esthetic motive on the part of the speaker is slang's reflection of the personality, the outward, clearly visible characteristics of the speaker. By and large, the man who uses slang is a forceful, pleasing, acceptable personality. Morality and intellect (too frequently not considered virtues in the modern American man) are overlooked in slang, and this had led to a type of reverse morality; many words, once standing for morally good things, are now critical. No one, for example, though these words were once considered complimentary, wants to be called a *prude* or *Puritan*. Even in standard usage they are mildly derisive.

Moreover, few of the many slang synonyms for drunk are derogatory or critical. To call a person a standard drunk may imply a superior but unsophisticated attitude toward drinking. Thus we use slang and say someone is *boozed up, gassed, high, potted, stinking, has a glow on,* etc., in a verbal attempt to convey our understanding and awareness. These slang words show that we too are human and know the effects of excessive drinking.

In the same spirit we refer to people sexually as *big ass man, fast, John, sex pot, shack job, wolf,* etc., all of which accept unsanctioned sexual intercourse as a matter of fact. These words are often used in a complimentary way and in admiration or envy. They always show acceptance of the person as a "regular guy." They are never used to express a moral judgment. Slang has few complimentary or even purely descriptive words for "virgin," "good girl," or "gentleman." Slang has *bag, bat, ex, gold digger, jerk, money mad, n.g., old lady, square,* etc.; but how many words are there for a good wife and mother, an attractive and chaste woman, an honest, hard-working man who is kind to his family, or even a respected elderly person? Slang— and it is frequently true for all language levels—always tends toward degradation rather than elevation. As slang shows, we would rather share or accept vices than be excluded from a social group. For this reason, for self-defense, and to create an aura (but not the fact) of modernity and individuality, much of our slang purposely expresses amorality, cynicism, and "toughness."

Reverse morality also affects slang in other ways. Many use slang just because it is not standard or polite. Many use slang to show their rebellion against *boobs, fuddy-duddies, marks,* and *squares.* Intellectuals and politicians often use slang to create the "common touch" and others use slang to express either their anti-intellectualism or avant-garde leanings. Thus, for teen-agers, entertainers, college students, beatniks, jazz fans, intellectuals, and other large groups, slang is often used in preference to standard words and expressions. Slang is the "official" modern language of certain vociferous groups in our population.

In my work on this dictionary, I was constantly aware that most American slang is created and used by males. Many types of slang words—including the taboo and strongly derogatory ones, those referring to sex, women, work, money, whiskey,[3] politics, transportation, sports, and the like—refer primarily to male endeavor and interest. The majority of entries in this dictionary could be labeled "primary masculine use." Men belong to more sub-groups than do women; men create and use occupational cant and jar-

[3] It would appear that the word having the most slang synonyms is *drunk*.

gon; in business, men have acquaintances who belong to many different sub-groups. Women, on the other hand, still tend to be restricted to family and neighborhood friends. Women have very little of their own slang.[4] The new words applied to women's clothing, hair styles, homes, kitchen utensils and gadgets are usually created by men. Except when she accompanies her boy friend or husband to *his* recreation (baseball, hunting, etc.) a woman seldom mingles with other groups. When women do mingle outside of their own neighborhood and family circles, they do not often talk of the outside world of business, politics, or other fields of general interest where new feminine names for objects, concepts, and viewpoints could evolve.

Men also tend to avoid words that sound feminine or weak. Thus there are sexual differences in even the standard vocabularies of men and women. A woman may ask her husband to set the table for dinner, asking him to put out the *silver, crystal,* and *china*—while the man will set the table with *knives, forks, spoons, glasses,* and *dishes.* His wife might think the *table linen* attractive, the husband might think the *tablecloth* and *napkins* pretty. A man will buy a *pocketbook* as a gift for his wife, who will receive a *bag.* The couple will live under the same roof, the wife in her *home,* the man in his *house.* Once outside of their domesticity the man will begin to use slang quicker than the woman. She'll get into the *car* while he'll get into the *jalopy* or *Chevvie.* And so they go: she will learn much of her general slang from him; for any word she associates with the home, her personal belongings, or any female concept, he will continue to use a less descriptive, less personal one.

Males also use slang to shock. The rapid tempo of life, combined with the sometimes low boiling point of males, can evoke emotions—admiration, joy, contempt, anger—stronger than our old standard vocabulary can convey. In the stress of the moment a man is not just in a standard "untenable position," he is *up the creek.* Under strong anger a man does not feel that another is a mere "incompetent"—he is a *jerk.* . . .

Men also seem to relish hyperbole in slang. Under many situations, men do not see or care to express fine shades of meaning: a girl is either a *knockout* or a *dog,* liquor either *good stuff* or *panther piss,* a person either has *guts* or is *chicken,* a book is either *great* or nothing but *crap.* Men also like slang and colloquial wording because they express action or even violence: we *draw pay, pull a boner, make a score, grab some sleep, feed our face, kill time*—in every instance we tend to use the transitive verb, making ourselves the active doer.

The relation between a sub-group's psychology and its cant and jargon is interesting, and the relation between an individual's vocabulary and

---

[4] Women who do work usually replace men at men's jobs are less involved in business life than men, and have a shorter business career (often but an interim between school and marriage). The major female sub-groups contributing to American slang are: airline stewardesses, beauty-parlor operators, chorus girls, nurses, prostitutes, and waitresses.

psychological personality is even more so. Slang can be one of the most revealing things about a person, because our own personal slang vocabulary contains many words used by choice, words which we use to create our own image, words which we find personally appealing and evocative—as opposed to our frequent use of standard words merely from early teaching and habit. Whether a man calls his wife *baby, doll, honey, the little woman, the Mrs.,* or *my old lady* certainly reveals much about him. What words one uses to refer to a mother (*Mom, old lady*), friend (*buddy, bunkie, old man*), the bathroom (*can, John, little boy's room*), parts of the body and sex acts (*boobies, gigi, hard, laid, score*), being tired (*all in, beat*), being drunk (*clobbered, high, lit up like a Christmas tree, paralyzed*), and the like, reveal much about a person and his motivations.[5]

The basic metaphors, at any rate, for all levels of language depend on the five senses. Thus *rough, smooth, touch; prune, sour puss, sweet; fishy, p.u., rotten egg; blow, loud; blue, red, square.* In slang, many metaphors refer to touch (including the sense of heat and cold) and to taste.

Food is probably our most popular slang image. Food from the farm, kitchen, or table, and its shape, color, and taste suggest many slang metaphors. This is because food can appeal to taste, smell, sight, and touch, four of our five senses; because food is a major, universal image to all people, all sub-groups; because men work to provide it and women devote much time to buying and preparing it; because food is before our eyes three times every day.

Many standard food words mean money in nonstandard use: *cabbage, kale, lettuce.* Many apply to parts of the body: *cabbage head, cauliflower ear, meat hooks, nuts, plate of meat.* Many food words refer to people: *apple, cold fish, Frog, fruitcake, honey, sweetie pie.* Others refer to general situations and attitudes: to *brew* a plot, to receive a *chewing out,* to find oneself *in a pickle* or something *not kosher,* to be unable to *swallow* another's story, to ask *what's cooking?* Many drunk words also have food images: *boiled, fried, pickled*; and so do many words for nonsense: *applesauce, banana oil, spinach.* Many standard food words also have sexual meanings in slang. The many food words for money, parts of the body, people, and sex reveal that food means much more to us than mere nourishment. When a *good egg brings home the bacon* to his *honey,* or when a *string bean* of a *sugar daddy* takes his *piece* of *barbecue* out to get *fried* with his hard-earned *kale,* food images have gone a long way from the farm, kitchen, and table.

Sex has contributed comparatively few words to modern slang,[6] but

[5] For just the last example, *clobbered* may indicate that a drinker is punishing himself, *high* that he is escaping, *lit up like a Christmas tree* that he is seeking attention and a more dominant personality, and *paralyzed* that he seeks punishment, escape or death.

[6] Many so-called bedroom words are not technically slang at all, but are sometimes associated with slang only because standard speech has rejected them as taboo. However, many of these taboo words do have further metaphorical meanings in slang.

these are among our most frequently used. The use of sex words to refer to sex in polite society and as metaphors in other fields is increasing. Sex metaphors are common for the same conscious reasons that food metaphors are. Sex appeals to, and can be used to apply to, most of the five senses. It is common to all persons in all sub-groups, and so we are aware of it continually.

Slang words for sexual attraction and for a variety of sexual acts, positions, and relationships are more common than standard words. Standard non-taboo words referring to sex are so scarce or remote and scientific that slang is often used in referring to the most romantic, the most obscene, and the most humorous sexual situations. Slang is so universally used in sexual communication that when "a man meets a maid" it is best for all concerned that they know slang.[7] Slang words for sex carry little emotional connotation; they express naked desire or mechanical acts, devices, and positions. They are often blunt, cynical and "tough."

The subconscious relating of sex and food is also apparent from reading this dictionary. Many words with primary, standard meanings of food have sexual slang meanings. The body, parts of the body, and descriptions of each, often call food terms into use: *banana, bread, cheese cake, cherry, jelly roll, meat,* etc. Beloved, or simply sexually attractive, people are also often called by food names: *cookie, cup of tea, honey, peach, quail, tomato,* etc. This primary relation between sex and food depends on the fact that they are man's two major sensuous experiences. They are shared by all personalities and all sub-groups and they appeal to the same senses—thus there is bound to be some overlapping in words and imagery. However, there are too many standard food words having sexual meanings in slang for these conscious reasons to suffice. Sex and food seem to be related in our subconscious.

Also of special interest in the number of slang expressions relating sex and cheating. Used metaphorically, many sex words have secondary meanings of being cheated, deceived, swindled, or taken advantage of, and several words whose primary meaning is cheating or deceiving have further specific sexual meanings: *cheating, make, royal screwing, score, turn a trick,* etc. As expressed in slang, sex is a trick somehow, a deception, a way to cheat and deceive us. To curse someone we can say *screw you,* which expresses a wish to deprive him of his good luck, his success, perhaps even his potency as a man.[8] Sex is also associated with confusion, exhausting tasks, and

---

[7] On the other hand, Madame de Staël is reported to have complimented one of her favorite lovers with "speech is not his language."

[8] See F. P. Wood, "The Vocabulary of Failure," *Better English,* Nov., 1938, p. 34. The vocabulary of failure is itself very revealing. Failure in one's personality, school, job, business, or an attempted love affair are all expressed by the same vocabulary. One gets the *brush off,* the *gate,* a *kiss off,* or *walking papers* in both business and personal relationships. As the previous discussion of counter-words demonstrates, slang allows no distinction or degree among individual failures. Incompetence does not apply to just one job or facet

disaster: *screwed up, snafu,* etc. It seems clear, therefore, that, in slang success and sexual energy are related or, to put it more accurately, that thwarted sexual energy will somehow result in personal disaster.

Language is a social symbol. The rise of the middle class coincided with the period of great dictionary makers, theoretical grammarians, and the "correct usage" dogma. The new middle class gave authority to the dictionaries and grammarians in return for "correct usage" rules that helped solidify their social position. Today, newspaper ads still implore us to take mail-order courses in order to "learn to speak like a college graduate," and some misguided English instructors still give a good speaking ability as the primary reason for higher education.

The gap between "correct usage" and modern practice widens each day. Are there valid theoretical rules for speaking good English, or should "observed usage" be the main consideration? Standard words do not necessarily make for precise, forceful, or useful speech. On the other hand, "observed usage" can never promise logic and clarity. Today, we have come to depend on "observed usage," just as eighteenth- and nineteenth-century social climbers depended on "correct usage," for social acceptance.

Because it is not standard, formal, or acceptable under all conditions, slang is usually considered vulgar, impolite, or boorish. As this dictionary shows, however, the vast majority of slang words and expressions are neither taboo, vulgar, derogatory, nor offensive in meaning, sound, or image. There is no reason to avoid any useful, explicit word merely because it is labeled "slang." Our present language has not decayed from some past and perfect "King's English," Latin, Greek, or pre-Tower of Babel tongue. All languages and all words have been, are, and can only be but conventions mutually agreed upon for the sake of communicating. Slang came to America on the Mayflower. In general, it is not vulgar, new or even peculiarly American: an obvious illustration of this is the polite, old French word *tête,* which was originally slang from a Latin word *testa*—cooking pot.

Cant and jargon in no way refer only to the peculiar words of undesirable or underworld groups. Slang does not necessarily come from the underworld, dope addicts, degenerates, hoboes, and the like. Any cultural sub-group develops its own personal cant and jargon which can later become general slang. All of us belong to several of these specific sub-groups using our own cant and jargon. Teen-agers, steel workers, soldiers, Southerners, narcotic addicts, churchgoers, truck drivers, advertising men, jazz musicians, pickpockets, retail salesmen in every field, golf players, immigrants from every country, college professors, baseball fans—all belong to

---

of life—either one belongs or is considered unworthy. This unworthiness applies to the entire personality, there are no alternate avenues for success or happiness. One is not merely of limited intelligence, not merely an introvert, not merely ugly, unknowing, or lacking in aggression—but one is a failure in all these things, a complete *drip, jerk,* or *square.* The basic failure is that of personality, the person is not a mere failure—he is an outcast, an untouchable; he is taboo.

typical sub-groups from which slang originates. Some of these sub-groups are colorful; most are composed of prosaic, average people.

Many people erroneously believe that a fundamental of slang is that it is intentionally picturesque, strained in metaphor, or jocular. Picturesque metaphor (and metonymy, hyperbole, and irony) does or should occur frequently in all levels of speech. Picturesque metaphor is a frequent characteristic of slang, but it does not define slang or exist as an inherent part of it. The picturesque or metaphorical aspect of slang is often due to its direct honesty or to its newness. Many standard usages are just as picturesque, but we have forgotten their original metaphor through habitual use. Thus slang's *jerk* and *windbag* are no more picturesque than the standard *incompetent* and *fool*. *Incompetent* is from the Latin *competens* plus the negating prefix *in-* and = "unable or unwilling to compete"; *fool* is Old French, from the Latin *follis* which actually = "bellows or wind bag"; slang's *windbag* and the standard *fool* actually have the same metaphor.

As for picturesque sounds, I find very few in slang. Onomatopoeia, reduplications, harsh sounds and pleasing sounds, even rhyming terms, exist on all levels of speech. Readers of this dictionary will find no more picturesque or unusual sounds here than in a similar length dictionary of standard words. Many slang words are homonyms for standard words.

As has been frequently pointed out, many slang words have the same meaning. There seems to be an unnecessary abundance of counter-words, synonyms for "drunk," hundreds of fad words with almost the same meaning, etc. This is because slang introduces word after word year after year from many, many sub-groups. But slang is a scatter-gun process; many new words come at the general public; most are ignored; a few stick in the popular mind.

Remember that "slang" actually does not exist as an entity except in the minds of those of us who study the language. People express themselves and are seldom aware that they are using the artificial divisions of "slang" or "standard." First and forever, language is language, an attempt at communication and self-expression. The fact that some words or expressions are labeled "slang" while others are labeled "jargon" or said to be "from the Anglo-Saxon" is of little value except to scholars. Thus this dictionary is a legitimate addition to standard dictionaries, defining many words just as meaningful as and often more succinct, useful, and popular than many words in standard dictionaries.

COMPREHENSION QUIZ

1. Which of the following statements is false?
   a. American slang includes expressions not accepted as good, formal usage by the majority of the American public.

b. Standard usage comprises words used and accepted by most Americans under any circumstances or degree of formality.
c. Slang is found in writing more often than in speech.
d. Colloquialisms are not considered formal enough for business correspondence.

2. The sentence, "Cousin, y'all talk mighty fine," is an example of
   a. dialect.
   b. cant.
   c. jargon.
   d. argot.

3. Which of the following statements is true?
   a. All slang passes eventually into standard speech.
   b. Jargon is the conversational, familiar idiom used by members of a specific age group.
   c. Rarely do new slang words and usages evolve from specific situations.
   d. Slang is fully intelligible only to initiates.

4. The growth of American slang is helped by
   a. the mobility of our population.
   b. the existence of the Academy of Correct English.
   c. official attempts to purify our speech.
   d. the traditions of New England.

5. Which of the following cultural conditions do *not* contribute to the creation of a large slang vocabulary?
   a. Acceptance of new objects, situations, and concepts.
   b. Existence of a large number of diversified subgroups.
   c. A society dominated and regulated by ritual.
   d. Democratic mingling between subgroups and the dominant culture.

6. Slang seems to prefer
   a. foreign words or terms.
   b. short words.
   c. polysyllabic words.
   d. a kind of reverse morality of expression.

7. Most American slang is created and used by
   a. ethnic groups.
   b. males.
   c. the major female subgroups.
   d. jazz musicians.

DISCUSSION QUESTIONS

1. Compare Flexner's definition of "slang" with that given in your dictionary. Do the definitions differ in any significant way?
2. Is there a practical reason why few slang words and expressions appear in standard dictionaries?
3. Why is most American slang created and used by males, rather than by females?

4. How do Flexner's observations about slang support the essays by Kenyon, Francis, and Marckwardt?

WRITING SUGGESTIONS

1. What is a "sub-culture," as Flexner uses the term? What sub-cultures do you belong to? In what respects does each have its own slang?
2. On pages 166–167 Flexner describes two hypothetical users of slang. Write a similar study of your own language patterns.
3. Make a list of the slang terms used on your campus for the following words or terms: an attractive girl; money; an automobile; to be intoxicated; a popular student on the campus.
4. Why are some words referring to aspects of sex regarded as taboo, while others having the same meanings are acceptable?

Recommended Readings to Part IV

Babcock, C. Heston. *The Ordeal of American English*. Boston: Houghton Mifflin, 1961.

Bryant, Margaret M. *Current American Usage*. New York: Macmillan, 1962.

Hook, J. N., and E. G. Mathews. *Modern American Grammar and Usage*. New York: Ronald Press, 1956.

Malmstrom, Jean, and Annabel Ashley. *Dialects—U.S.A*. Champaign, Ill.: National Council of Teachers of English, 1963.

Marckwardt, Albert H. *American English*. New York: Oxford University Press, 1958.

Pyles, Thomas. *Words and Ways of American English*. New York: Random House, 1952.

Warfel, Harry R., and Donald J. Lloyd. *American English in Its Cultural Setting*. New York: Alfred A. Knopf, 1956.

The Student and His Dictionary

V

How to Read
a Dictionary

by MORTIMER J. ADLER

The dictionary invites a playful reading. It challenges anyone to sit down with it in an idle moment only to find an hour gone by without being bored. Recently I noticed an advertisement for a dictionary as a wonder book. "Astonished Actually Means Thunderstruck" was the headline, written obviously in the hope that the prospective buyer would be thunderstruck, or wonderstruck, enough to look further. And the rest of the ad listed such tidbits as a "*disaster* literally means 'the stars are against you!", or "to tantalize is to torment with the punishment of Tantalus as told in Greek mythology."

While I do not think astonishment is the dictionary's main mission in life, I cannot resist reporting some of the things I learned accidentally while thumbing its pages, in the course of writing this article. I discovered that the word "solecism" derives from Soli, the name of a Greek colony in Cicilia, whose inhabitants were thought by the Athenians to speak bad Greek; hence, "solecism" was probably the equivalent in Greek slang for a Bostonian's contemptuous reference to "New Yorkese." I learned that "coal" originally meant charred wood. It was then applied to mineral coal when this was first introduced, under such names as "sea-coal" and "pit-coal." Now that mineral coal is the more common variety, we redundantly refer to charred wood as "charcoal." I was edified by the fact that the drink "Tom and Jerry" derives its name from the two chief characters in Egan's "Life of London" (1821), that in England a low beer joint is called a "Tom and Jerry Shop," and that indulgence in riotous behavior is called "to tom and jerry." I had always thought that a forlorn hope was really a hope

From Mortimer J. Adler, "How to Read a Dictionary," *Saturday Review of Literature*, December 13, 1941. Copyright 1941 by The Saturday Review Company, Inc. Copyright 1967 by Saturday Review, Inc. Reprinted by permission of *Saturday Review* and the author.

on the verge of turning into despair, but it seems that it isn't a hope at all.
"Hope" here is a misspelling of the Dutch word "hoop" meaning heap. A
forlorn hope is a storming party, a band of heroes who are willing to end
up in a heap for their country's cause. And most shocking of all was the
discovery that one theory about the origin of the magician's "hocus pocus"
accounts for it as a corruption of *"hoc est corous"*—the sacred words accompanying the sacrament of the Eucharist. This, together with the reversal
in meaning of "dunce"—from the proper name of Duns Scotus, the subtlest
doctor of the Church, to naming a numb-skull—provides a two word commentary on the transition from the Middle Ages to modern times.

The staid modern dictionary is full of such wit even when it doesn't
try to be funny, as Dr. Johnson did when he defined "oats" as "a grain which
in England is generally given to horses, but in Scotland supports the people." Look up "Welsh rabbit," for example, or "scotch capon" or "swiss
steak," and you will discover gentle jokes about national shortcomings in
diet.

I find that what interests me most of all are the shifts in meaning of
common words in daily use. From meaning an attendant on horses, "marshall" has come to mean a leader of men; though also originating in the
stable, "constable" has gone in the reverse direction from signifying an
officer of highest rank to denoting a policeman; "boon" has done an about-
face by becoming the gift which answers a petition, having been the prayer
which asked for it; "magistrate" and "minister" have changed places with
each other in the ups and downs of words, for in current political usage,
"magistrate" usually names a minor official, whereas "minister" refers to
a *major* diplomatic or cabinet post. It is often hard to remember that a
minister is a *servant* of the people, and harder still to recall the precise point
of religious controversy which caused the substitution of "minister" for
"priest" as the name for one who served in the performance of sacerdotal
functions. And readers of our Constitution should have their attention
called to a shift in the word "citizen" from meaning any one who, by birth
or choice, owes allegiance to the state, to the narrower designation of those
who are granted the right to vote. Similarly, "commerce" has narrowed in
meaning; like "trade," it once meant every dealing in merchandise, but now
is distinguished from industry according to the difference between distrib-
uting commodities and producing them.

The word "commerce" reminds me of one other sort of incidental
inquiry the dictionary lures you into. You discover that "commerce" and
"mercenary" have the same root in *"mercis,"* wares, and that leads you to
the closely related root *"merces,"* pay or reward, which is embodied in the
word "mercy." If you start this game of research, you will find such roots as
"spec" from *"spectare"* meaning to look at or see, which generates a family
of 246 English words (species, speculate, specimen, specify, spectacle, inspect,
respect, aspect, etc.); or *"press"* from *"primo"* meaning to squeeze, which

has an equally large family (impress, repress, pressing, compress, suppress, oppress, depress, express, etc.).

It is almost as hard to stop writing about the dictionary in this way as to stop reading one when you are in hot pursuit of the mysteries of human speech. But, over and above such fascinations, the dictionary has its sober uses. To make the most of these one has to know how to read the special sort of book a dictionary is. But, before I state the rules, let me see if I can explain why most people today don't use dictionaries in a manner befitting the purpose for which they were originally intended.

In its various sizes and editions, the dictionary is an unlisted best-seller on every season's list. To be able to get along without one would be a sign of supreme literacy—of complete competence as a reader and writer. The dictionary exists, of course, because there is no one in that condition. But, if the dictionary is the necessity we all acknowledge, why is it so infrequently used by the man who owns one? And, even when we do consult it, why do most of us misuse the dictionary or use it poorly?

The answer to both questions may be that few of us make efforts at reading or writing anything above the present level of our literary competence. The books—or maybe it is just the newspapers and magazines—we read, and the things we write, don't send us to the dictionary for help. Our vocabularies are quite adequate, because the first rule in most contemporary writing is the taboo against strange words, or familiar words in strange senses.

Of course, there are always people (not excluding college graduates) who have difficulty with spelling or pronouncing even the common words in daily discourse. That, by the way, is the source of the most frequent impulse to go to the dictionary. There is nothing wrong about this. The dictionary is there to render this simple service—in fact, Noah Webster began his career as the compiler of a spelling book which sold in the millions. But my point remains—the dictionary has other and more important uses, and the reason we do not generally avail ourselves of these services is not our superiority, but rather our lack of need as the life of letters is currently lived.

The history of dictionaries, I think, will bear me out on this point. The Greeks did not have a dictionary, even though "lexicon" is the Greek word for it. They had no need for foreign language dictionaries because there was no literature in a foreign language they cared to read. They had no need for a Greek word-book because the small educated class already knew what such a book would contain. This small group of literate men would have been, like the modern French Academy, the makers of the dictionary, the arbiters of good usage. But at a time when so sharp a line separated the learned from the lewd (which, in an obsolete usage, means *unlettered*), there was no occasion for the few men who could make a dictionary to prepare one for the others.

George Santayana's remark about the Greeks—that they were the only uneducated people in European history—has a double significance. The masses were, of course, uneducated, but even the learned few were not educated in the sense that they had to sit at the feet of foreign masters. Education, in that sense, begins with the Romans, who went to school to Greek pedagogues, and became cultivated through contact with Greek culture. It is not surprising, therefore, that the first dictionaries were glossaries of Homeric words. The earliest lexicon which is still extant is such a glossary, prepared by a Greek, Apollonius, in the fifth century of our era, obviously intended to help Romans read the "Iliad" and "Odyssey" of Homer, as well as other Greek literature which employed the Homeric vocabulary. Most of us today need similar glossaries to read Shakespeare well.

There were dictionaries in the Middle Ages—a famous Latin one by the Spaniard, Isidore of Seville, which was really a philosophical work, a sort of encyclopedia of worldly knowledge accomplished by discussions of the most important technical terms occurring in learned discourse. There were foreign-language dictionaries in the Renaissance (both Latin and Greek) made necessary by the fact that the *humane letters* which dominated the education of the period were from the ancient languages. Even when the vulgar tongues—English, French, or Italian—gradually displaced Latin as the language of learning, the pursuit of learning was still the privilege of the few. Under such circumstances, dictionaries were intended for a limited audience, mainly as an aid to reading the most worthy literature. In attempting to compile a standard dictionary, Dr. Johnson derived his norms from the usage of the best writers, on the theory that this would furnish a guide to others who tried to read them, or who tried to write as well.

We see, then, that from the beginning the educational motive dominated the making of dictionaries, though, as in the case of Dr. Johnson, and the work of the French and Italian Academies, there was also an interest in preserving the purity and order of the language. As against the latter interest, the *Oxford English Dictionary,* begun in 1857, was a new departure, in that it did not try to dictate the best usage, but rather to present an accurate historical record of every type of usage—the worst as well as the best, taken from popular as well as stylish writing. But this conflict between the mission of the lexicographer as self-appointed arbiter and his function as historian can be regarded as a side-issue, for the dictionary, however constructed, is primarily an educational instrument. And the problem is whether that instrument is currently well used.

Our own Noah Webster is in a sense the hero of the story. Alarmed by the state into which learning had fallen after the Revolutionary War, Webster sought to make a one volume dictionary which would serve in the self-education of the semi-literate masses. He was concerned with the masses, not the elite, and with self-education, at a time when this country had not yet become democratic enough to regard the public education of all its children as a primary obligation of the state. The Webster dictionary was probably one of the first self-help books to become a popular best-seller. And the paradox is that now, with public education widely established in this country, with "literacy" as universal as suffrage, the self-help potentialities of a dictionary are seldom realized by the millions who own one. I am not thinking merely of children from progressive schools who cannot use a dictionary because they do not know the alphabet. I am thinking of all the products of contemporary education who, not being taught or inspired to read the great and difficult books, have little use for the dictionary. *How much better educated was the self-read man whom Webster helped!*

This brief history of dictionaries is relevant to the rules for reading and using them well. One of the first rules as to how to read a book is to know what sort of book it is. That means knowing what the author's intention was and what sort of thing you can expect to find in his work. If you look upon a dictionary merely as a spelling book or guide to pronunciation, you will use it accordingly. If you realize that it contains a wealth of historical information, crystallized in the growth of the language, you will pay attention, not merely to the variety of meanings which are listed above under each word, but to their order.

And above all if you are interested in advancing your own education, you will use a dictionary according to its primary intention—as a help in reading books that might otherwise be too difficult because their vocabulary includes technical words, archaic words, literary allusions, or even familiar words used in now obsolete senses. The number of words in a man's vocabulary is as definite as the number of dollars he has in the bank; equally definite is the number of senses in which a man is able to use any given word. But there is this difference: a man cannot draw upon the public treasury when his bank-balance is overdrawn. But we can all draw upon the dictionary to get the coin we need to carry on the transaction of reading anything we want to read.

Let me be sure that I am not misunderstood. I am not saying that a dictionary is all you need in order to move anywhere in the realms of literature. There are many problems to be solved, in reading a book well, other than those arising from the author's vocabulary. And even with respect to vocabulary, the dictionary's primary service is on those occasions when you are confronted with a technical word or with a word that is wholly new to you—such as "costard" (an apple), or "hoatzin" (a South American bird) or "rabato" (a kind of flaring collar). More frequently the problem of interpretation arises because a relatively familiar word seems to be used in a strange sense. Here the dictionary will help, but it will not solve the problem. The dictionary may suggest the variety of senses in which the troublesome word can be used, but it can never determine how the author you are reading used it. That you must decide by wrestling with the context. More often than not, especially with distinguished writers, the word may be given a special, an almost unique, shade of meaning. The growth of your own vocabulary, in the important dimension of multiple meanings as well as in mere quantity of words, will depend, first of all, upon the character of the books you read, and secondly, upon the use you make of the dictionary as a guide. You will misuse it—you will stultify rather than enlighten yourself—if you substitute the dictionary for the exercise of your own interpretative judgment in reading.

This suggests several other rules as to how *not* to read a dictionary. There is no more irritating fellow than the man who tries to settle an argument about communism, or justice, or liberty, by quoting from Webster. Webster and all his fellow lexicographers may be respected as authorities on word-usage, but they are not the ultimate founts of wisdom. They are no Supreme Court to which we can appeal for a decision of those fundamental controversies which, despite the warnings of semanticists, get us involved with abstract words. It is well to remember that the dictionary's authority can, for obvious reasons, be surer in the field of concrete words, and even in the field of the abstract technical words of science, than it ever can be with respect to philosophical words. Yet these words are indispensable if we are going to talk, read, or write about the things that matter most.

Another negative rule is: Don't swallow the dictionary. Don't try to get word-rich quick, by memorizing a lot of fancy words whose meanings are unconnected with any actual experience. Merely verbal knowledge is almost worse than no knowledge at all. If learning consisted in nothing but knowing the meanings of words, we could abolish all our courses of study, and substitute the dictionary for every other sort of book. But no one except a pedant or a fool would regard it as profitable or wise to read the dictionary from cover to cover.

In short, don't forget that the dictionary is a book about words, not about things. It can tell you how men have used words, but it does not define the nature of the things the words name. A Scandinavian university undertook a "linguistic experiment" to prove that human arguments always reduce to verbal differences. Seven lawyers were given seven dictionary definitions of truth and asked to defend them. They soon forgot to stick to the "verbal meanings" they had been assigned, and became vehemently involved in defending or opposing certain fundamental views about the nature of truth. The experiment showed that discussions may start about the meanings of words, but that, when interest in the problem is aroused, they seldom end there. Men pass from words to things, from names to natures. The dictionary can start an argument, but only thought or research can end it.

If we remember that a dictionary is a book about words, we can derive from that fact all the rules for reading a dictionary intelligently. Words can be looked at in four ways.

(1) *Words are physical things*—writable marks and speakable sounds. There must, therefore, be uniform ways of spelling and pronouncing them, though the uniformity is often spoiled by variations.

(2) *Words are parts of speech.* Each single word plays a grammatical role in the more complicated structure of a phrase or a sentence. According to the part it plays, we classify it as a certain part of speech—noun or verb, adjective or adverb, article or preposition. The same word can vary in different usages, shifting from one part of speech to another, as when we say "Man the boat" or "Take the jump." Another sort of grammatical variation in words arises from their inflection, but in a relatively uninflected language like English, we need to pay attention only to the conjugation of the verb (infinitive, participle, past tense, etc.), the case of the noun (singular and plural), and the degree of the adjective (especially the comparative and superlative).

(3) *Words are signs.* They have meanings, not one but many. These meanings are related in various ways. Sometimes they shade from one into another; sometimes one word will have two or more sets of totally unrelated meanings. Through their meanings words are related to one another—as synonyms sharing in the same meaning even though they differ in its shading; or as antonyms through opposition or contrast of meanings. Furthermore, it is in their capacity as signs that we distinguish words as proper or common names (according as they name just one thing or many which are alike in some respect); and as concrete or abstract names (according as they point to some thing which we can sense, or refer to some aspect of things which we can understand by thought but not observe through our senses).

Finally, (4) *words are conventional.* They mean or signify natural things, but they themselves are not natural. They are man-made signs. That is why every word has a history, just as everything else man makes has a time and place of origin, and a cultural career, in which it goes through certain transformations. The history of words is given by their etymological derivation from original word-roots, prefixes, and suffixes; it includes the account of their physical change, both in spelling and pronunciation; it tells of their shifting meanings, and which among them are archaic and obsolete, which are current and regular, which are idiomatic, colloquial, or slang.

A good dictionary will answer all your questions about words under these four heads. The art of reading a dictionary (as any other book) consists in knowing what questions to ask about words and how to find the answers. I have suggested the questions. The dictionary itself tells you how to find the answers. In this respect, it is a perfect self-help book, because it tells you what to pay attention to and how to interpret the various abbreviations and symbols it uses in giving you the four varieties of information about words. Anyone who fails to consult the explanatory notes and the list of abbreviations at the beginning of a dictionary can blame only himself for not being able to read the dictionary well. Unfortunately, many people fail here, as in the case of other books, because they insist upon neglecting the prefatory matter—as if the author were just amusing himself by including it.

I think these suggestions about how to read, and how not to misuse, a dictionary are easy to follow. But like all other rules they will be followed well only by the man who is rightly motivated in the first place. And, in the last place, they will be wisely applied only by the man who remembers that we are both *free* and *bound* in all our dealings with language, whether as writers or readers.

> "When I use a word," Humpty-Dumpty said in a rather scornful tone, "it means just what I choose it to mean—neither more nor less."
> "The question is," said Alice, "whether you can make words mean so many different things."
> "The question is," said Humpty-Dumpty, "which is to be master—that's all."

COMPREHENSION QUIZ

1. Adler says the first rule in most contemporary writing is
    a. to avoid using strange words.
    b. avoid using familiar words in strange ways.
    c. avoid using words with few or no synonyms.
    d. both (a) and (b).
2. The source of the most frequent impulse to go to the dictionary is
    a. to check the spelling of a word.
    b. to check the meaning.
    c. to find a synonym.
    d. to check the part of speech.
3. The first people to be educated in the sense that they studied under foreign masters, were the
    a. Romans.
    b. Greeks.
    c. Spartans.
    d. French.
4. Which of the following was not considered a "vulgar tongue" according to Adler?
    a. English.
    b. French.
    c. Latin.
    d. Italian.
5. The growth of your own vocabulary, especially in multiple meanings of words, depends on
    a. the character of the books you read.
    b. the use you make of the dictionary as a guide.
    c. the use of the thesaurus in conjunction with the dictionary.

d.   both (a) and (b).

6.   According to Adler, words can be looked at in all of the following ways, except
    a.   as parts of speech.
    b.   as physical things.
    c.   as signs.
    d.   as natural things.

7.   You have only yourself to blame for not reading the dictionary well, if you do not
    a.   add vocabulary words at the rate of three per day.
    b.   check pronunciation and explanatory notes at the beginning of the dictionary.
    c.   master the pronunciation of words so as to move to the more important uses.
    d.   none of these.

8.   According to Adler, the hero of the story of the dictionary is
    a.   Dr. Johnson.
    b.   George Santayana.
    c.   Noah Webster
    d.   Isidore Seville.

DISCUSSION QUESTIONS

1.   What are some of the words that have developed in the past months and will undoubtedly go into the next editions of dictionaries?
2.   What is the primary intention of the dictionary, according to Adler?
3.   Why does Adler put quote marks around the word *literacy* in the phrase, "with 'literacy' as universal as suffrage"?
4.   Comment upon the statement that, "The number of words in a man's vocabulary is as definite as the number of dollars he has in the bank."
5.   How would Adler feel about the "Build-Your-Vocabulary-in-Thirty-Days" type of book? Explain.
6.   What do you think Adler means in his final sentence when he says, "We are both *free* and *bound* in all our dealings with language"?
7.   What do you understand to be the point of the quote from *Alice in Wonderland* at the end of this essay?
8.   Why does Adler say, "The dictionary can start an argument, but only thought or research can end it"? In what way can a dictionary start an argument? After all, doesn't it settle, rather than start arguments?

WRITING SUGGESTIONS

1.   Defend or reject Adler's assertion that, "The reason we do not avail ourselves of the services a dictionary offers is not our superiority but rather our lack of need as the life of letters is currently lived."

2.   Examine the procedures used in preparation of a dictionary, or in revising a presently existing one.

3.   Adler reminds us that words are man made signs, and thus every word has a history. Using an unabridged dictionary, cite the history of each of the following words: perfume, insulated, bugle, and algebra.

Preface
to Random House Dictionary

by JESS STEIN

Language is an indispensable instrument of human society. It is the means by which individuals understand each other and are enabled to function together as a community. Indeed, it is unlikely that any human organization could either be formed or long maintained without language. Certainly, in the absence of communication, the complex structure of modern society would be utterly impossible.

The effectiveness of human society, therefore, is largely dependent upon the clarity, accuracy, and efficiency with which language is used or understood. As man's voice reaches now with ease—by radio, by cable, by television—across continents and oceans, the importance of what he says becomes paramount.

But language, unlike such phenomena as breathing and eating, is not biologically inherent; it is not instinctively present. The infant must learn the power and uses of language; he must gain it by conscious effort and by discipline. Sound by sound, word by word, the child acquires this wondrous vehicle for making his wants known, for expressing his feelings and thoughts, for understanding what others wish him to know or do. And, constantly expanding and improving his command of language as he becomes an adult, he develops the capacity for thought and communication on the most abstract and sophisticated planes. Language, as a social convention, thus becomes one of the prime characteristics of man rising above a simple animal existence.

In man's language is to be found the true mirror of man himself. His lexicon is an index to his ideas and passions, his inventions and achievements, his history and hopes. As man extends the horizon of his knowledge, he extends simultaneously the range of his language—devising new words, new meanings, new symbols.

Thus, the remarkable explosion of knowledge in the middle of the twentieth century—the invention of computers and other cybernetic machines, the great new areas of medical discovery, the total revision and expansion of the physical sciences, the exploration of outer space by manned flight and by transmitted signal, and innumerable other developments—has been extensively reflected in our language. Large areas of vocabulary that did not exist until recently—in nuclear physics, in biochemistry, in mathematics, in psychology and sociology, and in dozens of other fields—now press insistently upon the student, the businessman, and the general reader. In every aspect of daily life the necessity for ready access to clear and authoritative information is steadily increasing.

If modern man is to function well in his society, one of his necessities, surely, is to keep pace with the dynamic growth of his language. To meet such a need *The Random House Dictionary of the English Language* has been prepared. It is an entirely new dictionary, written in midcentury for twentieth-century users. Because it is fully up to date and thoroughly reliable, the *RHD* will provide the user with all the information he is likely to need about meaning, spelling, pronunciation, usage, etymology, and other language matters. As a general-purpose reference book, the *RHD* meets the requirements of students and laymen and satisfies the quality standards of leading scholars and authorities. The broad sweep of the English language is fully covered here, including foreign words and phrases, biographical terms, geographical terms, abbreviations, titles of major literary works, and many other types of information frequently sought.

In the planning and preparation of this dictionary, we have endeavored to preserve all that is worthy in the great lexicographic traditions of Samuel Johnson, Noah Webster, James A. H. Murray, William Craigie, William Dwight Whitney, and others. We have resisted the temptation to introduce novelty in the guise of innovation, but we have carefully employed those new ideas and methods that represent genuine advances in modern lexicography. This viewpoint has governed us during the twenty years since publication of *The American College Dictionary,* which has been widely praised for its balanced application of linguistics, its lucid use of scholarship, and its unflagging awareness of the importance of communicating with the reader. The *ACD* established a new standard for desk dictionaries, and it is our hope that the *RHD* will set a new high standard for larger dictionaries.

Throughout our work we have had the advantage of working closely with hundreds upon hundreds of scholars and experts who helped us frame our basic principles, guided us in the myriad decisions that had to be made, and worked directly with us on the manuscript itself. At one stage of our progress, we were also able to confirm the acceptability of our policies by a long questionnaire submitted under unrevealed origin to more than ten thousand teachers, librarians, and writers. In addition, many hundreds of other authorities were consulted on specific questions, and all gave most generously and enthusiastically of their special knowledge and judgment. The comprehensive range represented by our consultants was matched by their wide distribution throughout the United States, England, and other parts around the world.

In the preparation of the *RHD,* our permanent lexicographic staff made full use of its departmental resources—our large file of citations from newspapers, magazines, and books; glossaries and indexes; special diction-aries and lists; textbooks and concordances; reference books and learned studies, and so on. This was supplemented by extensive use of many major public and university libraries, plus the facilities of many governments, private institutions, and professional organizations.

Our central concern throughout the editing of the *RHD* has been communication with the user. In the writing of definitions, for example, we have tried to avoid ingeniously concise wordings that are meaningful only to the writer. We have been guided by the premise that a dictionary editor must not only record; he must also teach. We have tried to express ourselves clearly and simply, using normal English and normal punctuation and capitalization. We have often added illustrative examples after defini-tions in order to give the reader as much help in understanding the mean-ing and use of the word as reasonably possible. Particularly useful too, we believe, is the coverage given in the *RHD* to idiomatic expressions, a cov-erage that enhances the informative value of this book, especially to those who are not native speakers of English.

The pronunciation system used in the *RHD* has, we believe, the two-fold merit of simplicity and accuracy. We have used a minimum of symbols —and those used are, in the main, the traditional ones. As a result, the reader will have little difficulty in reading our phonetic transcriptions; he will only rarely need to check a symbol in the key and, when he does, he will find a condensed key conveniently at the bottom of every odd-numbered page. Whenever common variant pronunciations exist, our transcriptions show them, generally in the order of frequency of occurrence. When the variants represent national differences, a geographic label is used to guide the user in his choice. In the transcriptions, our pronunciation editors have drawn upon every source of information available to them, including scholarly reports, tape recordings, polls of informants, etc. Throughout their work, our pronunciation staff has had the benefit of advice and guidance by Professor Arthur J. Bronstein. Every pronunciation in this dictionary, unless specifically restricted, is an acceptable one among cultivated speakers in what has aptly been described as "the language of well-bred ease."

The etymologies in the *RHD,* prepared by a group of internationally recognized authorities under the senior direction of Professor Kemp Malone, provide the user with an accurate account of the origin and history of the English vocabulary. All significant published research in this field has been utilized and, in addition, members of the etymological staff have frequently incorporated new findings of their own. As a general rule, the etymologies in this dictionary trace words back to their earliest attested forms; hypothetical forms and dubious conjectures have been excluded.

Numerous other features of the *RHD*—synonym lists and studies, antonym lists, usage notes, pictures and diagrams, spot maps, special charts and tables, to mention some—carry further the central principles of accuracy and clarity that guided us throughout.

And finally, that lexicographer's Scylla and Charybdis: Should the dictionary be an authoritarian guide to "correct" English or should it be so antiseptically free of comment that it may defeat the user by providing him with no guidance at all? There is, we believe, a linguistically sound middle course. Language, most people agree, is never static—except when dead. It has a capacity for constant change and growth that enables it to serve effectively the requirements of the society in which it exists. It is, therefore, the function of a dictionary to provide the user with an exact record of the language he sees and hears. That record must be *fully* descriptive. Since language is a social institution, the lexicographer must give the user an adequate indication of the attitudes of society toward particular words or expressions, whether he regards those attitudes as linguistically sound or not. The lexicographer who does not recognize the existence of long-established strictures in usage has not discharged his full responsibility. He has not been objective and factual; he has reported selectively, omitting references to a social attitude relevant to many words and expressions. He does not need to express approval or disapproval of a disputed usage, but he does need to report the milieu of words as well as their meanings. In this dictionary, on the basis of extensive research and thoughtful consideration, we have used usage labels to guide the reader to effective and appropriate use of words. A special panel of linguists under Professor Raven I. McDavid, Jr., has reviewed and, where necessary, amended the usage labels throughout the *RHD*.

In addition, to answer some of the frequently troublesome questions of usage, we have often appended to an entry a brief usage note. These usage notes are not arbitrary personal judgments; they are reports on the do's and don'ts urged by many users of English. The notes were prepared under the skilled direction of Mr. Theodore M. Bernstein of *The New York Times* and then reviewed by a group of editors and teachers.

This preface has given me the valued privilege of presenting *The Random House Dictionary* to its users on behalf of the many hundreds of scholars and editors who worked so devotedly to create this dictionary. It could not have been possible without them. Nor could it have been possible without the encouraging faith and remarkable patience of the officers and directors of Random House, whose sole instruction to us was to produce the best dictionary we possibly could.

COMPREHENSION QUIZ

1. Language is an indispensable instrument of human society for all but which of the following?
   a. A means of understanding each other.
   b. As aids in the functioning of society.
   c. The complex structure of society depends on language.
   d. A way of finding the meaning to communication between peoples.
2. Unlike breathing and eating, language is *not*
   a. rhythmical.
   b. biologically inherent.
   c. completely necessary.
   d. demanding.
3. The lexicon of man is
   a. a catalogue of words.
   b. a dream of his world.
   c. an index to his ideas.
   d. an indication of his ability to understand.
4. This "Preface" states that of central concern in the preparation of the RHD was
   a. good usage.
   b. accurate description.
   c. "correct" English.
   d. communication with the user.

DISCUSSION QUESTIONS

1. Discuss the emphasis this "Preface" placed on balanced—middle course—lexicography.
2. Why isn't one unabridged dictionary enough for one language?

WRITING SUGGESTIONS

1. Compare the "Preface" of Webster's Third to this one.
2. Write a brief paper on the term "Scylla and Charybdis."

Tongues,
Like Governments

by J. M. EDELSTEIN

". . . Tongues, like governments, have a natural tendency to degeneration . . ." said Samuel Johnson in the preface to his *A Dictionary of the English Language* (London, 1755). Johnson's dictionary was an unsuccessful attempt to check the tendency. *The Random House Dictionary of the English Language* is the latest event in the long history of the corruption of the language and a victory for the linguists who believe that they need only to record and not to discriminate. No one who is lucky enough to own a copy of *Webster's Second Unabridged* will want to get rid of it for either the new *Random House Dictionary* or the *Webster's Third New International Unabridged Dictionary* which came out in 1961.

The Random House Dictionary has some commendable qualities and features: it is relatively cheap as unabridged dictionaries go ($25.00 compared to $47.50 and up, depending on the binding, for the *Webster's Third*); it is legible, adequately illustrated, thumb-indexed, and on good paper. It is more than a dictionary ("a book containing a selection of the words of a language . . ."—*Random House Dictionary*) for it contains a large amount of colorful and peripheral material such as a directory of colleges and universities, concise foreign language dictionaries (French, Spanish, German and Italian), a basic style manual, lists of major reference works, of important dates in history, of the Presidents *and* the Vice Presidents of the United States, and lists of national parks, oceans, seas, principal lakes, noted waterfalls, major rivers, islands, deserts, volcanoes, and major mountain peaks. It reprints the Declaration of Independence, the Constitution and the Charter of the United Nations; it provides coastline measurements and air distances; and, finally, there is an elaborate world atlas. In all, 394 pages

From J. M. Edelstein, "Tongues, Like Governments," *The New Republic*, November 26, 1966. Reprinted by permission of *The New Republic*, © 1966, Harrison-Blaine of New Jersey, Inc.

are given over to its encyclopedic supplement and the atlas—almost one-fifth of the entire volume of 2,059 pages.

The lexicon proper continues the downward trend toward anarchy in language and usage which was given such a vigorous and discouraging push by the publication of *Webster's Third* five years ago. The philosophy of Mr. Jess Stein, editor in chief, and his staff of more than 350 people who labored for seven years with the help of four computers and about $3,000,000 to produce *The Random House Dictionary* is a permissive one. It is a philosophy of language which supports not the precise and the exact, but the vague and the ambiguous. It confuses "standard" with standards, and it ignores tradition and authority. At its worst, the result of such a philosophy is its contribution to the degeneration of the language. At its best, the result is mediocrity.

We are surrounded and bombarded today by officialese and jargon, by pretentiously wordy phrasing, by advertising and show-business lingo, by what is chic and fashionable, by the prose of publishers' blurbs. *The Random House Dictionary* blesses them all. It perpetuates the popular delusion that what is clear, effective, powerful, distinctive, or beautiful is not only outmoded, but is also snobbish and undemocratic. In his preface, Mr. Stein says: "In man's language is to be found the true mirror of man himself. His lexicon is an index to his ideas and passions, his inventions and achievements, his history and hopes." If these assertions are valid, and I believe that they are, then *The Random House Dictionary* reflects a sad state of affairs. Its language is an expression of the pseudo egalitarianism of our times. Its norm is the lowest common denominator. Its appeal is to the broadest possible market. . . .

COMPREHENSION QUIZ

1. The quotation by Samuel Johnson at the beginning of this essay says that "Tongues, like governments, have a natural tendency to
   a. improve."
   b. remain stationary."
   c. degeneration."
   d. none of the above.
2. Edelstein recommends the
   a. Random House Dictionary of the English Language.
   b. Webster's Second Unabridged Dictionary.
   c. Webster's Third New International Unabridged Dictionary.
   d. Johnson's Dictionary of the English Language.
3. The Random House Dictionary was prepared by a staff of more than
   a. 50.
   b. 150.

    c.   250.
    d.   350.
4. According to Edelstein, The Random House Dictionary's philosophy is
    a.   authoritarian.
    b.   prescriptive.
    c.   traditional.
    d.   permissive.
5. The author claims that The Random House Dictionary appeals to
    a.   the broadest possible market.
    b.   professional users of the language.
    c.   admirers of Webster's Second Unabridged Dictionary.
    d.   the highest common denominator.

DISCUSSION QUESTIONS

1. Does The Random House Dictionary have any redeeming qualities, according to Edelstein? Does he find it more to his liking than the Webster's Third?
2. Edelstein says that The Random House Dictionary "reflects a sad state of affairs." What is that "sad state"? According to Edelstein, how could it be corrected?
3. According to Edelstein, what is the relationship between change and corruption in language? Can you cite any "corrupt" forms or examples?

WRITING SUGGESTIONS

Summarize the differences between Stein (page 191) and Edelstein in their views on the purpose of a dictionary. Indicate which you believe is more nearly accurate.

Language
and Lexicons

Sirs:

Mr. J. M. Edelstein, who reviewed the *Random House Dictionary of the English Language* . . . demonstrates that he does not want to understand either the task of linguists or those of lexicographers; regrettably, he wishes to remain prejudiced or uninformed. He simply encourages one to keep his copy of *Webster's Second Unabridged* because it is, for some unsupported reason, excluded from "the long history of the corruption of the language." He seems to suggest that color, size of print, and similar peripheral matters (admittedly important in selling the dictionary) take precedence over the lexicographer's main purpose—to present an accurate, authoritative (and not authoritarian) record of words and their usage; Mr. Edelstein does not discuss any specific entries of words.

Because he overlooks any advancements made in the studies of language in the last two centuries, he makes various outlandish assertions: "The lexicon proper continues the downward trend toward anarchy in language and usage . . ."; the philosophy of Mr. Jess Stein, together with his staff, "supports not the precise and the exact, but the vague and the ambiguous"; this philosophy "ignores tradition and authority"; the "norm" of their dictionary "is the lowest common denominator"; and so on.

Mr. Edelstein categorically subscribes to the capricious notion that "the only ruler" linguists "obey" is change. Neither linguists nor lexicographers have decreed change, for it has always, as he undoubtedly knows, operated within language. One can rightly ask, why is change to be viewed as "corruption?" What is a corrupt form? How is this form singled out and condemned? It can, nevertheless, be observed what standard and nonstandard forms are, since the standard ones—representing a cultural level—reflect the usage of the majority of formally educated speakers in the American society who usually recognize the nonstandard ones (also representing a cultural

From Wallace L. Pretzer, "Language and Lexicons," *The New Republic*, December 17, 1966. Reprinted by permission of *The New Republic*, © 1966, Harrison-Blaine of New Jersey, Inc.

level). To label nonstandard forms as "corrupt" suggests the establishment of a Legion of Decency or a Board of Purity whose duties would be to compose sacred, inflexible laws of language.

Usage is, of course, "real and various"; Mr. Edelstein apparently thinks that linguists do not think so. Both linguists and lexicographers would know that a speaker or a writer varies his usage in light of various dimensions with respect to methodology (whether it be a matter of speech or of writing), to region, social class, age, occupation, and to situation. It is unrealistic to view language in simple ways and to expect lexicographers, and certainly linguists, to arbitrate, fix, or control usage by appealing to some supreme linguistic god. Samuel Johnson knew that he could not do so.

Wallace L. Pretzer
BOWLING GREEN STATE UNIVERSITY

COMPREHENSION QUIZ

1. Pretzer's letter is a rebuttal to Edelstein's review of
   a. Samuel Johnson's dictionary.
   b. Webster's Second Unabridged Dictionary.
   c. Webster's Third Unabridged Dictionary.
   d. the Random House Dictionary.
2. Pretzer charges that Edelstein
   a. overlooks any advancements made in the studies of language in the last two centuries.
   b. is too permissive in his attitude toward language and dictionaries.
   c. wants to make usage the sole arbiter of correctness.
   d. neglects to consider the importance of color, size of print, and type size in the latter's review.
3. Which of the following statements would Pretzer accept?
   a. The only rule linguists obey is change.
   b. Usage is real and various.
   c. There exists today a downward trend toward anarchy in language and usage.
   d. Usage should be regulated by the creation of an academy of linguists.
4. According to the author of this article, which of the following is *not* a factor when speakers and writers vary their usage?
   a. Region.
   b. The doctrine of correctness.
   c. Social class.
   d. Situation.

DISCUSSION QUESTIONS

1. Re-read the first paragraph of Pretzer's letter. Does he accurately state Edelstein's argument?

2. What kind of information properly belongs in a dictionary, in addition to listings of words?
3. What is the tone of Pretzer's letter?

WRITING SUGGESTIONS

1. Pretzer and Edelstein disagree on the purpose of a dictionary. Write a theme in which you summarize briefly the position of each author; then indicate, with supporting evidence, which viewpoint is more forceful and logical.
2. Is it true that "the only ruler" that linguists "obey" is change? If it is not true, then what determines "correctness" for the linguist?

Sabotage
in Springfield

by WILSON FOLLETT

Of dictionaries, as of newspapers, it might be said that the bad ones are too bad to exist, the good ones too good not to be better. No dictionary of a living language is perfect or ever can be, if only because the time required for compilation, editing, and issuance is so great that shadows of obsolescence are falling on parts of any such work before it ever gets into the hands of a user. Preparation of *Webster's Third New International Dictionary of the English Language* began intensively in the Springfield establishment of G. & C. Merriam Company in 1936, but the century was nine months into its seventh decade before any outsider could have his first look at what had been accomplished. His first look is, of course, incompetent to acquaint him with the merits of the new work; these no one can fully discover without months or years of everyday use. On the other hand, it costs only minutes to find out that what will rank as the great event of American linguistic history in this decade, and perhaps in this quarter century, is in many crucial particulars a very great calamity.

Why should the probable and possible superiorities of the Third New International be so difficult to assess, the shortcomings so easy? Because the superiorities are special, departmental, and recondite, the shortcomings general and within the common grasp. The new dictionary comes to us with a claim of 100,000 new words or new definitions. These run almost overwhelmingly to scientific and technological terms or meanings that have come into existence since 1934, and especially to words classified as ISV (belonging to the international scientific vocabulary). No one person can possibly use or even comprehend all of them; the coverage in this domain, certainly impressive to the nonspecialist, may or may not command the

From Wilson Follett, "Sabotage in Springfield," *The Atlantic Monthly*, January, 1962. Reprinted by permission of Mrs. Margaret Follett.

admiration of specialists. It is said that historians of the graphic arts and of architecture were displeased with the 1934 Webster, both for its omissions and for some definitions of what it included in their fields. Its 1961 successor may have disarmed their reservations; only they can pronounce.

But all of us may without brashness form summary judgments about the treatment of what belongs to all of us—the standard, staple, traditional language of general reading and speaking, the ordinary vocabulary and idioms of novelist, essayist, letter writer, reporter, editorial writer, teacher, student, advertiser; in short, fundamental English. And it is precisely in this province that Webster III has thrust upon us a 'dismaying assortment of the questionable, the perverse, the unworthy, and the downright outrageous.

Furthermore, what was left out is as legitimate a grievance to the ordinary reader as anything that has been put in. Think—if you can—of an unabridged dictionary from which you cannot learn who Mark Twain was (though *mark twain* is entered as a leadsman's cry), or what were the names of the apostles, or that the Virgin was Mary the mother of Jesus of Nazareth, or what and where the District of Columbia is!

The disappointment and the shock are intensified, of course, because of the unchallenged position earned by the really unabridged immediate predecessor of this strange work. *Webster's New International Dictionary,* Second Edition (1934), consummated under the editorship of William Allan Neilson, at once became the most important reference book in the world to American writers, editors, teachers, students, and general readers—everyone to whom American English was a matter of serious interest. What better could the next revision do than extend the Second Edition in the direction of itself, bring it up to date, and correct its scattering of oversights and errata?

The 1934 dictionary had been, heaven knows, no citadel of conservatism, no last bastion of puristical bigotry. But it had made shrewd reports on the status of individual words; it had taken its clear, beautifully written definitions from fit uses of an enormous vocabulary by judicious users; it had provided accurate, impartial accounts of the endless guerrilla war between grammarian and antigrammarian and so given every consultant the means to work out his own decisions. Who could wish the forthcoming revision any better fortune than a comparable success in applying the same standards to whatever new matter the new age imposed?

Instead, we have seen a century and a third of illustrious history largely jettisoned; we have seen a novel dictionary formula improvised, in great part out of snap judgments and the sort of theoretical improvement that in practice impairs; and we have seen the gates propped wide open in enthusiastic hospitality to miscellaneous confusions and corruptions. In fine, the anxiously awaited work that was to have crowned cisatlantic linguistic scholarship with a particular glory turns out to be a scandal and a disaster. Worse yet, it plumes itself on its faults and parades assiduously cultivated sins as virtues without precedent.

Examination cannot proceed far without revealing that Webster III, behind its front of passionless objectivity, is in truth a fighting document. And the enemy it is out to destroy is every obstinate vestige of linguistic punctilio, every surviving influence that makes for the upholding of standards, every criterion for distinguishing between better usages and worse. In other words, it has gone over bodily to the school that construes traditions as enslaving, the rudimentary principles of syntax as crippling, and taste as irrelevant. This revolution leaves it in the anomalous position of loudly glorifying its own ancestry—which is indeed glorious—while tacitly sabotaging the principles and ideals that brought the preceding Merriam-Webster to its unchallengeable pre-eminence. The Third New International is at once a resounding tribute of lip service to the Second and a wholesale repudiation of it—a sweeping act of apology, contrition, and reform.

The right-about-face is, of course, particularly evident in the vocabulary approved. Within a few days of publication the new dictionary was inevitably notorious for its unreserved acceptance as standard of *wise up, get hep* (it uses the second as a definition of the first), *ants in one's pants, one for the book, hugeous, nixie, passel, hepped up* (with *hepcat* and *hepster*), *anyplace, someplace,* and so forth. These and a swarm of their kind it admits to full canonical standing by the suppression of such qualifying status labels as *colloquial, slang, cant, facetious,* and *substandard.* The classification *colloquial* it abolishes outright: "it is impossible to know whether a word out of context is colloquial or not." Of *slang* it makes a chary occasional use despite a similar reservation: "No word is invariably slang, and many standard words can be given slang connotations or used so inappropriately as to become slang." *Cornball* is ranked as slang, *corny* is not.

The overall effect signifies a large-scale abrogation of one major responsibility of the lexicographer. He renounces it on the curious ground that helpful discriminations are so far beyond his professional competence that he is obliged to leave them to those who, professing no competence at all, have vainly turned to him for guidance. If some George Ade of the future, aspiring to execute a fable in slang, were to test his attempt by the status labels in Webster III, he would quickly discover with chagrin that he had expressed himself almost without exception in officially applauded English. With but slight exaggeration we can say that if an expression can be shown to have been used in print by some jaded reporter, some candidate for office or his speech writer, some potboiling minor novelist, it is well enough credentialed for the full blessing of the new lexography.

This extreme tolerance of crude neologisms and of shabby diction generally, however, is but one comparatively trifling aspect of the campaign against punctilio. We begin to sound its deeper implications when we plunge into the definitions and the copious examples that illustrate and support them. Under the distributive pronoun *each* we find, side by side: "(each of them is to pay his own fine) (each of them are to pay their own fine)." Where could anyone look for a neater, more succinct way to outlaw the dusty dogma that a pronoun should agree in number with its antecedent? Here is the same maneuver again under another distributive, *everybody*: "usu. referred to by the third person singular (everybody is bringing his own lunch) but sometimes by a plural personal pronoun (everybody had made up their minds)." Or try *whom* and *whomever*: "(a . . . recruit whom he hoped would prove to be a crack salesman) (people . . . whom you never thought would sympathize) . . . (I go out to talk to whomever it is) . . . (he attacked whomever disagreed with him)." It is, then, all right to put the subject of a finite verb in the accusative case—"esp. after a preposition or a verb of which it might mistakenly be considered the object."

Shall we look into what our dictionary does with a handful of the more common solecisms, such as a publisher might introduce into a cooked-up test for would-be copy editors? Begin with *center around* (or *about*). It seems obvious that expressions derived from Euclidean geometry should make Euclidean sense. A center is a point; it is what things are around, not what is around them; they center *in* or *on* or *at* the point. The Second Edition defined the Great White Way as "That part of Broadway . . . centering about Times Square"—patently an oversight. Is it the same oversight that produces, in the Third: *"heresy . . . 3*: a group or school of thought centering around a particular heresy"? We look up *center* itself, and, lo: "(a story to tell, centered around the political development of a great state) . . . (more scholarship than usual was centered around the main problems)," followed by several equivalent specimens.

Here is *due to*. First we come on irreproachable definitions, irreproachably illustrated, of *due* noun and *due* adjective, and we think we are out of the woods. Alas, they are followed by the manufacture of a composite preposition, *due to*, got up solely to extenuate such abominations as "the event was canceled due to inclement weather." An adjective can modify a verb, then. And here is a glance at that peculiarly incriminating redundancy of the slipshod writer, *equally as*: "equally opposed to Communism as to Fascism." The intolerable *hardly than* or *scarcely than* construction is in full favor: "hardly had the birds dropped than she jumped into the water and retrieved them." The sequence *different than* has the double approbation of editorial use and a citation: conjunctive *unlike* means "in a manner that is different than," and a passage under *different* reads "vastly different in size than it was twenty-five years ago." Adjectival *unlike* and conjunctive *unlike* both get illustrations that implicitly commend the unanchored and grammarless modifier: "so many fine men were outside the charmed circle that, unlike most colleges, there was no disgrace in not being a club man"; "unlike in the gasoline engine, fuel does not enter the cylinder with air on the intake stroke."

This small scattering should not end without some notice of that darling of the advanced libertarians, *like* as a conjunction, first in the meaning of *as,* secondly (and more horribly) in that of *as if.* Now, it is well known to the linguistic historian that *like* was so used for a long time before and after Langland. But it is as well known that the language rather completely sloughed off this usage; that it has long been no more than a regional colloquialism, a rarely seen aberration among competent writers, or an artificially cultivated irritant among defiant ones. The *Saturday Evening Post,* in which *like* for *as* is probably more frequent than in any other painstakingly edited magazine, has seldom if ever printed that construction except in reproducing the speech or tracing the thoughts of characters to whom it might be considered natural. The arguments for *like* have been merely defensive and permissive. Not for centuries has there been any real pressure of authority on a writer to use *like* as a conjunction—until our Third New International Dictionary decided to exert its leverage.

How it is exerted will appear in the following: "(impromptu programs where they ask questions much like I do on the air) . . . (looks like they can raise better tobacco) (looks like he will get the job) (wore his clothes like he was . . . afraid of getting dirt on them) (was like he'd come back from a long trip) (acted like she felt sick) . . . (sounded like the motor had stopped) . . . (the violin now sounds like an old masterpiece should) (did it like he told me to) . . . (wanted a doll like she saw in the store window) . . . (anomalies like just had occurred)."

By the processes represented in the foregoing and countless others for which there is no room here, the latest Webster whittles away at one after another of the traditionary controls until there is little or nothing left of them. The controls, to be sure, have often enough been overvalued and overdone by pedants and purists, by martinets and bigots; but more often, and much more importantly, they have worked as aids toward dignified, workmanlike, and cogent uses of the wonderful language that is our inheritance. To erode and undermine them is to convert the language into a confusion of unchanneled, incalculable williwaws, a capricious wind blowing whithersoever it listeth. And that, if we are to judge by the total effect of the pages under scrutiny—2720 of them and nearly 8000 columns of vocabulary, all compact in Times roman—is exactly what is wanted by the patient and dedicated saboteurs in Springfield. They, if they keep their ears to the ground, will hear many echoes of the despairing cry already wrung from one editorial assistant on a distinguished magazine that still puts its faith in standards: "Why have a Dictionary at all if anything goes?"

The definitions are reinforced, it will have been conveyed, with copious citations from printed sources. These citations occupy a great fraction of the total space. They largely account for the reduction in the number of entries (from 600,000 to 450,000) and for the elimination of the Gazetteer, the Biographical Dictionary, and the condensed key to pronunciation and symbols that ran across the bottoms of facing pages—all very material deprivations. Some 14,000 authors, we are told, are presented in the illustrative quotations—"mostly from the mid-twentieth century."

Can some thousands of authors truly worth space in a dictionary ever be found in any one brief period? Such a concentration can hardly fail to be, for the purposes of a dictionary, egregiously overweighted with the contemporary and the transient. Any very short period, such as a generation, is a period of transition in the history of English, and any great mass of examples drawn primarily from it will be disproportionately focused on transitional and ephemeral elements. To say that recording English *as we find it today* is precisely the purpose of a new dictionary is not much of a retort. For the bulk of the language that we use has come down to us with but minor, glacially slow changes from time out of mind, and a worthy record of it must stand on a much broader base than the fashions of yesterday.

It is, then, a mercy that among the thousands of scraps from recent authors, many of them still producing, we can also find hundreds from Shakespeare, the English Bible, Fielding, Dickens, Hawthorne, Melville, Henry James, Mark Twain, and so on. But the great preponderance of latter-day prose, little of it worth repeating and a good deal of it hardly worth printing in the first place, is likely to curtail by years the useful life of the Third New International.

So much is by the way. When we come to the definitions proper we face something new, startling, and formidable in lexicography. The definitions, all of them conformed to a predetermined rhetorical pattern, may be products of a theory—Gestaltist, perhaps?—of how the receiving mind works. The pattern, in the editor's general preface, is described as follows: "The primary objective of precise, sharp defining has been met through development of a new dictionary style based upon completely analytical one-phrase definitions throughout the book. Since the headword in a definition is intended to be modified only by structural elements restrictive in some degree and essential to each other, the use of commas either to separate or to group has been severely limited, chiefly to elements in apposition or in series. The new defining pattern does not provide for a predication which conveys further expository comment."

This doctrine of the strictly unitary definition is of course formulated and applied in the interest of a logical integrity and a simplification never before consistently attained by lexical definitions. What it produces, when applied with the rigor here insisted on, is in the first place some of the oddest prose ever concocted by pundits. A typical specimen, from the definition of the simplest possible term: "*rabbit punch* . . . : a short chopping blow delivered to the back of the neck or the base of the skull with the edge of the hand opposite the thumb that is illegal in boxing." When the idea, being not quite so simple, requires the one-phrase statement of several components, the definition usually turns out to be a great unmanageable and unpunctuated blob of words strung out beyond the retentive powers of most minds that would need the definition at all. Both theory and result will emerge clearly enough from a pair of specimens, the first dealing with a familiar everyday noun, the second with a mildly technical one:

> groan . . . *1:* a deep usu. inarticulate and involuntary often strangled sound typically abruptly begun and ended and usu. indicative of pain or grief or tension or desire or sometimes disapproval or annoyance.

> kymograph . . . *1:* a recording device including an electric motor or clockwork that drives a usu. slowly revolving drum which carries a roll of plain or smoked paper and also having an arrangement for tracing on the paper by means of a stylus a graphic record of motion or pressure (as of the organs of speech, blood pressure, or respiration) often in relation to particular intervals of time.

About these typical definitions as prose, there is much that any good reader might well say. What must be said is that the grim suppression of commas is a mere crotchet. It takes time to read such definitions anyway; commas in the right places would speed rather than slow the reading and would clarify rather than obscure the sense, so that the unitary effect— largely imaginary at best—would be more helped than hurt. In practice, the one-phrase design without further expository predication lacks all the asserted advantages over a competently written definition of the free conventional sort; it is merely more difficult to write, often impossible to write well, and tougher to take in. Compare the corresponding definitions from the Second Edition:

> groan . . . A low, moaning sound; usually, a deep, mournful sound uttered in pain or great distress; sometimes, an expression of strong disapprobation; as, the remark was received with *groans.*

> kymograph . . . *a* An automatic apparatus consisting of a motor revolving a drum covered with smoked paper, on which curves of pressure, etc., may be traced.

Everyone professionally concerned with the details of printed English can be grateful to the new Webster for linking the parts of various expressions that have been either hyphenated compounds or separate words—*highlight, highbrow* and *lowbrow, overall, wisecrack, lowercase* and *uppercase,* and so on. Some of the unions now recognized were long overdue; many editors have already got them written into codes of house usage. But outside this small province the new work is a copy editor's despair, a propounder of endless riddles.

What, for example, are we to make of the common abbreviations *i.e.* and *e.g.*? The first is entered in the vocabulary as *ie* (no periods, no space), the second as *e g* (space, no periods). In the preliminary list, "Abbreviations Used in This Dictionary," both are given the customary periods. (Oddly, the list translates its *i.e.* into "that is," but merely expands *e.g.* into "exempli gratia.") Is one to follow the vocabulary or the list? What point has the seeming inconsistency?

And what about capitalization? All vocabulary entries are in lowercase except for such abbreviations as ARW (air raid warden), MAB (medical advisory board), and PX (post exchange). Words possibly inviting capitalization are followed by such injunctions as *cap, usu cap, sometimes not cap, usu cap 1st A, usu cap A&B*. (One of the small idiosyncrasies is that "usu.," the most frequent abbreviation, is given a period when roman, denied it when italic.) From *america,* adjective—all proper nouns are excluded—to *american yew* there are over 175 consecutive entries that require such injunctions; would it not have been simpler and more economical to capitalize the entries? A flat *"cap,"* of course, means "always capitalized." But how often is "usually," and when is "sometimes"? We get dictionaries expressly that they may settle such problems for us. This dictionary seems to make a virtue of leaving them in flux, with the explanation that many matters are subjective and that the individual must decide them for himself—a curious abrogation of authority in a work extolled as "more useful and authoritative than any previous dictionary."

The rock-bottom practical truth is that the lexicographer cannot abrogate his authority if he wants to. He may think of himself as a detached scientist reporting the facts of language, declining to recommend use of anything or abstention from anything; but the myriad consultants of his work are not going to see him so. He helps create, not a book of fads and fancies and private opinions, but a Dictionary of the English Language. It comes to every reader under auspices that say, not "Take it or leave it," but rather something like this: "Here in 8000 columns is a definitive report of what a synod of the most trustworthy American experts consider the English language to be in the seventh decade of the twentieth century. This is your language; take it and use it. And if you use it in conformity with the principles and practices here exemplified, your use will be the most accurate attainable by any American of this era." The fact that the compilers disclaim authority and piously refrain from judgments is meaningless: the work itself, by virtue of its inclusions and exclusions, its mere existence, is a whole universe of judgments, received by millions as the Word from on high.

And there we have the reason why it is so important for the dictionary maker to keep his discriminations sharp, why it is so damaging if he lets them get out of working order. Suppose he enters a new definition for no better reason than that some careless, lazy, or uninformed scribbler has jumped to an absurd conclusion about what a word means or has been too harassed to run down the word he really wanted. This new definition is going to persuade tens of thousands that, say, *cohort,* a word of multitude, means one associate or crony "(he and three alleged housebreaking cohorts were arraigned on attempted burglary charges)" or that the vogue word *ambivalence,* which denotes simultaneous love and hatred of someone or something, means "continual oscillation between one thing and its opposite (novels . . . vitiated by an ambivalence between satire and sentimentalism)." To what is the definer contributing if not to subversion and decay? To the swallower of the definition it never occurs that he can have drunk corruption from a well that he has every reason to trust as the ultimate in purity. Multiply him by the number of people simultaneously influenced, and the resulting figure by the years through which the influence continues, and a great deal of that product by the influences that will be disseminated through speech and writing and teaching, and you begin to apprehend the scope of the really enormous disaster that can and will be wrought by the lexicographer's abandonment of his responsibility.

COMPREHENSION QUIZ

1. Webster's Third New International Dictionary has ——— new words or new definitions.
   a. 10,000
   b. 50,000
   c. 100,000
   d. 150,000
2. The Second Edition of Webster's unabridged dictionary was published in
   a. 1914.
   b. 1924.
   c. 1934.
   d. 1944.
3. Follett believes the Third
   a. has abrogated its responsibility.
   b. fails to heed the usage of journalists.
   c. relies too heavily on traditional controls.
   d. represents a victory over the linguists.
4. According to the author, definitions in the Third
   a. use too many commas.
   b. are too brief.
   c. are more logical than those in the Second.
   d. are difficult to read.
5. In his article, Follett
   a. laments the disappearance of the classification *colloquial.*
   b. welcomes the appearance of neologisms.

c.   praises the entries for *each* and *everybody*.
d.   criticizes the inclusion of an expanded gazetteer and biographical dictionary.

DISCUSSION QUESTIONS

1.   According to Follett, why are the superiorities of the Third New International Dictionary so difficult to assess? What, if anything, does he find to praise in the Third?
2.   In the third paragraph Follett says that "all of us" may form judgments about language. Does this contradict anything he says later in his article?
3.   How would you describe the tone and language of Follett's article?
4.   Follett laments the lack of controls over language in the Third. What "controls" does he probably have in mind? How reliable are they?
5.   Does the inclusion of a word in the dictionary imply that it is "officially applauded" by the editors?
6.   What does the Third recommend concerning the use of *like* as a conjunction?
7.   How, according to Follett, did the editor of Webster's Third "abrogate his authority"?

WRITING SUGGESTIONS

1.   Defend the Third's treatment of *each* and *everybody*.
2.   Should editors of dictionaries prescribe standards of "correctness"? Or is their duty merely to describe and record usage? Write a theme presenting your views.
3.   How justified is Follett's criticism of the prose style of the definitions in the Third? Try rewriting its definition of *rabbit punch*.

But What's a Dictionary For?

by BERGEN EVANS

The storm of abuse in the popular press that greeted the appearance of *Webster's Third New International Dictionary* is a curious phenomenon. Never has a scholarly work of this stature been attacked with such unbridled fury and contempt. An article in the *Atlantic* viewed it as a "disappointment," a "shock," a "calamity," "a scandal and a disaster." The New York *Times,* in a special editorial, felt that the work would "accelerate the deterioration" of the language and sternly accused the editors of betraying a public trust. The *Journal* of the American Bar Association saw the publication as "deplorable," "a flagrant example of lexicographic irresponsibility," "a serious blow to the cause of good English." *Life* called it "a non-word deluge," "monstrous," "abominable," and "a cause for dismay." They doubted that "Lincoln could have modelled his Gettysburg Address" on it—a concept of how things get written that throws very little light on Lincoln but a great deal on *Life.*

What underlies all this sound and fury? Is the claim of the G. & C. Merriam Company, probably the world's greatest dictionary maker, that the preparation of the work cost $3.5 million, that it required the efforts of three hundred scholars over a period of twenty-seven years, working on the largest collection of citations ever assembled in any language—is all this a fraud, a hoax?

So monstrous a discrepancy in evaluation requires us to examine basic principles. Just what's a dictionary for? What does it propose to do? What does the common reader go to a dictionary to find? What has the purchaser of a dictionary a right to expect for his money?

Before we look at basic principles, it is necessary to interpose two brief statements. The first of these is that a dictionary is concerned with words.

From Bergen Evans, "But What's a Dictionary For?," *The Atlantic Monthly*, May, 1962. Reprinted by permission of the author.

Some dictionaries give various kinds of other useful information. Some have tables of weights and measures on the flyleaves. Some list historical events, and some, home remedies. And there's nothing wrong with their so doing. But the great increase in our vocabulary in the past three decades compels all dictionaries to make more efficient use of their space. And if something must be eliminated, it is sensible to throw out these extraneous things and stick to words.

Yet wild wails arose. The *Saturday Review* lamented that one can no longer find the goddess Astarte under a separate heading—though they point out that a genus of mollusks named after the goddess is included! They seemed to feel that out of sheer perversity the editors of the dictionary stooped to mollusks while ignoring goddesses and that, in some way, this typifies modern lexicography. Mr. Wilson Follett, folletizing (his mental processes demand some special designation) in the *Atlantic,* cried out in horror that one is not even able to learn from the Third International "that the Virgin was Mary the mother of Jesus"!

The second brief statement is that there has been even more progress in the making of dictionaries in the past thirty years than there has been in the making of automobiles. The difference, for example, between the much-touted Second International (1961) is not like the difference between yearly models but like the difference between the horse and buggy and the automobile. Between the appearance of these two editions a whole new science related to the making of dictionaries, the science of descriptive linguistics, has come into being.

Modern linguistics gets its charter from Leonard Bloomfield's *Language* (1933). Bloomfield, for thirteen years professor of Germanic philology at the University of Chicago and for nine years professor of linguistics at Yale, was one of those inseminating scholars who can't be relegated to any department and don't dream of accepting established categories and procedures just because they're established. He was as much an anthropologist as a linguist, and his concepts of language were shaped not by Strunk's *Elements of Style* but by his knowledge of Cree Indian dialects.

The broad general findings of the new science are:

1. All languages are systems of human conventions, not systems of natural laws. The first—and essential—step in the study of any language is observing and setting down precisely what happens when native speakers speak it.

2. Each language is unique in its pronunciation, grammar, and vocabulary. It cannot be described in terms of logic or of some theoretical, ideal language. It cannot be described in terms of any other language, or even in terms of its own past.

3. All languages are dynamic rather than static, and hence a "rule" in any language can only be a statement of contemporary practice. Change is constant—and normal.

4. "Correctness" can rest only upon usage, for the simple reason that there is nothing else for it to rest on. And all usage is relative.

From these propositions it follows that a dictionary is good only insofar as it is a comprehensive and accurate description of current usage. And to be comprehensive it must include some indication of social and regional associations.

New dictionaries are needed because English has changed more in the past two generations than at any other time in its history. It has had to adapt to extraordinary cultural and technological changes, two world wars, unparalleled changes in transportation and communication, and unprecedented movements of populations.

More subtly, but pervasively, it has changed under the influence of mass education and the growth of democracy. As written English is used by increasing millions and for more reasons than ever before, the language has become more utilitarian and more informal. Every publication in America today includes pages that would appear, to the purist of forty years ago, unbuttoned gibberish. Not that they are; they simply show that you can't hold the language of one generation up as a model for the next.

It's not that you mustn't. You *can't*. For example, in the issue in which *Life* stated editorially that it would follow the Second International, there were over forty words, constructions, and meanings which are in the Third International but not in the Second. The issue of the New York *Times* which hailed the Second International as the authority to which it would adhere and the Third International as a scandal and a betrayal which it would reject used one hundred and fifty-three separate words, phrases, and constructions which are listed in the Third International but not in the Second and nineteen others which are condemned in the Second. Many of them are used many times, more than three hundred such uses in all. The Washington *Post,* in an editorial captioned "Keep Your Old Webster's," says, in the first sentence, "don't throw it away," and in the second, "hang on to it." But the old Webster's labels *don't* "colloquial" and doesn't include "hang on to," in this sense, at all.

In short, all of these publications are written in the language that the Third International describes, even the very editorials which scorn it. And this is no coincidence, because the Third International isn't setting up any new standards at all; it is simply describing what *Life,* the Washington *Post,* and the New York *Times* are doing. Much of the dictionary's material comes from these very publications, the *Times,* in particular, furnishing more of its illustrative quotations than any other newspaper.

And the papers have no choice. No journal or periodical could sell a single issue today if it restricted itself to the American language of twenty-eight years ago. It couldn't discuss half the things we are interested in, and its style would seem stiff and cumbrous. If the editorials were serious, the public—and the stockholders—have reason to be grateful that the writers on these publications are more literate than the editors.

And so back to our questions: what's a dictionary for, and how, in 1962, can it best do what it ought to do? The demands are simple. The common reader turns to a dictionary for information about the spelling, pronunciation, meaning, and proper use of words. He wants to know what is current and respectable. But he wants—and has a right to—the truth, the full truth. And the full truth about any language, and especially about American English today, is that there are many areas in which certainty is impossible and simplification is misleading.

Even in so settled a matter as spelling, a dictionary cannot always be absolute. *Theater* is correct, but so is *theatre*. And so are *traveled* and *travelled, plow* and *plough, catalog* and *catalogue,* and scores of other variants. The reader may want a single certainty. He may have taken an unyielding position in an argument, he may have wagered in support of his conviction and may demand that the dictionary "settle" the matter. But neither his vanity nor his purse is any concern of the dictionary's; it must record the facts. And the fact here is that there are many words in our language which may be spelled, with equal correctness, in either of two ways.

So with pronunciation. A citizen listening to his radio might notice that James B. Conant, Bernard Baruch, and Dwight D. Eisenhower pronounce *economics* as ECKuhnomiks, while A. Whitney Griswold, Adlai Stevenson, and Herbert Hoover pronounce it EEKuhnomiks. He turns to the dictionary to see which of the two pronunciations is "right" and finds that they are both acceptable.

Has he been betrayed? Has the dictionary abdicated its responsibility? Should it say that one *must* speak like the president of Harvard or like the president of Yale, like the thirty-first President of the United States or like the thirty-fourth? Surely it's none of its business to make a choice. Not because of the distinction of these particular speakers; lexicography, like God, is no respecter of persons. But because so widespread and conspicuous a use of two pronunciations among people of this elevation shows that there *are* two pronunciations. Their speaking establishes the fact which the dictionary must record.

Among the "enormities" with which *Life* taxes the Third International is its listing of "the common mispronunciation" *heighth.* That it is labeled a "dialectal variant" seems, somehow, to compound the felony. But one hears the word so pronounced, and if one professes to give full account of American English in the 1960s, one has to take some cognizance of it. All people do not possess *Life's* intuitive perception that the word is so "monstrous" that even to list it as a dialect variation is to merit scorn. Among these, by the way, was John Milton, who, in one of the greatest passages in all literature, besought the Holy Spirit to raise him to the "highth"

of his great argument. And even the *Oxford English Dictionary* is so be-
nighted as to list it, in full boldface, right alongside of *Height* as a variant
that has been in the language since at least 1290.

Now there are still, apparently, millions of Americans who retain, in
this as in much else, some of the speech of Milton. This particular pronunciation seems to be receding, but the *American Dialect Dictionary* still
records instances of it from almost every state on the Eastern seaboard
and notes that it is heard from older people and "occasionally in educated
speech," "common with good speakers," "general," "widespread."

Under these circumstances, what is a dictionary to do? Since millions
speak the word this way, the pronunciation can't be ignored. Since it has
been in use as long as we have any record of English and since it has been
used by the greatest writers, it can't be described as substandard or slang.
But it is heard now only in certain localities. That makes it a dialectal
pronunciation, and an honest dictionary will list it as such. What else can
it do? Should it do?

The average purchaser of a dictionary uses it most often, probably, to
find out what a word "means." As a reader, he want to know what an author
intended to convey. As a speaker or writer, he wants to know what a word
will convey to his auditors. And this, too, is complex, subtle, and forever
changing.

An illustration is furnished by an editorial in the Washington *Post*
(January 17, 1962). After a ringing appeal to those who "love truth and
accuracy" and the usual bombinations about "abdication of authority" and
"barbarism," the editorial charges the Third International with "pretentious and obscure verbosity" and specifically instances its definition of "so
simple an object as a door."

The definition reads:

> a movable piece of firm material or a structure supported usu. along one side
> and swinging on pivots or hinges, sliding along a groove, rolling up and down,
> revolving as one of four leaves, or folding like an accordion by means of which
> an opening may be closed or kept open for passage into or out of a building,
> room, or other covered enclosure or a car, airplane, elevator, or other vehicle.

Then follows a series of special meanings, each particularly defined and,
where necessary, illustrated by a quotation.

Since, aside from roaring and admonishing the "gentlemen from Springfield" that "accuracy and brevity are virtues," the *Post's* editorial fails to
explain what is wrong with the definition, we can only infer from "so
simple" a thing that the writer takes the plain, downright, man-in-the-
street attitude that a door is a door and any damn fool knows that.

But if so, he has walked into one of lexicography's biggest booby traps:
the belief that the obvious is easy to define. Whereas the opposite is true.

Anyone can give a fair description of the strange, the new, or the unique. It's the commonplace, the habitual, that challenges definition, for its very commonness compels us to define it in uncommon terms. Dr. Johnson was ridiculed on just this score when his dictionary appeared in 1755. For two hundred years his definition of a network as "any thing reticulated or decussated, at equal distances, with interstices between the intersections" has been good for a laugh. But in the merriment one thing is always overlooked: no one has yet come up with a better definition. Subsequent dictionaries defined it as a mesh and then defined a mesh as a network. That's simple, all right.

Anyone who attempts sincerely to state what the word *door* means in the United States of America today can't take refuge in a log cabin. There has been an enormous proliferation of closing and demarking devices and structures in the past twenty years, and anyone who tries to thread his way through the many meanings now included under *door* may have to sacrifice brevity to accuracy and even have to employ words that a limited vocabulary may find obscure.

Is the entrance to a tent a door, for instance? And what of the thing that seals the exit of an airplane? Is this a door? Or what of those sheets and jets of air that are now being used, in place of old-fashioned oak and hinges, to screen entrances and exits. Are they doors? And what of those accordion-like things that set off various sections of many modern apartments? The fine print in the lease takes it for granted that they are doors and that spaces demarked by them are rooms—and the rent is computed on the number of rooms.

Was I gypped by the landlord when he called the folding contraption that shuts off my kitchen a door? I go to the Second International, which the editor of the *Post* urges me to use in preference to the Third International. Here I find that a door is

> The movable frame or barrier of boards, or other material, usually turning on hinges or pivots or sliding, by which an entranceway into a house or apartment is closed and opened also, a similar part of a piece of furniture, as in a cabinet or bookcase.

This is only forty-six words, but though it includes the cellar door, it excludes the barn door and the accordion-like thing.

So I go on to the Third International. I see at once that the new definition is longer. But I'm looking for accuracy, and if I must sacrifice brevity to get it, then I must. And, sure enough, in the definition which raised the *Post's* blood pressure, I find the words "folding like an accordion." The thing *is* a door, and my landlord is using the word in one of its currently accepted meanings.

We don't turn to a work of reference merely for confirmation. We all have words in our vocabularies which we have misunderstood, and to come on the true meaning of one of these words is quite a shock. All our complacency and self-esteem rise to oppose the discovery. But eventually we must accept the humiliation and laugh it off as best we can.

Some, often those who have set themselves up as authorities, stick to their error and charge the dictionary with being in a conspiracy against them. They are sure that their meaning is the only "right" one. And when the dictionary doesn't bear them out they complain about "permissive" attitudes instead of correcting their mistake.

The New York *Times* and the *Saturday Review* both regarded as contemptibly "permissive" the fact that one meaning of one word was illustrated by a quotation from Polly Adler. But a rudimentary knowledge of the development of any language would have told them that the underworld has been a far more active force in shaping and enriching speech than all the synods that have ever convened. Their attitude is like that of the patriot who canceled his subscription to the *Dictionary of American Biography* when he discovered that the very first volume included Benedict Arnold!

The ultimate of "permissiveness," singled out by almost every critic for special scorn, was the inclusion in the Third International of *finalize*. It was this, more than any other one thing, that was given as the reason for sticking to the good old Second International—that "peerless authority on American English," as the *Times* called it. But if it was such an authority, why didn't they look into it? They would have found *finalize* if they had.

And why shouldn't it be there? It exists. It's been recorded for two generations. Millions employ it every day. Two Presidents of the United States —men of widely differing cultural backgrounds—have used it in formal statements. And so has the Secretary-General of the United Nations, a man of unusual linguistic attainments. It isn't permitting the word but omitting it that would break faith with the reader. Because it is exactly the sort of word we want information about.

To list it as substandard would be to imply that it is used solely by the ignorant and the illiterate. But this would be a misrepresentation: President Kennedy and U Thant are highly educated men, and both are articulate and literate. It isn't even a freak form. On the contrary, it is a classic example of a regular process of development in English, a process which has given us such thoroughly accepted words as *generalize, minimize, formalize,* and *verbalize.* Nor can it be dismissed on logical grounds or on the ground that it is a mere duplication of *complete.* It says something that *complete* doesn't say and says it in a way that is significant in the modern bureaucratic world: one usually *completes* something which he has initiated but *finalizes* the work of others.

One is free to dislike the word. I don't like it. But the editor of a dictionary has to examine the evidence for a word's existence and seek it in context to get, as clearly and closely as he can, the exact meaning that it conveys to those who use it. And if it is widely used by well-educated, literate, reputable people, he must list it as a standard word. He is not compiling a volume of his own prejudices.

An individual's use of his native tongue is the surest index to his position within his community. And those who turn to a dictionary expect from it some statement of the current status of a word or a grammatical construction. And it is with the failure to assume this function that modern lexicography has been most fiercely charged. The charge is based on a naive assumption that simple labels can be attached in all instances. But they can't. Some words are standard in some constructions and not in others. There may be as many shades of status as of meaning, and modern lexicography instead of abdicating this function has fulfilled it to a degree utterly unknown to earlier dictionaries.

Consider the word *fetch,* meaning to "go get and bring to." Until recently a standard word of full dignity ("Fetch me, I pray thee, a little water in a vessel"—I Kings 17:10), it has become slightly tainted. Perhaps the command latent in it is resented as undemocratic. Or maybe its use in training dogs to retrieve has made some people feel that it is an undignified word to apply to human beings. But, whatever the reason, there is a growing uncertainty about its status, and hence it is the sort of word that conscientious people look up in a dictionary.

Will they find it labeled "good" or "bad"? Neither, of course, because either applied indiscriminately would be untrue. The Third International lists nineteen different meanings of the verb *to fetch.* Of these some are labeled "dialectal," some "chiefly dialectal," some "obsolete," one "chiefly Scottish," and two "not in formal use." The primary meaning—"to go after and bring back"—is not labeled and hence can be accepted as standard, accepted with the more assurance because the many shades of labeling show us that the word's status has been carefully considered.

On grammatical questions the Third International tries to be equally exact and thorough. Sometimes a construction is listed without comment, meaning that in the opinion of the editors it is unquestionably respectable. Sometimes a construction carries the comment "used by speakers and writers on all educational levels though disapproved by some grammarians." Or the comment may be "used in substandard speech and formerly also by reputable writers." Or "less often in standard than in substandard speech." Or simply "dial."

And this very accurate reporting is based on evidence which is presented for our examination. One may feel that the evidence is inadequate or that the evaluation of it is erroneous. But surely, in the face of classification so much more elaborate and careful than any known heretofore, one cannot fly into a rage and insist that the dictionary is "out to destroy . . . every vestige of linguistic punctilio . . . every criterion for distinguishing between better usages and worse."

Words, as we have said, are continually shifting their meanings and connotations, and hence their status. A word which has dignity, say, in the vocabulary of an older person may go down in other people's estimation. Like *fetch*. The older speaker is not likely to be aware of this and will probably be inclined to ascribe the snickers of the young at his speech to that degeneration of manners which every generation has deplored in its juniors. But a word which is coming up in the scale—like *jazz*, say, or, more recently, *crap*—will strike his ear at once. We are much more aware of offenses given us than of those we give. And if he turns to a dictionary and finds the offending word listed as standard—or even listed, apparently—his response is likely to be an outburst of indignation.

But the dictionary can neither snicker nor fulminate. It records. It will offend many, no doubt, to find the expression *wise up,* meaning to inform or to become informed, listed in the Third International with no restricting label. To my aging ears it still sounds like slang. But the evidence—quotations from the *Kiplinger Washington Letter* and the *Wall Street Journal*—convinces me that it is I who am out of step, lagging behind. If such publications have taken to using *wise up* in serious contexts, with no punctional indication of irregularity, then it is obviously respectable. And finding it so listed and supported, I can only say that it's nice to be informed and sigh to realize that I am becoming an old fogy. But, of course, I don't have to use it (and I'll be damned if I will! "Let them smile, as I do now, At the old forsaken bough Where I cling").

In part, the trouble is due to the fact that there is no standard for standard. Ideas of what is proper to use in serious, dignified speech and writing are changing—and with breathtaking rapidity. This is one of the major facts of contemporary American English. But it is no more the dictionary's business to oppose this process than to speed it up.

Even in our standard speech some words are more dignified and some more informal than others, and dictionaries have tried to guide us through these uncertainties by marking certain words and constructions as "colloquial," meaning "inappropriate in a formal situation." But this distinction, in the opinion of most scholars, has done more harm than good. It has created the notion that these particular words are inferior, when actually they might be the best possible words in an informal statement. And so—to the rage of many reviewers—the Third International has dropped this label. Not all labels, as angrily charged, but only this one out of a score. And the doing so may have been an error, but it certainly didn't constitute "betrayal" or "abandoning of all distinctions." It was intended to end a certain confusion.

In all the finer shades of meaning, of which the status of a word is only one, the user is on his own, whether he likes it or not. Despite *Life's* artless assumption about the Gettysburg Address, nothing worth writing is written *from* a dictionary. The dictionary, rather, comes along afterwards and describes what *has been* written.

Words in themselves are not dignified, or silly, or wise, or malicious. But they can be used in dignified, silly, wise, or malicious ways by dignified, silly, wise, or malicious people. *Egghead,* for example, is a perfectly legitimate word, as legitimate as *highbrow* or *long-haired.* But there is something very wrong and very undignified, by civilized standards, in a belligerent dislike for intelligence and education. *Yak* is an amusing word for persistent chatter. Anyone could say, "We were just yakking over a cup of coffee," with no harm to his dignity. But to call a Supreme Court decision *yakking* is to be vulgarly insulting and so, undignified. Again, there's nothing wrong with *confab* when it's appropriate. But when the work of a great research project, employing hundreds of distinguished scholars over several decades and involving the honor of one of the greatest publishing houses in the world, is described as *confabbing* (as the New York *Times* editorially described the preparation of the Third International), the use of this particular word asserts that the lexicographers had merely sat around and talked idly. And the statement becomes undignified—if not, indeed, slanderous.

The lack of dignity in such statements is not in the words, nor in the dictionaries that list them, but in the hostility that deliberately seeks this tone of expression. And in expressing itself the hostility frequently shows that those who are expressing it don't know how to use a dictionary. Most of the reviewers seem unable to read the Third International and unwilling to read the Second.

The *American Bar Association Journal,* for instance, in a typical outburst ("a deplorable abdication of responsibility"), picked out for special scorn the inclusion in the Third International of the word *irregardless.* "As far as the new Webster's is concerned," said the *Journal,* "this meaningless verbal bastard is just as legitimate as any other word in the dictionary." Thirty seconds spent in examining the book they were so roundly condemning would have shown them that in it *irregardless* is labeled "nonstand"—which means "nonstandard," which means "not conforming to the usage generally characteristic of educated native speakers of the language." Is that "just as legitimate as any other word in the dictionary"?

The most disturbing fact of all is that the editors of a dozen of the most influential publications in America today are under the impression that *authoritative* must mean *authoritarian.* Even the "permissive" Third International doesn't recognize this identification—editors' attitudes being not yet, fortunately, those of the American people. But the Fourth International may have to.

The new dictionary may have many faults. Nothing that tries to meet an ever-changing situation over a terrain as vast as contemporary English can hope to be free of them. And much in it is open to honest, and informed, disagreement. There can be linguistic objection to the eradication of proper names. The removal of guides to pronunciation from the foot of every page may not have been worth the valuable space it saved. The new method of defining words of many meanings has disadvantages as well as advantages. And of the half million or more definitions, hundreds, possibly thousands, may seem inadequate or imprecise. To some (of whom I am one) the omission of the label "colloquial" will seem meritorious; to others it will seem a loss.

But one thing is certain: anyone who solemnly announces in the year 1962 that he will be guided in matters of English usage by a dictionary published in 1934 is talking ignorant and pretentious nonsense.

COMPREHENSION QUIZ

1. Modern linguistics gets its charter from
    a.   Strunk's *Elements of Style*.
    b.   Bloomfield's *Language*.
    c.   the writings of Wilson Follett.
    d.   Webster's Second Edition.
2. Which of the following statements would be accepted by modern linguists?
    a.   All languages are systems of natural laws.
    b.   Each language can be described in terms of a theoretical, ideal language.
    c.   All languages are static rather than dynamic.
    d.   "Correctness" can rest only upon usage.
3. Evans claims that articles attacking Webster's Third were in publications
    a.   written in the language that the Third describes.
    b.   known for their inaccuracy and unreliability.
    c.   ignored by the editors of the Third.
    d.   read by few Americans.
4. "Theater" and "theatre" are examples of
    a.   slang.
    b.   argot.
    c.   jargon.
    d.   variants.
5. In his discussion of "economics," Evans claims that
    a.   an incorrect pronunciation has been accepted by the majority of speakers.
    b.   Dwight D. Eisenhower mispronounces the word.
    c.   both pronunciations are acceptable.
    d.   a good dictionary should ignore widespread use of an obviously incorrect pronunciation.
6. To demonstrate that the obvious is not easy to define, Evans discusses the Third's definition of
    a.   "car."
    b.   "door."
    c.   "man."
    d.   "dog."

7. The ultimate of "permissiveness," singled out by almost every critic, was the inclusion in the Third International of
   a. "finalize."
   b. "minimize."
   c. "formalize."
   d. "verbalize."

DISCUSSION QUESTIONS

1. Why are new dictionaries needed? Why is Webster's Second no longer adequate today?
2. What does the fact that many readers want certainty in a dictionary suggest about their concept of "correctness"?
3. Examine several entries in Webster's Third. What is your reaction to its style of definition? Is the absence of a pronunciation key at the bottom of the page a serious weakness?
4. What was the basis of the editors' decision to abandon the label *colloquial?* What is Evans' opinion of this decision?

WRITING SUGGESTIONS

1. Re-read the four principles of linguistics listed by Evans in the eighth paragraph. How would Follett react to each of them?
2. Evans says that one of lexicography's biggest booby traps is the belief that the obvious is easy to define. Without the use of a dictionary, write a definition of the following words: *chair; school; paper; food.*
3. What is the Third's concept of "correct" English? Does it conflict with anything you have been taught in high school rhetoric and grammar textbooks?

Recommended Readings to Part V

Gove, Philip B. (ed.). *The Role of the Dictionary*. New York: Bobbs-Merrill, 1967.
Ives, Sumner. "A Review of *Webster's Third New International Dictionary*," *Word Study, 37* (1960), 7–8.
Marckwardt, Albert H. "Dictionaries and the English Language," *The English Journal* (May, 1963), pp. 336–345.
Sledd, James, and Wilma R. Ebbitt. *Dictionaries and That Dictionary*. Chicago: Scott, Foresman, 1962.

The Structure VI
of English

How to Talk
to a Martian

by G. R. SHIPMAN

Of all the stock characters in science fiction that I wish the BEMs would eat alive, number one on my list is the Telepathic Martian.

You know the one I mean. His spaceship lands in an Iowa cornfield one hot July day. The nation panics; a frantic Defense Department throws a cordon around the farm; the yokels take to the woods; reporters and TV cameramen trample on inquisitive scientists; the Chicago *Tribune* gets out an extra to warn us that the whole thing is probably a Fair Deal plot. Then, as the world and his wife sit with their ears glued to the radio, the hatches of the spaceship open and the Martian emerges to tell us he wishes us well and only wants to save our civilization from self-destruction.

In American English, no less. By some miracle the authors never explain, this visitor from outer space can not only project his thoughts into human brains, but can force them to rearrange his extraterrestrial ideas into the patterns of American speech. Every listener in the surrounding throng hears the Martian's off-the-cuff eloquence in the same way, and not even the most ignorant bystander ever translates a Martian thoughtwave by an "ain't" or a "he don't." Given the enormous cultural differences between Martians and ourselves, you'd expect large blank spots where earthly languages have no equivalents for Martian concepts. But no—we always read their signals one hundred per cent.

Of course there are variations on the telepathy theme. Sometimes the Martian has a walkie-talkie translating machine that picks up his native garglings, whirls them around for a few microseconds in its electronic insides, and sends them out of its loudspeaker in pure United States. Sometimes he seems to have learned English by reading our lips with a super-super-telescope. There may be still other gimmicks I haven't read about. But

From G. R. Shipman, "How to Talk to a Martian," *Astounding Science Fiction* (now *Analog Science Fiction-Science Fact*), October, 1953. Copyright © 1953 by Street & Smith Publications, Inc.

I have yet to see a science-fiction opus that meets this problem of communication across cultural boundaries head-on and tries to solve it by extrapolating from our present techniques.

The fact is, most science-fiction writers don't know such techniques exist.

At that, the writers are no more naive than most of the educated public. In this century descriptive linguistics has made such strides that we can already crack the code of extraterrestrial speech; yet the average intelligent reader has barely heard of the science. People who keep up with modern chemistry and physics can still talk about the study of language in terms handed down from the days when astrology was considered an exact science. They still refer to the study of language as "philology," and have a vague idea that philologists look for "roots" the way a pig looks for truffles. Well, calling the modern science of linguistics "philology" is like calling atomic physics "natural philosophy"—a subject my grandmother studied, without apparatus, when she was a student at a "female seminary."

Fortunately, the linguists haven't waited to be appreciated. They have simply gone on working while the world choked itself in yards and yards of cultural lag, and one of the reasons we won the war was that they knew their business. Thanks to them, GI's in many remote jungles and on lonely atolls learned exotic languages fast—and were really able to talk to the natives. The technique of learning strange tongues that the linguists had worked out with American Indians was equally applicable to Chinese or Russian, and brought results much sooner than traditional methods.

Some of these same linguists are also anthropologists, for language is the indispensable key to an alien culture. When the time comes to establish communication with Martians or any other race from Outside, the linguistic anthropologists will be the ones who forge the link. If beings from another planet use speech or any recognizable analogue, they will be able to decode it with the same techniques they have used to decode Salish or Navaho or Kwakiutl. (Those are American languages, by the way.)

The linguist doesn't need any impressive apparatus—only a pencil and paper, and perhaps a tape recorder. He gets along faster if he has an "informant," a native speaker of the language who has some other language in common with the linguist. There won't be any such informants aboard the spaceship, but, as we'll see later, it's possible to learn Martian without them.

When a linguist works with a human informant, he begins by asking him to say things like "Good morning," "How do you feel?" "What color is that apple?" and "I'm sure it's going to rain tonight." He writes the answers down in the most exact phonetic transcription possible, with a translation of each phrase. He does this even if the language has an alphabet of its own. Most languages, however, are unwritten, and phonetic script is the only way to record them.

The first few jottings in the linguist's notebook are simply odds and ends, as meaningless as ten answers in a Gallup poll. But as the entries pile up, patterns begin to emerge. By skillful questioning, the linguist wheedles more sentences out of the informant to confirm his hunches about the pattern. After he has filled a good many pages, he has enough material to peel out all the verb-forms, variations of the noun, and relevant categories. He is almost ready to write a grammar.

Not quite ready, though; he first has to be sure of the sound-system. Sounds are usually the first units to be analyzed, because they are the smallest elements into which human speech can be divided, and because all the rest of his work depends on his understanding of how they pattern. Though the number of noises that human tongues, lips, and larynges can make is almost infinite, no one language ever uses more than a small fraction of them. Moreover, no naive speaker is aware of all the sounds he makes. He is conscious only of *classes of sounds* that are functional in his language.

To show what "functional" means, let's turn the tables and imagine that a Martian linguist is trying to get the hang of certain American English consonants. His ears and sound spectrograph have recorded a rather large variety of noises made by closing the lips. He might arrange some words containing these sounds into a table like this:

	1	2	3
Voiceless	*pat*	*spat*	*tap*
Voiced	*bat*	———	*tab*

All these words contain sounds called *labial stops,* made by closing the lips and checking the breath-stream for an instant. The stops in the first, or "voiceless" row, are made with the vocal cords relaxed. Those in the "voiced" row are made while the vocal cords are tense and vibrating. Our conventional way of writing these sounds is with the letter p and b.

We write the labial stops in *pat, spat,* and *tap* with the same letter, but to the Martians and their instruments they will not sound exactly alike. The p_1 of *pat* has a puff of breath after the lip-closure that isn't heard after the p_2 of *spat.* If you doubt it, light a match, hold it near your lips, and say the two words, in a low voice but aloud. The flame flickers after the p of *pat,* doesn't it? Perhaps it even goes out. In *tap* we have another variety, p_3, which is made by closing the lips and banking up the breath without a following explosion. This is an *imploded* stop.

In the "voiced" row the Martians can find only two words; English has no words beginning with *sb.* The b_1 of *bat* is exploded like p_1, but the vocal cords vibrate while the lips close. The b_3 of *tab* is imploded like p_3, but again the vocal cords vibrate in the process. You can verify all this with another match.

Now let's suppose the Martian linguist does a little experimenting with these sounds. He says to his human informant, "Pat me," using p_1. The informant gently strokes the Martian's fur. The Martian again says "Pat me," using p_2. The informant may notice something strange about the Martian's pronunciation, but again he gives him a gentle pat.

On the next trial, the Martian actuates his vocal cords and says, not "Pat me," but "Bat me." The results are somewhat startling. Instead of being gently stroked, the Martian intercepts a stunning blow over the head from a blunt instrument. Nursing a dented cranium, he retires to his laboratory and records an important discovery: The acoustic difference between p_1 and b_1 is correlated with a striking (pun intended) difference in meaning, but the acoustic difference between p_1 and p_2 does not affect the meaning at all.

Did you realize the three p's were different before you started to experiment? Probably not, unless you have already studied phonetics. The reason is that the little variations are automatic adjustments to other sounds preceding or following. We are no more conscious of making these adjustments than we are of using every individual muscle we employ in walking. Thus p_1 occurs only at the beginning of a syllable, p_2 only after s, p_3 only at the end of a word. Since one sound never poaches on another's territory, we say the three p's are in *complementary distribution*.

With b_1 of *bat*, the situation is altogether different. It occurs at the beginning of a syllable in exactly the same relative position as p_1 in *pat*. The two sounds, which are acoustically distinct, are not in complementary distribution but in *contrast*. We are conditioned to respond to their acoustic difference. For us, *pat* and *bat* are two different words, as the growing lump on the Martian's skull attests.

Since a voiceless p-sound can contrast with a voiced b-sound in at least some positions, linguists sum up the difference by saying that sounds which have some features in common and can contrast with other sounds in the same relative position belong to different classes called *phonemes*—first syllable like "phone." All the different varieties of p are members of $/p/$ phoneme, and all the b's belong to the $/b/$ phoneme. (The slants are the linguist's shorthand sign to show that he is talking about a phoneme, not one of its members. The members are written in square brackets: $[p_1]$, $[p_2]$, $[p_3]$.)

This phonemic contrast of voiced and voiceless sounds is a pervading feature of English. In the following pairs, the first word begins with a voiceless consonant, the second with a voiced consonant. Otherwise the initial consonants are exactly alike; try it and see:

    tame : dame
    came : game
     fat : vat
    Chet : jet
    sell : Zell

These remarks hold good for English, but not necessarily for other languages. The distinction between voiced and voiceless consonants which is so meaningful to us may not even be perceptible to speakers of other languages which do not have it. Leonard Bloomfield tells us that the Menomini Indians heard Scandinavian lumberjacks called "Swedes" and translated the word by *sayewenet,* "one who is sweet." In Menomini there is a phoneme that includes sounds like our *t* and *d.* Since these sounds never contrast, the Indians were not aware that to English-speakers *t* and *d* sound quite different. The Chinese, on the other hand, think that our p_1 and p_2 are quite different, because their own language has contrasts between sounds similar to them.

Unless we understand the phonemic structure of a language, we cannot describe it accurately. A good deal of the English grammatical system, for instance, depends on the contrast of voiced and voiceless consonants. The past-tense ending that we write -*ed* is pronounced like *t* after voiceless consonants. Compare *locked, slapped,* with *logged, rigged.* Now imagine a Menomini Indian without phonemic training trying to write a grammar of English for his people. He would make a pretty awful mess of the section on the past tense of verbs.

Another advantage of phonemics is that it cuts down the number of sound-features we need to talk about in a grammar to manageable size. Few languages use more than two or three dozen phonemes, but the number of positional variants may be several times as many. Another advantage is that a phonemic—not phonetic—transcription is the best basis for a system of writing. If we assign a letter to each phoneme, a native speaker will automatically put the variants in the right places. For languages that have never been written, phonemics speeds up the task of making illiterate people literate.

The phonemes of a language are the "bricks" it uses to build up words and sentences. The way these "bricks" are laid together is purely arbitrary. There is no fancy philosophical reason why three English phonemes in one order mean a fish, *shad,* and in reverse order a punctuation mark, *dash.* It just *is* that way, by social custom. But this combination of phonemes in an arbitrary order enables a language to say a good deal with a limited number of basic elements. The thirty phonemes of my Midwestern pronunciation are enough to build up all the words in Webster's dictionary.

If the inhabitants of other planets use speech-sounds as we do, their language should yield to analysis by our methods as easily as any Earth language. The same would be true if they use any combination of other types of visual, audible, or tactile signals. A language might be based on musical notes of varying pitch and duration. An idealist named Francois Sudré once invented a language, Solresol, whose entire vocabulary was formed by combining the names of the seven notes of the musical scale, *do, re, mi, fa, sol, la, ti.* Solresol, which the inventor hoped would become the international language, could be spoken, sung, or played on any instrument except a drum. The Mazateco Indians of southern Mexico actually have a "whistle speech" beside their spoken language. Telegraph and blinker codes and the hand alphabets of the deaf-and-dumb substitute electronic impulses or gestures for letters, which in turn represent phonemes more or less exactly. In one of Gilbert K. Chesterton's stories, a professor invented a language of dance steps.

Whatever the "bricks" of Martian language may be, it should be possible to discover them as we discover the sound-patterns of earthly speech. Finding the larger patterns—words and sentences—into which they fit will be the real drudgery. Some languages have grammatical patterns so different from those of European speech that it is quite impossible to draw up a list of word-for-word equivalents. English is a somewhat extreme example of a pattern that is fairly rare. It breaks down its ideas into short units of expression—words—that undergo little change in form to show their relationship. The order of words is much more significant in English than their endings, and changing the order changes the meaning. "The man kicked the boy" is quite different from "The boy kicked the man." Chinese, which has no word-endings at all, is another language where order is supremely important. On the other hand, Latin and many other languages show relationship by changing endings. The three words *Marcus Mariam amat* may be combined in six ways, but in any order they mean "Mark loves Mary." The only way to make the affection mutual is to change the form of two words to *Maria Marcum amat,* "Mary loves Mark."

In still other languages, ideas that we express by separate words are fused into one utterance. Nootka, an Indian language of Vancouver Island, has such a structure. According to the late Benjamin Lee Whorf, Nootka *tlihisma* means "the boat is grounded on the beach" and *lashtskiqistama,* "the boat is manned by picked men." In many languages, the parts of such expressions have no more independent existence than the *-ed* of English *kicked.*

Look at those Nootka examples again, because we are going to use them to expose the Telepathic Martian for the fraud he is. The English translations of the Nootka sentence-words are constructed much alike. Both are statements about a boat, and we could formulate them: "The boat is *x*-ed preposition *y.*" Our speech-habits lead us to think that the two situations they describe must be something alike because our verbal descriptions of them are alike. Nootka shows that it isn't necessarily so. The parts of the two utterances mean:

    tlih: "moving pointwise" hence, "traveling as in a canoe"
      is: "on the beach"
  lash: "pick, choose"

tskiq: "reminder, result"
 ista: "in a canoe as crew"
  ma: (third person singular ending)

So the first expression means more or less: "It is on the beach pointwise as an event of canoe motion" and the second, "They are in the boat as a crew of picked men" or "The boat has a crew of picked men." Neither of the Nootka expressions contains anything you can dissect out and say, "This means *boat.*" The canoe is referred to only by implication.

Now the Indian and the paleface see the same canoe on the same beach. Both could identify it and its picked crew from a photograph and agree that the snapshot recorded the same event. But the two observers, conditioned by totally different linguistic systems, make a totally different set of "abstracts" or "isolates" from the observed event. In our way of looking at it, we have to specify the boat, or canoe, as an explicit element. For the Indian, the fact that a boat is concerned is implied by his choice of certain other elements. *Tlih,* "moving pointwise," has to apply to a canoe, just as "rolled" in English has to apply to a round or cylindrical object. Yet the English and the Nootka formulations are equally clear to another speaker of the same language. To the Indian, our English way of lumping together events that seem totally distinct to him must be perplexing and illogical.

The seventeenth-century philosophers used to speculate about "general grammar." All languages—so they reasoned—are attempts to translate the "reality" of the universe; a single logic underlies all of them. Our increased knowledge makes it seem more likely that the opposite is true. Languages do not depend on universal logic; logic depends on the structure of languages. *For any human being, "reality" is the sum total of the abstracts his language can make from observed events.*

Here is an example, also from Whorf, of two very different ways of regarding time. All human beings are aware that some things happen later than others. European languages express the "passage of time" in terms similar to those used to describe extension in space. We cut time into units of days, months, and years as we cut length into feet, yards, and miles. Nothing seems more natural to us; we speak of "a long day" and "a long pole." But a language like Hopi shows the analogy is not universal. English says "ten days" and "ten houses," but we can never experience ten days at once as we can see ten houses at once. *Houses* is a real plural; *days* is an imaginary plural.

Now Hopi has no imaginary plurals. For a Hopi Indian, the idea "ten days is longer than nine days" becomes "the tenth day is later than the ninth." He does not conceive of "ten days" as a length of time—see our spatial metaphor again?—cut up into shorter "lengths" called days, but as the recurrence of a phenomenon in a cycle. Hence a Hopi cannot multiply

ten days by two to get twenty days, and the idea of describing time by words
that also refer to space or matter would hardly occur to him. In fact, the
idea of time as a continuous flow would be quite strange. No Hopi Einstein,
uninfluenced by European ideas, would ever evolve the notion of a four-
dimensional space-time continuum. His mathematical picture of the universe
would have no more in common with ours than a Greek painting has with a
canvas by Picasso.

Now, perhaps, you begin to understand why I want to feed the Telepathic Martian and his universal translating machine to the BEM's. If
human languages can be so different as English and Nootka, the grammatical
categories of Martian speech must be something completely outside our
experience. The Telepathic Martian's thoughtwaves would have to be so
powerful that they could make our brain cells aware of logical and grammatical relationships that have no equivalent whatever in our language.

Imagine, for the sake of the argument, that a telepathic English-speaking American and a telepathic Nootka-speaking American sit down for a
chat. The only thoughts they could have in common would be mental pictures. The English-speaker might be able to project an image of his family
and his bungalow, and the Nootka might succeed in making the white man
visualize his squaw and his canoe. But how does the white man translate into
pictures: "I paid off the mortgage on my house last year"? How do you
visualize a mortgage to an Indian who barely understands money? Is the
mortgage "on" the house the same way the shingles are on it? How do you
picture the past-tense notion in "paid" and the concept "last year"?

See what I mean? When the Martians land, we'll have to learn their
language in the same laborious way we have learned Nootka and Salish and
all the rest. Though there won't be any informants on their spaceship, we
can teach them a limited amount of English by the time-honored process of
ostensive definition. This means pointing at a chair and saying "chair," or
dropping a brick and remarking "I just dropped a brick." Simple verbs can
be acted out, like *eat, wash, shave, cut, scratch, draw, write*. For more complicated ideas, we might begin by verbalizing arithmetical or mathematical
statements, like "two and two make four" or "The square of the hypotenuse
of a right triangle is equal to the sum of the squares of the other two sides."
Presumably the Martians could teach us some of their language in the same
way. It would be slow, but not impossible.

If twentieth-century science can already suggest a way to talk to Martians, science-fiction writers have an obligation to base their fantasies of the
future on the knowledge of the present. Science fiction, to be enjoyed by an
intelligent reader, has to be plausible. Recently I read a story that was
spoiled for me because of one elementary error. An extraterrestrial character
in it spoke English with a phony foreign accent in which all the *t*'s became *s*'s.
Yet this outlander, who couldn't manage our *t*-sound, had one in his own
name! You don't have to be a Ph.D. in linguistics to see the howler.

In the best science fiction, the gadgets of the future are logical developments of those we already have. Good writers send their spacefarers to other planets in ways that are already known to be possible, and devise imaginary civilizations that follow logically from the conditions we know to exist on other worlds. I hope to live long enough to read stories that cope with the problem of interplanetary communication as realistically as we now do with interplanetary travel. As a first step, I move we bury the Telepathic Martian and his walkie-talkie interpreter under six feet of solid mars.

COMPREHENSION QUIZ

1. In describing encounters between Martians and speakers of English, writers of science fiction
   a. demonstrate a surprising familiarity with linguistic techniques.
   b. allow for the enormous cultural differences between Martians and ourselves.
   c. resort to variations of the telepathy theme.
   d. employ techniques used by American soldiers in World War Two.
2. An "informant" is, in linguistic terms,
   a. a native speaker of the language who has some other language in common with the linguist.
   b. a person trained in the language of another culture for purposes of espionage.
   c. a linguist who studies the dialects of primitive tribes.
   d. none of the above.
3. Which of the following statements is true?
   a. Sounds are usually the first units to be analyzed.
   b. Most languages have written alphabets.
   c. Most native speakers are aware of all the sounds they make.
   d. Philology is the study of the roots of words.
4. "Voiceless" consonants are those made
   a. in a low voice.
   b. with the vocal cords relaxed.
   c. by inhaling the breath.
   d. with the vocal cords tense and vibrating.
5. We cannot describe a language accurately unless we understand
   a. its history.
   b. its literature.
   c. its alphabet.
   d. its phonemic structure.
6. Which of the following statements is false?
   a. For any human being, "reality" is the sum total of the abstracts his language can make from observed events.
   b. Languages do not depend on universal logic; logic depends on the structure of languages.

c.   The grammatical categories of Martian speech must be something completely outside our experience.

d.   All languages are attempts to translate the "reality" of the universe; a single logic underlies all of them.

DISCUSSION QUESTIONS

1.   Does the English alphabet correspond to the number of phonemes there are in English? Consult the pronunciation key of a collegiate dictionary for examples of the many phonemes in our language.
2.   Shipman's essay was written in 1953. Are his comments in the sixth paragraph valid today?
3.   What are the characteristics of all languages, according to Shipman? Do they correspond with those listed by Hill (page 36)?
4.   The author cites wartime uses of linguistics. Can you think of any peacetime uses, as well?
5.   On the basis of Shipman's essay, what are the three characteristics you would look for if you were analyzing a strange language?

WRITING SUGGESTIONS

1.   What would be the advantages of a universal language? Is English adequate for such a task, or would an artificial language such as Esperanto be more practical?
2.   Write an imaginative essay describing the initial attempts of a Martian and an Earthman attempting to communicate with one another.

Transformational Grammar

by PAUL ROBERTS

. . . Immediate-constituent grammar was a product of linguistics—largely American linguistics—of the 1930s and 40s. It was most available to the general reader in a book called *The Structure of English* by Charles Carpenter Fries of the University of Michigan, published in 1952. The grammar was characterized by certain fundamental tenets which still characterize work in linguistics and presumably always will:

1. *That language is primarily speech and only secondarily writing.* This is not to degrade writing or to say that it is not properly the central concern of the school system. It is only to indicate the actual relationship of writing and speech. Writing is a symbolization of speech and not vice versa. We approach writing and its problems more easily if we understand what it is.

2. *That word classes (parts of speech and their subgroups) can be identified only by their distribution, their formal characteristics, and the like that they share.* Efforts to define them on the basis of meaning are doomed to failure. Such definitions turn out always to be either false or circular.

3. *That correctness in language is a relative matter, not an absolute one.* There are no *linguistic* considerations for preferring one variety of English to another, but only sociological ones. In the sight of both God and logic, "He brung it" is no better and no worse than "He flung it." But to say that correctness is a sociological matter is not to say that it is unimportant. Obviously children being educated must learn that "He brung it" is not what educated people say. . . .

Immediate-Constituent Grammar

Immediate-constituent analysis makes the basic assumption that sentences can be viewed as being made up of two-part constructions on a series of levels. A sentence consists of two main parts (two immediate constituents); each of those parts consists of two parts; each of those of two parts, until one gets down to the ultimate constituents, the smallest meaningful units in the sentence—i.e., words or morphemes. For many sentences this structure can be shown very easily:

```
        The little girls walked to the store.
        The little girls / walked to the store.
      The / little girls   walked / to the store.
   The   little / girls    walk   / ed   to / the store.
 The   little   girl / s    walk   ed   to   the / store.
```

Not only did this analysis provide interesting insights into the nature of the sentence, but it proved to have various useful practical applications in solving problems of modification and the like.

However, there were certain types of constructions to which immediate-constituent analysis proved difficult to apply. What are the immediate constituents, for example, of "Did the little girls walk to the store?" If it consists of two parts, what are they? The further one tried to push the concept of immediate constituents, the more one confronted problems to which only uncertain or arbitrary answers could be given.

This difficulty, along with many others that had troubled linguistics, was surmounted by the development of transformational analysis, which was certainly the most interesting advance of linguistic science in the 1950s. . . .

Transformational Grammar

Transformational analysis begins with the assumption that the sentences of English or of any language are of two basic types: *kernel sentences* and *transformed sentences*. The heart of the grammar is a relatively small set of kernel or basic-sentence types. These are basic in the sense that they cannot be derived from any sentences or sentence types underlying them. They are the foundation on which all else is built. All the rest of the language can be most economically described as a series of changes rung on the kernel sentences, as transformations of them.

Thus, for example, the sentence "John saw Bill" is a kernel sentence. The following are all transformations of it:

Did John see Bill?	Who saw Bill?
John didn't see Bill.	Whom did John see?
John did see Bill.	Where did John see Bill?
John saw Bill, didn't he?	John's seeing Bill
Bill was seen by John.	that John saw Bill
Bill wasn't seen by John.	for John to see Bill

And so on.

. . . What we might try to do in this place is to see some of the more general consequences of transformational analysis and some of its relationship both to immediate-constituent grammar and to prescientific grammar.

One thing that transformational analysis demonstrates is that immediate-constituent analysis applies wholly and simply *only to kernel sentences.* Indeed, transformational analysis provides, for the kernel, a much more powerful proof of immediate-constituent theory than was ever possible before. It is quite easy to show that any kernel sentence can be evolved by a simple forking process, each higher or more general unit splitting into two lower or more particular units until actual words are reached:

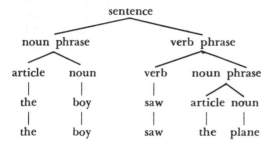

This process, refined to take into account the various types of predicates possible in English and to indicate the grammatical agreements necessary and the compatibility of various word groups, can display the whole kernel of English in a relatively small space. The entire kernel is produced by simple forking into immediate constituents.

But this system will not work to produce all of English sentences. One cannot produce "Did the boy see the plane?" for example, in this fashion. The easiest way to arrive at "Did the boy see the plane?" is to describe the changes made in the statement to produce the question. "Did the boy see the plane?" is a transformation of "The boy saw the plane." Like all transformations, it involves additions, the switching around of things, and the like. Its production requires rules or directions of a fundamentally different sort than the rules and directions which produce kernel sentences. Because it cannot be reached by a simple forking process, immediate-constituent analysis does not apply to it, or at least does not apply in the same simple way that it applies to the kernel.

It must be emphasized that transformational analysis is much more than simply a neater or more defensible way of describing language. It goes a long way to describe how languages are learned in the first place. It explains something of how virtually all human beings, even the dullest, manage to grasp and use at least one language. Language appears as a finite and comprehensible system. We somehow, as children, learn the kernel plus the rules for transforming the kernel into the various structures permitted by the language. This makes the possibilities infinite, and makes it possible for us to produce sentences which are completely grammatical but which we have never specifically learned. Given the kernel sentence "The boy saw the plane" and knowledge of how to make that kind of statement into a yes/no question, we can produce "Did the boy see the plane?" without ever having heard the question previously. Thus grasp of a finite system permits us to produce infinitely many grammatical sentences.

We are led from here to a much better understanding of the complex question of grammaticality. What do we mean when we say a sentence is or is not grammatical? We obviously can't mean that it makes sense. The sentence "Chicago is a dish of fried sofas" makes no sense, but we accept it as wholly grammatical. Neither do we mean that a grammatical sentence is one that occurs frequently in a language. "Chicago is a dish of fried sofas" has a zero frequency in English. It has, presumably, never occurred before. Yet it is quite as grammatical as, say, "Chicago is the hog butcher of the world."

Immediate-constituent grammar tends to make and describe an inventory. In theory, at least, it simply records the sentences—more precisely, a sample of the sentences—that have occurred in a language and then describes their features. Transformational analysis goes much further than this. It seeks to figure out the grammatical system of a language and then project it. Thus it not only recognizes sentences as grammatical because they have occurred but also undertakes to predict what sentences will be grammatical when and if they occur in the future.

Word Classes

The problem of grammaticality is closely connected with the problem of definition of word classes, something that has plagued students and teachers of grammar since at least the time of Aristotle. Grammars previous to transformational analysis have tended to begin with the smallest units and work up to the sentence unit. One begins by describing the sounds, then shows how these go together to make morphemes, how these make words, how the words are arranged in word classes, and how the word classes go together to form sentences. In this process, definition is crucial. One had to find some way of identifying each class and fencing it off from its neighbors. Both scientific and prescientific grammars spent much time in this pursuit with no really satisfactory conclusion. Thus we find in grammars of one sort or another the following definitions of *adjective:*

1. A word that modifies a noun. (Absurd. This would put *bad* and *bank* in the same class: "a bad robber," "a bank robber.")

2. A word that indicates a quality. (Absurd. This puts *courageous* and *courage* in the same class: "He's courageous," "He has courage.")

3. A word that patterns with *very*. (Absurd. This puts *old* and *much* in the same class: "very old," "very much.")

4. A word that takes the endings /ər/ and /əst/ (*-er, -est*). (Absurd. This puts *fine* and *tear* in the same class: *fine, finer, finest*— /fayn/, /faynər/, /faynəst/; *tear, terror, terraced*— /ter/, /terər/, /terəst/.)[1]

Thus, though some of the definitions proposed work pretty well in a general sort of way, all of them encounter absurdity when pushed to conclusion. Transformational analysis does not solve the problem by providing better definitions in the same sense of *definition*. Rather it avoids the problem altogether by beginning with the largest, most abstract level—sentence—and working down to the concrete items. Every higher-level concept is automatically defined by indicating what it consists of on the next level down. There is never any need to frame a definition of *sentence*, because the whole grammar is a definition of sentence. The whole grammar is a level-to-level description of the make-up of sentences in some particular language. . . .

We start with some such rule as this:

$$S \rightarrow NP + VP$$

S stands for *sentence*. The arrow means "rewrite as." Formulas of this type define the term to the left of the arrow by the terms given to the right of the arrow. The formula $S \rightarrow NP + VP$ means that any sentence consists of an *NP* and a *VP*, whatever they are. (*NP* stands for *noun phrase*, and *VP* for *verb phrase*, but the terms and symbols are arbitrary; we could just as well write $S \rightarrow X + Y$; the meaning of *NP* and *VP*, or *X* and *Y*, will be indicated in successive rules below.)

$$NP \rightarrow T + N$$
$$T \rightarrow \text{the, a}$$
$$N \rightarrow \text{man, boy, table} \ldots$$

Thus an *NP* is shown to consist of a *T* and an *N*, and *T* and *N* are defined, as we arrive at the concrete level, by showing the words, or examples of the words, that occur in these classes—articles and nouns. We would come at adjective in the *VP:*

$$VP \rightarrow Aux + V$$
$$Vi$$
$$V \rightarrow Vt + NP$$
$$Vs + Adj$$
$$Vi \rightarrow \text{occur, arrive} \ldots$$
$$Vt \rightarrow \text{see, find} \ldots$$
$$Vs \rightarrow \text{seem, appear} \ldots$$
$$Adj \rightarrow \text{old, fine} \ldots$$

[1] Chomsky's example.

The class *adjective,* when it appears, appears as a set of words. But it is a set of words in a complex, a piece in the pattern that goes to make up grammatical English sentences. Classroom experience shows that when word classes are approached in this direction, the problem of definition largely vanishes. It just isn't there any more. Teacher and student are relieved of the burden and enabled to proceed to examination of the actual characteristics of the sentences of English.[2]

A transformational grammar is intended to produce all grammatical sentences of a language and only those. That is, if you follow out all the possibilities given in the rules, you eventually can construct all the grammatical sentence types, but you will not produce any sentences that are not grammatical. This clearly necessitates the subdivision of word classes. If, for example, we have a sentence type "noun-verb-noun" and if the verb class contains all verbs with no differentiation, we would be able to derive not only the grammatical "The boy saw the table" but also "The boy occurred the table," which is not grammatical. So we must subdivide verb into transitive, intransitive, and various other subclasses, as traditional grammar has done, too.

We come eventually, however, to a point at which grammatical subclassification stops. This is the point where grammar leaves off and semantics begins. For example, there is no *grammatical* way to rule out the sentence "Chicago is a dish of fried sofas." There is no grammatical way to classify the words *Chicago, dish, fried,* and *sofa* to keep them from coming together in this order, though semantic groupings might be possible. This is why we say that the sentence, though semantically absurd, is perfectly grammatical. . . .

It would be a mistake to make too much of the newness of transformational analysis or to suggest that it is a rejection of the work in linguistics of the past or is unrelated to that work. Much of transformational analysis is implicit in immediate-constituent grammars—in such books as Fries's *The Structure of English* or Francis's *Structure of American English* or Lloyd and Warfel's *American English in Its Cultural Setting.* In all these works we find descriptions of basic-sentence types (something that looks very much like the kernel) and descriptions of the mechanism for expanding the basic sentences (something that looks very much like transformation). All these books share with transformational analysis the same kind of interest in speech, in form and function, in language as a signaling system. All look at the same language in the same objective way, working from the same data to very similar conclusions. . . .

Transformational analysis is more truly conceived as a going-on, as a

---

[2] These examples are not intended to display the actual content of a transformational grammar, either a scholarly or a textbook one. A full grammar would have to be considerably more elaborate in the area shown and would proceed differently in respect to some particulars. . . .

building on earlier work. Penetrating more profoundly into very general questions concerning the nature of language, of grammar, of linguistics, it gains a vantage point from which to discern more promising new routes to the solution of old problems. It explains conclusions which before were only intuited. Often, in working with immediate-constituent grammar, one felt that beyond certain points progress became steeply difficult. The description was right as far as it went, but one couldn't take it farther. In transformational analysis one doesn't have this sense of a blocking-off. One feels that the way is open from a rough and general sketch to a complete and satisfying description of English. If this also is illusory, the illusion is at least not easily dispelled. . . .

COMPREHENSION QUIZ

1. The most interesting advance of linguistic science in the 1950's was the development of
   a. morphemes.
   b. transformational analysis.
   c. immediate-constituent grammar.
   d. immediate-constituent analysis.
2. Basic to the grammar of transformational analysis is
   a. the kernel sentence.
   b. the transformed sentence.
   c. both (a) and (b).
   d. neither (a) nor (b).
3. Roberts contends that once we learn the kernel, plus the rules for transforming the kernel into the various structures permitted by the language, the possibilities for different sentences from that kernel
   a. are at least one thousand.
   b. are really limited by our various vocabularies.
   c. are infinite.
   d. are not much different from those under immediate-constituent grammar.
4. The definitions for classes of words, or parts of speech under traditional grammar can be shown to be absurd when pushed to a conclusion. Transformational analysis does not solve the problem of definition by providing better definitions, but rather by
   a. making pattern sentences.
   b. beginning with the smallest part of a sentence, the morpheme.
   c. avoiding definitions.
   d. being grammatically incorrect and semantically absurd.
5. Transformational analysis actually is
   a. a radical departure from earlier grammar.
   b. designed to replace older grammar.
   c. a building on earlier grammar, refined.

    d.   none of these.
6. One main problem with immediate-constituent analysis was that it applied wholly to
    a.   only the transformed sentences.
    b.   only kernel sentences.
    c.   only certain word classes.
    d.   all of these.

DISCUSSION QUESTIONS

1. Why does Roberts say that the problem of definition or word classes has plagued students and teachers since Aristotle?
2. What do you understand the terms "scientific" and "prescientific" grammar to mean as used in this essay?
3. Why is it necessary to subdivide word classes? Has this subdividing made learning transformational analysis easier or more complex?
4. What was Roberts' purpose in using the example by Chomsky in showing the absurdity of the traditional definition of adjectives?
5. Explain Roberts' meaning when he said, "The whole grammar [transformational] is a level-to-level description of the make-up of sentences in some particular language."
6. Would this type of grammatical approach work in a nonsubject-predicate form of language such as the Chinese have?

WRITING SUGGESTIONS

1. Write a 250 to 500 word explanation of the difference between immediate-constituent grammar and transformational analysis.
2. Defend the value of transformational grammar against a typical college freshman whose disclaimer is, "I had a hard time learning regular grammar and now you tell me I have to start all over!"

Generative Grammar: Toward Unification and Simplification

by OWEN THOMAS

The grammatical theories of Noam Chomsky, Morris Halle, and their followers are widely discussed but only rarely, if at all, are they applied to the teaching of English grammar in secondary schools. The reasons for this lack of application are many, varied, and complex, and even the primary reasons make an almost overwhelming list:

1. Chomsky, the generally acknowledged leader of the group, published the original statement of the theory less than ten years ago and, consequently, the development of the theory is still in its early stages.

2. The explications of his theory have been directed more toward linguists, psychologists, and mathematicians than toward teachers of English grammar.

3. The criticisms of his theory by other linguists have generated more heat than light, and most secondary school teachers—who, after all, neither are nor need be linguists—have prudently rejected the opportunity to be burned.

4. The secondary school teacher, even if he should be curious, has no effective way of satisfying his curiosity since, almost without exception (according to the two-score catalogues I checked), departments of English offer no courses in comparative grammar.

Unfortunately, these reasons (and I have idealistically ignored the inertia of school boards and the conservatism of traditionally trained parents) have caused many teachers of English to assume that generative grammar—though perhaps "correct" in some mathematical sense—is pedagogically un-

From Owen Thomas, "Generative Grammar: Toward Unification and Simplification," *English Journal*, February, 1962. Reprinted with the permission of the National Council of Teachers of English and Owen Thomas.

adaptable to the needs of a secondary school curriculum.[1] Such an assumption, I feel, is false.

This personal feeling is based largely upon the response to a course, "English Grammar for Teachers," that I conducted in the summer of 1961 at Indiana University. The thirty students in the class were of widely varying backgrounds and experience. Some had just completed their second year of college work; others had been teaching for more than twenty years. All of them, however, although they didn't know it until the end of the eight-week session, were subjects in an experiment that the liberal administration of Indiana University permitted me to conduct. Briefly, and this is something of an over-simplification, we hoped to answer one question: what do secondary school teachers—not professional linguists—think of generative grammar?

The answer proved the validity of the question. Without exception, the students were convinced that certain deductions from the theories of Chomsky could be applied systematically to the teaching of grammar, not only in the secondary school but with equal effectiveness in the elementary school. . . .

What, then, is the theory? And how can his theory be applied to the teaching of grammar? Before answering these questions, we must consider his definition of grammar: a grammar is a device for generating the sentences of a language. Thus (to belabor the point), if a student understands the grammar of a language, he can construct grammatically correct sentences in that language. No grammar, however, can tell a student which of two grammatically correct sentences is *stylistically* better. Such judgments are outside the realm of grammar; they are solely matters of taste and must be taught accordingly.

"Kernel" Sentences

After having defined the limits of his theory, Chomsky introduces a basic concept: that of a group of "kernel" sentences. A kernel sentence is "simple, active, declarative," and Chomsky feels that "all other sentences" are derived from kernel sentences by means of "transformations." Roughly, a "transformation" is a rule that either introduces new elements into kernel sentences (e.g., adjectives, negatives), or rearranges the elements of a kernel sentence (e.g., to produce an interrogative sentence), or both (e.g., to produce a passive sentence). Chomsky implies, therefore, that passive, interrogative, and negative sentences, and sentences containing, for example, adjectives,

---

[1] The terms "transformational grammar" and "generative grammar" are sometimes used interchangeably. The latter term, however, seems to be supplanting the former. This trend was particularly noticeable at the recent (summer, 1961) meeting of the Commission on English, which debated some of the questions considered in this article.

adverbs, and conjunctions, are all more complex or "sophisticated" than kernel sentences.

Not surprisingly, Chomsky's "kernel sentence" bears a strong resemblance to the simple "subject-verb-complement" sentence of traditional grammar. He states that a kernel sentence is composed of a "noun phrase plus a verb phrase." A "noun phrase" (symbol: NP) consists simply of an article (T) plus a noun (N), and the presence of the article is optional.[2] A "verb phrase" (VP) consists of an auxiliary (Aux) plus a main verb (V) plus a noun phrase (and this last "noun phrase" is, of course, similar to the traditional "complement"); the noun phrase contained within the verb phrase is also optional. This may seem confusing at first reading, but the symbolic representation is straightforward and easy to understand:[3]

Sentence → NP + VP (where the arrow means "rewrite," i.e., "rewrite
   Sentence as NP plus VP")
NP → T + N
VP → Aux + V + NP

Thus, the following are "noun phrases":

John, the boy, a dog, the men

And the following are "verb phrases":

reads, eats the apple, may bury a bone, have bought the farm

Therefore, the following are "kernel sentences":

John reads.
The boy eats the apple.
A dog may bury a bone.
The men have bought the farm.

Chomsky thus simplifies the descriptions of English (such as that from Fries, quoted above) by limiting these descriptions to a relatively small number of simple sentences. All other sentences are "generated from" (i.e., built upon) these kernel sentences by applying certain constant and *invariable* transformations, and the constancy of the transformation is, for most teachers of English, a major feature of Chomsky's theory.

Thus, given a kernel sentence (e.g., "The men have bought the farm"), we may generate a passive sentence ("The farm has been bought by the men"), a negative sentence ("The men haven't bought the farm"), a "yes-or-no" interrogative sentence ("Have the men bought the farm?"), two "wh-"

---

[2] More properly, I feel, the "article" should be called a "determiner" according to a definition such as that of Sledd in *A Short Introduction to English Grammar*, p. 207.

[3] This is the simplest possible presentation. Copyright laws being what they are, we cannot duplicate the presentation, and it must suffice to say that those rules, for example, pertaining to "noun phrase singular" (NP) are equally explicit, self-consistent, and easy to understand.

interrogative sentences ("What have the men bought?" and "Who has bought the farm?"), and even combinations of these sentences (e.g., a negative-passive: "The farm hasn't been bought by the men"). Furthermore, with still other transformations we may introduce adverbs, adjectives, and prepositional phrases into any or all of these sentences ("Who has finally bought the old farm on the hill?").[4]

These transformations, it is worth repeating, are invariable. Given a kernel sentence of a particular form (and Chomsky defines the required form precisely), then any and all related non-kernel sentences can be generated by applying the appropriate (and quite simple) transformation. One specific example will serve to illustrate these remarks. The "passive transformation" may be given in the following form:

> To derive a passive sentence, we first need a kernel "string" containing the following elements: a noun phrase (NP), an auxiliary (Aux), a verb (V), and a second noun phrase (NP). These might be represented as follows:
>
> $[NP_1] + [Aux] + [V] + [NP_2]$
>
> To transform this string into a "passive string," the four basic elements are rearranged and three other elements are (invariably) added, as follows:
>
> $[NP_2] + [Aux] + be + en + [V] + by + [NP_1]$
>
> The "en" which is added is the so-called "past participle morpheme."
>
> Finally, the resultant string is converted into an English sentence by inserting appropriate parts of speech into the string.
>
> Thus, given the kernel sentence:
>
> [The man] + [has] + [eaten] + [the apple]
>
> we may apply the transformation to produce:
>
> [The apple] + has + be + en + [eaten] + by + [the man]
>
> This, of course, reduces to: "The apple has been eaten by the man."[5]

Such is the nature of Chomsky's major contribution toward the simplification of grammar. In addition, he makes another quite important contribution: he divides all of grammar into three parts. The first part presents

[4] There is quite obviously a relationship between Chomsky's kernel sentences and simple traditional diagraming, and even between those transformations which add adjectives and phrases to the kernel and those diagrams which indicate the subordinate position of adjectives and phrases. Transformations, however, indicate the exact nature of subordination; more importantly, they indicate the exact nature of the relationship between a kernel sentence and the associated passive, negative, and interrogative sentences.

[5] For purposes of illustration, the transformation, as given, is somewhat simplified as the reader may see for himself by substituting, for example, a plural subject or object into the kernel. Such refinements, however, are easily and systematically handled through certain so-called "obligatory" transformations. The principle, at any rate, is invariable.

those rules that pertain to kernel sentences ("phrase structure"), and here his theory will certainly draw upon the work of the structuralists. The second part presents rules that generate non-kernel sentences ("transformational structure"). And the third part presents the rules that are necessary to account for such irregular forms as "child, children" and "buy, bought" ("morphological structure"), and this part of his theory will probably draw upon the work of the historical grammarians (e.g., Jespersen).

The theory, then, is not too difficult for an adult to understand. And most persons acquainted with Chomsky's work, including the members of my class, feel that his theories provide the only logical explanation currently available for the intuitive sense which most native speakers have of a relationship between active and passive, or positive and negative, or declarative and interrogative sentences. But we may legitimately ask whether transformations can be taught to secondary school pupils. This is essentially the same question we asked above: "how can Chomsky's theory be applied to the teaching of grammar?" To answer this question completely would be to write a text, or at least a syllabus, for a course on methods of teaching grammar. Obviously, nothing of that sort is being attempted here. But during the final meetings of my class, we reached agreement on a number of points that will probably be included in any text that is written.

Application to Sentence Structure

We agreed, for example, that the study of grammar has one primary function: to enable a student to construct grammatically correct sentences. The most significant advance that an understanding of Chomsky's theory permits is the organization of this study according to increasing ("graduated") levels of sophistication in sentence construction. Thus, we should first teach the use of the kernel sentence (terminology is unimportant and should be subordinate to an understanding of the kernel form, i.e., to an understanding of a sentence that is "simple, declarative, active, with no complex verb or noun phrases"). The following sentences are typical kernel sentences:

1. The boy hit the ball.
2. The girl bought the dress.
3. The teacher ate the apple.
4. John loves Mary.

Conversely, the following sentences are *not* kernel sentences:

5. The ball was hit by the boy.
6. The girl didn't buy the dress.
7. Did the teacher eat an apple?
8. Who loves Mary?

Secondary school pupils, the class agreed, could construct kernel sentences of their own. Next they could be taught to construct passive sentences from their kernels; then, negative sentences, "yes-or-no" interrogative sentences, and "wh-" interrogative sentences. At each step, the teacher can point out the recurring elements of the resultant sentences (i.e., the underlying form). The repetition would familiarize the student—unconsciously, perhaps, but nonetheless effectively—with the basic form, and the ordering of the exercises—in gradually increasing levels of complexity—would enable the student to build his confidence systematically.

Students may then combine their sentences, for example, the passive and the negative (and the teacher may note that the passive is formed before the negative is added). After (and sometimes during) exercises of this type, the teacher may introduce adjectives, adverbs, and prepositional phrases, noting that any of these may appear in any sentence form.[6]

Of course, in any presentation, certain definitions are required, but the definitions should be introduced only when they are necessary, that is, only when a student needs a "label" to discuss the elements he is, in fact, using. Thus, "noun" and "verb" should be defined when the students are being taught the form of the kernel sentence. (I feel Sledd's definitions are quite appropriate.) In this way, those parts of speech that are simplest to define (and for the student to understand) are taught first, and the hard-to-define (and to understand) parts of speech, such as the "preposition" and the "conjunction," are postponed until the student has developed familiarity and confidence with the simpler and more important forms.

There are still other benefits to be derived from an understanding of Chomsky's theories. Transformations *per se*, as we have noted, probably cannot be taught to pre-college students; but from any transformation a teacher can deduce several invariable rules. For example, from the passive transformation we can deduce such rules as the following (and the list is by no means exhaustive):

1. There can be no passive voice unless a kernel sentence contains a subject and its object.
2. There can be no passive voice without an auxiliary verb or verbs. (If there is only one auxiliary, it must be a form of *to be*.)
3. The subject of the kernel sentence invariably follows the verb in the related passive sentence and is invariably introduced with the word "by."
4. The main verb in a passive sentence is invariably in the past participial form.

Similar rules, it is worth repeating, can be derived from any transformation, and the form of the transformation guarantees that there are no exceptions to these rules.

---

[6] A method such as that advocated by D. M. Wolfe ("Grammatical Autobiography," *English Journal*, XLIX, 1 [January 1960], pp. 16–21) would be quite suitable for this kind of study.

In brief, then, Chomsky's theories are not difficult to understand. They are, in fact, a means of systematizing the almost countless "rules" of both traditional and structural grammarians. And most importantly, an understanding of Chomsky's theories permits a teacher to select and arrange grammatical elements in the most logical order and to build effectively upon preceding material. As teachers, we can hardly ask more of any theory.

COMPREHENSION QUIZ

1. The explication or detailed descriptions of Chomsky's theory have been directed principally toward all of the following except
    a. linguists.
    b. English grammar instructors.
    c. psychologists.
    d. mathematicians.
2. According to the Thomas essay, a device for generating the sentences of a language is called
    a. a morpheme.
    b. a kernel sentence.
    c. a grammar.
    d. a transformation.
3. The kernel sentence is most similar to which of these traditional grammar sentences?
    a. The subject-verb.
    b. The verb-subject.
    c. The subject-verb-indirect object.
    d. The subject-verb-complement.
4. The symbolic representation for "John eats the apple" would be shown as
    a. $NP \rightarrow T + N$.
    b. $VP \rightarrow Aux + V \cdot NP$.
    c. sentence $\rightarrow NP + VP$.
    d. sentence $\rightarrow VP + NP$.
5. Chomsky divides all of grammar into
    a. two parts.
    b. three parts.
    c. eight parts.
    d. an infinite number of parts.
6. Which of the following is not correctly called a "kernel sentence?"
    a. Who eats candy?
    b. Phil slapped a single.
    c. Bill hates work.
    d. The ladies have sold the ice cream.
7. According to this essay, Chomsky's theories
    a. are not difficult to understand.
    b. are a means of systematizing the myriad rules in grammar.

    c. both (a) and (b).

    d. neither (a) nor (b).

8. In generative grammar, a rule that introduces new elements into the "kernel" or rearranges the elements of the kernel is called a

    a. determiner.

    b. morphological structure.

    c. transformation.

    d. all of these.

DISCUSSION QUESTIONS

1. What is meant by a "kernel string"? What is the difference between it and a kernel sentence?

2. Do you agree with Thomas that generative grammar is adaptable to the needs of the secondary school curriculum?

3. Has there been any change in the availability of courses in comparative grammar since this article was written in 1962?

4. What differences are there, if any, between transformational grammar and generative grammar?

5. What are Chomsky's three parts or divisions for all grammar?

6. What is the logical explanation for the intuitive sense which most native speakers have?

7. Thomas gives a list of four rules which he deduced from the passive transformation. He says the list is "by no means exhaustive." Can you deduce two additional rules to add to the four Thomas already has?

WRITING SUGGESTIONS

1. Explain in detail the concepts of morphological structure, which are briefly mentioned in this article.

2. Make a biographical sketch of Noam Chomsky, including a listing of his writings.

3. List the pro and con arguments, as you see them, for introducing transformational-generative grammar into the secondary schools.

Recommended Readings to Part VI

Bach, Emmon. *An Introduction to Transformational Grammars*. New York: Holt, Rinehart and Winston, 1964.

Chomsky, Noam. *Syntactic Structures*. The Hague: Mouton, 1957.

Fodor, Jerry A., and Jerrold J. Katz (eds.). *The Structure of Language*. Englewood Cliffs, N.J.: Prentice-Hall, 1964.

Francis, W. Nelson. *The Structure of American English*. New York: Ronald Press, 1958.

Fries, Charles C. *The Structure of English*. New York: Harcourt, Brace & World, 1952.

Gleason, II. A. *An Introduction to Descriptive Linguistics*, rev. ed. New York: Holt, Rinehart and Winston, 1961.

Jespersen, Otto. *Growth and Structure of the English Language*. Garden City, N.Y.: Doubleday, 1955.

Roberts, Paul. *English Sentences*. New York: Harcourt, Brace & World, 1962.

Whitehall, Harold. *Structural Essentials of English*. New York: Harcourt, Brace & World, 1956.

Word Lore VII

Trials
of a Word-Watcher

by CHARLTON OGBURN, JR.

Recently I was at a party at which one of the guests spoke of a collision of airplanes in mid air. "Mid air," another of the guests—a magazine editor —repeated with a smile. "Airplanes always collide in *mid* air. One wonders where else in the air they could collide." His manner was amused, off-hand.[1] But I did not miss the working of his jaw-muscles, the clenching of his fists. Here, confronted by a pet abomination, was a fellow-martyr to that condition known by the inadequate and not very descriptive term of *purism,* defined by the *Oxford English Dictionary* as "scrupulous or exaggerated observance of, or insistence upon, purity or correctness, esp. in language or style."

Until that moment I had employed the expression *mid air* with contentment and assurance. I now felt that all my life my intelligence had been insulted by it. I experienced the exhilaration of an obsessive collector who unexpectedly acquires a prize. At the same time, my heart sank as I recognized that I had taken on another distraction, an increment to a burden under which I was already staggering. A sultan who has added a notable beauty to a harem already ruinous in its demands upon him would know what I mean.

Purism is like alcoholism or drug-addiction. Once it takes hold, the victim's most heroic efforts of will to combat it are likely to prove inadequate. I had found this out during the years I spent in the government. I was supposed to be an official charged (in government terminology) with substantive responsibilities. Yet all the while, possibly because of the kind

[1] The author's system of hyphenation has been followed faithfully throughout this article.

of thing I had to spend my time reading, I found myself falling ever more
deeply under the sway of an ever-proliferating array of bugaboos of syntax
and vocabulary and becoming a mere compulsive proof-reader. "Cannot help
but believe new regime certain grow disenchanted its present internatl
assocs," I would read in a telegram from an overseas post, but instead of
considering whether my superiors should not be "alerted" (ugh!) to the
opportunities such a development would open for the U. S., I would be sent
off on a tangent by the reporting officer's English. "It is not enough that he
cannot but believe," I would mutter. "It is not enough that he cannot help
believing. Nothing will do but that he *cannot help but* believe!"

One does not, of course, have to be a fetishist about words to be put off
by the flatulent jargon endemic in bureaucracies. ("Prior to implementation
of approved directives, all concerned agencies will consult as to appropriate
instrumentalities.") But worse than that, to one who suffers from morbid
inflammation of the word-consciousness, are the affronts to grammar habitually employed in the government with an air of professionalism—such as,
for example, "hopefully" used to mean "I hope" or "it is to be hoped." You
read, "Hopefully, the government of X will see the error of its present course
in time," and your morning is ruined. You start imagining where the precedent could lead: "Fearfully, the government of X will not see its error in
time. . . . Expectfully, the U. S. will have to bail it out."

Then there is that "effective immediately" routine, with which notices
begin. I used to have a day-dream in which I got back at my superiors who,
among their other trying ways, permitted this travesty of English. In it, I
would appear before them to reply to the charge of having failed to comply
with an order stating, for example, *Effective immediately, all chairmen of
inter-agency committees will keep this office informed of all meetings held
and of the action taken.* "I am not," I would say with devastating tren-
chancy, "an immediately effective chairman."

While my colleagues were striving to forge new links with our partners
in the Free World (working out "agreed positions" to be set forth in "agreed
texts"—as if you *could* agree a position or a text!) I was fighting the battle
of "presently." The government had been swept by a vogue for this word.
"Now" was becoming almost as rare in official disseminations as "eftsoons."
In a carefully controlled voice, I would explain in a drafting committee, as
if I had not done so in a score of others, that "presently" did not mean "at
present." It meant "in the immediate future." Not only were the results of
my efforts disappointing, to say the least, but one of my associates whom
I *had* impressed came to me one day with an aggrieved air and a tale of
having lost a dollar by betting that "presently" had just the sense I had
said only to find that "at present" loomed as large as any other among the
meanings given in his dictionary. He had, if you please, looked it up in
Webster's! I had patiently to explain that *Webster's* would accept any
usage if enough word-slingers gave it currency.

Preserved from Vainglory

The pathological word-watcher, it should be made clear, is no more apt to rejoice in his fixation than is the book-keeper who cannot see a row of figures on a license-plate or railroad-car without adding them up. He can hardly help realizing that just as a philatelist who devotes his life to Mauritian issues is likely to become fairly expert in his field, so is a person who gives the better part of his attention to the pitfalls of English—even if his family goes in want, as it is apt to. Actually, if he is like me—I being one who as a child was sent to progressive schools, where I was taught no formal grammar—he may be unable to parse "The cat sat on the mat" or guess what is being talked about when hanging participles or gerunds are brought up. He may, like me, be unable to spell and have to depend upon his wife to catch mistakes in what he writes, usually the same ones over and over again. (Says mine, "Absense isn't going to make *my* heart grow fonder until you learn that it ends with an 's-e,' not a 'c-e.' "[2] The word-watcher is also preserved from vainglory by the lack of conspicuous popular demand for what he has to offer.

"Will I type this up in triplicate?" my secretary used to ask. She was an Irish-American lass from New Hampshire. "I don't know," I would reply. "Shall you?" Her eyes would travel to the bronze paper-cutter on my desk. Before she came finally to sink it in my neck, however, she married a military attaché on home leave from Helsinki and that was the last I saw of her.

It is difficult to administer correctives in such a way as to make them appreciated; that is the point. I have heard purists resort to the device of repeating the offender's erring statement in correct form, reflectively, as if unaware that they had altered the expression but trusting him to benefit from the example. Thus, when he hears the sentence, "If the information would leak out we'd be in trouble," the purist will, after thinking it over, muse, "Umm. Yes. If it should leak out, that would be too bad." But possibly because a slight stress on the *should* is almost unavoidable, this may provoke the testy retort, "What's the matter, did I say something wrong again?"

An alternative method is for the purist to pretend to be a partner of the offender's in fallibility and interestedly speculate upon the unseemly locution as upon one he himself might well have employed. "Whether we go or not depends upon the weather," he repeats with a faint smile at the ceiling, weighing the words. "Curious, isn't it, how we put in that 'or not' after 'whether' even when it is subsumed under the word 'whether' itself; that is to say [*chuckle*], regardless of *whether or not* it is needed." I have never heard anyone get away with this.

[2] She says I have got it wrong again. It seems only honest for me to leave it as it is, however.—*C. O., Jr.*

I do not mean to imply that the purist is motivated primarily by the desire for gratitude in setting others to rights. In the case of a reiterated corruption of the language it is a matter of self-preservation. I discovered the limits of what one can take in connection with the policy papers put out by the National Security Council, the nation's supreme policy-making body in foreign affairs. For years I steeled myself to the notation at the head of these papers. It read, "The President approves NSC 168 [or whatever] and directs its implementation." But human nerves can bear just so much. In a meeting with the Secretary of the Council something inside me finally snapped. "The President directs its implementation, you say? He does nothing of the kind!" I cried "His subordinates do that!" My voice was shrill. "What you mean is, 'The President directs that it be implemented.' Good God, man! What . . . what . . ." I threw up my hands. It was held that the prolonged crisis in Southeast Asia had been too much for me.

Why does anyone fall into this "exaggerated observance of . . . correctness, esp. in language or style"? Psychologists tell us that excessive concern with detail is a form of escapism originating in a basic sense of insecurity. They are no doubt right. So are most human pursuits—coin-collecting, cigarette-smoking, reading, drinking, big-game-hunting, girl-chasing, money-making, probably even psychology-studying. Anyone who has not got a basic sense of insecurity and an over-riding desire to escape has fewer brains than a rabbit. As for why the compulsion leads in some persons to purism instead of to some less generally irritating and more socially acceptable extravagance, my guess is that it is a matter of the influences one comes under in one's formative years.

One of my early memories is of my grandfather's refusing to attend the local Methodist church any longer because of the minister's abuse of English. " '*That* much,' '*that* important,' " he scoffed. "Are we to have 'that' foisted upon us as an adverb? Is the minister's time *that* important that he cannot say 'as important as that'?" To have moved my grandparent—otherwise the gentlest, most forbearing of men—to such impatience, the offense, I judged, must have been heinous. Indeed, I conceived the notion at an early age that violations of the canons of English were almost as reprehensible as violations of the moral code, and that there were canons to right of us, canons to left of us, canons in front of us.

That does not mean I learned easily. I can still hear my father saying, time after time, "Not different *than*. Different *from*." And, "Not *in back of*. *Back of*, or *behind*." It must have taken years for such delinquencies to be extirpated from my juvenile prattle, with my mother working at it as conscientiously as my father. I remember from boyhood the astonishment in the face of a friend of mine when, upon my asking if I had to "stay home," my mother replied that I could not stay home now or ever. "Home is not an adverb. You stay *at* home." Her condemnation of the use of "place" for "where" in "eat some place" or "going some place" was (and still is) so unsparing—how can you eat a place or go a place?—that I cannot meet with the usage without a sense of imminent disaster, and I can never speak of church-goers or theater-goers without a twinge of conscience. Can you go a church? Should there not be a "to" in there somewhere? To-church-goers? Go-to-churchers?

I must be at least as hard on my children as my parents were on me. I sometimes wonder that they have not given up talking altogether, for they seldom get three sentences out consecutively without being brought up short by their mother or father. (They catch it from both sides, for the wife of a purist is either another purist or a good prospect for a divorce-lawyer.)

"Not 'I did it already.' Say, 'I've already done it.' "

"Not '*Robin* Hood.' 'Robin *Hood.*' You wouldn't say '*John* Smith.' "

"Not 'They're both alike.' 'They're alike.' It wouldn't be possible for just one of them to be alike."

"Not 'The Matthews.' 'The Matthewses.' . . . Yes, I know they've got 'The Matthews' on their mailbox. It's still wrong. One Matthews, two Matthewses."

"Not 'I feel badly.' That would mean 'that your sense of feeling is impaired. Say, 'I feel bad.' "

" 'Escapers,' not 'escapees.' . . . I don't care what they say in school or in the newspapers. 'Employees' are persons who are employed. 'Payees' are persons who are paid. 'Escapees' would be persons who are escaped—the guards, that is."

I Just Know It—That's All

The two girls get their own back, however. Not only do I hear them correcting their friends, but they correct me.

"Why do you say 'idear' and 'Canader'?" one of the sprites asks.

"Well, it's this way," I explain. "New Englanders and Southerners, like President Kennedy and your father—and like the English—don't sound *r*'s except when they precede vowels. We say . . . let's see . . . 'Baltimoah, Maryland,' But 'Baltimo*rr r*and Ohio.' We separate the vowel sounds by sounding the *r*. So when we get two vowel sounds in succession, one at the end of one word, one at the beginning of the next, we tend to put in an *r* from force of habit, even when it doesn't belong there. We say 'the ide*ah* wasn't mine,' but then we're apt to say 'the ide*arr* is a good one.' Same with Canada. 'Canad*ah* goose' but 'Canad*arr* ale.' "

"But it's wrong, isn't it?"

"You could say it's colloquial."

"Wrong."

"Well, yes."

The girls are just beginning to learn that relying on my authority has its risks. For example, I know that "Do you have?" means "Do you ordinarily have?" or "Do you make a practice of having?" whereas "Have you?" or "Have you got?" means "Are you in possession of the object at present?" I know it is incorrect to say, "Do you have a pencil with you?" It is just as incorrect as it would be to say, "Have you [or have you got] a good time in the country?" But I cannot cite any rules of syntax that make this so. I just know it, that's all. I know by the way it sounds and because I've had it on good authority. To insist upon what you know is right, tolerating no divergent opinion, when you cannot say why it is right, takes character. But it does not always win arguments.

There is the further complicating fact that, like any confirmed word-watcher, I supplement the accepted rules of English with others of my own devising. Or, as I prefer to think of it, I discover hitherto unformulated principles. One of these is my law of A-or-An-Before-H. This law states that "a" shall be used before a word beginning with "h" if the accent is on the first syllable of that word (provided the "h" is sounded) but that if the accent is on a subsequent syllable, "an" shall be used. Thus we are to speak of *a* history but *an* historical novel, *a* hexagon, but *an* hexagonal figure. Neat, isn't it? I should add that the law permits no exception. True, "an hotel" may sound a little affected or precious, but a people which has the Saviour in the Sermon on the Mount speaking an "an hill" (the translators of the King James Bible having of course lacked the benefit of my law) should certainly have the resolution to say "an hotel" in a clear, unfaltering voice. I demand nothing less from my offspring—who, by the way, regard the word "hotel" as a queer derivative of "motel"—and the fact that nobody but me recognizes my law does not move me.

The Hyphen, Alas!

It is the misfortune of the purist to appear arrogant when all he is doing is being right. Perhaps much may be forgiven him in recognition of his being committed to a losing cause. Poor sod, as the British would say, he is driven on the one hand to pursue a perfection perhaps unattainable this side of the grave (at least the ugly suspicion insinuates itself that the only purity of speech is to be found in total silence, of which language is in its entirety a corruption) and on the other to cling to positions that irresistibly are eroded away beneath him; for, like the noblest headlands, destined to be undermined by the remorseless seas, it is the fate of language to deteriorate. (I am aware that some would say evolve.) I, for example, have given the best years of my life to the hyphen—and to what end?

The hyphen is being done away with—indefensibly, ruthlessly, as if a conspiracy had been formed against it. And we must understand that if the hyphen goes, so does the very conception of the structure of English.

The hyphen permits us to shorten "a railroad operated by the state" to "a state-operated railroad." But in National Intelligence Estimates costing tens of thousands of dollars each we may read "a state operated railroad" or even "a state owned and operated railroad"—a phrase in which the parts of speech are impossible to identify and one devoid of meaning. We may read of "Western oriented regimes," which can mean only Western regimes facing east, and of "white collar workers," which could mean either workers with white collars or white men who work on collars.

Writers who should know better do not show it. John Hersey gives us *The Child Buyer,* apparently believing that a child buyer is one who buys children, whereas in fact it is a child who buys. And Joseph W. Alsop in his book *From the Silent Earth* (his exciting book, I must admit) may think he is describing a helmet encrusted with boar's tusks in his phrase "a boar's tusk-encrusted helmet" but what he is actually describing is a tusk-encrusted helmet belonging to a boar. (He did use one hyphen, though.)

Where is this leading? It has already led, as I can report from my own observation, to a headline reading "Child Chasing Fox Found Rabid" and to an advertisement suggesting "For the pet lover on your Christmas list, a perfect little four-poster bed for the corner of the living room."

One would expect the nation to draw back from the brink while there is time, but I am pessimistic. The hyphen is disappearing, and neither the purist's outrage nor his lamentations will save it, I fear, or retard the degeneration of the English language into mouthfuls of words indiscriminately spewed forth. He pounds the table till his wattles shake, and it does no good.

And yet the purist—even such as I—has his vindications. Do you know why Mariner I, the "probe" aimed at Mars, went off course into oblivion? I ask you, do you know? Because, in all the complicated instructions fed into its guidance system, one hyphen was inadvertently omitted. One tiny hyphen that requires you only to extend your little finger to the upper right-hand corner of the keyboard. It cost the American people two million bucks.

And if you ask me, it served them damned well right.

COMPREHENSION QUIZ

1. Ogburn would be among those who say that language, over the years is
   a. changing.
   b. evolving.
   c. receding.
   d. deteriorating.
2. The author implies that the principal criterion for acceptance of a definition in Webster's Dictionary is
   a. actual meaning.

    b.   currency of usage.
    c.   original meaning.
    d.   none of these
3. Ogburn admits that his "exaggerated observance of correctness, especially in language" may be
    a.   a form of hostility.
    b.   a carryover from his childhood.
    c.   a form of escapism.
    d.   an attempt at rationalizing his lack of effort.
4. To Ogburn, violations of the canons of English are almost as reprehensible as
    a.   not going to church.
    b.   violations of conscience.
    c.   violations of the moral code.
    d.   ignorance of one's own language.

DISCUSSION QUESTIONS

1. What does Ogburn mean by "the flatulent jargon endemic in bureaucracies"?
2. Exactly what is grammatically objectionable with using words such as "hopefully, fearfully, expectfully, etc." mentioned disdainfully by Ogburn in the first section of his essay?
3. What is the intended effect of Ogburn's use of the word "eftsoons"? Does he succeed?
4. What comments do you imagine Margaret M. Bryant would have on this essay, in view of her position concerning the use of words, as set forth in the essay, "Usage" which appears in this text?
5. Notice Ogburn's use of "canons" in the sentence, "Indeed, I conceived the notion at an early age . . ." In what two senses does he use this word?
6. What is the tone of this essay? How serious does Ogburn want to be taken when he says that "language is in its entirety a corruption of total silence"?
7. Consult a handbook of English usage and discuss the correct usage of the hyphen. What examples of the misuse of hyphens can you locate?
8. Do you agree with the writer when he says that it is incorrect to say "Do you have a pencil?"

WRITING SUGGESTIONS

1. Write a directive in the style of bureaucratic government. Then rewrite it as Ogburn would prefer.
2. Write a tongue-in-cheek sort of reply to Ogburn, scolding him for his outdated stubbornness.
3. The writer speaks of "the canons of English." Write a paper explaining what they are and how they are established.

Milk, Beards, Thongs, and the Spiral Nebulae

by BERGEN EVANS

In World War II, in an experiment in secret communication that would have delighted James Bond, the Navy placed Navajo Indians on various ships and simply had them talk to each other in Navajo.

The assumption that an intimate knowledge of idiomatic Navajo would be rare among Japanese naval officers was probably well founded. But since a discussion of wickiups or wampum would have been of little value to the Navy, it must also have been assumed that an Old Stone Age language of desert nomads could be adapted and expanded to deal with the technicalities and complexities of modern naval warfare, with navigation, degaussing, air cover, firepower, radar, and the like—as it could, surprising as it may seem. Actually, its adaptation would only be a dramatic illustration of what almost every language has done in the past two or three centuries and continues to do as we plunge on into the vast unknown.

Consider, for instance, one of the most startling recent adventures of human awareness, the realization that certain astronomical bodies hitherto assumed to be galaxies are something wholly different—infinitely distant, fantastically enormous, incredibly radioactive. In comparison to them the hydrogen bomb is ludicrously insignificant.

With what words can we meet them? How does the mind reach out to touch anything so bewildering? "Quasi-stellar radio sources" is all the astonished astronomers yet can call them. "A thrilling mystery, an exciting enigma," Northwestern's Professor Hynek exclaims. "The most bizarre and puzzling objects ever observed through a telescope," says Cal Tech's Professor Jesse L. Greenstein. Perhaps the product of "catastrophic implosion," ventures Fred Hoyle, the Cantabrigian cosmologist.

Well, that's a beginning at least; and an examination of four of the

From Bergen Evans, "Milk, Beards, Thongs, and the Spiral Nebulae," *The Atlantic Monthly*, July, 1965. Reprinted by permission of the author.

more recondite-seeming terms employed—galaxy, bizarre, enigma, and catastrophic—comforts us with the assurance that although our heads are farther above the clouds than ever, our feet are still firmly on the earth.

Galaxies are so called because they resembled the Milky Way, which was *the* galaxy until we learned there were others. And *galaxy* is simply an extension of the Greek word for milk. Galactose is milk sugar.

Bizarre is almost as bizarre for a word as 3C 273 is for a star. It is the Basque word for beard. Basque is a tiny island of non-Indo-European speech in the vast sea of English, Italian, Russian, Romanian, and other related Indo-European tongues. And while people did not perceive formerly that most European languages were, in a sense, mere dialectal variations, they did perceive that Basque was mighty peculiar. It was said that the devil had tried for seven years to learn Basque and had finally abandoned the attempt. Some said that even the Basques themselves did not understand it.

Now, whether the Basques wore strange beards or whether any word of theirs was thought in itself to carry a suggestion of strangeness, or whatever, no one knows. But we do know that the Italian *bizarro,* which had been borrowed from the Spaniards, who had borrowed it from the Basques, came to mean capricious, unaccountable. And since Italy then set the fashion, what was bizarre to the Italians was bizarre to the rest of Europe too.

Enigma goes back to a Greek word meaning to speak in riddles, to speak darkly. And back of that it seems to have meant a fable or an allegory. And even further back it is related, seemingly, to a mumbling plea to be excused from some task or duty.

The root meaning of *catastrophe* is a strap or leather thong. And since such thongs were often twisted or plaited for greater strength, or perhaps because something fastened with such a thong was more manageable and could be turned and handled more easily, out of the idea of the thong came the idea of twisting or turning. And the verb that conveyed this idea—the Greek *strephein*—was applied to the turning and wheeling of the chorus in the Greek tragedies, giving us the *strophe* and the *antistrophe* and the *apostrophe.* And at the end of the play, the *katastrophe,* the downturning, the disaster which overwhelmed the protagonist, in the great poetry of the famed tragedians so moves us, even yet, to pity and fear, that the word remains our term for the greatest conceivable collapse or disaster.

So—much more like the Navajos than we thought—with a leather thong, some milk, a ludicrous beard, and a mumbled excuse, we go once more to comprehend the incomprehensible.

Astronomy is a glorious thing, certeyn. And so is speech.

COMPREHENSION QUIZ

1. Bergen Evans is on the faculty of
   a.   UCLA.
   b.   Northwestern.
   c.   Harvard.
   d.   MIT.
2. An "implosion" was used in this selection to mean
   a.   a great distance beyond known space.
   b.   radio activity within galaxies.
   c.   a bursting inwards.
   d.   none of these.
3. As used in this essay, "Basque" means
   a.   a representation of avant-garde thinking.
   b.   a name given to a small island of non-Indo-European speech, located in the midst of Indo-European tongues.
   c.   the European name for "beard," from which the word "bizarre" was derived.
   d.   None of these.

DISCUSSION QUESTIONS

1. Is the long, mysterious title of this selection appealing? Appropriate? What was Evans' intent in devising such a title?
2. Why were the Navajo Indians encouraged to speak to each other in their native tongue?
3. Was Evans trying to draw an implicit relationship between the universe of space and the universe of language?
4. What are some of the other dramatic adaptations our language has had to make in the past 20 years?

WRITING SUGGESTIONS

1. Make a report on the "Quasi-stellar radio sources" mentioned in the article.
2. Evans is highly regarded as an authority on English usage. Review some of his articles and the contributions he has made to language study.
3. Make a list of 25 words which were not in our dictionaries a few years ago, but which have appeared in recent editions.

The Big Mystery
in Small Words

by MARIO PEI

In the literary segment of every language there are words that stump the experts, both as to meaning and as to derivation. The Romans of the late Republic admitted that they were puzzled concerning some of the words that appeared in their more ancient laws and treaties. "What did our ancestors mean?" asks Polibius in the second century B.C. Here archaism and forgetfulness, coupled with ignorance of etymology, supply the explanation. We know more about the meaning and origin of some of those words than did the Romans of the pre-Augustan age.

The medieval French ballads of François Villon contain dozens of words that are unclear to modern scholars. Here the fault lies with Villon's use of *jobelyn,* the thieves' cant of his period. It is likely that many of the words he used were unfamiliar even to the upper social strata of his own day.

Dante scholars have wondered for centuries about the meaning of the words Dante puts into the mouth of Pluto at the beginning of the Seventh Canto of the *Inferno: "Pape Satan, Pape Satan Aleppe!"* Pluto seems bewildered and unpleasantly surprised at the invasion of his nether realm by visitors from the world of the living, and the best bet is that he is calling upon his superior, Satan, to eject them. *Aleppe* is then interpreted as the Italian rendering of *aleph,* the first letter of the Hebrew alphabet. This would give Satan the Status of "No. 1" demon, head of the infernal hierarchy, but leaves *pape* unexplained. Could Dante, whose antipapal leanings had led to his expulsion from Guelph-dominated Florence, be ironically comparing Satan to the Pope?

Ingenious, but utterly incredible, is the explanation supplied centuries later by Benvenuto Cellini. He states that at the Paris court, which he had

had occasion to visit, the chief usher, or bouncer, was nicknamed Satan, and that Dante, who had also been to Paris—though at a much earlier period—was giving a covert Italianized version of a French *"Paix, Satan, paix! Allez!"* ("Peace, Satan, peace! Go!").

Both the Bible and the eleventh-century French *Chanson de Roland* repeat at the end of stanzas words which make no sense. The Biblical word is *selah,* given untranslated in the English King James version, which comes repeatedly in the Psalms and occasionally elsewhere, and to which Semitic scholarship has been unable to assign a meaning or derivation. Greek versions sometimes render it by *diapsalma,* "that which comes between verses," but this begs the question. The word is generally interpreted to be a musical direction indicating a pause or rest.

The *Chanson de Roland,* most famous of medieval French epics, reported to have been sung by William's men at the Battle of Hastings, often makes use of a similar word, *aoi,* at the end of its *laisses,* or stanzas of unequal length. Is this just a vocalization, meant to be intoned by the *jongleur* for musical effect? Is it a nonsense-word designed to mark the end of a *laisse?* If so, why is it not universally used throughout the poem? Why does it appear in no other contemporary or subsequent work? Above all, does it have a meaning? Theories abound. One of the most elaborate is that *aoi* is the continuator of Latin *avoco,* "I am calling away or off," "I am interrupting," and that it gives rise to our nautical *ahoy,* which most sources list as a mere interjection. But it must be mentioned that *ahoy's* first recorded appearance is in 1751, a trifle late for connection with the *aoi* of the late eleventh century.

When we leave the rarefied atmosphere of literature and step down among the common words of everyday usage, we are amazed at the large number of such words, most of them monosyllabic and high in the frequency scale, which have no known origin or source. Dictionaries of word etymologies are always at pains to tell us what our big, long words come from, and what their original meaning was. They just as regularly avoid telling us about the short words of common use. They are merely following the course of least resistance. Some measure of uncertainty attaches to terms like *dream, drama, tube, small, boss, kiss, gay, ask, to mean.* We can trace them easily enough to their immediate source, Greek, Latin, or Germanic. Beyond that, we are in doubt, because the Greek, Latin, or Germanic root has no cognates in the other Indo-European branches, as it should have.

This raises the possibility that the particular language in which they first appeared may have borrowed from outside the Indo-European family. Could, for example, Greek have taken *drama* from Semitic? Could Latin have done the same with the word which gives us *tube* and all its derivatives? Could the pan-Germanic *dream* root be of Semitic origin? Could there have been an earlier, unrecorded link, or even a downright affiliation, between the Semitic and our own Indo-European languages?

There are, of course, plenty of Semitic words in the tongues of the West. Many of them, like *alcohol, algebra, cotton, alkali, zenith, syrup, assassin,* came in from Arabic during and after the Crusades. Others are the good old Biblical words from Hebrew and Aramaic which spread with Christianity and the Bible, words like *amen, abbot, jubilee, sabbath* and *sabaoth, seraph* and *cherub, hosannah* and *hallelujah.* Normally, their formation and meaning are crystal-clear, though they do lend themselves to the process of folk etymology, the type of legend whereby *sirloin* is attributed to a mythical king who liked loin of beef so much that he knighted it and said: "Rise, sir loin!" Actually, sirloin is just the French *sur longe*: "above the loin."

Sabaoth is the Hebrew plural of *saba*, "army," used in a possessive relation, so that "Lord Sabaoth" means "Lord of hosts." *Hosannah* is the Aramaic *hoshi ah nna*, "pray save us now." *Jubilee*, despite legends to the contrary, comes from Hebrew *yobel*, "ram's horn," which seems to give rise even to our *yodel* and *yowl. Hallelujah* is the Hebrew *hallelu-yah*, "praise ye Jahweh"; but the Italian folk legend would have it that at the time when Christ's body lay in the sepulcher, it was guarded by three Roman legionaries who happened to be, respectively, a Roman, a Piedmontese from northern Italy, and a German mercenary. When Our Lord rose from the dead and stood before them, they were at first stricken speechless. Then the Roman broke out into a single exclamation of amazement: "Ha!" The more articulate man from Piedmont cried out: "L'e lu!" which in present-day Piedmontese dialect means: "It's him!" The German could only stammer out his agreement: "Ja!" And so *hallelujah* came into being.

Among words of this type there is one, not Biblical, concerning which doubt lingers: *abracadabra*. It is attested in both Greek and medieval Latin, but does not appear in English until 1696. One version, supported by the appearance in Greek of the variant *abrasadabra*, takes the word back to Abrasax, a name devised for the Lord of Heaven by Basilides the Gnostic, who lived and taught in Alexandria in the second century of our era. More plausible, perhaps, is derivation from Aramaic *abhadda kedabrah*, "vanish at this word," a suitable incantation for warding off maladies or other evils.

It is easy enough to construct a list of words of one syllable whose origin is mysterious. But first let us look at a group of three words of purely American and quite recent origin: *blizzard, jitney*, and *sundae*. Earliest recorded appearance of *blizzard* is in 1829, but with the meaning of "sharp blow." It is only in 1870 that it assumes the sense of a snowstorm accompanied by high winds and sub-zero temperatures. The *Oxford English Dictionary* tentatively suggests affiliation with an English dialectal *blizzer*, ultimately associated with *blaze*, while Eric Partridge, in his *Origins*, offers *blizz* and *blaze* with an *-ard* suffix, which is usually derogatory. The *Random House Dictionary*, most recent on the market, carries it back to Anglo-Saxon *blysa*, "torch," and *blysian*, "to burn," but does not seem too sure of itself. *Webster's Third International* gives up, and labels its source "unknown." It does the same with *jitney,* which first appears in 1915. Here Random House calls it "slang for 5 cents," which still tells us nothing, and only Partridge ventures to connect it with Old French *geter,* modern *jeter,* "to throw," and its modern derivative *jeton,* "coin-shaped token."

For *sundae,* first recorded in 1904, Random House says nothing but "special use of Sunday"; Webster III calls it an "alteration of spelling"; Partridge suggests that it may originally have been served only on Sunday; and Oxford offers the entrancing theory that sundaes were made up of what was left over from Sunday sales of ice cream and related items. Another, unofficial, source claims that the sundae arose in a Puritanically-minded Midwestern town where the sale of ice cream sodas was forbidden on the Sabbath, but unfizzed ice cream was allowed, even if doctored up with other food ingredients. The peculiar spelling, paralleling that of the feminine name *May—Mae—*could be attributed to American creativeness in orthography. (After all, it was Andrew Jackson who said that it was a mighty poor mind that couldn't think of more than one way to spell a word.)

Here are fourteen common English monosyllables, each of which poses a problem: *bad, big, blab, chat, dad, fit, fog, fun, girl, job, lad, lass, put,* and for good measure, *slum.*

Bad starts its career as the thirteenth-century Middle English *baedde* or *badde,* which has no direct counterpart in Anglo-Saxon (*yfel,* the ancestor of *evil,* is the regular word there). There are, however, such Anglo-Saxon words as *baeddel,* "hermaphrodite," *baedling,* "effeminate," and even a verb *baedan,* "to defile." Could it be that *bad* itself simply did not have the good fortune to be recorded in any of the Anglo-Saxon writings that have come down to us? Or should we listen to Partridge's enticing alternative of derivation from Celtic *bados,* "wide open" (to evil ideas)?

Big is Middle English *bigge,* but again does not appear in Anglo-Saxon. Here the general theory is that it may have been a Scandinavian importation from the days of the Danelaw and King Cnut. There is a Scandinavian *bugge,* meaning "important man," which would give our "Mr. Big" an archaic flavor. Partridge complicates the matter with the possibility of relationship to *bug,* to Latin *bucca* ("cheek," "inflated cheek"), and even to Celtic *beccus,* "beak."

Blab is the late Middle English *blabbe,* said to be derived, by the process of cutting off the ending, from *blaeberen,* which gives us *blabber.* But *blaeberen* itself is said to be an "echoic" word, one coined on the basis of the sound produced by the object, which again injects a note of uncertainty (does blabbering really sound like *blabber*?).

Chat is Middle English, and said to be a cut-off form of *chatter,* first attested in 1540. This in turn is said to be an echoic word, formed on the basis of the sound striking the ear, like *blab.* Perhaps so.

Dad first appears in 1500. All agree that it is child talk, and that it has a very wide range (Irish *daid,* Welsh *tad,* Latin, Greek, Sanskrit *tata,* Gothic *atta,* Slavic *otets*). The best guess seems to be that the child is trying, in all these languages, to utter the word *pater* or something similar (the *pater-father* root is practically universal in Indo-European), and substitutes a dental for a labial in the first syllable, either because the dental is easier to articulate, or because he is anticipating the dental in the second syllable. What concerns us is from which of these sources English took its *dad.* On the basis of both form and chronology, Irish or Welsh would seem to be the most likely candidates.

Fit (in the sense of "a fit of anger," not that of "to fit a dress") goes all the way back to Anglo-Saxon *fitt,* where it has the meaning of "strife." Random House suggests a secondary meaning, "a round of a fight." The question then arises whether *fitt* is linked to Anglo-Saxon *feoht* and *feohtan,* which give us *fight,* as a noun and as a verb. The evidence for the link is not as clear as it might be.

Fog does not show up until 1544, in the form *fogge.* A Scandinavian source seems most likely. Danish has *fog* as "spray" or "snow," Old Norse has *fjuk* in the same sense, *fuka* as "sea-fog." Again the time element comes into play. Is this a relatively late borrowing from Danish, or did it come in with the pre-Hastings Danes and lie unrecorded until the sixteenth century?

Fun, too, is late (1685), and is at first used only as a verb, *to fun,* meaning "to cheat, hoax, cajole, make a fool of." Partridge alone links it to *fond,* which he derives from Middle English *fonned,* the past participle of *fonnen,* "to be silly, make a fool of." Beyond that, he suggests Celtic origin (Irish *fonn,* "pleasure," "folly"; Welsh *gwan,* "feeble," "faint"). To a modern observer, it is interesting to note how a word which in origin was a verb turns into a noun, then into an adjective ("fun dress," "fun party," even "Fun City").

Girl is given as Middle English and obscure by both Oxford and Webster. Random House links Middle English *girle, gurle* with Anglo-Saxon *gyrlgyden,* "virgin goddess," and with Low German *göre,* "young person (some Scottish dialects still use *girl* to refer to the young of either sex). Partridge admits this possibility, but also advances Anglo-Irish *girleen* and the hypothesis of a borrowing from Irish *caile, cailin* (the word familiar to most as *colleen*).

Job, from 1557, seems at first to have had the meaning of "lump" (a lump of work?), and Webster definitely links it to *gob.* If this is right, then it goes back to Old French *gober,* from which we get *gobble* and even *gobbledegook.* French in turn gets it from Welsh-Breton *gob,* "snout" or "beak." So far as English is concerned, the semantic link seems weak, and we can't really blame Random House for rejecting it.

Lad is Middle English *ladde,* originally meaning "serving man." Both Random House and Partridge, however, advance the Anglo-Saxon proper name *Ladda* as a possible source.

Lass appears in Middle English in the form *lasce*. Oxford theorizes that this may be linked to Swedish *lösk kona,* "unmarried woman," while Partridge suggests that *lasce* or *lasse* may be a cutdown form of *laddesse, lad* with a feminine suffix.

Put is generally linked to Anglo-Saxon *putian, potian,* "to thrust, push, goad," and Old Norse *pota,* "to thrust," is advanced by Random House. Partridge alone suggests that it may be echoic.

Slum is a quite modern word, first appearing in 1812, and labeled "cant" by Oxford. There is general silence as to its derivation save from Partridge, who says it may come from *slumber,* in the sense that slum areas, which lexicographers took good care not to wander into, may have unjustly acquired the reputation of being sleepy and quiet.

These elements of mystery and doubt connected with our shortest and most common words could easily be duplicated in every language. That they are most numerous in English is perhaps due to the extremely varied sources from which we have obtained our vocabulary. They also account for the tendency of our popular etymologists to deal with words like *rhododendron* and *sesquipedalian* in preference to *fog* and *girl*. But there is an added psychological trait that enters the picture. The long words we have to think about. The short ones we use without thinking.

COMPREHENSION QUIZ

1. The vast number of English words whose ancestries are in doubt is due to
   a. the failure of the Anglo-Saxons to keep accurate records.
   b. the destruction of the monasteries during the English Reformation.
   c. the extremely varied sources from which we have obtained our vocabulary.
   d. the linguistic consequences of the invention of the printing press.
2. Which of the following language families is not a member of the Indo-European family?
   a. Semitic.
   b. Greek.
   c. Latin.
   d. Germanic.
3. Pei says that most of the words of unknown origin or source
   a. are polysyllabic and rarely used.
   b. were first used by medieval French poets.
   c. are uniform in their early spellings.
   d. are monosyllabic and high in the frequency scale.
4. The Aramaic phrase, "Vanish at this word," has given us the word
   a. "amen."
   b. "hosannah."
   c. "hallelujah."
   d. "abracadabra."

5. Pei suggests that the spelling of "sundae" may be attributed to American creativeness in
   a. etymology.
   b. orthography.
   c. philology.
   d. phonology.

DISCUSSION QUESTIONS

1. Why are short words more difficult to trace, rather than longer words?
2. What popular explanations have you heard for the origins of any of the words mentioned by Pei?
3. Look up the term "Indo-European" in your dictionary. What are the major families in this group? Does it include Hebrew, Chinese, or Swahili?

WRITING SUGGESTIONS

1. For an interesting excursion through political and linguistic history, trace the history of the following terms: "O.K."; "Uncle Sam"; "Kilroy"; "G.I."
2. Look up one of the following terms in at least three different collegiate dictionaries and an unabridged dictionary. Write a report presenting the various explanations and theories of the origins of the word.

"lousy"   "snafu"   "mugwump"

I Mean,
After All!

by EDMUND WARE SMITH

"You know," "I mean," "What I mean" and the even more deadly "But I mean, after *all*," are mannerisms that infect our daily conversation like a verbal pox. One shrinks from calling them idiom, for much of our idiom is effective and honorable. They deserve an entirely new word, one denoting full derogation and distaste. The word I propose is "odiom," with the plural "odia," stemming from the Latin verb *odisse,* which means "to hate."

Let us begin with one of the commonest and deadliest of odia, "you know."

When someone says, "*You* know," what is it you are supposed to know? He isn't asking you if you know. He is telling you that you do. But what is it? It must be something. But if you know, why is he telling you in the first place? That's something you will never know.

The same goes for "I mean." People who corrode their sentences with "I mean's" are trying desperately to convey something. They don't know what it is. So they don't mean anything. If they do mean something, and can't say it, they should be helped to find an interpreter.

Among these first samples of odia, the superlative outrage is "But I mean, after *all*."

All what? What all? After what all? What mean? The answer, straight across the board, is zero. "But I mean, after *all*" (sometimes both "mean" and "all" are underscored) is commonly used by people (usually girls) who haven't developed any particular meaning and only a very trifling all. All sounds like a lot, the way they say it. I say you could get it on a pinhead.

Here's what could happen to the opening sentences of one of our language's celebrated orations when treated to an odiom or two:

From Edmund Ware Smith, "I Mean, After *All!*," *Redbook Magazine,* July, 1963. Copyright © 1963 by McCall Corporation, New York. Reprinted by permission of Brandt & Brandt, New York.

"Friends, Romans, countrymen, lend me your ears. But I *mean,* after *all,* we come to bury Caesar, not to—*you* know—praise him."

The odiom is guaranteed to paralyze intelligent conversation.

"If you get what I mean" and "If you follow me" are direct insults. They imply that whoever is using them has a private pipeline to some reservoir of omniscience denied to you. The implication is that you are excluded from the Inner Group, underprivileged and too dumb to belong.

Another member of an inner group is the girl who starts or ends every other paragraph with "Do you realize?" This girl often is overstimulated with the experience of education. She wants you to realize some of the things *she* realizes, and this is kind of her. But she also wants you to realize that she is simply loaded with knowledge, and this is not so kind of her. Among her friends, you can be sure, there are at least two other girls who incline toward the use of "basically" and "incidentally."

"In my opinion" is another conversation-stopper. Who else's opinion? This odiom is employed by someone who wants you to think he is a man of acumen whose opinion is weighty. He isn't, and it isn't. Walk away from him.

Another man to shun is the one who is explaining something he wants you to feel is a bit too knotty for your limited comprehension. He looks at you as if you had lost a few bolts and says: "Let me put it this way."

If he had known what he was talking about to begin with, he would have put it that way, thus eliminating the labor of putting it another way.

"Let-me-put-it-this-way's" first cousin is a phrase people use as a kind of showcase in which to display their vocabularies or virtuosity. They start every crushing new paragraph with the ominous words "In other words."

If they had been talking sense in the first place, their first words would have been enough words. Their other words, besides being superfluous, are nothing but a seamy device to anchor themselves on stage. To listen to them for more than a minute or two is like being brained with a vacuum.

Another vacuum, more and more prevalent of late, is the speaker who is in love with numbers. He feels that he is loaded with items of import and he likes to count them for you, ticking them off on his fingers: "Number one . . . number two . . ."

He must know many more numbers than these, but I have left them out because he rarely gets beyond number two. I don't know why it is, but something happens to number three and all the others. Have you ever wondered what, say, number eight would be? Or number eleven? A lot of lost material there somewhere. But to date this numbers racket has not been followed through.

An exception could be President Kennedy's speech on the Cuban crisis. He made numbers one through seven without a hitch; but his case is unusual, if not unique. He had seven things to say.

Next we come to three of our most repulsive odia: "Frankly," "Candidly" and "To be honest with you."

The user of these is simply telling you that all his previous utterances have been false. So why should you believe him now? He has branded himself a suspicious character.

"Let me tell you something!" and "You want to know something?" are borderline odia, and not too poisonous. These phrases prepare you for a great revelation and the shock that never comes. That's the nice thing about them.

But there is nothing nice to be said for "anyway" and "so." I have heard a horrifying number of women take off on a prolonged burst of rhetoric, spray-hitting targets miles from their original theme, and terminating with a sort of interstellar "anyway" or "so." Sometimes the "so" is elongated to "so-o-o-o-o," and sometimes "anyway" comes out unaccountably as "any-who-o-o." I am not certain what these odia signify—whether the ladies are back on the fairway or just out of breath.

The final odiom on our list is "Let me finish," and this is the death cry of the man who already *has* finished. Long ago. The interruptions and drifting attention of his audience should have given him the message. He doesn't hear it. He presses on, ever and anon crying: "Let me finish!"

He uses it as a verbal bridge from island to island in the dead sea of parlor filibuster. He is the living proof that the odiom must be swept clean from our spoken language.

But now let *me* finish.

COMPREHENSION QUIZ

1. The author of this selection suggests his dislike for phrases like "You know" and "I mean, after *all*," by calling them
   a. a verbal pox.
   b. deadly phrases.
   c. idioms.
   d. common fallacies.
2. The author suggests a new word that would denote derogation and distaste:
   a. ocarina.
   b. odic.
   c. odiom.
   d. odium.
3. This essay states that the common expressions and phrases are guaranteed
   a. to bore the reader.
   b. to render useless the language.
   c. to paralyze intelligent conversation.
   d. to enervate cognitive discourse.

4. President Kennedy's speech on the Cuban missile crisis had seven points—an exception to the author's notion that numbers should be avoided. The reason was that
   a. Kennedy was, after all, the President.
   b. he had seven things to say.
   c. seven is considered a magical number.
   d. saying seven things was easy for Kennedy.

DISCUSSION QUESTIONS

1. Are the common expressions cited by the author as odious as he claims? Do they have any redeeming qualities?
2. Explain the author's intention in his concluding sentence.
3. How do such phrases as "I mean, after *all*," and "In my opinion" develop? Do they really mean something quite different from their obvious, literal meaning?
4. Which of the expressions in Smith's article do you often use? Do you agree with his opinion of their sincerity?

WRITING SUGGESTIONS

1. Many observers of American speech patterns would argue that the phrases attacked by Smith have a valuable use. If you agree, write a theme explaining your views.
2. Construct a social situation—a party, for example—and describe the various "types" of people present by pointing out the kinds of "odia" they might use.

The Language
of Democracy

by EMILE CAPOUYA

Some years ago Mr. Edmund Wilson complained—bootlessly, it appears
—about what was then a new solecism, the word "massive" used to qualify
things that are not, cannot be, massive. Mr. Wilson observed that the adjective properly describes a physical object whose mass is considerable, and
by extension a physical object of large size and great weight. Grants of
credits to foreign nations, or retaliation against them for their warlike acts,
could not, as in John Foster Dulles's usage, be massive. They could be other
things, including wise or foolish, but, by the genius of the language, "massive" was a quality denied to threats or blandishments as to gossamer or
moonshine. As we all know, Mr. Wilson's complaint has been massively
ignored. Oddly enough, the error flourishes only among those who pass for
educated. The workman will refer correctly to a massive casting; one has
to ascend as high as the Personnel Department to hear of massive lay-offs,
and to the Olympus of the board room itself to learn of plans for a massive
expansion of sales.

Clearly, there is a class of persons whose careers depend on their being
able to summon words that can kill seven at a blow. And the principle of
selection seems to be the same that Dryden attributed to a poetaster of his
day: "He fagotted his verses as they fell,/And if they rhymed and rattled, all
was well." Or, as the floorwalker said when discovered with his hand in the
till, "Go away. Can't you see I'm too drunk to know what I'm doing?" It
must be some such intoxication that induces a man who is looking for a
job to claim that he is "seeking a position." Seeking, as if it were the Grail
he was after. And position. But on second thought, I suppose we must sympathize with his reluctance to say "job," a word with an unfortunate history,

some part of which survives in "jobbery," and that in one ugly monosyllable tells you anyway more than you want to know about work done not for love but for money. In the same way, I suppose we should forgive the unfortunate who promises to "contact" us. Life has dealt with him so harshly that he shies away from touching his fellows, to the point where he refuses even to get in touch with them—or call or write—unless he can put it in Latin, which is impersonal, antiseptic, and high-toned. But still, there is a powerful temptation when we are told, "I'll contact you," to answer, "Don't contact us. We'll contact *you*." Or as the children say, in much better English, "Not if we see you first."

Those examples of the high-pressure vocabulary suggest that it is not necessarily the long word or the one of learned origin that is chosen when the situation calls for overkill capacity. The desiderata seem to be abstractness, remoteness, and something that suggests a connection with science or technology. The use of "type" in place of "kind" or "sort" is by now almost universal. "What type of person is he?" says Everybody, making unconscious obeisance to the god of the shop and the laboratory. If he feels a special reverence for the stock-shelves of the Parts Department, he may contract the expression further to, "What type person is he?" The answer comes, "Oh, a high-type person," and the hyphenated construction expresses the mechanical analogy that the speaker has at the back of his mind. The high-type person is being compared to a double-action model, or an overhead-cam model, or a quick-release model. In fine, to a manufactured object, machined to definite specifications, and with all the kinks and bugs ironed out.

Some of the popular technicizing terms appear to have come into the language under the influence of the German scientists we captured in 1945 and who have been making rockets for us ever since. (I wonder if the Russians owe a similar linguistic debt to the Germans *they* captured and who are making their rockets.) "Breakthrough" sounds German to me, and I certainly don't remember hearing the word before the Second World War, though the nation was equally given to celebrating trifles in those days. "Fallout" is another example of the *furor Teutonicus*, I imagine, and a number of unfortunate formations on the same pattern—"dropout," "cookout." Here, though, I think we must distinguish between promiscuous neologisms and native examples of more legitimate ancestry, for example, Mark Twain's expression, "a regular old toreout," which is probably born of metathesis from the time-honored "a real old rip." And "blowout," of course, meant a gorgeous feast long before it came to mean the bursting of an automobile tire. Some forms that are not particularly attractive in themselves are ennobled by their associations. "Sit-down" has an honorable origin, and so does the new "sit-in" and the brand-new "teach-in." But nothing can quite make up for the inherent gracelessness of such words. They are, as it were, the warrant-officers among words, neither enlisted men nor yet gentlemen-by-act-of-congress. For "holdout" and "standout" it is hard to imagine an excuse.

Speaking of the German language, when I was a boy the announcement, "Hopefully, I'll go next week," or I'll go, hopefully, next week," conveyed a very different message than it does nowadays. Firstly, it told us that the speaker was a foreigner, or possibly a religious enthusiast, given the unexpectedly insistent adverb. But in either case, it meant that a spirit of hope would accompany him on his peregrinations. "Hopefully" could be nothing but an adverb expressing the frame of mind in which he would carry out the action. Now, as it happens, the Germans have an expression, *hoffentlich*, whose colloquial use is, "*Hoffentlich* I go next week." Who do you suppose won the last world war? The most respectable periodicals in the country are printing contributions by the most respected writers, in which "hopefully" means "I hope to" or "I hope that." But before 1945 those writers would have had to say what they meant.

This is as good a point as any to consider the contention of some modern lexicographers that usage is the final arbiter of elegance. That claim is most often advanced in defense of vulgar neologisms, or just plain vulgarity, and it represents itself as being objective, scientific, and democratic. Objectivity and science in this context mean statistics, and democracy means the linguistic prejudices of the lexicographer. But surely those words have loftier meanings? Democracy, for example, is not a taste for plebescite, but a passion for political responsibility. And since it is a passion, it flourishes only among people who are capable of being passionate. In this connection, then, counting noses is not being objective but merely uninterested—and also disingenuous. For when the dictionary-makers I am referring to appeal to usage, they do not specify whose usage they have in mind. They would like to have it appear that they mean just folks, the backbone of the nation. However, the majority of the population, including me, can scarcely get through a spoken sentence without using expressions that are technically blasphemous or obscene, and yet such expressions are not to be found in the popular word-books compiled on folksy principles. So that their message comes down to this: If your speech is notably graceless, corrupt, and ignorant, don't you mind. Your neighbors are in the same fix. And I'm a lexicographer, and I say it's all right.

The reason for being starchy in such matters, and passionate rather than permissive, is that the language of cultivated speakers and writers is precise, subtle, and beautiful. The cultivated speaker, of course, is not necessarily the person who has a degree in linguistics. Indeed, nowadays the conversation of the professional middle class, from whom we might expect cultivated speech, is like the imitation whipped cream dispensed from those grease-gun affairs in soda fountains. It is synthetic, without either calories or flavor, and it is delivered under high pressure. For nourishing speech, one has to go to the country. But the point of art is to improve on nature, and turn rude energy to something express and moving. In one of his poems Paul Goodman boasts of "Excellent sentences I make,/Better than any other man's." That's the spirit. And now, if you please, what is the source of Mr. Goodman's affection for the expression—repeated dozens of time in his prose works—This, that, or the other thing is *importantly* true? That usage is a curious example of provincialism, in which the province is just about limited to Mr. Goodman. I suppose we do know why he does it. He is a man of the world, and he has learned that truth can be trivial. He means to put us on notice: "Not this truth, dear reader. I made it myself, and I can attest that it is importantly true." Possibly, but need he brandish a solecism in order to persuade us?

But if "importantly" is Mr. Goodman's very own solecism, he shares a barbarism with half the nation. After reciting a list of facts, he will say, "Now, this means. . . ." Or after delivering himself of one of his character-istically illuminating aphorisms, he will explain, "This is because. . . ." English makes a subtle distinction between "this" and "that" in such cases. When the thing referred to is an argument or a proposition, it is felt to be an abstraction, remote rather than near at hand, yonder rather than right here, and so we say, "That is because . . . ," using the particle that suggests spatial separation. I think that German and Yiddish have influenced Ameri-can English to the point that for many persons "this" and "that" represent an embarrassment of riches. But Mr. Goodman does make "excellent sen-tences" in prose and verse when he is in the vein, and therefore one wants to say to him apropos of his lapses what Hamlet says to Laertes during the fencing match: "You do but dally; I pray you, pass with your best violence; I am afeared you make a wanton of me."

COMPREHENSION QUIZ

1. Errors in the use of the word "massive" flourished, according to this article
   a. among working men.
   b. among those who pass for educated.
   c. in board rooms of corporations.
   d. both (b) and (c).
2. Capouya uses "poetaster" to mean
   a. one who writes poetry.
   b. a mere versifier.
   c. a literary critic.
   d. none of these.
3. The author suggests that the criteria for using a "high pressure" vocabulary include all *except*
   a. abstractness.

b. remoteness.

c. obtuseness.

d. something suggesting a connection with science.

4. When it comes to accepting the "popular" usage of words, the writer of this
    article would rather be

a. permissive than passive.

b. permissive than passionate.

c. passive than passionate.

d. passionate than permissive.

DISCUSSION QUESTIONS

1. In the sentence, " 'What type of person is he?' says Everybody, . . .," why is
    "Everybody" capitalized? Is the inference intended to be sarcastic?

2. What is Capouya's attitude toward usage, rules, and language "correctness"?

3. The author asks us to distinguish between "promiscuous neologisms and native
    examples of more legitimate ancestry. . . ." What does he mean? What deter-
    mines the correctness of new words?

4. Why must one "go to the country for nourishing speech"?

5. What might Paul Goodman say in his own defense, in the light of Capouya's
    attack?

WRITING SUGGESTIONS

1. Write a reply to Capouya's indictment; argue from the viewpoint of a lexi-
    cographer.

2. If you agree with Capouya, write a defense of the principles of purism.

Recommended Readings to Part VII

Brown, Roger. *Words and Things.* New York: Free Press, 1958.

Gellner, Ernest. *Words and Things.* London: Gollancz, 1959.

Mathews, Mitford M. *Words: How to Know Them.* New York: Holt, Rinehart and Winston, 1956.

McKnight, George H. *English Words and Their Background.* New York: Appleton-Century-Crofts, 1923.

Partridge, Eric. *Name into Words.* New York: Macmillan, 1949.

Potter, Simeon. *Our Language.* Harmondsworth, England: Pelican Books, 1950.

Ullmann, Stephen. *Words and Their Use.* New York: Philosophical Library, 1951.

Semantics: VIII
What Do You Mean?

Semantics
and Common Sense

by LOUIS B. SALOMON

Semantics is usually defined as the study of meanings, and, since words are the chief (though by no means only) vehicles of meaning, it is assumed that the semanticist's attention is directed primarily to language. A skeletal definition, this will do for a starter, with the understanding that much of the ensuing discussion must serve incidentally to flesh out the skeleton, showing the nature and limits of the study by example rather than by explicit formula.

Let it be said at the outset that [here] semantics will be treated not as a body of subject-matter, like physics or chemistry or history, in which the data are largely, if not universally, agreed upon, but rather as a method of approach, in which many questions are asked but few given final answers. Among semanticists themselves there are wide areas of disagreement as to both their technical nomenclature and their view of the symbolic process by which minds communicate with other minds, or consciousness communicates with itself, so to speak, in the process we call thought. The only principle you are asked to accept as axiomatic is, as Thoreau put it, "It is the man determines what is said, not the words." Or, as it might be paraphrased: "Words don't mean; people mean."[1]

The degree of precision and certainty that can be achieved in the analysis of meaning, in any case, is limited by one or more built-in impediments. Words constitute not only the materials to be studied but to some extent the instruments with which we do our probing and almost exclusively the means by which we report on the results. Key terms such as *word, meaning,*

[1] Although, in speaking about Word X, we shall often use the common locutions "Word X means . . . ," "the meaning of Word X," and so forth, it should be remembered that . . . these forms of expression are always a convenient shorthand for the more awkward-sounding "What people mean by Word X," and so forth.

truth must either be taken on faith or explained by means of verbal formulations made up of "words" that have "meaning" and which add up to a statement that has value only in proportion to its "truth." A rider on a merry-go-round ultimately comes back to the starting point, no matter how many valuable lessons he may have learned while swinging round the circuit.

Another dilemma of circularity attends the decision whether to begin an examination of language with the meaning of words as separate entities or with the meaning of words organically incorporated into sentences. Either choice has inescapable drawbacks.

In practice we do not communicate by means of words apart from their relationship to sentence texture; therefore investigating the meaning of a word *per se* is pretty much like studying a lung dissected out of the living organism. We do, it is true, have one-word sentences, like "Go!", but the meaning here is not merely the equivalent of any one of the definitions of *go* in a dictionary; it includes the imperative intention of the speaker, which resides not in the word itself but in the context of punctuation or tone of voice that makes it a sentence.

On the other hand, if we start with sentences, we have to take it for granted that we are agreed on the meanings of the separate words that compose the sentences—a very risky assumption indeed. Thus, the decision has to be made as arbitrarily as the choice of a number to bet on at roulette. We shall begin with words, but in the course of their treatment we shall constantly have to illustrate points with sentences to show that words are not merely museum specimens; then, when we come to sentences we shall have to show that what look like identical sentences may have very different meanings, hence for practical purposes be different sentences, depending on the interpretation of one or more words therein.

Meanings of "Meaning"

Another perplexity in any inquiry into meaning grows out of the fact that some of the words indispensable to such an inquiry are commonly used in a number of *different* senses; the first of these variables being the word *meaning* itself. In fact, a good many of the stumbling blocks that seem to impede a solution for semantic quandaries tend to look less formidable once one has accepted the apparent paradox that the question "What is the meaning of ——?" may have more than one valid answer, or quite possibly *no* valid answer expressible in other words.

Take a look at some of the more conspicuous branchings of the word in its natural linguistic habitat:

1. "Life has lost its meaning for me."

The nearest verbal equivalent for *meaning* would probably be: *sense of purpose.*

2. "Nuclear war means the end of civilization."

We could obviously substitute *will result in* for *means*.

3. "You mean a lot to me."

Mean suggests something on the order of *are worth* or *have importance*.

4. "She may not accomplish much, but she means well."

Means clearly implies *has intentions* or *makes efforts, regardless of the effects*.

5. "A falling barometer means a change in the weather."

Here we have a more complicated case. For *means* we might substitute *is a sign of*—but what does *that* mean? Suppose we define a sign as the first of a pair of phenomena which we have observed almost invariably to occur in the same chronological order, so that when we see *A* we expect very shortly to see *B*. Although *A* is not the cause of *B*—there were storms before barometers were invented—we have learned from experience that when "the glass" is falling we had better take in sail, or cover the lawn furniture, or call off our plans for a picnic. In other words, a sign may be said to tell us something, in the sense that it influences our behavior or state of mind. The influence may have a logical basis (for example, meteorologists, by a series of inferences, have decided that the condition which causes the barometer to fall serves also as a cause of storms), but it does not have to. If after each time we saw a falling star we found a fifty-cent piece within the next two minutes, or after each time a black cat crossed our path we stumbled and fell, we might after many and frequent repetitions come to feel that we had "discovered the meaning" of the first event; and if after several hundred such sequences the second event failed to occur, we might feel that the first event had somehow failed us, or told us something untrue.

It is on this sign level that we "communicate" with animals. To Pavlov's dogs the bell became a sign of dinner, and when they heard it they salivated: that is, evinced a signal reaction. You can teach Fido that if, when he hears the name *Mary*, he goes to his mistress he will get a biscuit or at least a pat on the head, and thereafter if anyone mentions the name *Mary* in his hearing he will go to her, or look for her if she is not in his line of vision.

6. "*Democracy* means: a government of the people, by the people, for the people."

7. "If you want to know the meaning of Beethoven's *Fifth Symphony*, listen to it."

It is with these last two, disparate as they may be in some respects, that this book is chiefly concerned. Here we have to do with symbolization: the process by which a vocal sound or its written representation or a set of musical tones or an arrangement of pigments enables a sending mind to evoke in a receiving mind (the two may be the same) an image of a thing or a class of things, a concept or feeling or a class of concepts or feelings. Instead of impelling a single motor response or arousing an expectation of another event, a symbol causes an image, concept, or feeling to be flashed on a screen, as it were, either for the sake of the esthetic satisfaction derived from the symbolic utterance itself or as a subject for the operations of discursive reason, or for a combination of the two.

To Fido the sound *Mary* operates as a sign pointing the way to biscuit or caress. Even in a human mind, signal reactions *may* be evoked by the name of a being or concept (for example, the word *God* to a militant atheist, *work* to a confirmed loafer); but in so far as it functions symbolically the name triggers a mechanism that calls up out of the storehouse of the user's memory his entire image of, and personal attitude toward, Mary or democracy, then shuts itself off to leave the way clear for the questions: "Well, what about Mary? What about democracy?"

Symbols may well be more than mere vehicles for communication; they may be an indispensable ingredient of thought itself. The question of whether it is possible to think without using language has been much debated, and no final answer is offered here. Suffice it that (a) the question hinges primarily upon what we mean by *think,* and (b) it is difficult to conceive of anything that we should ordinarily call thought apart from conceptualization—that is to say, a process which by nature lends itself to, if not demands, symbolic treatment, regardless of whether the concept antedates the explicit symbol or vice versa. As Ernst Cassirer put it, introducing a value judgment, "All truly strict and exact thought is sustained by the *symbolics* and *semiotics* on which it is based."

The meaning of a symbol, unlike the meaning of a sign, is imputed by the users of the symbol, and is constantly subject to change at the pleasure of the users. There is, of course, no guarantee that two users will impute the same meaning to a given symbol, whether it be discursive like *democracy* or esthetic like Beethoven's *Fifth Symphony*; agreement is a matter rather of social convenience than of either logical necessity or moral obligation.

Words as Units of Meaning

So much for the many-faceted ambiguity of the term *meaning.* Once we have stipulated that we are going to focus on those aspects represented in Examples 6 and 7, and that our topic in the main has to do with the meaning of words, it sounds as though we might proceed directly to business —and so we might, were it not for a still further semantic snag in the topic-statement itself. Can we safely assume that we know what a word is, or, to put it in a form more suitable to our methodology, can we assume that we agree on what we mean by the word *word*?

There are at least two sets of specialists whose professional concern requires them to answer this question as categorically as possible: the dictionary-makers, for whom it is the starting-point of their entire enterprise, and the telegraph companies, with their down-to-earth, down-to-pocketbook rule that messages are charged by the word. The linguistic approach is exemplified by entries in two standard American dictionaries, one of which defines *word* as "the smallest unit of speech that has meaning when taken by itself"; the other calls it "an element which can stand alone as an utterance, not divisible into two or more parts similarly characterized; thus *boy* and *boyish,* but not *-ish* or *boy scout,* the former being less than a word, the latter more." Or if you choose the more pragmatic test you will find that if you send the Emerson quotation on the title page of this book as a telegram you will be charged the current rate for twenty-five words; that a telegraphed reference to New Zealand will cost you the charge for two words, a reference to Ireland for one word.

Either standard leaves some questions still unanswered. Is the concept represented by *New Zealand* any less unitary than that represented by *Ireland?* Why is *-ish* less than a word, while *ism* ranks as a full-grown specimen? Why is *boy scout* more than a word? Why, for instance, if a two-word boy scout feels chilly on his one-word campground, does he pull up a two-word camp chair in front of his one-word campfire? Anyone who seeks a strictly logical answer to such questions is chasing will-o'-the-wisps (chargeable in telegrams as a single word, because of the hyphens) in a semantic bog. We do not use language half so rationally as we like to think we do, and perhaps the only realistic answer to our initial query is that a word is any meaningful speech sound or set of speech sounds, from *a* or *I* to *antidisestablishmentarianism,* which according to current convention is represented *in writing* with a space before and after. Surely *won't* is neither more nor less a unit of meaning than *will not;* yet both the dictionary-makers and the telegraph companies classify *won't* as one word, *will not* as two. Furthermore, any adequate dictionary of the English language lists and defines hundreds of entries that by this standard consist of two or more words each: for example, *woolly bear, lapis lazuli, stumbling block, matter of course, tongue and groove, je ne sais quoi.*

It is true, of course, that the spoken language must have come into existence long before writing was invented, and that except for deaf-mutes all of us learn to speak before we learn to write. But it is also true that in an age of almost universal literacy we spend the greater part of our life so compulsively manipulating and being manipulated by the written language that we have come, whether we admit it to ourselves or not, to regard the written convention as the controlling one when it comes to separating the parts of a sentence into smaller units of meaning.

A totally illiterate speaker of English, on the one hand, would be hard put to determine how many words there are in the demand which he hears and speaks as *Gimmeanapple.* The readers, on the other hand, would probably all agree, after a moment's pause for picturing the same phonetic sequence written in standard English, to call it four words. Indeed, it is a common experience for a reader to learn the meaning of a word through seeing it often enough in print, without ever having heard it spoken, and even, in a language so unphonetically spelled as English, with a very mistaken notion of its accepted pronunciation in the spoken language.[2] Furthermore, many modern words owe their origin entirely to the written language: some of them, like *G.I.* or *O.K.*, being pronounced as individual letters rather than syllables; others, like *Wac, laser, scuba,* or *snafu* (called acronyms), having been manufactured by putting together the initial letters of several ordinary written words.

Mere linguistic vagaries, however, are not our chief concern here; the point to be observed is that the conventions of the written language exercise a semantic influence in themselves, because, once having committed ourselves to the principle that a word is a unit of meaning, we feel constrained to find such unity in every verbal symbol like *boyish* and deny it to every verbal symbol like *boy scout,* overlooking the fact that the latter could just as easily be, and may very likely come some day[3] to be, written either *boy-scout* or *boyscout.* Why, if there is any consistent semantic rationale behind word separation, do we write *fifteen* as one word, *twenty-five* as a hyphenated compound, *five hundred* as two words, *five hundred thousand* as three, *five million* as two?

This absence of logical system in word separation is by no means confined to the English language. For our "of the," French has two words *de la* before feminine nouns, one word *du* (contraction, we are told, for *de le,* but the Frenchman never says or writes *de le*) before masculine nouns. For our "begin," German uses the one word *anfangen* in the infinitive form but splits it up into two words in *ich fange an* ("I begin"). Swedish *verk* means "work," but Swedish has an enclitic article with which the separate preceding article may or may not be used as an addition; thus the equivalent of "the work" can be either the one word *verket* or the two words *det verket.* In French the definite article is customarily used before nouns of certain kinds regardless of context; thus, the Frenchman says *la France,* but we would sound merely silly if we translated it as "the France" (though we sound quite sensible when we speak of "the Netherlands," "the Bowery," "the Bronx").

Even if we accept the written convention as a guide to what constitutes a word, there are still a couple of reservations to be noted. In the first place, we have some "words" that perhaps do not have any meaning (in the ordinary sense) at all. The most obvious group consists of interjections used as mere introductory noises to ease the tone of discourse or to avoid a momentary silence while we decide what we are going to say next. The dictionaries

---

[2] [This writer], during his youth, coupled the printed word misled with the sound represented by the capitalized portion of the *MICE'LL Die.*

[3] The one-word form *someday* is already making a bid for acceptance in respectable publications. Why shouldn't it, somehow, sometime?

recognize some of these (for instance, *O, oh, well, now*) while mostly ignoring others such as *uh, mm, mph,* which occur just as frequently in both spoken and written dialogue. Then too, modern English has certain purely formal additives that appear in some constructions but not in others: the *to* of *You need to work,* as contrasted with *You need not work;*[4] the *Did* of *Did you work?* as contrasted with *You worked* (in much earlier English, as in most other languages still, the interrogative form *Worked you?* was standard). Finally, we have some compound verbs in which "words" are interchangeable with their apparent opposites: when you enter data on a routine form or questionnaire, you are filling it in (or out); when you reduce the speed of your car, you are slowing up (or down), and so forth. If the substitution of *out* for *in, down* for *up,* produces no change in the meaning of the whole expression, this at least raises a question as to whether these words (in such expressions) have what we should ordinarily call meaning.

The second query has to do with (1) identical-sounding words like *base* and *bass* in "He did a base act" or "He has a bass voice"; (2) the various uses of *base* in "He did a base act," "He stole second base," "The Navy has set up a base on Guam," "The addition of an acid to a base produces a salt"; and (3) the uses of the written symbol *bass* to represent different sounds in "He has a bass voice" and "He caught a black bass." Words that are pronounced alike, regardless of how spelled, are called homophones; those that are spelled alike, regardless of how pronounced, are called homographs; in (2) we have words that are both at the same time.[5] Are these all different words, or the same words with different meanings or spellings or pronunciations? This is what we shall learn later to call a purely verbal question (that is, the answer tells merely what, in this context, we choose to mean by *same* or *different*), but together with the other points raised about *word* it helps to reveal the complexity cloaked by such simple-sounding formulas as "unit of meaning," "saying the same thing in fewer words," "making one word do the work of three," and "word-for-word translation."

It may thus point up some of the problems that dictionary-makers and semanticists encounter.

---

[4] The whole question of the separate *to* as the sign of the modern English infinitive, as contrasted with other inflectional signs like the *-ed* of the past tense, is of considerable linguistic interest, to say nothing of all the rhetorical pother over whether a "split" infinitive is bad or not.

[5] Note that an illiterate would have no way of knowing whether homophones were also homographs; a deaf and blind person, though ever so expert at reading Braille, would have no way of knowing whether homographs were also homophones.

COMPREHENSION QUIZ

1. Semantics is usually defined as
   a. the study of etymology.
   b. the science of language.
   c. the study of meanings.
   d. the investigation of regional dialects.
2. Which one of the following does the process of symbolization *not* include?
   a. A vocal sound or its written representation.
   b. A set of musical tones or an arrangement of pigments.
   c. A single motor response or arousing an expectation of another event.
   d. A concept or feeling or a class of concepts or feelings.
3. With respect to the question of whether it is possible to think without using language, Salomon
   a. offers no final answer.
   b. regards language as vitally necessary to the ability to think.
   c. believes that thinking occurs on several levels in addition to the verbal.
   d. says that investigations into the structure of brain cells will yield an answer within the near future.
4. The author focuses on the meaning of
   a. sounds.
   b. words.
   c. sentences.
   d. longer units of communication.
5. Which of the following statements is *not* true?
   a. The spoken language must have come into existence long before writing was invented.
   b. Most of us regard the written convention as the controlling one when it comes to separating the parts of a sentence into smaller units of meaning.
   c. The spelling of English is, to a large extent, unphonetic.
   d. There are no modern words that owe their origin entirely to the written language.
6. Which of the following groups of words do not have any meaning (in the ordinary sense) at all?
   a. Interjections used as introductory noises to ease the tone of discourse.
   b. Formal additives that appear in some constructions but not in others.
   c. Compound verbs in which "words" are interchangeable with their apparent opposites.
   d. Symbols based on social convenience rather than logical necessity or moral obligation.

DISCUSSION QUESTIONS

1. Salomon regards words as the chief vehicles of meaning. What are some other methods of conveying meaning?

2. How valid is the following statement: "I know what I mean, but I don't know how to say it"?
3. What is the "dilemma of circularity"? Describe an instance of this occurrence in your own life.
4. It has been suggested that the basis of most disagreements—personal as well as national—is the failure to understand one another's real meaning. Do you agree?
5. If words never have exactly the same meaning, how do people succeed in communicating?

WRITING SUGGESTIONS

1. Define one of the following words: "meaning"; "truth"; "word."
2. We often have signal reactions to verbal symbols like "mother" and "communist." Analyze the reactions provoked by several other words; consider, for example, "Negro," "flag," and "women and children."
3. Explain why it is impossible for anyone to decide for others what words mean.

Classification

by S. I. HAYAKAWA

When a legal distinction is determined . . . between night and day, childhood and maturity, or any other extremes, a point has to be fixed or a line has to be drawn, or gradually picked out by successive decisions, to mark where the change takes place. Looked at by itself without regard to the necessity behind it, the line or point seems arbitrary. It might as well be a little more to the one side or the other. But when it is seen that a line or point there must be, and that there is no mathematical or logical way of fixing it precisely, the decision of the legislature must be accepted unless we can say that it is very wide of any reasonable mark.

—OLIVER WENDELL HOLMES

For of course the true meaning of a term is to be found by observing what a man does with it, not by what he says about it.

—P. W. BRIDGMAN

Giving Things Names

The figure below shows eight objects, let us say animals, four large and four small, a different four with round heads and another four with square heads, and still another four with curly tails and another four with straight tails. These animals, let us say, are scampering about your village, but since at first they are of no importance to you, you ignore them. You do not even give them a name.

One day, however, you discover that the little ones eat up your grain, while the big ones do not. A differentiation sets itself up, and abstracting the common characteristics of A, B, C, and D, you decide to call these *gogo;* E, F, G, and H you decide to call *gigi.* You chase away the *gogo,* but leave the *gigi* alone. Your neighbor, however, has had a different experience; he

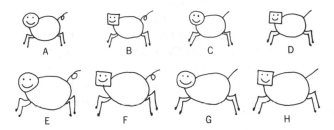

finds that those with square heads bite, while those with round heads do not. Abstracting the common characteristics of B, D, F, and H, he calls them *daba,* and A, C, E, and G he calls *dobo.* Still another neighbor discovers, on the other hand, that those with curly tails kill snakes, while those with straight tails do not. He differentiates them, abstracting still another set of common characteristics: A, B, E, and F are *busa,* while C, D, G, and H are *busana.*

Now imagine that the three of you are together when E runs by. You say, "There goes the *gigi*"; your first neighbor says, "There goes the *dobo*"; your other neighbor says, "There goes the *busa.*" Here immediately a great controversy arises. What is it really, a *gigi,* a *dobo,* or a *busa?* What is its *right name?* You are quarreling violently when along comes a fourth person from another village who calls it a *muglock,* an edible animal, as opposed to *uglock,* an inedible animal—which doesn't help matters a bit.

Of course, the question, "What is it *really?* What is its *right name?*" is a nonsense question. By a nonsense question is meant one that is not capable of being answered. Things can have "right names" only if there is a necessary connection between symbols and things symbolized, and we have seen that there is not. That is to say, in the light of your interest in protecting your grain, it may be necessary for you to distinguish the animal E as a *gigi;* your neighbor, who doesn't like to be bitten, finds it practical to distinguish it as a *dobo;* your other neighbor, who likes to see snakes killed, distinguishes it as a *busa.* What we call things and where we draw the line between one class of things and another depend upon the interests we have and the purposes of the classification. For example, animals are classified in one way by the meat industry, in a different way by the leather industry, in another different way by the fur industry, and in a still different way by the biologist. None of these classifications is any more final than any of the others; each of them is useful for its purpose.

This holds, of course, for everything we perceive. A table "is" a table to us, because we can understand its relationship to our conduct and interests; we eat at it, work on it, lay things on it. But to a person living in a culture where no tables are used, it may be a very big stool, a small platform, or a meaningless structure. If our culture and upbringing were different, that is to say, our world would not even look the same to us.

Many of us, for example, cannot distinguish between pickerel, pike, salmon, smelts, perch, crappies, halibut, and mackerel; we say that they are "just fish, and I don't like fish." To a seafood connoisseur, however, these distinctions are real, since they mean the difference to him between one kind of good meal, a very different kind of good meal, or a poor meal. To a zoologist, even finer distinctions become of great importance, since he has other and more general ends in view. When we hear the statement, then, "This fish is a specimen of the pompano, *Trachinotus carolinus,*" we accept this as being "true," even if we don't care, not because that is its "right name," but because that is how it is *classified* in the most complete and most general system of classification which people most deeply interested in fish have evolved.

When we name something, then, we are classifying. *The individual object or event we are naming, of course, has no name and belongs to no class until we put it in one.* To illustrate again, suppose that we were to give the *extensional* meaning of the word "Korean." We would have to point to all "Koreans" living at a particular moment and say, "The word 'Korean' denotes at the present moment these persons: A_1, A_2, A_3 . . . A_n." Now, let us say, a child, whom we shall designate as Z, is born among these "Koreans." *The extensional meaning of the word "Korean," determined prior to the existence of Z, does not include Z.* Z is a new individual belonging to no classification, since all classifications were made without taking Z into account. Why, then, is Z also a "Korean"? *Because we say so.* And, saying so— fixing the classification—we have determined to a considerable extent future attitudes toward Z. For example, Z will always have certain rights in Korea; he will always be regarded in other nations as an "alien" and will be subject to laws applicable to "aliens."

In matters of "race" and "nationality," the way in which classifications work is especially apparent. For example, the present writer is by birth a "Canadian," by "race" a "Japanese," and is now an "American." Although he was legally admitted to the United States on a Canadian passport as a "non-quota immigrant," he was unable to apply for American citizenship until after 1952. According to American immigration law (since 1952 as well as before), a Canadian entering the United States as a permanent resident has no trouble getting in, unless he happens to be of Oriental extraction, in which case his "nationality" becomes irrelevant and he is classified by "race." If the quota for his "race"—for example, Japanese—is filled (and it usually is), and if he cannot get himself classified as a non-quota immigrant, he is not able to get in at all. Are all these classifications "real"? Of course they are, and *the effect that each of them has upon what he may and may not do constitutes their "reality."*

The writer has spent his entire life, except for short visits abroad, in Canada and the United States. He speaks Japanese haltingly, with a child's vocabulary and an American accent; he does not read or write it. Nevertheless, because classifications seem to have a kind of hypnotic power over some people, he is occasionally credited with (or accused of) having an "Oriental mind." Since Buddha, Confucius, General Tojo, Mao Tse-tung, Pandit Nehru, Syngman Rhee, and the proprietor of the Golden Pheasant Chop Suey House all have "Oriental minds," it is difficult to know whether to feel complimented or insulted.

When is a person a "Negro"? By the definition accepted in the United States, any person with even a small amount of "Negro blood"—that is, whose parents or ancestors were classified as "Negroes"—is a "Negro." *It would be exactly as justifiable to say that any person with even a small amount of "white blood" is "white."* Why do they say one rather than the other? Because the former system of classification *suits the purposes of those making the classification.* Classification is not a matter of identifying "essences," as is widely believed. It is simply a reflection of social convenience and necessity— and different necessities are always producing different classifications.

There are few complexities about classifications at the level of dogs and cats, knives and forks, cigarettes and candy, but when it comes to classifications at high levels of abstraction—for example, those describing conduct, social institutions, philosophical and moral problems—serious difficulties occur. When one person kills another, is it an act of murder, an act of temporary insanity, an act of homicide, an accident, or an act of heroism? As soon as the process of classification is completed, our attitudes and our conduct are to a considerable degree determined. We hang the murderer, we lock up the insane man, we free the victim of circumstances, we pin a medal on the hero.

Unfortunately, people are not always aware of the way in which they arrive at their classifications. Unaware of those characteristics of the extensional Mr. Miller not covered by classifying him as "a Jew," and attributing to Mr. Miller all the characteristics *suggested* by the affective connotations of the term with which he has been classified, they pass final judgment on Mr. Miller by saying, "Well, a Jew's a Jew. There's no getting around that!"

We need not concern ourselves here with the injustices done to "Jews," "Roman Catholics," "Republicans," "red-heads," "chorus girls," "sailors," "brass-hats," "Southerners," "Yankees," "school teachers," "government regulations," "socialistic proposals," and so on, by such hasty judgments or, as it is better to call them, fixed reactions. "Hasty judgments" suggests that such errors can be avoided by thinking more slowly; this, of course, is not the case, for some people think very slowly with no better results. What we are concerned with is the way in which we block the development of our own minds by such automatic reactions.

To continue with our example of the people who say, "A Jew's a Jew. There's no getting around that!"—they are, as we have seen, confusing the denoted, extensional Jew with the fictitious "Jew" inside their heads. Such persons, the reader will have observed, can usually be made to admit, on being reminded of certain "Jews" whom they admire—perhaps Albert

Einstein, perhaps Associate Justice Arthur Goldberg, perhaps Jascha Heifetz, perhaps Mort Sahl—that "there are exceptions, of course." They have been compelled by experience, that is to say, to take cognizance of at least a few of the multitude of "Jews" who do not fit their preconceptions. At this point, however, they continue triumphantly, "But exceptions only prove the rule!"[1] —which is another way of saying, "Facts don't count."

The writer, who lives in Marin County, California, once attended hearings at the county court house concerning a proposed ordinance to forbid racial discrimination in the rental and sale of housing. (Such discrimination in Marin is chiefly directed against Negroes.) He was impressed by the fact that a large majority of those who rose to speak were in favor of the ordinance; but he was also impressed by the number who, though maintaining that they counted Negroes among their best and most admired friends, still spoke heatedly against a law that would, by forbidding racial discrimination in the sale and rental of housing, enable Negroes to live anywhere in the county. Presumably, all the Negroes whom they loved and admired were "exceptions," and the stereotyped "Negro" remained in their heads in spite of their experience.

People like this may be said to be impervious to new information. They continue to vote for their party *label,* no matter what mistakes their party makes. They continue to object to "socialists," no matter what the socialists propose. They continue to regard "mothers" as sacred, no matter which mother. A woman who had been given up both by physicians and psychiatrists as hopelessly insane was being considered by a committee whose task it was to decide whether or not she should be committed to an asylum. One member of the committee doggedly refused to vote for commitment. "Gentlemen," he said in tones of deepest reverence, "you must remember that this woman is, after all, a mother."[2] Similarly such people continue to hate "Protestants," no matter which Protestant. Unaware of characteristics left out in the process of classification, they overlook, when the term "Republican" is applied to the party of Abraham Lincoln, the party of Warren Harding, the party of Herbert Hoover, and the party of Dwight Eisenhower, the rather important differences between them.

Cow₁ Is Not Cow₂

How do we prevent ourselves from getting into such intellectual blind alleys, or, finding we are in one, how do we get out again? One way is to

[1] This extraordinarily fatuous saying originally meant, "The exception *tests* the rule" —*Exceptio probat regulam*. This older meaning of the word "prove" survives in such an expression as "automobile proving ground."

[2] One wonders how this committee member would have felt about Elizabeth Duncan, executed for murder in San Quentin in 1962, whose possessive love of her son led her to hire assassins to kill her pregnant daughter-in-law.

remember that practically all statements in ordinary conversation, debate, and public controversy taking the form, "Republicans are Republicans," "Business is business," "Boys will be boys," "Women drivers are women drivers," and so on, are *not true*. Let us put one of these back into a context in life.

> "I don't think we should go through with this deal, Bill. Is it altogether fair to the railroad company?"
> "Aw, forget it! *Business is business,* after all."

Such an assertion, although it looks like a "simple statement of fact," is not simple and is not a statement of fact. The first "business" *denotes* transaction under discussion; the second "business" invokes the *connotations* of the word. The sentence is a *directive,* saying, "Let us treat this transaction with complete disregard for considerations other than profit, as the word 'business' suggests." Similarly, when a father tries to excuse the mischief done by his sons, he says, "Boys will be boys"; in other words, "Let us regard the actions of my sons with that indulgent amusement customarily extended toward those whom we call 'boys,' " though the angry neighbor will say, of course, "Boys, my eye! They're little hoodlums; that's what they are!" These too are not informative statements but directives, directing us to classify the object or event under discussion in given ways, in order that we may feel or act in the ways suggested by the terms of the classification.

There is a simple technique for preventing such directives from having their harmful effect on our thinking. It is the suggestion made by Korzybski that we add "index numbers" to our terms, thus: $Englishman_1$, $Englishman_2$, $Englishman_3$, . . . ; cow_1, cow_2, cow_3, . . . ; $Frenchman_1$, $Frenchman_2$, $Frenchman_3$, . . . ; $communist_1$, $communist_2$, $communist_3$, . . . The terms of the classification tell us what the individuals in that class have in common; *the index numbers remind us of the characteristics left out.* A rule can then be formulated as a general guide in all our thinking and reading: Cow_1 is not cow_2; Jew_1 is not Jew_2; $politician_1$ is not $politician_2$, and so on. This rule, if remembered, prevents us from confusing levels of abstraction and forces us to consider the facts on those occasions when we might otherwise find ourselves leaping to conclusions which we might later have cause to regret.

"Truth"

Most intellectual problems are, ultimately, problems of classification and nomenclature. Some years ago there was a dispute between the American Medical Association and the Antitrust Division of the Department of Justice as to whether the practice of medicine was a "profession" or "trade."

The American Medical Association *wanted* immunity from laws prohibiting "restraint of trade"; therefore, it insisted that medicine *is* a "profession." The Antitrust Division *wanted* to stop certain economic practices connected with medicine, and therefore it insisted that medicine *is* a "trade." Partisans of either side accused the other of perverting the meanings of words, and of not being able to understand plain English.

Can farmers operate oil wells and still be "farmers"? In 1947 the attorney general of the state of Kansas sued to dissolve a large agricultural cooperative, Consumers Cooperative Association, charging that the corporation, in owning oil wells, refineries, and pipe-lines, was exceeding the statutory privileges of purchasing cooperatives under the Cooperative Marketing Act, which permits such organizations to "engage in any activity in connection with manufacturing, selling, or supplying to its members machinery, equipment or supplies." The attorney general held that the cooperative, under the Act, could not handle, let alone process and manufacture, general farm supplies, but only those supplies used in the marketing operation. The Kansas Supreme Court decided unanimously in favor of the defendant (CCA). In so deciding, the court held that gasoline and oil *are* "farm supplies," and producing crude oil *is* "part of the business of farming." The decision which thus enlarged the definition of "farming" read,

> This court will take judicial notice of the fact that in the present state of the art of farming, gasoline . . . is one of the costliest items in the production of agricultural commodities. . . . Anyway, gasoline and tractors are here, and this court is not going to say that motor fuel is not a supply necessary to carrying on of farm operations. . . . Indeed it is about as well put as can be on Page 18 of the state's Exhibit C where the defendant (CCA) says: "*Producing crude oil, operating pipe-lines and refineries, are also part of the business of farming. It is merely producing synthetic hay for iron horses. It is 'off-the-farm farming' which the farmer, in concert with his neighbors, is carrying on.* . . . Production of power farming equipment, then, is logically an extension of the farmers' own farming operations." (Italics supplied.)

Is a harmonica player a "musician"? Until 1948, the American Federation of Musicians had ruled that the harmonica was a "toy." Professional harmonica players usually belonged, therefore, to the American Guild of Variety Artists. Even as distinguished a musician as Larry Adler, who has often played the harmonica as a solo instrument with symphony orchestras, was by the union's definition "not a musician." In 1948, however, the AFM, finding that harmonica players were getting popular and competing with members of the union, decided that they were "musicians" after all—a decision that did not sit well with the president of AGVA, who promptly declared jurisdictional war on the AFM.[3]

[3] "The S.F. Police Dept. Bagpipe Band . . . will soon be decked out in the traditional finery of bagpipers. Pan-Am is flying over from Scotland 21 uniforms. . . . The

Thurman Arnold tells of another instance of a problem in classification:

A plaster company was scraping gypsum from the surface of the ground. If it was a mine, it paid one tax; if a manufacturing company, it paid another. Expert witnesses were called who almost came to blows, such was their disgust at the stupidity of those who could not see that the process was essentially mining, or manufacturing. A great record was built up to be reviewed by the State Supreme Court on this important question of "fact."[4]

Is aspirin a "drug" or not? In some states, it is legally classified as a "drug," and therefore it can be sold only by licensed pharmacists. If people want to be able to buy aspirin in groceries, lunchrooms, and pool halls (as they can in other states), they must have it reclassified as "not a drug."

Is medicine a "profession" or a "trade"? Is the production of crude oil "a part of farming"? Is a harmonica player a "musician"? Is aspirin a "drug"? Such questions are commonly settled by appeals to dictionaries to discover the "real meanings" of the words involved. It is also common practice to consult past legal decisions and all kinds of learned treatises bearing on the subject. The decision finally rests, however, not upon appeals to past authority, but upon *what people want*. If they want the AMA to be immune from antitrust action, they will go to the Supreme Court if necessary to get medicine "defined" as a "profession." If they want the AMA prosecuted, they will get a decision that it is a "trade." (They got, in this case, a decision from the Court that it did not matter whether the pracice of medicine was a "trade" or not; what mattered was that the AMA had, as charged, *restrained* the trade of Group Health Association, Inc., a cooperative which procured medical services for its members. The antitrust action was upheld.)

If people want agricultural cooperatives to operate oil wells, they will get the courts to define the activity in such a way as to make it possible. If the public doesn't care, the decision whether a harmonica player is or is not a "musician" will be made by the stronger trade union. The question whether aspirin is or is not a "drug" will be decided neither by finding the dictionary definition of "drug" nor by staring long and hard at an aspirin tablet. It will be decided on the basis of where and under what conditions people want to buy their aspirin.

In any case, society as a whole ultimately gets, on all issues of wide public importance, the classifications it wants, even if it has to wait until all the members of the Supreme Court are dead and an entirely new court is appointed. When the desired decision is handed down, people say, "Truth has triumphed." *In short, society regards as "true" those systems of classification that produce the desired results.*

---

pipers, by the way, don't have to belong to the Musicians Union since the bagpipe is classified as 'an instrument of war.' Has there ever been any doubt?" Herb Caen in the San Francisco *Chronicle*.

4 *The Folklore of Capitalism* (1938), p. 182.

The scientific test of "truth," like the social test, is strictly practical, except for the fact that the "desired results" are more severely limited. The results desired by society may be irrational, superstitious, selfish, or humane, but the results desired by scientists are only that our systems of classification produce predictable results. Classifications, as amply indicated already, determine our attitudes and behavior toward the object or event classified. When lightning was classified as "evidence of divine wrath," no courses of action other than prayer were suggested to prevent one's being struck by lightning. As soon, however, as it was classified as "electricity," Benjamin Franklin achieved a measure of control over it by his invention of the lightning rod. Certain physical disorders were formerly classified as "demonic possession," and this suggested that we "drive the demons out" by whatever spells or incantations we could think of. The results were uncertain. But when those disorders were classified as "bacillus infections," courses of action were suggested that led to more predictable results.

Science seeks only the *most generally useful* systems of classification; these it regards for the time being, until more useful classifications are invented, as "true."

COMPREHENSION QUIZ

1. According to Hayakawa, the question, "What is it *really*? What is its *right name?*"
   a. is a nonsense question.
   b. is capable of being answered.
   c. can yield the true essence of the object referred to.
   d. can be answered only after analyzing the object.
2. Which of the following statements is false?
   a. The individual object or event we are naming has no name and belongs to no class until we put it in one.
   b. Classification systems derive their "reality" from the effects they have upon the objects so classified.
   c. Classification is a matter of identifying "essences."
   d. Classification is a reflection of social convenience and necessity.
3. The sentence, "Business is business, after all," is
   a. a simple statement of fact.
   b. an informative statement.
   c. an example of the avoidance of confusing levels of abstraction.
   d. a directive.
4. Which of the following statements is true?
   a. Society regards as "true" those systems of classification that produce the desired results.
   b. Science seeks only the most generally useful systems of classification.

c.   The results desired by scientists are only that our systems of classification produce predictable results.

d.   All of the above.

5.   The author relates a personal anecdote concerning

a.   his doctoral program at the University of Wisconsin.

b.   the difficulties he experienced while learning the English language.

c.   a hearing he attended concerning a proposed housing ordinance.

d.   the virtues of having an "Oriental mind."

DISCUSSION QUESTIONS

1.   How do labels or classifications help to give an object its "reality"?

2.   Humor is often based on shifts of classification. Can you think of any jokes or puns that utilize this technique?

3.   How does the scientific test of "truth" differ from the social test? Which is more widely adopted? Which endures longer?

WRITING SUGGESTIONS

1.   Many of us fall back upon stereotypes when responding to or considering a class-word or classification. To illustrate this fact, select one of the following terms and describe the picture that comes to mind: "Grandmother"; "Boy Scout"; "communist"; "professor" "football hero."

2.   Hayakawa says that our systems of classification are merely reflections of social convenience and necessity. In a theme, describe such a classification system, showing how it fulfills "social convenience and necessity."

3.   Cite an example based on your own observation of the confusion between "cow_1, cow_2, cow_3, . . ."

4.   The author claims that most intellectual problems are ultimately problems of classification and nomenclature. Describe such a problem.

Our Symbol-Laden Culture

by JOHN C. CONDON, JR.

Millions of Americans begin their day something like this: A radio alarm clock awakens them, perhaps with music, and later with news. They dress according to the fashion and what the weather report recommends; they listen to the news of prison riots, of wars in far-off lands, or sports scores from across the nation. A famous man has died, and the millions are saddened, if only briefly. They may gobble down a vitamin pill but then skip breakfast, quickly brush their teeth, and hurry off to work. If they drive, they watch their speedometer to stay under the legal limit while keeping track of how much time they still have to arrive at their destination on time. This is how the day begins.

For a day to commence (and continue) in this manner these millions must have accepted a very sophisticated and complex set of symbols, for there is very little in the description that is not heavily endowed with symbols. *The clock* that wakes one—a revolutionary change from not so many centuries ago, when the sunrise or a rooster did the job with the result that days varied considerably from season to season. With the invention of the clock, the abstract notion of time was arbitrarily marked off into convenient units. *The clothing*—a choice of formal or casual, of coat and tie for men, of heels for women; how many buttons on the coat, how wide the tie, how high the heels, all of these arbitrary decisions are quite unrelated to the more practical purpose of keeping the body comfortable. This is not to say that style means nothing to these millions, for the hyperbolic woman "would rather *die* than be caught in last year's style!" *The news reports* that enrage or sadden them are of people they have never met, of events they can never know, of places they have never been. Nevertheless, for these millions the names on the news "mean" more than the names of their neighbors. The *vitamin pill* appears to be like thousands of other pills, but the label on the bottle is impressive with its fine print of unpronounceable names. And besides, anything that costs that much must have *something*. They compulsively brush their teeth, because they believe that brushing prevents cavities (though most do not really know why). They drive on the right side of the street because they agreed to do so. They agree to travel at a speed that traffic signs permit and assume that their speed is correct when a needle on the dashboard points to the appropriate number. And the millions hurry to their destinations because they have agreed to begin work at nine, and being too early will communicate something undesirable to their colleagues (and themselves, perhaps) and being too late will communicate something else to their bosses. Out of respect for the millions, we will end the story before the day's *work* begins.

The history of human civilization is a history of the increasing importance of the symbolic dimension of life. An underdeveloped society has far fewer codes of behavior than does a complex civilization. Susanne Langer[1] has said that "the symbol-making function is one of man's primary activities, like eating, looking, or moving about." And because we can note that the symbolic functions pervade the other primary functions and even can come to replace the "basic needs," it is essential that we examine closely the symbols we live by.

Of Mice and Men, Signs and Symbols

There are many metaphors for what language is for man. It is a tool, a map, a weapon, a toy, a surrogate, a mask—many metaphors for the many functions of language. All of the functions of language, if they are to aid man, in some ways affect that most basic need of any living organism, survival. From the premise that survival is desirable, it follows that the language that best aids survival is the best language. The implication of this conclusion is the subject of most of this chapter.

Darwin's thesis holds for man as well as for any animal: that when the survival mechanism of any creature fails, that animal ceases to exist. What the bee or the beaver needed to survive in 1666 is the same mechanism the bee or beaver employs in 1966. And if conditions should change greatly in those three hundred years, the bee and beaver will join the brontosaurus. The skill for survival is built into the animals, a literal and complete "design for living." Adopt another skill as occasion demands, the animal cannot.

But man is something different. Man has developed a physiology slightly different from his nearest simian brother. Man possesses a forebrain (cortex)

[1] Susanne Langer, *Philosophy in a New Key* (Cambridge: Harvard University Press, 1942), p. 41.

larger than the "closest ape," and this distinction, which is one of degree, permits a behavior that is utterly different in kind. With his enlarged forebrain man can perform an exercise more marvelous than any of the animals he sometimes praises: man is able to think. And, as W. Grey Walter[2] puts it, physiologically speaking, *Cogito ergo sum* is true for man; man exists (survives) because he can think.

> Man . . . is specifically what he is by virtue of thought, and owes his survival in the struggle for existence to the development of that supreme function of the brain. He is sapiens, the thinking species of the genus homo. The discerning, discreet and judicious one, even if he does not always live up to all these meanings of the name he has given himself.

Because no animal possesses the more fully developed forebrain that makes language possible, the communication skills of an animal are rather limited. In nature, animals have many ingenious (to us) ways of warning of danger or of flirting with a mate or of passing on useful information. Bees give directions to each other by dancing. Porpoises seem to have a small vocabulary of meaningful noises that they burble at each other. In captivity, animals can be taught some new skills: parrots are accustomed to saying a few words in public, and even old dogs can learn a few new tricks. The young ape can be taught to outperform the human infant. One ape has been taught to mouthe a half-dozen words. Recently, too, some chimpanzees have learned to perform simple arithmetic exercises, using a machine constructed for this purpose. But only the lowest level of what could be called a "verbal skill" can be learned by any creature besides man. Anything sophisticated, such as the linking together of several symbols, is beyond even the brightest ape. A rat may learn to find its way through a maze by trial and error, but it cannot plan the trip by studying a map.

In terms of survival, man's ability to think means many things. It means, first of all, that man can adapt himself to new or changing conditions. It took Noah to build the ark, for even if the animals could sense the storm, they could not call themselves together to weather it out. The ability to think means also that man gives himself skills he was not born with. It is true that man was not made to fly, but in two generations he has become the most skillful flier known. The ability to think means that to a great extent man can create the kind of environment he wants to live in; only man can now live comfortably at any point on the earth, or under the seas or even away from the earth.

Unfortunately, along with the marvelous achievements of man come blunders and stupidity and cruelty that are unknown even to a rat. For though man can turn the desert into a garden, can plan his community, his

---

[2] W. Grey Walter, *The Living Brain* (New York: W. W. Norton, 1953), p. 15.

birthrate, and increase his lifespan, only man can also plan his death or the death of his entire species. And no white rat would flee his property because a black rat had moved into the hole next door.

The ability to use language means the ability to transfer something of experience into symbols and *through the symbolic medium to share experience*. Man, through his ability to use language, is capable of learning from the past. Man has thus advanced while other creatures have not, cannot. Because man's experience is built upon experience, change accelerates at a geometric rate. Witness the developments in the past fifty years as compared to the previous fifteen hundred. As we enter the "Age of the Computer," the promises for man are almost incredible. Never before has the retrieval and analysis of information been possible with the speed or accuracy permitted by this cybernetic revolution. To transfer the symbolic experience into meaningful human behavior is, of course, another task, a task that, up until now, man has not always taken onto himself.

To briefly review, man is distinguished physiologically from animals by an enlarged forebrain or cortex that makes language and thought possible. Through language man can express his experience in symbols, and through those symbols he can share his experiences with his fellow man. The sharing of meaningful experiences results in the change we call learning. As man learns he advances, or at least changes, from generation to generation. Animals, which are capable of communicating in varied but comparatively limited ways, cannot learn from each other, cannot change, cannot advance.

This distinction between man and animals finds its counterpart in the kinds of communication performed by each. Animals can learn to respond to *signs,* but only man can use *symbols.* Susanne Langer expresses the difference by saying that signs announce but symbols remind. That is, animals can emit and receive cries signifying food or sex or danger. But an animal cannot contemplate the nature of food and thereby decide it might be a good idea to go on a diet.

Another distinction between sign and symbol is the difference in number of possible responses. A sign stands in a one-to-one relationship with an experience (or object, or the like); a symbol suggests many possible responses. A sign of danger, such as a loud noise, may only stimulate an animal to flee. The symbol *danger* may mean many things, of which fleeing might be the least useful. The variety of responses with which man may respond to symbols gives him increased flexibility and requires him to pause for consideration of the most appropriate response before acting. To jump at every warning is to put man at the level of the rabbit.

Mark Twain[3] once made this same observation when he noted that we sometimes behave like animals instead of behaving like people:

[3] Bernard DeVoto (ed.), *The Portable Mark Twain* (New York: Viking, 1946), p. 563.

We should be careful to get out of an experience only the wisdom that is in it—and stop there lest we be like the cat that sits down on a hot stove lid. She will never sit down on a hot stove-lid again, and that is well; but also she will never sit down on a cold one anymore.

To go from cat to mouse, we may recall Wendell Johnson's remark on this distinction: "To a mouse, cheese is cheese; that's why mousetraps work."

In times of stress man does often respond to a word (symbol) as if it were a sign: he reacts signally. As he does so he acts more like an animal than a human being. A letter to the editors of the *Christian Science Monitor*[4] describes such an incident in Boston:

During a big meeting in Boston, I took 16 women from all over the country, to a downtown restaurant via the subway. None of these women had even seen a subway before, and were very timid about the ride.

We arrived at the subway at the rush hour, and after warning and pushing, we all got on, and were immediately scattered throughout the car.

I got to talking and forgot about the station; when all of a sudden I realized that we were at our stop. The door was open, and I didn't know how long we had to get off.

I realized instantly that I had to get every one of these 16 women off that car, or we would probably not see each other again, at least that week! So, I just shut my eyes, jumped to my feet, and shouted: "We get off here!" at the top of my voice.

Everyone of the 16 shot to her feet, with little cries of excitement. The other people sitting with them leaped to their feet, too, and started following us as we rushed for the door. Even the motorman jumped up and looked around.

The man who had been sitting next to me, with his briefcase on his knees, his hat on top, had been peacefully reading his newspaper, when I jumped to my feet and shouted. He jammed his hat on his head, grabbed his briefcase, and started after me. Suddenly he realized that he did NOT want to get off at that station. He gave me a reproachful look, which I returned with an apologetic one.

If we smile at the situation and think, "how human," we should think twice—for how *un*human, how animal-like the reactions were.

Man creates a few signs for his immediate reactions. The alarm-clock buzzer, the class bell, and the stop sign are each designed by man to elicit one appropriate and immediate response. But such signs are few. Inappropriate signal reactions are, unfortunately, more common. Whether we jump to conclusions, refuse to listen to information because of a label we have given its source ("don't believe anything *she* says"), or blush at certain words, we are also responding signally. Such reactions fail to use the resources of

4 Letter by Martha E. Tull to the *Christian Science Monitor*, October 14, 1963.

language as they might best be used. Learning to use language intelligently begins by learning not to be used by language.

COMPREHENSION QUIZ

1. All of the following are used in this essay as metaphors for what language is to man, except
   a. a mask.
   b. a surrogate.
   c. a sponge.
   d. a toy.
2. Because man's experience is built upon experience, change accelerates
   a. quickly.
   b. steadily.
   c. at a geometric rate.
   d. at an arithmetic rate.
3. The sharing of meaningful experiences results in the change called
   a. learning.
   b. reasoning.
   c. symbolic reception.
   d. none of these.
4. While man can use symbols, animals respond to
   a. symbols.
   b. stimuli.
   c. noises.
   d. signs.
5. Communication skills of animals are rather limited because they possess no
   a. fully developed language.
   b. ability to form words with the lips or mouth.
   c. fully developed forebrain.
   d. vortex.
6. In addition to the primary activities of eating and looking about, man also has that
   a. symbol-making function.
   b. sign-making activity.
   c. both (a) and (b).
   d. neither (a) nor (b).
7. The difference between signs and symbols can be expressed by saying that
   a. symbols announce while signs remind.
   b. symbols remind while signs announce.
   c. a symbol suggests only one possible response.
   d. a sign suggests many possible responses.
8. The author suggests that man is far superior to animals in every area except
   a. reasoning.
   b. cruelty to others of his same species.

   c.   mobility.
   d.   ability at nonverbal communication.

DISCUSSION QUESTIONS

 1. Can you explain how a symbolic function can come to replace a "basic need"?
 2. If change is ever accelerating, what problems can you see for language?
 3. What does the author mean by saying "To transfer the symbolic experience into meaningful human behavior is . . . a task that, up to now man has not always taken on himself."
 4. The difference between a sign and a symbol was brought out in the essay. Can you cite clearly an example of each?
 5. What are some examples of man's response to signs rather than symbols?
 6. How can you illustrate the statement, "To jump at every warning is to put man at the level of the rabbit"?
 7. Of what value might the knowledge about the characteristics of signs and symbols be to a soldier in training for the battlefield? How about a football team training for a crucial game?
 8. What is your understanding of the term "cybernetic revolution"?
 9. Why did the author place the word "work" in italics? (It appears at the end of the second paragraph of the article.)
10. Does any animal possess, or approach possession of, the capability to use symbols?
11. Can you explain how one might be "used" by language, as the author suggests in his last sentence?

WRITING SUGGESTIONS

 1. Write a short humorous article based generally on the material in this article, and entitled, "To a Mouse, Cheese Is Cheese."
 2. Write an explanation of the differences between signs and symbols. Include in your paper several examples of the use of both of these two. The last paragraph of this essay may be helpful.
 3. Write a 500 word essay on the subject, "Learning to Use Language Intelligently Begins by Learning Not to Be Used by Language."

Prejudice: Linguistic Factors

by GORDON W. ALLPORT

Without words we should scarcely be able to form categories at all. A dog perhaps forms rudimentary generalizations, such as small-boys-are-to-be-avoided—but this concept runs its course on the conditioned reflex level, and does not become the object of thought as such. In order to hold a generalization in mind for reflection and recall, for identification and for action, we need to fix it in words. Without words our world would be, as William James said, an "empirical sand-heap."

Nouns That Cut Slices

In the empirical world of human beings there are some two and a half billion grains of sand corresponding to our category "the human race." We cannot possibly deal with so many separate entities in our thought, nor can we individualize even among the hundreds whom we encounter in our daily round. We must group them, form clusters. We welcome, therefore, the names that help us to perform the clustering.

The most important property of a noun is that it brings many grains of sand into a single pail, disregarding the fact that the same grains might have fitted just as appropriately into another pail. To state the matter technically, a noun *abstracts* from a concrete reality some one feature and assembles different concrete realities only with respect to this one feature. The very act of classifying forces us to overlook all other features, many of which

From Gordon W. Allport, *The Nature of Prejudice*, Reading, Mass.: Addison-Wesley Publishing Company, Inc., 1954. Reprinted by permission of the publisher.

might offer a sounder basis than the rubric we select. Irving Lee gives the following example:

> I knew a man who had lost the use of both eyes. He was called a "blind man."
> He could also be called an expert typist, a conscientious worker, a good student,
> a careful listener, a man who wanted a job. But he couldn't get a job in the
> department store order room where employees sat and typed orders which
> came over the telephone. The personnel man was impatient to get the inter-
> view over. "But you're a blind man," he kept saying, and one could almost feel
> his silent assumption that somehow the incapacity in one aspect made the man
> incapable in every other. So blinded by the label was the interviewer that he
> could not be persuaded to look beyond it.[1]

Some labels, such as "blind man," are exceedingly salient and powerful. They tend to prevent alternative classification, or even cross-classification. Ethnic labels are often of this type, particularly if they refer to some highly visible feature, e.g., Negro, Oriental. They resemble the labels that point to some outstanding incapacity—*feeble-minded, cripple, blind man*. Let us call such symbols "labels of primary potency." These symbols act like shriek-ing sirens, deafening us to all finer discriminations that we might otherwise perceive. Even though the blindness of one man and the darkness of pig-mentation of another may be defining attributes for some purposes, they are irrelevant and "noisy" for others.

Most people are unaware of this basic law of language—that every label applied to a given person refers properly only to one aspect of his nature. You may correctly say that a certain man is *human, a philanthropist, a Chi-nese, a physician, an athlete*. A given person may be all of these; but the chances are that *Chinese* stands out in your mind as the symbol of primary potency. Yet neither this nor any other classificatory label can refer to the whole of a man's nature. (Only his proper name can do so.)

Thus each label we use, especially those of primary potency, distracts our attention from concrete reality. The living, breathing, complex indi-vidual—the ultimate unit of human nature—is lost to sight. As in the figure following, the label magnifies one attribute out of all proportion to its true significance, and masks other important attributes of the individual.

. . . a category, once formed with the aid of a symbol of primary po-tency, tends to attract more attributes than it should. The category labeled *Chinese* comes to signify not only ethnic membership but also reticence, impassivity, poverty, treachery. To be sure, . . . there may be genuine ethnic-linked traits making for a certain *probability* that the member of an ethnic stock may have these attributes. But our cognitive process is not cautious.

---

[1] I. J. Lee, *How Do You Talk about People?*, Freedom Pamphlet (New York, Anti-Defamation League, 1950), p. 15.

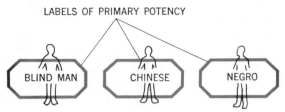

LABELS OF PRIMARY POTENCY

The labeled category, . . . includes indiscriminately the defining attribute, probable attributes, and wholly fanciful, nonexistent attributes.

Even proper names—which ought to invite us to look at the individual person—may act like symbols of primary potency, especially if they arouse ethnic associations. Mr. Greenberg is a person, but since his name is Jewish, it activates in the hearer his entire category of Jews-as-a-whole.

The anthropologist, Margaret Mead, has suggested that labels of primary potency lose some of their force when they are changed from nouns into adjectives. To speak of a Negro soldier, a Catholic teacher, or a Jewish artist calls attention to the fact that some other group classifications are just as legitimate as the racial or religious. If George Johnson is spoken of not only as a Negro but also as a *soldier,* we have at least two attributes to know him by, and two are more accurate than one. To depict him truly as an individual, of course, we should have to name many more attributes. It is a useful suggestion that we designate ethnic and religious membership where possible with *adjectives* rather than with *nouns*.

Emotionally Toned Labels

Many categories have two kinds of labels—one less emotional and one more emotional. Ask yourself how you feel, and what thoughts you have, when you read the words *school teacher,* and then *school marm.* Certainly the second phrase calls up something more strict, more ridiculous, more disagreeable than the former. Here are four innocent letters: m-a-r-m. But they make us shudder a bit, laugh a bit, and scorn a bit. They call up an image of a spare, humorless, irritable old maid. They do not tell us that she is an individual human being with sorrows and troubles of her own. They force her instantly into a rejective category.

In the ethnic sphere even plain labels such as Negro, Italian, Jew, Catholic, Irish-American, French-Canadian may have emotional tone for a reason that we shall soon explain. But they all have their higher key equivalents: nigger, wop, kike, papist, harp, cannuck. When these labels are employed we can be almost certain that the speaker *intends* not only to characterize the person's membership, but also to disparage and reject him.

Quite apart from the insulting intent that lies behind the use of certain labels, there is also an inherent ("physiognomic") handicap in many terms designating ethnic membership. For example, the proper names characteristic of certain ethnic memberships strike us as absurd. (We compare them, of course, with what is familiar and therefore "right.") Chinese names are short and silly; Polish names intrinsically difficult and outlandish. Unfamiliar dialects strike us as ludicrous. Foreign dress (which, of course, is a visual ethnic symbol) seems unnecessarily queer.

But of all these "physiognomic" handicaps the reference to color, clearly implied in certain symbols, is the greatest. The word Negro comes from the Latin *niger,* meaning black. In point of fact, no Negro has a black complexion, but by comparison with other blonder stocks he has come to be known as a "black man." Unfortunately *black* in the English language is a word having a preponderance of sinister connotations: the outlook is black, blackball, blackguard, blackhearted, black death, blacklist, blackmail, Black Hand. . . .

There is thus an implied value-judgment in the very concept of *white race* and *black race.* One might also study the numerous unpleasant connotations of *yellow,* and their possible bearing on our conception of the people of the Orient.

Such reasoning should not be carried too far, since there are undoubtedly, in various contexts, pleasant associations with both black and yellow. Black velvet is agreeable, so too are chocolate and coffee. Yellow tulips are well liked; the sun and moon are radiantly yellow. Yet it is true that "color" words are used with chauvinistic overtones more than most people realize. There is certainly condescension indicated in many familiar phrases: dark as a nigger's pocket, darktown strutters, white hope (a term originated when a white contender was sought against the Negro heavyweight champion, Jack Johnson), the white man's burden, the yellow peril, black boy. Scores of everyday phrases are stamped with the flavor of prejudice, whether the user knows it or not.[2]

Members of minority groups are often understandably sensitive to names given them. Not only do they object to deliberately insulting epithets, but sometimes see evil intent where none exists. Often the word Negro is spelled with a small *n,* occasionally as a studied insult, more often from ignorance. (The term is not cognate with white, which is not capitalized, but rather with Caucasian, which is.) Terms like "mulatto" or "octoroon" cause hard feeling because of the condescension with which they have often been used in the past. Sex differentiations are objectionable, since they seem doubly to emphasize ethnic difference: why speak of Jewess and not of Protestantess, or of Negress and not of whitess? Similar overemphasis is implied in terms like Chinaman or Scotchman; why not American man?

[2] L. L. Brown, "Words and White Chauvinism," *Masses and Mainstream* (1950), 3, pp. 3–11. See also *Prejudice Won't Hide! A Guide for Developing a Language of Equality* (San Francisco, California Federation for Civic Unity, 1950).

Grounds for misunderstanding lie in the fact that minority group members are sensitive to such shadings, while majority members may employ them unthinkingly.

The Communist Label

Until we label an out-group it does not clearly exist in our minds. Take the curiously vague situation that we often meet when a person wishes to locate responsibility on the shoulders of some out-group whose nature he cannot specify. In such a case he usually employs the pronoun "they" without an antecedent. "Why don't they make these sidewalks wider?" "I hear they are going to build a factory in this town and hire a lot of foreigners." "I won't pay this tax bill; they can just whistle for their money." If asked "who"? the speaker is likely to grow confused and embarrassed. The common use of the orphaned pronoun *they* teaches us that people often want and need to designate out-groups (usually for the purpose of venting hostility) even when they have no clear conception of the out-group in question. And so long as the target of wrath remains vague and ill-defined specific prejudice cannot crystallize around it. To have enemies we need labels.

Until relatively recently—strange as it may seem—there was no agreed-upon symbol for *communist*. The word, of course, existed but it had no special emotional connotation, and did not designate a public enemy. Even when, after World War I, there was a growing feeling of economic and social menace in this country, there was no agreement as to the actual source of the menace.

A content analysis of the *Boston Herald* for the year 1920 turned up the following list of labels. Each was used in a context implying some threat. Hysteria had overspread the country, as it did after World War II. Someone must be responsible for the postwar malaise, rising prices, uncertainty. There must be a villain. But in 1920 the villain was impartially designated by reporters and editorial writers with the following symbols:

> alien, agitator, anarchist, apostle of bomb and torch, Bolshevik, communist, communist laborite, conspirator, emissary of false promise, extremist, foreigner, hyphenated-American, incendiary, IWW, parlor anarchist, parlor pink, parlor socialist, plotter, radical, red, revolutionary, Russian agitator, socialist, Soviet, syndicalist, traitor, undesirable.

From this excited array we note that the *need* for an enemy (someone to serve as a focus for discontent and jitters) was considerably more apparent than the precise *identity* of the enemy. At any rate, there was no clearly agreed-upon label. Perhaps partly for this reason the hysteria abated. Since no clear category of "communism" existed there was no true focus for the hostility.

But following World War II this collection of vaguely interchangeable labels became fewer in number and more commonly agreed upon. The out-group menace came to be designated almost always as *communist* or *red*. In 1920 the threat, lacking a clear label, was vague; after 1945 both symbol and thing became more definite. Not that people knew precisely what they meant when they said "communist," but with the aid of the term they were at least able to point consistently to *something* that inspired fear. The term developed the power of signifying menace and led to various repressive measures against anyone to whom the label was rightly or wrongly attached.

Logically, the label should apply to specifiable defining attributes, such as members of the Communist Party, or people whose allegiance is with the Russian system, or followers, historically, of Karl Marx. But the label came in for far more extensive use.

What seems to have happened is approximately as follows. Having suffered through a period of war and being acutely aware of devastating revolutions abroad, it is natural that most people should be upset, dreading to lose their possessions, annoyed by high taxes, seeing customary moral and religious values threatened, and dreading worse disasters to come. Seeking an explanation for this unrest, a single identifiable enemy is wanted. It is not enough to designate "Russia" or some other distant land. Nor is it satisfactory to fix blame on "changing social conditions." What is needed is a human agent near at hand: someone in Washington, someone in our schools, in our factories, in our neighborhood. If we *feel* an immediate threat, we reason, there must be a near-lying danger. It is, we conclude, communism, not only in Russia but also in America, at our doorstep, in our government, in our churches, in our colleges, in our neighborhood.

Are we saying that hostility toward communism is prejudice? Not necessarily. There are certainly phases of the dispute wherein realistic social conflict is involved. American values (e.g., respect for the person) and totalitarian values as represented in Soviet practice are intrinsically at odds. A realistic opposition in some form will occur. Prejudice enters only when the defining attributes of "communist" grow imprecise, when anyone who favors any form of social change is called a communist. People who fear social change are the ones most likely to affix the label to any persons or practices that seem to them threatening.

For them the category is undifferentiated. It includes books, movies, preachers, teachers who utter what for them are uncongenial thoughts. If evil—befalls—perhaps forest fires or a rocket explosion—it is due to communist saboteurs. The category becomes monopolistic, covering almost anything that is uncongenial. On the floor of the House of Representatives in 1946, Representative Rankin called James Roosevelt a communist. Congressman Outland replied with psychological acumen, "Apparently everyone who disagrees with Mr. Rankin is a communist."

When differentiated thinking is at a low ebb—as it is in times of social crisis—there is a magnification of two-valued logic. Things are perceived as either inside or outside a moral order. What is outside is likely to be called "communist." Correspondingly—and here is where damage is done— whatever is called communist (however erroneously) is immediately cast outside the moral order.

This associative mechanism places enormous power in the hands of a demagogue. For several years Senator McCarthy managed to discredit many citizens who thought differently from himself by the simple device of calling them communists. Few people were able to see through this trick and many reputations were ruined. But the famous senator had no monopoly on the device. . . .

COMPREHENSION QUIZ

1. Which of the following labels tends to prevent alternative classification?
   a. Negro.
   b. Oriental.
   c. blind man.
   d. all of these.
2. Which of the following labels refers to the whole of a man's nature, according to Allport?
   a. physician.
   b. Mr. Ralph W. Wilson.
   c. astronaut.
   d. human.
3. A category, once formed with the aid of a symbol of primary potency,
   a. attracts few additional attributes.
   b. tends to repel other attributes.
   c. tends to attract more attributes than it should.
   d. none of these.
4. Labels of primary potency lose some of their force when changed from
   a. abstract to concrete nouns.
   b. nouns to pronouns.
   c. nouns to adjectives.
   d. concrete nouns to abstract nouns.
5. Allport says that often the word Negro is spelled with a small "n" which he attributes largely to
   a. a studied insult.
   b. prejudice.
   c. ignorance.
   d. a subtle evil intent.
6. The main objection to sex differentiation in use of primary potency labels is that
   a. they seem to doubly emphasize ethnic differences.
   b. minorities are sensitive in this area.

    c.   so many people do this unthinkingly.

    d.   both (a) and (c).

7. Allport speaks of the "orphaned" pronoun
   a. "I."
   b. "you."
   c. "those."
   d. "they."

8. When differentiated thinking is at a low ebb
   a. labels of primary potency are useless.
   b. labels of primary potency are most common.
   c. people feel that danger is near by.
   d. there is a magnification of two-valued logic.

DISCUSSION QUESTIONS

1. What are some of the probable attributes which come to your mind with the mention of the following labels of primary potency: "Catholic"; "Communist"; "hippie"; "convict"?
2. Can you list five every-day phrases stamped with the flavor of prejudice? For example: "sweat like a nigger" and "yellow streak."
3. From Allport's list of communist labels, select those which have also been applied to other persons. Have any of these been applied to you or your friends?
4. What does Allport mean by "two-valued logic"?
5. What group or groups in today's world suffer from the two-valued logic which exists? Explain your answer.
6. Allport tells us we speak of "Jewess" but not of "Protestantess"; "Negress," but not "whitess." Is this a valid objection, or does it seem to be picayune? Explain your answer. What other examples of this type of differentiation can you cite?
7. Have you ever tried to "pin down" a user of the orphaned pronoun "they"? What was your experience? Why do people use this vague term?
8. Allport says that until we label an out-group it does not clearly exist in our minds. What do you understand this to mean? Can you demonstrate this?

WRITING SUGGESTIONS

1. Write an analysis of all of the labels you have used or heard used to describe someone of an ethnic group, e.g. Jews, Irishmen, Negroes, Italians, et al.
2. Write an essay entitled, "Every Label Applied to a Given Person Refers Properly Only to One Aspect of His Nature."
3. Analyze the late Senator Joseph McCarthy's techniques for fighting "communism."
4. Identify a person you feel to be on the demagogue level. Analyze his or her techniques, applying points from Allport's article to support your analysis.

Ambiguity

by LIONEL RUBY

There are many obstacles in the path of successful communication, but ambiguity is undoubtedly the worst offender. An ambiguous word is one that may be understood in more than one sense. Thus a symbol may be interpreted differently by speaker and hearer; communicators and communicatees are at cross-purposes and there is no meeting of minds.

Most of the words in any language have more than one referent. This is in many ways a boon rather than an evil, for the range of possible meanings in any limited number of words is greatly increased. Our vocabularies are enlarged when one word has different meanings in different contexts; the single word then becomes the equivalent of many different words. In many cases the differences in referents may be on a "large" scale, as when the word "secretary" refers in turn to "a person who attends to correspondence," "an executive officer in the government," "a writing desk," and "a South African bird with long legs." There are many other words in which the differences in the referents are of a more subtle nature, the shifts in meaning being less obvious, as in the different ways in which the word "man" is used in the following contexts:

All *men* are mortal.
The child is father to the *man*.
Those were the days when *men* were *men*.
What a piece of work is *man!* How infinite in capacity!
The football team is under*manned*.

Successful communication occurs only when the reader correctly interprets the symbols used by the writer. . . . When the communication is successful then the communicator and the communicatee have their minds referred to the same referents; they have the same terms in mind. They have "come to terms." But ambiguous words are obstacles to such happy consummations; communication is frustrated. . . . When such failures of communication occur, the speaker and the hearer have different referents in mind.

But note that ambiguity is an evil only when it results in these frustrations of communication. In scientific discourse, where the aim is to achieve clear and precise reference, ambiguity is an unmitigated evil. But there are other fields of thought in which ambiguity may have certain desirable effects. This is the case in poetry, where ambiguity may sometimes contribute to the poetic effect by suggesting a rich aura of implied meanings: "Life is a tale told by an idiot, full of sound and fury, signifying nothing"; "Faith is the substance of things hoped for; the evidence of things not seen." In this manner poetry approximates the effects produced by music, which, among all of the arts, is certainly the most expressively ambiguous. One of the great charms of music lies in the ambiguity with which it expresses moods, so that each hearer may interpret the musical score in his own way. Ambiguity also has more mundane uses. Diplomatic language has developed the art of saying things ambiguously so that failure to agree will be masked by "face-saving" language. Finally, the ambiguous aspects of words are exploited as a rich source of humor. Gagsters and punsters thrive on the double-meanings of words. Our primary interest, of course, is to learn how to avoid ambiguity in scientific discourse.

Ambiguity is the direct opposite of synonymity (the use of synonymous words). An ambiguous word refers to several referents; in synonymity a single referent is referred to by several different words. "Spade" refers to at least two referents: a playing card and a garden implement. Fool, lout, simpleton, oaf, dunderhead, ninny, nincompoop, addle-pate, and dope, all refer to the same referent, or to substantially the same referent, since few synonymous words are absolutely identical in meaning. . . .

The Analysis of Ambiguity

Though many words have more than one meaning, the context of surrounding circumstances will usually clarify the sense in which the word is used. The initial ambiguity is often completely eliminated by the context. We shall be primarily concerned with examples in which the ambiguity is not eliminated by the context, with a resulting blockage of communication. . . .

When two or more interpretations of an author's language are possible, the reader does not know what is in the author's mind. We should be clear as to the task of the logician in analyzing instances of ambiguity. The logician cannot eliminate ambiguity; his primary task is to call attention to the fact that ambiguity occurs and to show the different ways in which it occurs. The logician can also help to make the reader sensitive to ambiguities in places where ambiguity might be unsuspected. The logician can also advise the reader to find out what was in the author's mind before the reader interprets ambiguous language. The reader's task here may be likened to that of a judge whose task is to decide what the legislature meant by the ambiguous language in a law. The court will investigate the circumstances in which the law was passed, the remarks of legislators concerning the intent of the law, and so on. In other words, the context will be studied for light on the probable meaning of the words.

We shall examine the manner in which ambiguity occurs in the use of words, phrases, and sentences. Ambiguity, as we know, is a fruitful source of humor, and we shall note some of the entertaining aspects of its various forms. Humorists deliberately use the ambiguities of language in various kinds of jokes and "gags." Finally, we shall examine some of the "fallacies" of ambiguity. This aspect of ambiguity is of greatest interest to the logician. The failure to recognize ambiguity often results in misinterpretations of meanings and in erroneous inferences.

The Types of Ambiguity

1. Simple Ambiguity

By *simple* ambiguity we shall mean the fact that single words or phrases may refer to more than one referent, even after we have examined their contexts. Verbal disagreements are based upon this type of ambiguity. Any statement containing a word which is ambiguous in its context exemplifies this vice: "The early Christians were communists." Since the word "communist" has more than one referent in this context, ambiguity exists. "Communists$_1$" means one who favors a system of social organization in which goods are held in common; "communist$_2$" means an advocate of "the dictatorship of the proletariat." Before we affirm or deny the truth of a statement we should find out what the writer means. Questions may also involve simple ambiguity, as in "Do you believe in God?" "God" means different things to different persons, and a yes-or-no-answer is inappropriate until we learn what referent the questioner has in mind. Spinoza, for example, defined God as "everything which exists." Spinoza was a deeply religious man whose pantheistic philosophy was permeated with devotion to God. The Catholic Church, however, has condemned his pantheism as equivalent to atheism.

Simple ambiguity is closely related to "vagueness," but should be distinguished from it. An ambiguous word has several distinct referents; a vague word lacks precision and definiteness in its reference. Thus, the question, "Has there been any progress during the past 2,000 years?" involves the use of the vague word "progress." The reader spontaneously responds to such a question with his own questions: "Progress in what sense?

In spiritual growth? In the advancement of the common man? In a material sense?" The word "progress" is vague rather than ambiguous, for in each case it means "advancement toward a definite goal," but the question does not specify the goal involved.

Vagueness, rather than ambiguity, will also be found in the following incident. In the summer of 1947 General Eisenhower was reported to have said that "the United States Army is a 'poor second' to that of Russia." Congressman Short asked, "In what sense?" In quantity? In quality? The United States Army has never been equal to the Russian army in size either in war or peace. Here too, "poor second" is not ambiguous, since it means "far behind the first," but its meaning is not precise.

Questions containing vague words cannot be answered without further clarification of their meaning. We should also note how careful thinking may result in the discovery that "clear" words are actually vague. Thus, the question "Is this building moving?" may appear to be clear. But we must ask: "In relation to which frame of reference?" In relation to the sun, this building is moving at a speed of eighteen miles per second. In relation to the earth, however, it is stationary.

Simple ambiguity has two forms, written and oral. The phonetic sound "teers" may stand for two different words: "tiers" and "tears." An amusing example of oral ambiguity based on this sound is found in the following:

> A reporter was describing a scene at the House of Commons to another reporter. "There, on the floor of the House, stood the Prime Minister speaking," he said, "back of him were the members of the Cabinet, in front of him sat the members of the Opposition, and in tiers around him sat the other members of the House."
>
> The second reporter was very young and very earnest. "Not really *tears*," he exclaimed. "Poor chaps!" (Albert Levi and Albert Frye, *Rational Belief,* Harcourt, Brace, 1941, p. 108.)

Simple ambiguity lies at the basis of much humor, especially in puns, as in Wordsworth's remark, "If I had a mind to, I could write like Shakespeare."

2. Amphiboly

"I shall lose no time in reading your manuscript," the noted critic wrote to the aspring young author. Should the author have been pleased with this message? Would the critic read his manuscript soon or never?

The critic's remark is an example of an amphibolous sentence. Its meaning is ambiguous though no *word* in the sentence is ambiguous. The ambiguity results from the way in which the words are put together in the sentence.

Amphiboly refers to the fact that the meaning of a sentence may be ambiguous, not because any of its words are ambiguous, but because the grammatical construction of the sentence permits several interpretations as to its meaning. The amphibolous sentence is capable of being understood in more than one sense. This may result in a failure in communication. A sentence combines words in order to express a thought. The referents have a certain relationship in the mind of the speaker. The grammatical construction of the sentence may fail to direct the hearer's mind to the relationship referred to by the speaker. The logician calls the reader's attention to these factors. The grammarian seeks to teach writers how to make themselves clear.

Vivid examples of amphiboly are found in humorous exaggerations of this fault. Thus, the following account was reportedly given by a newspaper reporter, with reference to the departure of the famous prewar dirigible from the Lakehurst airport: "The Graf Zeppelin was leaving the Lakehurst airport. Among the last to enter was Mrs. Smith, lone woman passenger. Slowly her huge nose was turned into the wind. Then, like some huge beast, she crawled along the grass . . ."

Grammarians have noted a type of error similar to amphiboly in the error called "the dangling participle," as in "Zooming along under her own power, Jane was fascinated by the spectacle of the glider before her." The participle "zooming" seems to refer to Jane. The words are unambiguous, but ambiguity results from the manner in which they are put together.

A famous historical source of amphiboly is found in the Delphic oracle, in ancient Greece. The oracle was certainly the most astute diplomat who ever lived and also the Nostradamus of its time, except that, unlike Nostradamus, the oracular pronouncements were right 100 per cent of the time. This success was due to the use of amphiboly. The oracle was consulted on the eve of great undertakings, in order to obtain its "inspired" predictions as to success or failure. The oracle always retained its reputation for infallibility because of the manner in which it made its pronouncements: "Apollo says that the Greeks the Persians shall subdue." Cyrus, the Persian King, sent messengers to the oracle for a prophecy concerning a projected war. The messengers were informed that "the King yet lives that Cyrus shall depose." The variant interpretations of these statements are obvious.

Amphibolous sentences of the type just noted may be called *completely* amphibolous in that the reader does not know how to interpret them correctly. In most cases, though two or more interpretations are possible, it will generally appear that one interpretation is more reasonable than the others, either from the context or the customs of speech. Thus, when a law court is presented with an amphibolous document, the "reasonable" interpretation will be applied. For example, a licensing agreement between the holder of a patent and the manufacturer provided that the manufacturer would pay the patentee "50¢ a unit for producing 5,000 units or less, and 30¢ a unit for all units of an output of over 5,000 units." The manufacturer claimed that when the output exceeded 5,000 units he was obligated to pay

30¢ per unit for *all* units produced. The court ruled that the agreement meant "50¢ for the first 5,000 units and 30¢ for all units in excess of 5,000." Otherwise the patentee would receive less royalties for a production of 6,000 units than he would receive for 4,000.

It is impossible to state whether a sentence is true or false until we understand its meaning. An amphibolous sentence must be given a definite interpretation before we can judge it as true or false. For example, a man says, "All women are not fickle." By this he may mean either that "some women are not fickle" or that "no women are fickle." If the speaker is available we should question him to determine what he meant. If he is not available, how shall we interpret the statement?

Note that the sentence takes the "All . . . are not . . ." formation. The logician adopts a rule of interpretation here, stating that all such statements shall be read as if they meant "*Not all* women are fickle" or "Some women are not fickle," unless he has clear evidence from the context or elsewhere that the speaker meant "No women are fickle." In the sentence "All human beings are not perfect" the speaker probably means "No human beings are perfect," but in "All Russians are not communists" he probably means "Some Russians are not communists."

Other types of amphiboly that require interpretation are such sentences as "All agree with me who are not ignorant of the facts." This may mean either "All who agree with me are persons who are not ignorant of the facts" or it may mean "All who are not ignorant of the facts agree with me." The speaker may mean either one, but in the absence of further evidence, the grammarian will adopt the latter interpretation as the more likely one.

3. Ambiguity in Emphasis

A unit of discourse may make different kinds of sense depending upon which of its parts we accent or emphasize. We should always seek to give writings the emphasis which the author intended them to have, but when the writing is ambiguous in this respect, the reader may be unable to determine where the proper emphasis lies. The full and complete meaning of a sentence may even require that we hear it spoken. Thus the invitation "I hope that you will come to dinner" may accent "I," "you," or "dinner" when it is spoken. When you leave, you say, "The dinner was very good." You may accent "dinner." It is for this reason that classroom instruction is superior to mere reading for most students, since the instructor gives oral emphasis to the most important words.

Ambiguity of emphasis occurs when a reader does not know which parts of a writing deserve chief emphasis. Troublesome cases of this sort occur when a writer presents somewhat conflicting points of view, as in Book V of Plato's *Republic,* concerning the nature and status of women in his ideal state. The reader will find "equalitarian" remarks such as, "The only difference between men and women consists in the fact that women bear and that men beget children," and "The differences between men and women do not justify different types of education for the two sexes. Women as well as men, should be trained to qualify as rulers of the state." But elsewhere Plato says that "women are inferior to men in all pursuits followed by each." Again, that "men and women possess the same qualities and differ only in their comparative strength and weakness." Does Plato believe that women are essentially the same as men, or does he hold that the weaker sex is the inferior sex? No one can answer this question with certainty.

When summaries are made of writings, ambiguity of emphasis may create similar difficulties. The summarizer should emphasize the most important elements. When excerpts and quotes are given they should be truly representative of the author's meaning. Summaries, however, open the door to many errors of carelessness or deliberate misinterpretation, to be discussed further under the "fallacies of ambiguity." Book reviewers are often accused of "not having read the whole book" when the author thinks that his position has been misinterpreted. The reviewer's misinterpretation, however, may be due in whole or in part to the author's failure to make his points clear. Or the author may state somewhat conflicting positions, as in the selections from Plato's *Republic*.

A different type of problem concerning emphasis or "accent" occurs in problems of punctuation. Literary scholars seek to interpret Shakespeare's meanings accurately, but there are variant readings of many of the plays. The Folio and the Second Quarto editions, the oldest sources, differ in many important respects. Consider the different possible readings of Hamlet's speech to Guildenstern (II, 2, 315). The Neilson and Hill version of the speech, based upon the Quarto version, is stated as follows:

> What a piece of work is a man! How noble in reason! How infinite in faculty! in form and moving! How express and admirable in action How like an angel in apprehension! How like a god!

The Everyman's edition, following the Folio version, prints the lines as follows:

> What a piece of work is man! How noble in reason! how infinite in faculty! in form and moving! How express and admirable in action! How like an angel in apprehension how like a god!

4. The Ambiguity of Significance

By this type we refer to statements whose semantical meaning may be clear, but whose factual significance is not. A statement may contain no ambiguous words, its sentence structure may convey an unambiguous meaning, and it may contain no ambiguities of emphasis. But its significance may be "ambiguous." As an illustration, consider the statement that there were 454 deaths due to traffic accidents in the United States during the Thanksgiving holiday weekend last year. The significance of such a statement is ambiguous in many respects. An isolated fact means something, of course. We all deplore the large number of deaths reported. But its full significance would require knowing whether the number was higher or lower than the number killed during the previous year's holiday weekend, and whether the figures for a non-holiday weekend are higher or lower.

It should be apparent that alertness to this kind of "ambiguity" is almost synonymous with the scientific attitude. Every statement whatsoever will have different kinds of significance depending upon its context or surrounding circumstances. It should also be obvious that this kind of "ambiguity" is not a genuinely semantical problem. We deal with it here only because it concerns a kind of uncertainty to which readers should be alerted, and because ambiguity in its broadest sense refers to doubtfulness or uncertainty.

Many other examples of such ambiguous isolated statements come to mind. "There are 3 million unemployed in the United States." Up or down since last month? In comparison with last year? What is the normal number of unemployed even in periods of "full employment?" Many statements are ambiguous to the uninitiated though not to well-informed. "You have 5 billion germs in your mouth." What is the significance of that fact to a non-physiologist? In all the examples cited we find statements whose referential meaning is unambiguous, but whose significance is subject to varying interpretations.

The significance of many statements is ambiguous until we answer the questions: "Who said it?" and "under what circumstances?" In the fall of 1947 a United States Congressman said, "We will be at war with Russia in one month." Who was the speaker? A responsible or an irresponsible talker? When we listen to criticism of the foreign or domestic policies of the federal administration, we should of course judge these criticisms on their own merits, but we should also be concerned with the background of the critic. Is he a member of the opposition party? Is he blindly partisan? In the absence of coercive evidence we will give greater or lesser weight to criticism depending upon the stature of the critic. If the speaker is thought to be impartial, greater weight will be given to his criticism. In a law court great weight is given to statements which are called "admissions against one's own interest."

Another important distinction concerns the question as to whether a statement is being made in jest or in earnest. "Smile when you call me that" is a type of comment which emphasizes the ambiguity of significance. Persons whose humor is "dry" often make ironical or sarcastical statements that should not be interpreted literally.

An amusing example of the ambiguity of significance occurred when the late Heywood Broun, a wit among drama critics, once wrote that a certain actor, *J*, was "the world's worst 'actor,' " Broun was sued for libel and acquitted. Sometime later, *J* appeared in another play, and Broun, reporting the performance, wrote: "Mr. *J* was not up to his usual standard last night."

The Fallacies of Ambiguity

Thus far we have noted four different types of ambiguity. When confronted with ambiguities we are not certain as to how we should interpret (1) single words or phrases, (2) the sense of a sentence, (3) the emphases or accents desired by the writer or speaker, or (4) the significance of a statement. The careful reader will be alert to the presence of these uncertainties. He will ask the appropriate questions in order to get information that will help to interpret the statements correctly.

A *fallacy* of ambiguity is a distortion of meaning or an error of reasoning based upon an incorrect interpretation of an ambiguous word or phrase. These errors of reasoning usually occur in *use* (by the writer). Distortions of meaning, on the other hand, occur in *interpretation* (by the reader).

Note that the presence of ambiguity is not, in itself, an "error." If a friend tells us that he shot a secretary (meaning a bird) on his last safari to Africa, we may or may not be aware of the ambiguity of the word "secretary." If we jump to the conclusion that he shot a beautiful female of the human species, this would be an error resulting from our faulty interpretation of the ambiguous word. We shall now examine two major fallacies arising from the various types of ambiguity: equivocation and accent.

1. Equivocation

The fallacy of equivocation is an error of use, rather than of interpretation, i.e., it is committed by writers and speakers rather than readers and listeners. It occurs when a writer (or speaker) uses an ambiguous word (or root or phrase) in more than one sense in a given unit of discourse, such equivocal use resulting in an unjustified inference. Some examples: A speaker says: "I am sure that communists really believe in God. It is generally agreed that for its followers communism is a religion, and religious people believe in God." The term "religion" is used in two different senses. Communism is a religion in the sense that its followers show an ardent devotion and fidelity to its tenets, but it is not a religion in the traditional sense of "conviction of the existence of a Supreme Being." The failure to distinguish these meanings resulted in an unjustified inference.

Our second example involves the ambiguous term "law." In its legal sense law means a rule regulating human conduct established by an appropriate governing body. In science, a law refers to the uniform behavior of natural events, i.e., to an order or pattern in nature that is regarded as unvarying under the given conditions. An example is the law of gravitation. It is impossible to "violate" such a law, nor can it have exceptions, for if there is an exception the behavior is not uniform and there is no law. A convenient way of distinguishing the two senses of law is to say that a law of nature is a *description* (of nature); a legal or civil law is a *prescription,* a command. Now suppose one were to argue as follows:

Science has discovered many laws of nature. This is proof that there is a God, for a law implies the existence of a lawgiver, and God is the great Lawgiver of the universe.

The term "law" is used equivocally in this argument. Law in the sense of an order or command implies the existence of a lawgiver or commander, but law in the sense of a description does not.

Equivocation may of course be used deliberately for the purposes of wit and humor. "Your argument is sound, nothing but sound." Thus Benjamin Franklin's pun, "If we don't hang together, we'll hang separately." Or the absurd syllogism, "Some dogs have shaggy ears. My dog has shaggy ears. Therefore, my dog is *some* dog."

Note that equivocation can occur only if the ambiguous term is used at least twice in the same unit of discourse. When an ambiguous word is used only once, this is simple ambiguity. It goes without saying that equivocation should be avoided in our discussions. A word should be used in the same sense throughout a unit of discourse. If we do not use our words consistently there can be no communication or reasoning.

2. Accent

The fallacy of "accent" is an error which results from giving an obviously improper accent or emphasis to the words in a sentence or to the ideas in a unit of discourse.

Such improper accenting or distortion of meaning may be done deliberately, in order to deceive, but usually occurs where there is ambiguity of emphasis. Misinterpretations may then occur because of careless writing or careless interpretation. We shall note three typical ways in which the fallacy occurs:

a. The incorrect emphasis of the words in a sentence

The commandment says, "Thou shalt not bear false witness against thy neighbor."

If one were to stress the word "neighbor," implying that it is permissible to bear false witness against those who are not our neighbors, this would be an obvious misinterpretation.

b. The incorrect interpretation of amphibolous sentences

If one were to interpret the example given earlier on p. 325 as meaning that *Jane* was zooming along under her own power, the amphibolous sentence would be misinterpreted.

c. Incorrect summaries

When a summary is made of an author's statements, it should represent his most important thoughts. When a unit of discourse is improperly summarized, the fault may lie, of course, with the author, whose meaning was not clear. On the other hand, the summarizer may distort the author's meaning either carelessly or with the intent to deceive. We shall now examine some of the forms in which this type of accent occurs.

The reader should always be on the alert when excerpts from a writing are presented. Dishonest examples of "excerpt-lifting" abound. A dramatic critic writes that he "liked all of the play except the lines, the acting, and the scenery." He is quoted as having said that "he liked all of it." Ironical remarks are open to this kind of misinterpretation. A schoolteacher tells her civics class that "communism is the best type of government if you care nothing for your liberty or your material welfare." She is quoted as having said that "communism is the best type of government." Unwitting errors of the same sort occur when a student fails to distinguish between a lecturer's own views and those which he quotes, or even between a speaker's own views and those which he attacks.

The careful thinker will always be on his guard against quotations taken out of their context and he will ask, "Let's have the whole of that quotation." This does not mean that quotations are improper, but only that quotations should be fair and accurate representations of the meaning of the author.

Newspaper headlines purportedly summarize the news, but may distort the meaning by improper emphasis. The "headline reader" is thereby misled. "Let me write the headlines," an editor once said, "and I care not who writes the news." Advertisements may achieve similar results by the use of large case type in bold letters. The "come-on" elements will be presented in large letters, and the less attractive ones will be minimized by the use of small type. A famous example is one that was used by Barnum to advertise the first Canadian concert of the Belgian violinist, Ysaye. It read,

THEIR EXCELLENCIES,
THE PRINCE AND PRINCESS OF BELGIUM

have been asked whether they

WILL ATTEND THE CONCERT OF YSAYE,
WORLD'S GREATEST VIOLINIST

A form of summary called "special pleading" or "stacking the cards" is perhaps of greatest importance in this connection. Speakers emphasize only those elements in a report which suit their purposes and omit the rest. This may be permissible practice for debaters and lawyers who seek to win a case, but it is not in the spirit of the seeker after truth. Thus, in the days when India was struggling for its independence, rioting was frequent. A pro-Indian spokesman on a radio panel was denouncing the British for their callous disregard of elementary decency and reported an incident in the House of Commons in which the Conservative members of parliament "stood up and cheered" when informed that the British Army in India had killed 500 Indians. His audience was profoundly shocked by this report. But another speaker on the same program then read from the full Parliamentary report of the incident. This report stated that many British soldiers had been killed during the rioting, that about 500 Indians had been killed, and the report ended with the Prime Minister's declaration that the government intended to preserve law and order at all costs. (Cheers from Conservative benches.)

Accent, of course, is sometimes a fruitful source of humor when the incorrect interpretation of accent or emphasis is deliberate. Thus, Humpty-Dumpty says to Alice: "They gave it me—for an unbirthday present." "I beg your pardon?" Alice said with a puzzled air. "I'm not offended," said Humpty-Dumpty.

Another: "Would you—be good enough"—Alice panted out after running a little farther, "to stop a minute—just to get one's breath again?" "I'm *good* enough," the King said, "only I'm not strong enough. You see, a minute goes by so fearfully quick. You might as well try to catch a bandersnatch!"

COMPREHENSION QUIZ

1. Ambiguity is the direct opposite of
   a. homonymity.
   b. synonymity.
   c. antonymity.
   d. phonomity.
2. The initial ambiguity of words is often eliminated by
   a. context.
   b. careful reading.
   c. use of the dictionary.
   d. none of these.
3. For most students, classroom instruction is superior to merely reading because
   a. ambiguity can be better identified.
   b. instructors give oral emphasis to the most important words.

    c.   reading does not permit the exchange of ideas that a classroom does.

    d.   the routine of a classroom tends to become more ingrained in one's habit patterns.

4. A statement announcing the number of golf courses built during last year would contain

    a.   the ambiguity of significance.

    b.   ambiguity of emphasis.

    c.   simple ambiguity.

    d.   amphiboly.

5. The fallacy of equivocation is committed by

    a.   speakers.

    b.   listeners.

    c.   readers.

    d.   none of these.

6. Equivocation can occur only if

    a.   an ambiguous term is used.

    b.   no ambiguous term is used.

    c.   the ambiguous term is used only once in the unit of writing.

    d.   the ambiguous term is used at least twice in the unit of writing.

7. A summary made of an author's writings should

    a.   represent his most commonly mentioned thoughts.

    b.   represent his most important thoughts.

    c.   be about one/fifth as long as the actual writing.

    d.   none of these.

8. Speakers emphasizing only those elements in a report which suit their purposes, while omitting the rest, are guilty of

    a.   ambiguity of scale.

    b.   equivocation.

    c.   stacking the cards.

    d.   amphiboly.

DISCUSSION QUESTIONS

1. What is a syllogism? Why does Ruby call his syllogism about dogs with shaggy hair absurd?

2. What are some common ambiguities which one may come across almost daily?

3. Explain the idea that "the presence of ambiguity is not, in itself, an error."

4. Many students complain about ambiguity in connection with test items. Bring to class examples of what you think are ambiguous questions and discuss them.

5. Show by illustration the difference between equivocation and simple ambiguity.

6. Bring to class three examples of excerpts you have taken from the daily newspaper. Sports pages and editorial sections are especially good sources for this.

7. What is implied in the quote from the essay "Let me write the headlines and I care not who writes the news"?

8. Rewrite the headlines of a recent copy of your student newspaper, distorting the news by improper emphasis. Do this to each story on page one.

WRITING SUGGESTIONS

1. Demonstrate your ability to differentiate between vagueness and ambiguity by writing five sentences containing vague statements, and five containing ambiguous statements.
2. Write a short article on a contemporary subject, and purposely insert vague words. Then rewrite the article, eliminating them.
3. Write a summary of a common fairy tale such as "The Three Bears," deliberately incorporating the ambiguous fallacy of accent as related to incorrect summaries.

Selection,
Slanting,
and Charged Language

by NEWMAN P. BIRK and GENEVIEVE B. BIRK

. . . [In this selection] we shall consider the way groups of words work together in larger contexts. Since words, singly or in groups, serve as symbols to convey knowledge, it is desirable here to consider a principle that underlies all knowledge and all use of words.

A. The Principle of Selection

Before it is expressed in words, our knowledge, both inside and outside, is influenced by the principle of selection. What we know or observe depends on what we notice; that is, what we select, consciously or unconsciously, as worthy of notice or attention. As we observe, the principle of selection determines which facts we take in.

Suppose, for example, that three people, a lumberjack, an artist, and a tree surgeon are examining a large tree in a forest. Since the tree itself is a complicated object, the number of particulars or facts about it that one could observe would be very great indeed. Which of these facts a particular observer will notice will be a matter of selection, a selection that is determined by his interests and purposes. A lumberjack might be interested in the best way to cut the tree down, cut it up, and transport it to the lumber mill. His interest would then determine his principle of selection in observing and thinking about the tree. The artist might consider painting a picture of the tree, and his purpose would furnish his principle of selec-

From Newman P. Birk and Genevieve B. Birk, *Understanding and Using English*, 4th Edition. Copyright © 1965 by The Odyssey Press, New York. Reprinted by permission of the publisher.

tion. The tree surgeon's professional interest in the physical health of the tree might establish a principle of selection for him. If each man were now required to write an exhaustive, detailed report on every thing he observed about the tree, the facts supplied by each would differ, for each would report those facts that his particular principle of selection led him to notice.[1]

The principle of selection holds not only for the specific facts that people observe but also for the facts they remember. A student suddenly embarrassed may remember nothing of the next ten minutes of class discussion but may have a vivid recollection of the sensation of the blood mounting, as he blushed, up his face and into his ears. In both noticing and remembering, the principle of selection applies, and it is influenced not only by our special interest and point of view but by our whole mental state at the moment.

The principle of selection then serves as a kind of sieve or screen through which our knowledge passes before it becomes our knowledge. Since we can't notice everything about a complicated object or situation or action or state of our own consciousness, what we do notice is determined by whatever principle of selection is operating for us at the time we gain the knowledge.

It is important to remember that what is true of the way the principle of selection works for us is true also of the way it works for others. Even before we or other people put knowledge into words to express meaning, that knowledge has been screened or selected. Before an historian or an economist writes a book, or before a reporter writes a news article, the facts that each is to present have been sifted through the screen of a principle of selection. Before one person passes on knowledge to another, that knowledge has already been selected and shaped, intentionally or unintentionally, by the mind of the communicator.

B. The Principle of Slanting

When we put our knowledge into words, a second process of selection, the process of slanting, takes place. Just as there is something, a rather mysterious principle of selection, which chooses for us what we will notice, and what will then become our knowledge, there is also a principle which operates, with or without our awareness, to select certain facts and feelings from our store of knowledge, and to choose the words and the emphasis that we shall use to communicate our meaning.[2] **Slanting** may be defined as

[1] Of course all three observers would probably report a good many facts in common— the height of the tree, for example, and the size of the trunk. The point we wish to make is that each observer would give us a different impression of the tree because of the different principle of selection that guided his observation.

[2] Notice that the "principle of selection" is at work as we *take in* knowledge, and that slanting occurs as we *express* our knowledge in words.

the process of selecting (1) knowledge—factual and attitudinal; (2) words; and (3) emphasis, to achieve the intention of the communicator. Slanting is present in some degree in all communication: one may *slant for* (favorable slanting), *slant against* (unfavorable slanting), or *slant both ways* (balanced slanting).

The favorable or unfavorable or balanced slanting of the subject matter is determined, as we have said, by the intention of the communicator: he selects the knowledge, the words, and the emphasis, and he adapts them to fit his intention and to achieve his purpose. Sometimes he slants his material consciously and deliberately; sometimes, especially in spontaneous or impulsive uses of language, he is unaware that he is making a choice, and after he has spoken, he may be surprised at what he has said. In such spontaneous utterances, slanting still occurs and is still controlled by intention, but the intention operates on a subconscious rather than a conscious level.

A lawyer engaged in presenting his concluding argument to a jury is likely to be sharply aware of his intention and very careful of the way he slants facts and words to achieve that intention, but the same lawyer in answer to a casual question about his golf game might without conscious awareness of intention or of slanting give a long and ecstatic account of how he sank a thirty-foot putt on the ninth green. In this account his unconscious intention (perhaps in this case his desire to have his audience admire his golfing skill) would determine what facts he selected and how he expressed himself. We can say, then, that although both intention and slanting are present in verbal communication, the communicator's awareness of them is subject to wide variation, and they may do their work at different mental levels. In the next three sections we shall examine separately each of the three basic devices of slanting; later we shall go on to consider passages in which these devices work together to produce charged language.

C. Slanting by Use of Emphasis

Slanting by use of the devices of emphasis is unavoidable,[3] for emphasis is simply the giving of stress to subject matter, and so indicating what is important and what is less important. In speech, for example, if we say that Socrates was *a wise old man,* we can give several slightly different meanings, one by stressing *wise,* another by stressing *old,* another by giving equal stress to *wise* and *old,* and still another by giving chief stress to *man.* Each different stress gives a different slant (favorable or unfavorable or balanced) to the

[3] When emphasis is present—and we can think of no instance in the use of language in which it is not—it necessarily influences the meaning by playing a part in the favorable, unfavorable, or balanced slant of the communicator. We are likely to emphasize by voice stress, even when we answer *yes* or *no* to simple questions.

statement because it conveys a different attitude toward Socrates or a different judgment of him. Connectives and word order also slant by the emphasis they give: consider the difference in slanting or emphasis produced by *old but wise, old and wise, wise but old.* In writing, we cannot indicate subtle stresses on words as clearly as in speech, but we can achieve our emphasis and so can slant by the use of more complex patterns of word order, by choice of connectives, by underlining heavily stressed words, and by marks of punctuation that indicate short or long pauses and so give light or heavy emphasis. Question marks, quotation marks, and exclamation points can also contribute to slanting.[4] It is impossible either in speech or in writing to put two facts together without giving some slight emphasis or slant. For example, if we have in mind only two facts about a man, his awkwardness and his strength, we subtly slant those facts favorably or unfavorably in whatever way we choose to join them:

More Favorable Slanting	*Less Favorable Slanting*
He is awkward and strong.	He is strong and awkward.
He is awkward but strong.	He is strong but awkward.
Although he is somewhat awkward, he is very strong.	He may be strong, but he's very awkward.

With more facts and in longer passages it is possible to maintain a delicate balance by alternating favorable and unfavorable emphasis and so producing a balanced effect.

All communication, then, is in some degree slanted by the *emphasis* of the communicator.

D. Slanting by Selection of Facts

To illustrate the technique of slanting by selection of facts, we shall examine three passages of informative writing which achieve different effects simply by the selection and emphasis of material. Each passage is made up of true statements or facts about a dog, yet the reader is given three different impressions. The first passage is an example of objective writing or balanced slanting, the second is slanted unfavorably, and the third is slanted favorably.

A. Balanced presentation

Our dog, Toddy, sold to us as a cocker, produces various reactions in various people. Those who come to the back door she usually growls and barks at (a milkman has said that he is afraid of her); those who come to the front door,

---

4 Consider the slanting achieved by punctuation in the following sentences: He called the Senator an honest man? *He* called the Senator an honest man? He called the Senator an honest man! He said one more such "honest" senator would corrupt the state.

she whines at and paws; also she tries to lick people's faces unless we have forestalled her by putting a newspaper in her mouth. (Some of our friends encourage these actions; others discourage them. Mrs. Firmly, one friend, slaps the dog with a newspaper and says, "I know how hard dogs are to train.") Toddy knows and responds to a number of words and phrases, and guests sometimes remark that she is a "very intelligent dog." She has fleas in the summer, and she sheds, at times copiously, the year round. Her blonde hairs are conspicuous when they are on people's clothing or on rugs or furniture. Her color and her large brown eyes frequently produce favorable comment. An expert on cockers would say that her ears are too short and set too high and that she is at least six pounds too heavy.

The passage above is made up of facts, verifiable facts,[5] deliberately selected and emphasized to produce a *balanced* impression. Of course not all the facts about the dog have been given—to supply *all* the facts on any subject, even such a comparatively simple one, would be an almost impossible task. Both favorable and unfavorable facts are used, however, and an effort has been made to alternate favorable and unfavorable details so that neither will receive greater emphasis by position, proportion, or grammatical structure.

B.   Facts slanted *against*

That dog put her paws on my white dress as soon as I came in the door, and she made so much noise that it was two minutes before she had quieted down enough for us to talk and hear each other. Then the gas man came and she did a great deal of barking. And her hairs are on the rug and on the furniture. If you wear a dark dress they stick to it like lint. When Mrs. Firmly came in, she actually hit the dog with a newspaper to make it stay down, and she made some remark about training dogs. I wish the Birks would take the hint or get rid of that noisy, short-eared, overweight "cocker" of theirs.

This unfavorably slanted version is based on the same facts, but now these facts have been selected and given a new emphasis. The speaker, using her selected facts to give her impression of the dog, is quite possibly unaware of her negative slanting.

Now for a favorably slanted version:

C.   Facts slanted *for*

What a lively and responsive dog! When I walked in the door, there she was with a newspaper in her mouth, whining and standing on her hind legs and

[5] *Verifiable facts* are facts that can be checked and agreed upon and proved to be true by people who wish to verify them. That a particular theme received a failing grade is a verifiable fact; one needs merely to see the theme with the grade on it. That the instructor should have failed the theme is not, strictly speaking, a verifiable fact, but a matter of opinion. Possibly student and teacher will not agree on this matter of opinion. That women on the average live longer than men is a verifiable fact; that they live better is a matter of opinion, a *value judgment*.

wagging her tail all at the same time. And what an intelligent dog. If you suggest going for a walk, she will get her collar from the kitchen and hand it to you, and she brings Mrs. Birk's slippers whenever Mrs. Birk says she is "tired" or mentions slippers. At a command she catches balls, rolls over, "speaks," or stands on her hind feet and twirls around. She sits up and balances a piece of bread on her nose until she is told to take it; then she tosses it up and catches it. If you are eating something, she sits up in front of you and "begs" with those big dark brown eyes set in that light, buff-colored face of hers. When I got up to go and told her I was leaving, she rolled her eyes at me and sat up like a squirrel. She certainly is a lively and an intelligent dog.

Speaker C, like Speaker B, is selecting from the "facts" summarized in balanced version A, and is emphasizing his facts to communicate his impression.

All three passages are examples of *reporting* (i.e., consist only of verifiable facts), yet they give three very different impressions of the same dog because of the different ways the speakers slanted the facts. Some people say that figures don't lie, and many people believe that if they have the "facts," they have the "truth." Yet if we carefully examine the ways of thought and language, we see that any knowledge that comes to us through words has been subjected to the double screening of the principle of selection and the slanting of language. Since a communicator usually cannot know all the facts and figures, he can give us only the ones he knows; and when he puts his knowledge into words, he necessarily slants by the emphasis he gives it. Because it is easy to give a biased impression in this way even without intending to do so, responsible communicators make an effort to supply a representative sampling of favorable and unfavorable details and to give a reasonably balanced slanting, particularly when they are evaluating something or are simply trying to give reliable information.

Wise listeners and readers realize that the double screening that is produced by the principle of selection and by slanting takes place even when people honestly try to report the facts as they know them. (Speakers B and C, for instance, probably thought of themselves as simply giving information about a dog and were not deliberately trying to mislead.) Wise listeners and readers know too that deliberate manipulators of language, by mere selection and emphasis, can make their slanted facts appear to support almost any cause.

In arriving at opinions and values we cannot always be sure that the facts that sift into our minds through language are representative and relevant and true. We need to remember that much of our information about politics, governmental activities, business conditions, and foreign affairs comes to us selected and slanted. More than we realize, our opinions on these matters may depend on what newspaper we read or what news commentator we listen to. Worth-while opinions call for knowledge of reliable facts and reasonable arguments for and against—and such opinions include beliefs about morality and truth and religion as well as about public affairs. Because complex subjects involve knowing and dealing with many facts on both sides, reliable judgments are at best difficult to arrive at. If we want to be fair-minded, we must be willing to subject our opinions to continual testing by new knowledge, and must realize that after all they *are* opinions, more or less trustworthy. Their trustworthiness will depend on the representativeness of our facts, on the quality of our reasoning, and on the standard of values that we choose to apply.

We shall not give here a passage illustrating the unscrupulous slanting of facts. Such a passage would also include irrelevant facts and false statements presented as facts, along with various subtle distortions of fact. Yet to the uninformed reader the passage would be indistinguishable from a passage intended to give a fair account. If two passages (B and C) of casual and unintentional slanting of facts about a dog can give such contradictory impressions of a simple subject, the reader can imagine what a skilled and designing manipulation of facts and statistics could do to mislead an uninformed reader about a really complex subject. An example of such manipulation might be the account of the United States that Soviet propaganda has supplied to the average Russian. Such propaganda, however, would go beyond the mere slanting of the facts: it would clothe the selected facts in charged words and would make use of the many other devices of slanting that appear in charged language.

E. Slanting by Use of Charged Words

In the passages describing the dog Toddy, we were illustrating the technique of slanting by the selection and emphasis of facts. Though the facts selected had to be expressed in words, the words chosen were as factual as possible, and it was the selection and emphasis of facts and not of words that was mainly responsible for the two distinctly different impressions of the dog. In the passages below we are demonstrating another way of slanting —slanting by the use of charged words. This time the accounts are very similar in the facts they contain; the different impressions of the subject, Corlyn, are produced not by different facts but by the subtle selection of charged words.

The passages were written by a clever student who was told to choose as his subject a person in action, and to write two descriptions, each using the "same facts." The instructions required that one description be slanted positively and the other negatively, so that the first would make the reader favorably inclined toward the person and the action, and the second would make him unfavorably inclined.

Here is the favorably charged description. Read it carefully and form your opinion of the person before you go on to read the second description.

CORLYN

Corlyn paused at the entrance to the room and glanced about. A well-cut black dress draped subtly about her slender form. Her long blonde hair gave her chiseled features the simple frame they required. She smiled an engaging smile as she accepted a cigarette from her escort. As he lit it for her she looked over the flame and into his eyes. Corlyn had that rare talent of making every male feel that he was the one man in the world.

She took his arm and they descended the steps into the room. She walked with an effortless grace and spoke with equal ease. They each took a cup of coffee and joined a group of friends near the fire. The flickering light danced across her face and lent an ethereal quality to her beauty. The good conversation, the crackling logs, and the stimulating coffee gave her a feeling of internal warmth. Her eyes danced with each leap of the flames.

Taken by itself this passage might seem just a description of an attractive girl. The favorable slanting by use of charged words has been done so skillfully that it is inconspicuous. Now we turn to the unfavorably slanted description of the "same" girl engaged in the "same" actions:

CORLYN

Corlyn halted at the entrance to the room and looked around. A plain black dress hung on her thin frame. Her stringy bleached hair accentuated her harsh features. She smiled an inane smile as she took a cigarette from her escort. As he lit it for her she stared over the lighter and into his eyes. Corlyn had a habit of making every male feel that he was the last man on earth.

She grasped his arm and they walked down the steps and into the room. Her pace was fast and ungainly, as was her speech. They each reached for some coffee and broke into a group of acquaintances near the fire. The flickering light played across her face and revealed every flaw. The loud talk, the fire, and the coffee she had gulped down made her feel hot. Her eyes grew more red with each leap of the flames.

When the reader compares these two descriptions, he can see how charged words influence the reader's attitude. One needs to read the two descriptions several times to appreciate all the subtle differences between them. Words, some rather heavily charged, others innocent-looking but lightly charged, work together to carry to the reader a judgment of a person and a situation. If the reader had seen only the first description of Corlyn, he might well have thought that he had formed his "own judgment on the basis of the facts." And the examples just given only begin to suggest the techniques that may be used in heavily charged language. For one thing, the two descriptions of Corlyn contain no really good example of the use of charged abstractions; for another, the writer was obliged by the assignment to use the same set of facts and so could not slant by selecting his material.

F. Slanting and Charged Language

Thus far we have dealt with one device or technique of slanting at a time. When slanting of facts, or words, or emphasis, or any combination of the three *significantly influences* feelings toward, or judgments about, a subject, the language used is charged language.

The way of determining whether or not a communication is charged is to ask: Does this communication strongly affect my emotions or attitudes or judgments? Does it express strong emotions, attitudes, or judgments of the communicator? Does it significantly affect the emotions, attitudes, or judgments of most people? If an expression strongly affects me, it is charged for me; if it expresses the strong feeling of the communicator, it is charged for him; and if it significantly affects most people, it is charged for them and can be said to be generally charged.

Of course communications vary in the amount of charge they carry and in their effect on different people; what is very favorably charged for one person may have little or no charge, or may even be adversely charged, for others. It is sometimes hard to distinguish between charged and uncharged expression. But it is safe to say that whenever we wish to convey any kind of inner knowledge—feelings, attitudes, judgments, values—we are obliged to convey that attitudinal meaning through the medium of charged language; and when we wish to understand the inside knowledge of others, we have to interpret the charged language that they choose, or are obliged, to use. Charged language, then, is the natural and necessary medium for the communication of charged or attitudinal meaning. At times we have difficulty in living with it, but we should have even greater difficulty in living without it.

Some of the difficulties in living with charged language are caused by its use in dishonest propaganda, in some editorials, in many political speeches, in most advertising, in certain kinds of effusive salesmanship, and in blatantly insincere, or exaggerated, or sentimental expressions of emotion. Other difficulties are caused by the misunderstandings and misinterpretations that charged language produces. A charged phrase misinterpreted in a love letter; a charged word spoken in haste or in anger; an acrimonious argument about religion or politics or athletics or fraternities; the frustrating uncertainty produced by the effort to understand the complex attitudinal meaning in a poem or play or a short story—these troubles, all growing out of the use of charged language, may give us the feeling that Robert Louis Stevenson expressed when he said, "The battle goes sore against us to the going down of the sun."

But however charged language is abused and whatever misunderstandings it may cause, we still have to live with it—and even by it. It shapes our attitudes and values even without our conscious knowledge; it gives purpose to, and guides, our actions; through it we establish and maintain relations with other people and by means of it we exert our greatest influence on them. Without charged language, life would be but half life. The relatively uncharged language of bare factual statement, though it serves its informative purpose well and is much less open to abuse and to misunderstanding, can describe only the bare land of factual knowledge; to communicate knowledge of the turbulencies and the calms and the deep currents of the sea of inner experience we must use charged language.

COMPREHENSION QUIZ

1. Our knowledge is influenced by the principle of selection
    a. before it is expressed in words.
    b. after the thought occurs.
    c. while the voice mechanism is operating.
    d. during our discussions with others.
2. The principle of selection holds for both
    a. facts people observe and facts they know.
    b. facts people remember and facts they tell others.
    c. facts people observe and facts they remember.
    d. facts people remember and facts they forget.
3. Slanting is a process of selecting
    a. knowledge, memory, and emphasis.
    b. knowledge, words, and emphasis.
    c. words, emphasis, and intention.
    d. intention, words, and knowledge.
4. The sentence "He is strong but awkward." is said to be slanted because of
    a. emphasis.
    b. position.
    c. blame.
    d. intention.
5. Worthwhile opinions call for knowledge of
    a. reliable facts and reasonable arguments for and against.
    b. reasonable arguments of logic.
    c. facts and opinions.
    d. description of all the conditions involved.

DISCUSSION QUESTIONS

1. Why do we sort out sense impressions in our minds? Why, for example, do some persons remember color while others remember shape and size?
2. Construct a list of characteristics for judging slanted writing. For example, knowing *when* and *where* the statement was made is important.

3. Discuss the slanting used by two national magazines covering the same event or person—a political candidate, for example.

WRITING SUGGESTIONS

1. Write three descriptive paragraphs of a sunset as a painter, a sailor, and a surfer might see it.
2. Write a paper that concerns some especially embarrassing moments and how the embarrassment affected your memory of the facts involved.
3. In a paper of definition, discuss the word "slanting."
4. Use this sentence for a writing assignment, "Charged language is difficult to live with and difficult to live without."

Recommended Readings to Part VIII

Austin, J. L. *How to Do Things with Words*. Cambridge, Mass.: Harvard University Press, 1962.

Breal, M. J. *Semantics*. New York: Dover, 1964.

Brown, Roger. *Words and Things*. New York: Free Press, 1958.

Chase, Stuart. *The Power of Words*. New York: Harcourt, Brace & World, 1959.

Hayakawa, S. I. *Language in Thought and Action*. New York: Harcourt, Brace & World, 1964.

Johnson, Wendell. *People in Quandaries*. New York: Harper & Row, 1946.

Korzybski, Alfred. *Selections from Science and Sanity*. Lakeville, Conn.: Institute of General Semantics, 1958.

Lee, Irving J. *Language Habits in Human Affairs*. New York: Harper & Row, 1941.

Lee, Irving J. *The Language of Wisdom and Folly*. New York: Harper & Row, 1949.

Ogden, C. K., and I. A. Richards. *The Meaning of Meaning*. New York: Harcourt, Brace & World, 1930.

Schaff, Adam. *Introduction to Semantics*. New York: Pergamon, 1962.

Ullmann, Stephen. *Words and Their Use*. New York: Philosophical Library, 1951.

Urban, W. M. *Language and Reality*. New York: Macmillan, 1939.

Ziff, Paul. *Semantic Analysis*. Ithaca, N.Y.: Cornell University Press, 1960.

IX

Language and the Creative Act: Composition and Literature

Words
Under a Mask

by SEYMOUR FERSH

"Why do men make mistakes?" asks Walter Lippmann, the U.S. writer
and political analyst, and answers, "Because an important part of human
behaviour is reaction to the pictures in their heads. Human behaviour takes
place in relation to a pseudo-environment—a representation, which is not
quite the same for any two individuals. What they suppose to be—not what
is—the reality of things. This man-made, this cultural environment which
has its being in the minds of men, is interposed between man as a biological
organism and external reality."

The problem is one of bringing "pictures in the mind" and "external
reality" into truer alignment. The best way—though certainly not an
infallible one—is through first-hand experiences, followed by audio-visual
representations, and lastly by words. It is through words, however, that most
of our "education" takes place and much is inevitably lost in the telling as
word descriptions are substituted for their real-life counterparts.

Consider words such as poverty, underdeveloped, hot, cold, democratic,
progressive, backward, and the like. Dictionaries carry definitions but people
carry connotations—and it is connotations which influence thinking and
rule behaviour. Moreover, connotations are not only personal, they are also
heavily cultural. A Frenchman, a Cambodian and a Tunisian or an Englishman, an Indian and an American may "understand" the words which each is
using when speaking French or English, but whether they will ever "understand" the nuances—the shades of delicate differences in meaning—is quite
another matter.

Throughout history many writers in many cultures have called attention to the fact that words misinform as well as inform, but it was not until
1897 that a Frenchman, Michel Breal, gave it the name "sémantique," or the

From Seymour Fersh, "Words Under a Mask," *UNESCO Courier*, February, 1965. Reprinted by permission of the *UNESCO Courier*.

science of meaning. More recently, in the 1920's in the United States, a movement called General Semantics, often referred to as G. S., was pioneered by Alfred Korzybski and subsequently popularized by researchers and writers, including Stuart Chase, Wendell Johnson, S. I. Hayakawa, and Irving Lee.

From these and other writers on the subject, we have drawn a number of examples to illustrate the contribution General Semantics can make to the study of other peoples and ways of living different from our own. We do not claim that greater attention to these and other General Semantics assumptions and techniques will in itself eliminate all problems of "meaning," but it should be incontestable that descriptions of "things out there" can and must be conveyed more precisely and with more accurate interpretation.

The nature of the world is one of dynamic flow—"a mad dance of electrons"—in which no two things are identical, no one thing remains the same and, as Heraclitus expressed it over two thousand years ago, "one cannot step in the same river twice."

The nature of man is that—unlike other living things—he can "receive gifts from the dead" through the use of his man-made language, but his internal experiences are literally "unspeakable." Abstractions take place when he tries to substitute words for reality.

The nature of languages is like that of a map; it is useful to the extent that it describes the territory accurately. Maps and territories are not the same, however, nor are words and reality interchangeable, though it is by no means uncommon for some people to react to words as they would to a slap in the face. And, of course, advertisers have long known that certain names appear to have the magical effect of seemingly impregnating themselves into a product. Who among us has not purchased an item recently because the name rather than the substance—often untried—appealed to our stream of connotations?

For example, South American (A) is not South American (B) is not South American (C) is not South American (D), etc. In other words, South American (teacher in Lima) is not South American (rural area worker in Brazil), etc. Although by convention we refer to the 150 million people who live in an area called South America as "South Americans," the truth is that no two "South Americans" are identical—including, of course, those who live in the same country or even in the same household. Considered in the same way, each of the estimated seventy-seven thousand million people who have inhabited the earth has been unique.

Statements which purport to talk about "a people" as if they were one entity must obviously be qualified. Questions such as "What do Africans think about Europeans?" are clearly unanswerable. Answerable questions—those which have some likelihood of being verified—are less dramatic and perhaps less satisfying, but that is the nature of the problem. It is only by taking liberties with language that we appear to be better informed than the data permit. Similarly, it may readily be seen that terms such as "Asian,"

"Moslem," "Oriental," and the like conceal differences as well as reveal group affinities.[1]

Japan (1840) is not Japan (1945) is not Japan (1965) is not Japan (1980), etc. Change is inevitable, though the rate varies. One who forgets this is certain to be shocked when confronted with the discrepancy between what he thinks (or remembers) is true and what is so.

The same may be used to connote different "realities," while similar events or experiences are sometimes called by different names.

For example, when someone says that it is hot, the word "hot" is more likely to represent the speaker's state of mind than it is to describe the current temperature reading. "Cold wave" could mean anything from 20 to 30 degrees below zero (F) in Alaska to 40 degrees above zero in New Delhi where, incidentally, a continuous string of days in the 90's in May would scarcely qualify as a "heat wave."

Very often, the addition by the speaker of the words "to me" and the addition by the listener of the words "to you" help to identify so-called statements of fact as really statements of opinion. Words whose meanings have become meaningless from being used to carry too heavy and too diversified loads of information should be set apart by enclosing them with quotation marks to alert the reader. Korzybski used to wiggle two fingers of each hand when speaking to achieve the same effect.

Consider this plea from ancient China, entitled, "On the Standard of Beauty":

> If a man sleeps in a damp place, he gets lumbago and may die. But what about an eel? And living up a tree is frightening and tiring to the nerves. But what about monkeys? What habitat can be said to be absolutely right? Then men eat flesh, deer eat grass, centipedes enjoy small worms, owls and crows delight in mice. Whose is the right taste, absolutely? Monkeys mate with ape, bucks with does, eels consort with fishes, while men admire great beauties such as Mao Chiang and Li Chi. Yet at the sight of these women the fish plunged deep into the water, birds flew from them aloft, and deer sped away. Who shall say what is the right standard of beauty? In my opinion, the doctrines of benevolence and righteousness and the paths of right and wrong are inextricably confused. How could I discriminate among them?[2]

No matter how complete a listing or how comprehensive an explanation, the possibility always remains open that something more might be said about the matter under consideration. All descriptions are "open-ended" with the last word unsaid. Completeness may be a goal, but like infinity it eludes mortal grasp. Thus for example, an examination of any culture or any

---

[1] For other aspects of this subject we refer the reader to "Twisted Images—How Nations See Each Other." *The Unesco Courier*, June 1955 (now out of print).

[2] *Through Asian Eyes*, compiled by Baldoon Dhingra. Charles E. Tuttle, Rutland, Vermont 1959.

country might include reference to its history, its development, its achievements and so on, but these would always be incomplete. No matter how extensive the treatise, a mental "etc." should be added to the last punctuation point. The practical effect of this orientation is to leave the door open, albeit a crack, for additional information which may be forthcoming.

This list of "devices" for applying General Semantics can be extended almost indefinitely. Here are a few more cautions to consider:

Let us try to use descriptive terms rather than those expressing approval or disapproval. For example, the words "clean" and "unclean" are relative. The comment that cow dung is used for fuel in many Afro-Asian villages often provokes reactions of disgust from many urban dwellers the world (1965) over. It may be instructive on this point to quote from an American, writing about his experience on the Great Plains of his country in 1879 when buffalo and cow dung (he calls them "chips") were commonly used for fuel:

> It was comical to see how gingerly our wives handled these chips at first. They commenced by picking them up between two sticks, or with a poker. Soon they used a rag, and then a corner of their apron. Finally, growing hardened, a washing after handling them was sufficient. And now? Now it is out of the bread, into the chips and back again—and not even a dust of the hands.

Let us try to use phrases which indicate certain conditions which should be considered with a statement. For example, awareness may be increased by using such phrases as "in our culture," "from our point of view," "at that time," and the like.

Miscalculations often arise through the mistaken notion that other cultures prize the same values as one's own. Here, for example, is what Aldous Huxley wrote following his first trip around the world in 1927:

> So the journey is over and I am back again where I started, richer by much experience and poorer by many exploded convictions, many perished certainties. For convictions and certainties are too often the concomitants of ignorance. Of knowledge and experience the fruit is generally doubt. It is doubt that grows profounder as knowledge more deeply burrows into the underlying mystery, that spreads in exact proportion as experience is widened and the perceptions of the experiencing individual are refined . . .
>
> . . . I set out on my travels knowing, or thinking that I knew, how men should live, how be governed, how educated, what they should believe. I knew which was the best form of social organization and to what end societies had been created. I had my views on every activity of life. Now, on my return, I find myself without any of these pleasing certainties . . .
>
> . . . The better you understand the significance of any question, the more difficult it becomes to answer it. Those who like to feel that they are always right

and who attach a high importance to their own opinions should stay at home. When one is travelling, convictions are mislaid as easily as spectacles, but unlike spectacles, they are not easily replaced.[3]

Let us try to move in the direction of substituting more precise words for vague ones. For example, it is often said that "heavy rains" fall on India during the monsoon season. The statement would carry more meaning if it were pointed out, for example, that Allahabad, a city in the Ganges Valley, and New York City both receive on the average 40 inches of rain annually with the significant difference that New York City gets from two to four inches monthly whereas Allahabad is hit by some 37 inches from June to October.

Let us become more alert to the ways in which cultural conditioning shapes our value judgments. An exercise in seeing one's own culture as it might be seen by a stranger is a useful start. Consider, for example, the following excerpt from an article called, "Body Ritual Among the Nacirema":

The focal point of the shrine is a box or chest which is built into the wall. In this chest are kept the many charms and magical potions without which no native believes he could live . . .

. . . The charm is not disposed of after it has served its purpose, but is placed in the charm-box of the household shrine. As these magical materials are specific for certain ills, and the real or imagined maladies of the people are many, the charm-box is usually full to overflowing. The magical packets are so numerous that people forget what their purposes were and fear to use them again.

While the natives are very vague on this point, we can only assume that the idea in retaining all the old magical materials is that their presence in the charm-box, before which the body rituals are conducted, will in some way protect the worshipper.[4]

Here under discussion has been the medicine cabinet in American (Nacirema—spelled backward), or almost any other western culture!

Let us become more suspicious of our own "wisdom." Anatole France once said of a man, "He flattered himself on being a man without prejudices; and this pretension itself is a very great prejudice." In "The Devil's Advocate: A Plea for Superstition," written in 1909, Sir James G. Frazer argued that so-called superstitions more often than not embody a realistic distillation of experience whereby the unitiated and unwary may receive tested guidance. Behind many "myths" are "truths" which have helped people to rationalize and maintain social order and organization.

[3] *Jesting Pilate,* Aldous Huxley, Harper & Row, New York, 1928.
[4] Horace Miner, in *American Anthropologist,* Vol. 58, No. 3, 1956.

Thus, for example, a "superstition" long held in some local area that a certain marsh is "haunted" may seem ridiculous at first but it may be a shorthand way of saying that the number of people who enter it and the number who emerge continually shows a marked discrepancy. Until the cause of deaths in the marsh—possibly malaria—is identified and dealt with, the local "respect" for the area is based on more than mere superstition.

Of course, much of what has been pointed out here will not come as a revelation. None of the ideas are new and, under different names, many of the General Semantics techniques have been used by intelligent people who have never heard of the word "semantics," let alone been exposed to the writings of Korzybski and others.

So much the better. Our concern is not so much with how people distinguish between a "map" and the physical territory which it describes, but that they do distinguish. George Orwell writes, "What is above all needed is to let the meaning choose the word, and not the other way about. . . . Probably it is better to put off using words as long as possible and get one's meaning as clear as one can through pictures and sensations."

No one is suggesting that all abstractions be distrusted. "In demanding that people cease reacting to abstract names as if they were realities-in-themselves," says S. I. Hayakawa, "we are merely saying in another way, 'Stop acting like suckers'." And until we do give more disciplined attention to words, we will continue to stockpile symbols and labels while the "precious commodities" which are being symbolized and labeled escape our detection and comprehension. The argument-ending gambit, "It is only a matter of semantics" must give way to the more sophisticated recognition that the "real" search for "meaning" often starts where words leave off.

COMPREHENSION QUIZ

1. This essay quotes Walter Lippmann concerning the reasons men make mistakes; he says that a part of human behavior is a reaction to the
    a. ground rules of communication.
    b. pictures in their heads.
    c. way that men see their families.
    d. method of understanding cybernetics.
2. The author states that connotations
    a. develop slowly.
    b. destroy the true meaning of words.
    c. influence thinking.
    d. add color to the world.
3. Semantics can be defined as
    a. the science of meaning.
    b. the code for words.

c. understanding based on sight.

d. pattern of repetition.

4. Abstractions take place when someone tries to substitute words for

a. meaning.

b. symbols.

c. techniques.

d. reality.

5. One of the cautions about language that the author suggests is

a. that we should all speak one tongue.

b. that we should substitute precise words for vague ones.

c. that some languages need more study than others.

d. that no man can be fully aware of the implications of his statements.

DISCUSSION QUESTIONS

1. Discuss this statement, "Miscalculations often arise through the mistaken notion that other cultures prize the same values as one's own."

2. How is language like a map?

3. Why are so many generalizations concerning "peoples" false?

WRITING SUGGESTIONS

1. Using this sentence as the basis, write a theme expressing your experience. "Let us become more alert to the ways in which cultural conditioning shapes our value judgments."

2. Choose any of the "cautions" which the author gives and write a theme on it.

Parts
of Speech
and Punctuation

by GERTRUDE STEIN

One of the things that is a very interesting thing to know is how you are feeling inside you to the words that are coming out to be outside of you.

Do you always have the same kind of feeling in relation to the sounds as the words come out of you or do you not. All this has so much to do with grammar and with poetry and with prose.

Words have to do everything in poetry and prose and some writers write more in articles and prepositions and some say you should write in nouns, and of course one has to think of everything.

A noun is a name of anything, why after a thing is named write about it. A name is adequate or it is not. If it is adequate then why go on calling it, if it is not then calling it by its name does no good.

People if you like to believe it can be made by their names. Call anybody Paul and they get to be a Paul call anybody Alice and they get to be an Alice perhaps yes perhaps no, there is something in that, but generally speaking, things once they are named the name does not go on doing anything to them and so why write in nouns. Nouns are the name of anything and just naming names is alright when you want to call a roll but is it any good for anything else. To be sure in many places in Europe as in America they do like to call rolls.

As I say a noun is a name of a thing, and therefore slowly if you feel what is inside that thing you do not call it by the name by which it is known. Everybody knows that by the way they do when they are in love and a writer should always have that intensity of emotion about whatever is the object about which he writes. And therefore and I say it again more and more one does not use nouns.

Now what other things are there beside nouns, there are a lot of other things beside nouns.

When you are at school and learn grammar grammar is very exciting. I really do not know that anything has ever been more exciting than diagraming sentences. I suppose other things may be more exciting to others when they are at school but to me undoubtedly when I was at school the really completely exciting thing was diagraming sentences and that has been to me ever since the one thing that has been completely exciting and completely completing. I like the feeling the everlasting feeling of sentences as they diagram themselves.

In that way one is completely possessing something and incidentally one's self. Now in that diagraming of the sentences of course there are articles and prepositions and as I say there are nouns but nouns as I say even by definition are completely not interesting, the same thing is true of adjectives. Adjectives are not really and truly interesting. In a way anybody can know always has known that, because after all adjectives effect nouns and as nouns are not really interesting the thing that effects a not too interesting thing is of necessity not interesting. In a way as I say anybody knows that because of course the first thing that anybody takes out of anybody's writing are the adjectives. You see of yourself how true it is that which I have just said.

Beside the nouns and the adjectives there are verbs and adverbs. Verbs and adverbs are more interesting. In the first place they have one very nice quality and that is that they can be so mistaken. It is wonderful the number of mistakes a verb can make and that is equally true of its adverb. Nouns and adjectives never can make mistakes can never be mistaken but verbs can be so endlessly, both as to what they do and how they agree or disagree with whatever they do. The same is true of adverbs.

In that way any one can see that verbs and adverbs are more interesting than nouns and adjectives.

Beside being able to be mistaken and to make mistakes verbs can change to look like themselves or to look like something else, they are, so to speak on the move and adverbs move with them and each of them find themselves not at all annoying but very often very much mistaken. That is the reason any one can like what verbs can do. Then comes the thing that can of all things be most mistaken and they are prepositions. Prepositions can live one long life being really being nothing but absolutely nothing but mistaken and that makes them irritating if you feel that way about mistakes but certainly something that you can be continuously using and everlastingly enjoying. I like prepositions the best of all, and pretty soon we will go more completely into that.

Then there are articles. Articles are interesting just as nouns and adjectives are not. And why are they interesting just as nouns and adjectives are not. They are interesting because they do what a noun might do if a noun was not so unfortunately so completely unfortunately the name of something. Articles please, a and an and the please as the name that follows cannot please. They the names that is the nouns cannot please, because after all you know well after all that is what Shakespeare meant when he talked about a rose by any other name.

I hope now no one can have any illusion about a noun or about the adjective that goes with the noun.

But an article an article remains as a delicate and a varied something and any one who wants to write with articles and knows how to use them will always have the pleasure that using something that is varied and alive can give. That is what articles are.

Beside that there are conjunctions, and a conjunction is not varied but it has a force that need not make any one feel that they are dull. Conjunctions have made themselves live by their work. They work and as they work they live and even when they do not work and in these days they do not always live by work still nevertheless they do live.

So you see why I like to write with prepositions and conjunctions and articles and verbs and adverbs but not with nouns and adjectives. If you read my writing you will you do see what I mean.

Of course then there are pronouns. Pronouns are not as bad as nouns because in the first place practically they cannot have adjectives go with them. That already makes them better than nouns.

Then beside not being able to have adjectives go with them, they of course are not really the name of anything. They represent some one but they are not its or his name. In not being his or its or her name they already have a greater possibility of being something than if they were as a noun is the name of anything. Now actual given names of people are more lively than nouns which are the name of anything and I suppose that this is because after all the name is only given to that person when they are born, there is at least the element of choice even the element of change and anybody can be pretty well able to do what they like, they may be born Walter and become Hub, in such a way they are not like a noun. A noun has been the name of something for such a very long time.

That is the reason that slang exists it is to change the nouns which have been names for so long. I say again. Verbs and adverbs and articles and conjunctions and prepositions are lively because they all do something and as long as anything does something it keeps alive.

One might have in one's list added interjections but really interjections have nothing to do with anything not even with themselves. There so much for that. And now to go into the question of punctuation.

There are some punctuations that are interesting and there are some punctuations that are not. Let us begin with the punctuations that are not.

Of these the one but the first and the most the completely most uninteresting is the question mark. The question mark is alright when it is all alone when it is used as a brand on cattle or when it could be used in decoration but connected with writing it is completely entirely completely uninteresting. It is evident that if you ask a question you ask a question but anybody who can read at all knows when a question is a question as it is written in writing. Therefore I ask you therefore wherefore should one use it the question mark. Beside it does not in its form go with ordinary printing and so it pleases neither the eye nor the ear and it is therefore like a noun, just an unnecessary name of something. A question is a question, anybody can know that a question is a question and so why add to it the question mark when it is already there when the question is already there in the writing. Therefore I never could bring myself to use a question mark, I always found it positively revolting, and now very few do use it. Exclamation marks have the same difficulty and also quotation marks, they are unnecessary, they are ugly, they spoil the line of the writing or the printing and anyway what is the use, if you do not know that a question is a question what is the use of its being a question. The same thing is true of an exclamation. And the same thing is true of a quotation. When I first began writing I found it simply impossible to use question marks and quotation marks and exclamation points and now anybody sees it that way. Perhaps some day they will see it some other way but now at any rate anybody can and does see it that way.

So there are the uninteresting things in punctuation uninteresting in a way that is perfectly obvious, and so we do not have to go any farther into that. There are besides dashes and dots, and these might be interesting spaces might be interesting. They might if one felt that way about them.

One other little punctuation mark one can have feelings about and that is the apostrophe for possession. Well feel as you like about that, I can see and I do see that for many that for some the possessive case apostrophe has a gentle tender insinuation that makes it very difficult to definitely decide to do without it. One does do without it, I do, I mostly always do, but I cannot deny that from time to time I feel myself having regrets and from time to time I put it in to make the possessive case. I absolutely do not like it all alone when it is outside the the word when the word is a plural, no then positively and definitely no, I do not like it and in leaving it out I feel no regret, there it is unnecessary and not ornamental but inside a word and its well perhaps, perhaps it does appeal by its weakness to your weakness. At least at any rate from time to time I do find myself letting it alone if it has come in and sometimes it has come in. I cannot positively deny but that I do from time to time let it come in.

So now to come to the real question of punctuation, periods, commas, colons, semi-colons and capitals and small letters.

I have had a long and complicated life with all these.

Let us begin with these I use the least first and these are colons and semi-colons, one might add to these commas.

When I first began writing, I felt that writing should go on, I still do feel that it should go on but when I first began writing I was completely possessed by the necessity that writing should go on and if writing should go on what had colons and semi-colons to do with it, what had commas to do with it, what had periods to do with it what had small letters and capitals to do with it to do with writing going on which was at that time the most profound need I had in connection with writing. What had colons and semi-colons to do with it what had commas to do with it what had periods to do with it.

What had periods to do with it. Inevitably no matter how completely I had to have writing go on, physically one had to again and again stop sometime and if one had to again and again stop some time then periods had to exist. Beside I had always liked the look of periods and I liked what they did. Stopping sometime did not really keep one from going on, it was nothing that interfered, it was only something that happened, and as it happened as a perfectly natural happening, I did believe in periods and I used them. I really never stopped using them.

Beside that periods might later come to have a life of their own to commence breaking up things in arbitrary ways, that has happened lately with me in a poem I have written called Winning His Way. . . . By the time I had written this poem about three years ago periods had come to have for me completely a life of their own. They could begin to act as they thought best and one might interrupt one's writing with them that is not really interrupt one's writing with them but one could come to stop arbitrarily stop at times in one's writing and so they could be used and you could use them. Periods could come to exist in this way and they could come in this way to have a life of their own. They did not serve you in any servile way as commas and colons and semi-colons do. Yes you do feel what I mean.

Periods have a life of their own a necessity of their own a feeling of their own a time of their own. And that feeling that life that necessity that time can express itself in an infinite variety that is the reason that I have always remained true to periods so much so that I say recently I have felt that one could need them more than one had ever needed them.

You can see what an entirely different thing a period is from a comma, a colon or a semi-colon.

There are two different ways of thinking about colons and semi-colons you can think of them as commas and as such they are purely servile or you can think of them as periods and then using them can make you feel adventurous. I can see that one might feel about them as periods but I myself never have, I began unfortunately to feel them as a comma and commas are servile they have no life of their own they are dependent upon use and convenience and they are put there just for practical purposes. Semi-colons

and colons had for me from the first completely this character the character
that a comma has and not the character that a period has and therefore and
definitely I have never used them. But now dimly and definitely I do see that
they might well possibly they might have in them something of the character
of the period and so it might have been an adventure to use them. I really
do not think so. I think however lively they are or disguised they are they
are definitely more comma than period and so really I cannot regret not
having used them. They are more powerful more imposing more pretentious
than a comma but they are a comma all the same. They really have within
them deeply within them fundamentally within them the comma nature.
And now what does a comma do and what has it to do and why do I feel
as I do about them.

What does a comma do.

I have refused them so often and left them out so much and did without
them so continually that I have come finally to be indifferent to them. I do
not now care whether you put them in or not but for a long time I felt very
definitely about them and would have nothing to do with them.

As I say commas are servile and they have no life of their own, and
their use is not a use, it is a way of replacing one's own interest and I do
decidedly like to like my own interest my own interest in what I am doing.
A comma by helping you along holding your coat for you and putting on
your shoes keeps you from living your life as actively as you should lead it
and to me for many years and I still do feel that way about it only now I do
not pay as much attention to them, the use of them was positively degrading.
Let me tell you what I feel and what I mean and what I felt and what I
meant.

When I was writing those long sentences of The Making of Americans,
verbs active present verbs with long dependent adverbial clauses became a
passion with me. I have told you that I recognize verbs and adverbs aided
by prepositions and conjunctions with pronouns as possessing the whole of
the active life of writing.

Complications make eventually for simplicity and therefore I have
always liked dependent adverbial clauses. I have liked dependent adverbial
clauses because of their variety of dependence and independence. You can
see how loving the intensity of complication of these things that commas
would be degrading. Why if you want the pleasure of concentrating on the
final simplicity of excessive complication would you want any artificial aid
to bring about that simplicity. Do you see now why I feel about the comma
as I did and as I do.

Think about anything you really like to do and you will see what I mean.

When it gets really difficult you want to disentangle rather than to cut
the knot, at least so anybody feels who is working with any thread, so anybody feels who is working with any tool so anybody feels who is writing any
sentence or reading it after it has been written. And what does a comma do,

a comma does nothing but make easy a thing that if you like it enough is easy enough without the comma. A long complicated sentence should force itself upon you, make you know yourself knowing it and the comma, well at the most a comma is a poor period that it lets you stop and take a breath but if you want to take a breath you ought to know yourself that you want to take a breath. It is not like stopping altogether which is what a period does stopping altogether has something to do with going on, but taking a breath well you are always taking a breath and why emphasize one breath rather than another breath. Anyway that is the way I felt about it and I felt that about it very very strongly. And so I almost never used a comma. The longer, the more complicated the sentence the greater the number of the same kinds of words I had following one after another, the more the very many more I had of them the more I felt the passionate need of their taking care of themselves by themselves and not helping them, and thereby enfeebling them by putting in a comma.

So that is the way I felt punctuation in prose, in poetry it is a little different but more so. . . . But that is the way I felt about punctuation in prose.

COMPREHENSION QUIZ

1. Miss Stein's article
    a. is particularly for the student who wants to know where he ought to place a comma.
    b. encourages writers to use more nouns and adjectives.
    c. is a plea for precision and clarity.
    d. expresses an antagonism to commas.
2. She says that she has never known anything more exciting than
    a. diagraming a sentence.
    b. learning a foreign language.
    c. meeting famous celebrities.
    d. writing a novel.
3. Of all the parts of speech, Miss Stein likes best of all the
    a. adjective.
    b. adverb.
    c. preposition.
    d. conjunction.
4. She finds the most uninteresting punctuation mark to be the
    a. comma.
    b. colon.
    c. period.
    d. question mark.
5. Her article deals with punctuation in
    a. prose.

b. poetry.
c. poetry and prose.
d. none of the above.

DISCUSSION QUESTIONS

1. How would you describe the rhythm and order of the words in this essay? Does Miss Stein's style suggest anything about her personality?
2. Is this essay really a defense of ambiguity, a protection against being taken too simply? Or is Miss Stein urging greater clarity and exactness in language?
3. How much "practical" advice concerning punctuation is to be found in this essay? Note, for example, her advice concerning the use of the comma.
4. Miss Stein says that she has never known anything more exciting than diagraming sentences. Does your experience compare with hers? Was diagraming profitable for you? Did it improve your writing?

WRITING SUGGESTIONS

1. Write an analysis of Miss Stein's prose style.
2. Do you agree with her comments about verbs and their superiority over nouns and adjectives? Write a theme in which you explain the principles one should keep in mind when selecting words.
3. Develop the following statement: "One of the things that is a very interesting thing to know is how you are feeling inside you to the words that are coming out to be outside of you."
4. At the end of this selection Miss Stein says that punctuation in poetry is different from punctuation in prose. Write an essay in which you give advice on punctuation to a prospective writer of poetry.

In the Beginning

by LAWRENCE E. NELSON

The generalizations about theme introductions in many composition handbooks are inadequate for most students. The standard handbook admonitions, "Be brief," "Be direct and sure," "Catch the reader's interest," and "Lead the reader to the subject," are empty phrases to beginning writers. A student confronted with the statement, "Let the reader know the business at hand," for example, might be willing to do just that. But he doesn't know how to go about this. Nor does he have the skill to "limit and fix his subject," or "concern himself with the history of the subject." These vague suggestions, rarely offered with examples, must be supplemented by explanations and concrete examples of how others have written introductions before young writers can be expected to begin themes skillfully.

To help my students improve their introductions, I prepared the following set of specific models. Each of them more or less fills the prescriptions given in most composition handbooks about what to do in an introduction. And equally important, each of them offers the student a concrete example of an introduction.

1. *Begin with a definition of a key word or phrase in your theme.* The semanticist, Hayakawa, begins an article about human reactions to words by defining what he means by "pattern of reaction," a key phrase used throughout his essay.

> The end product of education, yours and mine and everybody's, is the total pattern of reactions and possible reactions we have inside ourselves. If you did not have within you at this moment the pattern of reactions which we call "the ability to read English," you would see here only meaningless black marks on paper. Because of the trained patterns of response, you are (or are not) stirred to patriotism by martial music, your feelings of reverence are

From Lawrence E. Nelson, "In the Beginning," *English Journal*, March, 1966. Reprinted by permission of the National Council of Teachers of English and Lawrence E. Nelson.

aroused by the symbols of your religion, you listen more respectfully to the health advice of someone who has "M.D." after his name than to that of someone who hasn't. What I call here a "pattern of reactions," then, is the sum total of the ways we act in response to events, to words and to symbols.[1]

2. *Begin with a brief, vivid history of your subject.* Be careful to write only about its general history. Close regard to detail here would tend to shift your readers' attention from your topic to historical points which may not have any bearing on your theme. Aldous Huxley uses this approach in an essay on the influence of certain drugs:

In the course of history many more people have died for their drink and their dope than have died for their religion or their country. The craving for ethyl alcohol and the opiates has been stronger, in these millions, than the love of God, of home, of children; even of life. Their cry was not for liberty or death; it was for death preceded by enslavement. There is a paradox here and a mystery. Why should such multitudes of men and women be so ready to sacrifice themselves for a cause so utterly hopeless and in the ways so painful and so profoundly humiliating?[2]

3. *Begin with a direct statement of your position on an issue.* This bold technique is often very effective for an argumentative paper. Following is an example from Norbert Wiener's "Role of the Intellectual and the Scientist."

This book argues that the integrity of the channels of internal communication is essential to the welfare of society. This internal communication is subject at the present time not only to the threats which it has faced at all times, but to certain new and especially serious problems which belong peculiarly to our age. One among these is the growing complexity and cost of communication.[3]

4. *Begin with an analytical paragraph which states the major divisions of your paper.* This type of beginning is particularly useful for long papers or very involved topics which need a strong, controlling statement. Bertrand Russell uses this technique in a philosophic essay entitled, "The Expanding Mental Universe."

The effects of modern knowledge upon our mental life have been many and various, and seem likely, in the future, to become even greater than they have been hitherto. The life of the mind is traditionally divided into three aspects:

---

[1] S. I. Hayakawa, "How Words Change Our Lives." Used by special permission of *The Saturday Evening Post.* Copyright, 1958, by The Curtis Publishing Company.

[2] Aldous Huxley, "Drugs That Shape Men's Minds." Used by special permission of *The Saturday Evening Post.* Copyright, 1958, by The Curtis Publishing Company.

[3] Norbert Wiener, *The Human Use of Human Beings: Cybernetics and Society* (Boston: The Houghton Mifflin Company, 1950). Quoted by permission of the publisher.

thinking, willing, and feeling. There is no great scientific validity in this division, but it is convenient for purposes of discussion, and I shall, therefore, follow it.[4]

5. *Begin by describing your topic without naming it. Then name the topic in the next paragraph.* The "mystery beginning," as I call it, can be intriguing. It must not be used, however, to mock the reader by demanding that he play "guess what" for long. It is useful only when it catches reader attention and satisfies his curiosity in the second paragraph of the theme. For example, beginning an essay on the fathers of great men, Gilbert Highet says,

> The last group of teachers to discuss is one of the most important and effective. However, it is not really a group, but a collection of individuals, hardly any of whom knows or cares anything about the others. It exists now. It is self-perpetuating. It is given far less credit than it earns. Usually it is forgotten altogether by the public and sometimes by its pupils. But its work has been invaluable, and now ranks as teaching of the very finest type.
> These teachers are the fathers of great men, who taught them much of what they needed to become great. . . .[5]

6. *Begin with an anecdote which is relevant to your topic.* Anecdotal introductions are potent but sometimes inadvisable for high school writers, because they spend more time reading anecdotes than writing a paper. Sometimes students will attempt to alter their papers to fit their anecdotes and lose sight of the assignment. I advise students to use the anecdotal introduction sparingly. Here is a good example from *Harper's*:

> There is an anecdote, possibly apocryphal, about a woman at a cocktail party in Paris telling James Thurber how much she had enjoyed his "delightful sketches" in French translation. "Thank you," said Thurber. "It is undoubtedly true that my writing loses a good deal in the original."[6]

7. *Begin by making general statistics relevant to the individual.* A statistical beginning usually requires some research and a little mathematics, but the results are worth the labor. In an age of statistics this method is particularly effective. Here is how Jessica Mitford interprets a vast sum of money according to the individual's pocketbook.

> In 1960, Americans spent, according to the only available government estimate, $1.6 billion on funerals, setting thereby a new national and world rec-

4 Bertrand Russell, "The Expanding Mental Universe." Used by special permission of *The Saturday Evening Post.* Copyright, 1959, by The Curtis Publishing Company.

5 Gilbert Highet, *The Art of Teaching* (New York: Alfred A. Knopf, 1950). Quoted by permission of the publisher.

6 John A. Kouwenhoven, "The Trouble with Translation," *Harper's* (August 1962). Quoted by permission of *Harper's* Magazine.

ord. The $1.6 billion is, as we shall see, only a portion of what was actually spent on what the death industry calls "the care and memorialization of the dead." Even this partial figure if averaged out among the number of deaths, would amount to the astonishing sum of $942 for the funeral of every man, woman, child, and stillborn babe who died in the United States in 1960. This is a record unmatched in any previous age of civilization.[7]

8. *Begin by contrasting two opposing aspects of a topic.* The contrast may be between almost any two aspects—good and bad, past and present, weak and strong, happy and sad. The contrasting introduction should end with that aspect of the topic which is to be discussed in the essay. An example of this type of introduction from *The Atlantic* follows.

They say that in the old days lumbering was wasteful; the lumbermen would fell a tree and perhaps take only one good log out of the middle, leaving the other two to rot. Today the red-shirted, calk-booted, two-fisted woodsman has disappeared, along with the forlorn tarpaper flaps on the roofs of the old log camps. Yet the trees are coming down faster, if not more wastefully than of old, thanks to the chain saw that makes a forest look as if a gigantic mowing machine had gone over it.[8]

9. *Begin with a question or a series of questions which will be answered in the body of the essay.* This technique can be used with several variations. The introduction can be merely a bold, one-sentence paragraph which asks a question which the theme will answer. Or it can be a brief discussion of an issue which resolves itself in a question, such as is done in example two above. Another variation follows here. The writer asks a question initially, proffers a series of answers, and negates all of them to make way for the correct answer which is the body of the essay.

What is race? A myth, as some popular writers believe, or a rigid division of mankind into superior and inferior groups? A reverse freedom rider northward bound? America's greatest and most divisive unsolved problem? The white, black, yellow, red, and the brown races pictured in the school geography books? Or a relatively recent and superficial division of mankind?

No. Re-examined in the light of science and history, race is not exactly any of these. . . .[9]

10. *Begin with a brief narrative.* An essay which describes George Washington Carver begins with the following narrative introduction.

[7] Jessica Mitford, "The Undertaker's Racket," *The Atlantic* (June 1963). Quoted by permission of the author.

[8] Robert E. Pike, "Log Drive on the Connecticut," *The Atlantic* (July 1963). Quoted by permission of the author.

[9] Carleton S. Coon, "New Findings on the Origin of Races," *Harper's* (December 1962). Quoted by permission of *Harper's* Magazine.

The stooped old Negro shuffled along through the dust of an Alabama road at a curiously rapid rate. He was carrying an armful of sticks and wild flowers.[10]

This list of models is not complete, but it does serve as a useful supplement to many generalizations about the beginnings of themes. The student, once confronted with a model of how another writer has introduced an essay, can often see the sense of handbook suggestions more readily and apply them more effectively.

COMPREHENSION QUIZ

1. The author of this article finds the directions for theme introductions in many composition handbooks
   a. too detailed and elaborate.
   b. placing excessive emphasis on humor as an attention getting device.
   c. too vague, and rarely offered with examples.
   d. much improved over handbooks of 25 years ago.
2. To help his students improve their introductions, the author
   a. urged the students to concentrate initially on concluding paragraphs.
   b. compiled a list of "don'ts."
   c. required a minimum of three drafts before preparing the final copy.
   d. prepared a set of specific models.
3. Which of the following "openers" is *not* recommended?
   a. Begin with a direct statement of your position on an issue.
   b. Begin with an acknowledgment that yours is a very unpopular view.
   c. Begin with a brief history of your subject.
   d. Begin by contrasting two opposing aspects of a topic.
4. Nelson believes that the student, once confronted with a model of how another writer has introduced an essay,
   a. can recognize the weaknesses of handbook suggestions.
   b. can often see the sense of handbook suggestions more readily.
   c. can come to some appreciation of how easy the writing of theme introductions really is.
   d. can recognize, for the first time, the futility of imitating or studying other writers.
5. The basic idea of this article is that
   a. young writers need to have concrete examples of how others have written introductions.
   b. students should be encouraged to develop their own techniques of theme introductions.
   c. plagiarism is encouraged through the study of other's writing.
   d. theme introductions are far less important than theme endings.

[10] James Saxon Childers, "A Boy Who Was Traded for a Horse" in Rewey Belle Inglis and others, editors, *Adventures in American Literature* (New York: Harcourt, Brace and World, Inc., 1952). Quoted by permission of the author.

DISCUSSION QUESTIONS

1. Cite two examples of especially good openings of essays you have read.
2. List at least two other ways to begin a theme.

WRITING SUGGESTIONS

1. Write a short theme in which you offer advice to college freshmen concerning beginning a theme.
2. Using the advice given in this essay, write a brief introduction to three themes.

Reading Literature as Problem-Solving

by SEYMOUR B. CHATMAN

The fact that "reading literature" and "problem-solving" do not ordinarily rub shoulders is, I suppose, one more instance of the feud between the sciences and the humanities that so troubles us today. But science would not be so ominous to the humanist if he could accept Thomas Henry Huxley's view; Huxley felt that *all* men are scientists since "the method of scientific investigation is nothing but the expression of the necessary mode of working of the human mind." To the extent that each person constantly solves problems he is engaged in scientific activity. Part of what a reader does when he reads a poem, at least at the outset, is to solve a set of explicational problems. Why not help the beginning reader acquire the problem-solving attitude as a conscious piece of intellectual equipment? Granted that English teachers want to introduce values and ideals to students through literature, granted that we feel some obligation to induce inklings of esthetic enjoyment, of the breath and finer spirit which means so much to us, I wonder if sometimes we do not tend to underestimate a severe first-order problem which stands in the way—a problem which one could almost call (horrendous word) *mechanical*. To put it bluntly but realistically, a large number of our students never respond to literature because they never learn how to read it; I mean "read it" in the ordinary sense of making out what it says. Students, of course, lack life experience—most have not lived through a sufficient variety of emotional situations, or learned enough about men and manners to grasp the sophistications of the great authors. But more important for our purposes, they lack reading experience. At the risk of being universally condemned for a mechanist, let me say simply that they have not developed the requisite *linguistic apparatus* to read successfully.

From Seymour B. Chatman, "Reading Literature as Problem-Solving," *English Journal*, May, 1963. Reprinted by permission of the National Council of Teachers of English and Seymour B. Chatman.

It is useful to think of this apparatus as containing three mechanisms: grammatical, lexical, and interpretational. In each case, the cultivation of a problem-solving attitude can be a salutary and effective aid to the novice reader. Separating problems makes the student's job much easier, because it allows him to focus on one at a time. And as he progresses, he becomes his own diagnostician. In a sense, the real goal is to help the student develop a sense of problems. Once problems are recognizable, they can be solved; but if one does not have the faculty of recognition, he can only flounder.

Grammatical Analysis

The grammar of a language is the system by which its components are organized. Its study is the province of linguistics. But in reading, what one tries to achieve is a practical and operational rather than a theoretical control of grammatical organizations. The purpose of grammatical training, insofar as reading is concerned, should not be to develop some abstract ability to name structures, to "parse," but rather to learn how to make sense of sentences of various degrees of structural complexity. Poetry offers special problems because poets write complexly and idiosyncratically. Their sentences are long; ellipses abound; word order is frequently inverted; and the reference of pronouns or dependent constructions is not always immediately clear. Because of the pressures of meter and the general condensation of poetic language, syntax is simply more complex than what students are used to. An elementary but vital ability that they need to learn is quite literally to figure out who is doing what to whom. Consider just one problem by way of example, that of word order. Certainly the questions could not be more explicit: what is the subject, what is the verb, and what is the object? The feature by which we normally identify these functions, of course, is relative position: the subject and hence the doer precedes the verb and the object and hence the goal of the action follows. But in poetry the order frequently gets switched around, and it often requires some interpretive effort to decide what's what. Both subject and object may precede the verb, either in that order, subject first and object second, as in Pope's

Steel could the labor of the gods destroy

or in inverted order, as in Milton's

That glory never shall his wrath or might
Extort from me.

Or object may precede verb and subject follow, as in Milton's

Him followed his next mate.

Inversions catch the student unawares. He is not used to that slight but essential act of disentangling and "straightening out" sentence elements. It is not that disentangling is particularly hard: anybody with a native command of the language and a normal sense of context can usually make his way, providing he perceives that there is a problem that has to be solved, a problem which is sharp and specific, not at all fuzzy and vague, as students seem often to assume.

The best way to raise this problem to a conscious level is to require paraphrases. But paraphrases of a very special and limited sort: indeed, perhaps "paraphrase" is misleading as a name for this particular sort of exercise. The actual words of the original should not be changed; only their order. For example, the following revisions would be acceptable for the lines from Pope and Milton quoted above:

> Steel could destroy the labor of the gods.
> His wrath or might should never extort that glory from me.
> His next mate followed him.

A mechanical exercise you say, but a necessary one, since the problem *is* a mechanical one. Time enough for more sophisticated things once the rudimentary difficulties are solved. And, I have found, students are not impatient with this kind of drill; because it is concrete, it has the low-grade excitement of a puzzle, and they soon see its practical importance.

A bad job of disentangling can have startling results. A teacher I know[1] asked a high-school class to interpret lines from the *Ancient Mariner* which occur just after the albatross has been slain. The mariner, you will remember, is cursed by the other crew members for having killed the bird.

> Ah wretch! said they, the bird to slay,
> That made the breeze to blow.

The problem is that the phrase "the bird to slay," besides being a rather loose modifier of "wretch," has its object preceding rather than following its verb. The meaning, of course, is something like "The Mariner is a wretch for having slain the bird which made the breeze blow." The teacher received a wonderous collection of responses, the recitation of which will do more than theoretical words can to illustrate the severity of the problem. Consider these efforts to identify the wretch: One student thought it was the bird, and paraphrased:

> They said, "Ah wretch" to the bird they wanted to slay because he made the breezes blow.

One thought it was the speaker:

> Don't kill that bird, the wretch said, it broke the air in flight.

[1] Bertram Mott. See the *English Journal*, April 1963.

One took it personally:

> They said I am a wretch for slaying the bird which made the breezes blow.

One didn't identify the "wretch" at all, but thought it was some kind of exclamation, perhaps the nineteenth century equivalent of "Ah nuts!":

> As they were going to slay a bird which made the breeze blow, they said "Ah Wretch!"

Even where the wretch was properly identified, the passage remained unclear. Some couldn't understand why the mariner was a wretch. One thought that it was because he made the breeze blow:

> Ah wicked one! they said, the breeze started blowing because you killed the poor bird.

Two thought that he was a wretch because he needed urging to slay the bird (apparently taking the infinitive "to slay" as if it were an imperative). In one case, the bird needed to be slain because it caused the breeze:

> Ah wretch! they said, slay that bird that made the breeze blow.

But as wonderfully wrong-headed as these interpretations may be, they at least represent effort. Because their authors kept the exact words of the original, errors of position could be pointed to and discussed and some educational advance made. But what can you do with responses like:

> It is a shame that it is so windy

or

> They said to slay the bird that just flew by

or

> Ah retch they said as the movement of their ax which was to slay the bird escaped him?

Although syntactic confusion is common among novice readers, all too often it is too buried under the hazy and general verbiage of overambitious literary "appreciation" to be unearthed. The teacher has so much substantive and stylistic material to correct that specifically syntactic failures may slip by. But without interpretive fluency, the student has nothing; all else is air, mostly hot. Students can learn to solve syntactic problems when they learn to see them as problems, and the best way to achieve heightened awareness is through controlled practice and drill.

Lexical Analysis

The second mechanism which proficient readers apply to interpretive problems is *lexical*. It is the capacity to perceive the proper senses of words in context. Words are obstinately pluri-significational; they possess (or should we say "are possessed of"?) several meanings. Adept readers have learned that fact and make strenuous efforts to identify the precise sense which words take to themselves in specific instances. They are keen observers of context, and where trouble arises, they have a knack of sensing which word it is in the sentence that is causing difficulty. The sense of trouble, of sudden incoherence, is a sharp invitation to check the dictionary for unsuspected senses. Beginning students, on the other hand, are likely to feel a vague and hopeless sense of disorientation, from whose grip they rarely extricate themselves. The primary difficulty again is learning to size up the problem; once a problem is recognized, a solution is more than half achieved.

What often misleads students is the very commonness of some words. Most will dutifully look up words they've never seen before; what deceives them are words which they "know" perfectly well, but "know" in an inappropriate sense. A great step toward maturity in reading is the awareness that a common-place word may be just the one causing trouble. Unfortunately, their own nonsensical or puzzling or inane interpretations rarely become sufficiently depressing to most students to prompt them to ransack the dictionary for other possibilities. For example, confronted by Milton's

> And ye the breathing Roses of the Wood

do students rush to the dictionary to snatch the necessary but unusual sense of "breathing"—"giving off odors, redolent"? No, they're struck, committed to the ordinary yet inappropriate sense of "inhaling"; consequently the whole line misfires. It's all so comfortable but so meaningless. Another example from Donne's famous Holy Sonnet:

> Batter my heart, three person'd God; for, you
> As yet but knock, breathe, shine, and seek to mend.

Here "breathe" means "to inspire" in the most literal sense of that word, the implicit object being "me." But how many students can be expected to resist the dissatisfying assumption that the poet is asking God to inhale and exhale? In Pope's "Elegy to the Memory of an Unfortunate Lady," the lady's miserable funeral is lamented:

No friend's complaint, no kind domestic tear
Pleas'd thy pale ghost, or grac'd thy mornful bier.

The ordinary meaning of "complaint" obviously does not suit the context; the appropriate sense is "lament," as in a formal verse complaint. How many students, despite feeling vaguely troubled by the word, will check the dictionary for a more appropriate meaning. And what is the predictable response to Gray's lines

Lo where the rosy-bosom'd Hours

. . . . . .

Disclose the long-expecting flowers

where "disclosed" means "opened up," not "revealed," and "long-expecting" means "expected for a long while," not "pregnant"? Or to Keats' nightingale, which pours its song "abroad"—not in a foreign country, but "widely over a broad surface"?

The problem is to increase sensitivity to the possibilities of plurisignification—multiple meaning. Here a sequence of drills might be useful in inducing sensitivity. Students might first be asked to use contexts to identify the senses of certain words preselected by the instructor. Once they have achieved some competence in this process, they could be asked themselves to select words in given passages needing glosses. This second step is absolutely necessary; otherwise the entire first assignment becomes empty and meaningless. It is not enough for a student to be able to supply answers on demand; it is much more important that he learn how to sense the existence of lexical problems. The beginning reader must learn how to diagnose his situation, to learn what is holding him up.

Lexical adeptness means an ability to solve more complicated and wider-ranging problems as well. In Pope's "Rape of the Lock," for instance, the word "nymph" occurs repeatedly; sometimes it refers to real nymphs—the female members of Ariel's band of sylphs—but often it refers to living girls at Hampton Court. This provides a sophisticated challenge for sharpening lexical wits. The problem is even more challenging when it comes to important abstractions, words like "wit" and "judgment," which have so many senses in the eighteenth century.

Interpretation of Literature

The third reading mechanism in which problem-solving talent is useful can be called, for lack of a better term, *interpretational*. Interpreting may be defined as the art of making coherent sense—a consistent frame of meaning—out of a discourse. It is not uncommon that although a student understands the grammar of a passage and the meanings of all the words taken separately, he cannot give an accurate account of what the poem as a whole says. His difficulty may either be that he doesn't see any point at all, or that he ascribes an erroneous, sometimes a spectacularly erroneous point. For example, a student of mine read William Blake's poem entitled "London"—

> I wander thro' each charter'd street,
> Near where the charter'd Thames does flow
> And mark in every face I meet
> Marks of weakness, marks of woe, etc.

as a commentary on the seventeenth century English Revolution. A curious association of ideas suggested this interpretation to her: the word "charter'd" she felt, had a parliamentary ring to it; then there were references to the "black'ning" church (Anglican vs. Broadchurch) and the hapless soldier (of either side), and the fact that somewhere she had learned that Blake was interested in seventeenth century English art. So strong was her political assumption that she interpreted the mention of a marriage hearse in the sentence

>   I hear
> How the youthful Harlot's curse
> Blasts the new born Infant's tear
> And blights with plagues the Marriage hearse.

as a reference to the marriage of William of Orange and Mary!

The interpretational problem that faces students is specifically to learn how to perceive a poem's *probable* limits of reference. If one assumes, as I do, that each poem is a unified discourse, all of whose parts are necessary, interlocking, and mutually informing—as I. A. Richards puts it, a "raft of consents," all of whose "boards" agree to band together—then one need go outside the poem only to explain special allusions. The essential characteristics of any successful interpretation are probability and simplicity. A good interpretation of a poem is one that is probable in terms of the normal meanings of words and references, and one that is simple, that is, requires the least number of special presuppositions. It is simpler, for example, to assume that Blake is talking about 18th century London than 17th century London because he uses the first person and the present tense. This does not mean that poems describing former eras are never written in the first person, present tense, but rather that if they are, one can usually assume that they will contain other evidence to signal the fact, that one's decision about such matters necessarily depends upon a number of clues containing a certain redundancy of information.

One technique which seems to be useful for showing students how to stay on the right track is what my collaborator, Morse Peckham, has named the "interpretational hypothesis."[2] The term "hypothesis" is meant to suggest that every interpretation can be usefully worked out, line by line, and

---

[2] See our text, *Word, Meaning, Poem* (New York: Crowell, 1961).

without skipping a line, on the basis of a continuing sequence of normal probabilities. Interpretations, in this view, amount to highly educated guesses, since total and perfect communication is impossible, and a paraphrase is always an approximation. One would not dream of asserting that any interpretation is *true*, but only that it is adequate and reasonably reliable. In forming the hypothesis, one makes decisions only upon the evidence as it occurs, without jumping around in the poem. If a line or word is ambiguous, the various possibilities can be kept in mind until decisive information is secured; and even if a passage seems totally obscure, one should still try to form a hypothesis of what might be being said. Passivity is the greatest enemy of successful interpretation; we must assume that all poems say something, and that normal speakers of the language can, with effort, make sense of them.

The interpretational hypothesis, further, should proceed not only by paraphrase but also in the form of questions raised by the paraphrase: Who is the speaker? Who is the listener, if any? What is the occasion of the poem? What is the setting? What is the period of history? What state of mind is implied? What seems to be the point? What connotations are suggested over and above plain sense meanings? Perhaps the best way to demonstrate what I mean is simply to quote part of one of our Interpretational Hypotheses; it refers to the first four lines of Shakespeare's Sonnet 116:

Let me not to the marriage of true minds
Admit impediments; love is not love
Which alters when it alterations finds,
Or bends with the remover to remove.

The poem begins with an appeal. Do not permit me to admit the truth of the proposition that any obstacle can frustrate (or stand in the way of) the permanent devotion to each other of faithful minds. "Mind" is probably best thought of here as mental intention, as in "I have a mind to do so-and-so." But to whom is the request addressed? It has a peculiar urgency, coming as it does at the beginning of the poem without any prelude or explanation. It is as if the speaker were desperately crying out, "Don't let me do it! I don't want to!" The request implies a powerful impulse to do whatever the speaker is begging not to be permitted to do. It may be addressed to the beloved, or it may be addressed to the speaker himself. But if to the former, an insistence that there *are* no impediments would seem more likely. There is also the possibility that the speaker is addressing a third individual, a god or a friend. But since there is no information as to who such a person might be, it is best to adopt, until the poem requires us to do otherwise, the simplest hypothesis. We shall go on the assumption, therefore, that the speaker is addressing himself, and is, in some agony, attempting to quell his doubts about the permanence of love. "True" is used in the sense of "faithful in love," and is associated with "marriage," because to plight one's troth, to declare one's truth or faithfulness, precedes marriage. "Marriage of true minds," then, can be interpreted as the unchanging devotion to each other of personalities who have declared that they would maintain such devotion. The speaker is trying to resist considering the possibility that the declaration of love does not assure love's permanence, that "saying so does not make it so." If this hypothesis is correct, the doubts which the speaker is trying to suppress will make themselves apparent in the poem.

The first attempt to achieve conviction is by definition. An emotion which one has taken to be love is not really love which changes simply because its object (i.e. the beloved) has changed. Even if a partner in love (i.e. the beloved) exhibits a lessening or cessation of love, a true lover continues to love. Nor is an emotion really love if its direction is turned away from the beloved toward another love-object just because the beloved's emotion has shifted *its* direction toward another love-object (1.4). It follows that the speaker is not so much anxious about a change in the love of his partner as he is about what would happen to his own feelings if his partner's love changed. If, the implication is, the speaker's love should change as a consequence of a change in the beloved's love, then the speaker's love was not really love to begin with. That is, if it should turn out that there are impediments to a love which appears to be a true love, then it was not true love in the first place. But this conclusion is not satisfactory, because the speaker doesn't want to find out if his love is true or not; he wants to believe that there is no possibility that it is not true love. Does his anxiety stem from a suspicion, hidden even from himself, that there is such a possibility? Else, why all the shouting?[3]

There will be those, of course, who object that this sort of paraphrase is, to use a word popular in recent literary criticism, heretical, that it can never be a substitute for the poem itself. To which the response can be made: "Of course—no one claims that it *is* a substitute." One works out a paraphrase not to replace the poem, but to understand it. Poems are difficult pieces of discourse, and one of the best ways to recognize and resolve the difficulties is to put the poem into other words. This does not mean that the putting-into-other-words is the desired consummation. Quite the contrary. The student now possesses the poem more clearly than he ever could before. At this stage literary criticism can begin. Those who feel that poetry is a butterfly all too easily broken on a wheel will shudder at these suggestions; but perhaps that particular analogy has outlived its usefulness. It is more like a fruit with an intricate skin that has to be removed; or like the reproduction of a painting that has been cut up into a jig-saw puzzle and whose proper appreciation requires some piecing together. Either way you look at it—taking apart or putting together—reading poetry requires effort, specifically interpretive effort—making out the grammar, deciding on the meanings of words, and developing some theory of the point of it all. Certainly, let esthetics and value judgments follow, but let them be based on a firm and sophisticated understanding of what the poem says.

[3] From Morse Peckham and Seymour Chatman (eds.), *Word, Meaning, Poem*. Copyright © 1961 by Thomas Y. Crowell Company. Reprinted by permission of the publisher.

COMPREHENSION QUIZ

1. According to Chatman, the first step to "straightening out" the lines of a poem is
   a. to analyze the metrical pattern.
   b. to determine the rhyme scheme.
   c. to isolate the figures of speech.
   d. to make a paraphrase.
2. The author cites examples of faulty readings of lines taken from
   a. *The Ancient Mariner.*
   b. *The Wasteland.*
   c. *Ozymandias.*
   d. *Don Juan.*
3. Lexical analysis is
   a. the study of the derivation of words.
   b. the ability to unearth classical allusions through the use of a classical dictionary.
   c. the capacity to perceive the proper senses of words in context.
   d. none of the above.
4. What deceives most readers are
   a. foreign words and phrases.
   b. the words which they "know" perfectly well.
   c. rarely used and exotic, scientific terminology.
   d. all of the above.
5. Which of the following is *not* characteristic of a good interpretation of a poem?
   a. One that is simple; that is, requires the least number of special presuppositions.
   b. One that is probable in terms of the normal meanings of words and references.
   c. One that forces the reader to go outside the poem only to explain special allusions.
   d. One that assumes a poem has no probable limits of reference.
6. Chatman concludes by saying esthetics and value judgments of poetry should be based on
   a. a firm and sophisticated understanding of what the poem says.
   b. an insistence that the paraphrase is equivalent to the poem.
   c. the recognition that poems are not, in reality, difficult pieces of discourse.
   d. the words of the poet, rather than those of a paraphrase.

DISCUSSION QUESTIONS

1. Despite his title, Chatman restricts his comments to the understanding of poetry. Why? What is there about poetry that makes it more difficult to understand than prose?

2. Why is a paraphrase an inadequate substitute for a poem?
3. Chatman says that students lack life experience to grasp the sophistications of the great authors. Does this mean students are denied an understanding of poetry? What are some examples of "life experience" he might have in mind?
4. What requirements must be fulfilled by any interpretation of a poem that claims to state its "meaning"?

WRITING SUGGESTIONS

1. Write an answer to the following question: "Why do poets have to be so obscure?"
2. Develop the following topic into a theme: "How To Read A Poem."
3. Using Chatman's suggestions, select several lines from one of your favorite poems and show how lexical analysis aids in their interpretation.

What Is Style?

by F. L. LUCAS

When it was suggested to Walt Whitman that one of his works should be bound in vellum, he was outraged—"Pshaw!" he snorted, "—hangings, curtains, finger bowls, chinaware, Matthew Arnold!" And he might have been equally irritated by talk of style; for he boasted of "my barbaric yawp" —he would *not* be literary; his readers should touch not a book but a man. Yet Whitman took the pains to rewrite *Leaves of Grass* four times, and his style is unmistakable. Samuel Butler maintained that writers who bothered about their style became unreadable but he bothered about his own. "Style" has got a bad name by growing associated with precious and superior persons who, like Oscar Wilde, spend a morning putting in a comma, and the afternoon (so he said) taking it out again. But such abuse of "style" is misuse of English. For the word means merely "a way of expressing oneself, in language, manner, or appearance"; or, secondly, "a *good* way of so expressing oneself"—as when one says, "Her behavior never lacked style."

Now there is no crime in expressing oneself (though to try to *im*press oneself on others easily grows revolting or ridiculous). Indeed one cannot help expressing oneself, unless one passes one's life in a cupboard. Even the most rigid Communist, or Organization-man, is compelled by Nature to have a unique voice, unique fingerprints, unique handwriting. Even the signatures of the letters on your breakfast table may reveal more than their writers guess. There are blustering signatures that swish across the page like cornstalks bowed before a tempest. There are cryptic signatures, like a scrabble of lightning across a cloud, suggesting that behind is a lofty divinity whom all must know, or an aloof divinity whom none is worthy to know (though, as this might be highly inconvenient, a docile typist sometimes interprets the mystery in a bracket underneath). There are impetuous squiggles implying that the author is a sort of strenuous Sputnik streaking round the globe every eighty minutes. There are florid signatures, all curli-

From F. L. Lucas, "What Is Style?" *Holiday*, March, 1960. Reprinted by permission of the Executors of the late F. L. Lucas, Farrer & Company, London.

cues and danglements and flamboyance, like the youthful Disraeli (though these seem rather out of fashion). There are humble, humdrum signatures. And there are also, sometimes, signatures that are courteously clear, yet mindful of a certain simple grace and artistic economy—in short, of style.

Since, then, not one of us can put pen to paper, or even open his mouth, without giving something of himself away to shrewd observers, it seems mere common sense to give the matter a little thought. Yet it does not seem very common. Ladies may take infinite pains about having style in their clothes, but many of us remain curiously indifferent about having it in our words. How many women would dream of polishing not only their nails but also their tongues? They may play freely on that perilous little organ, but they cannot often be bothered to tune it. And how many men think of improving their talk as well as their golf handicap?

No doubt strong silent men, speaking only in gruff monosyllables, may despise "mere words." No doubt the world does suffer from an endemic plague of verbal dysentery. But that, precisely, is bad style. And consider the amazing power of mere words. Adolf Hitler was a bad artist, bad statesman, bad general, and bad man. But largely because he could tune his rant, with psychological nicety, to the exact wave length of his audiences and make millions quarrelsome-drunk all at the same time by his command of windy nonsense, skilled statesmen, soldiers, scientists were blown away like chaff, and he came near to rule the world. If Sir Winston Churchill had been a mere speechifier, we might well have lost the war; yet his speeches did quite a lot to win it.

No man was less of a literary aesthete than Benjamin Franklin; yet this tallow-chandler's son, who changed world history, regarded as "a principal means of my advancement" that pungent style which he acquired partly by working in youth over old *Spectators;* but mainly by being Benjamin Franklin. The squinting demagogue, John Wilkes, as ugly as his many sins, had yet a tongue so winning that he asked only half an hour's start (to counteract his face) against any rival for a woman's favor. "Vote for you!" growled a surly elector in his constituency. "I'd sooner vote for the devil!" "But in case your friend should not stand . . .?" Cleopatra, that ensnarer of world conquerors, owed less to the shape of her nose than to the charm of her tongue. Shakespeare himself has often poor plots and thin ideas; even his mastery of character has been questioned; what does remain unchallenged is his verbal magic. Men are often taken, like rabbits, by the ears. And though the tongue has no bones, it can sometimes break millions of them.

"But," the reader may grumble, "I am neither Hitler, Cleopatra, nor Shakespeare. What is all this to me?" Yet we all talk—often too much; we all have to write letters—often too many. We live not by bread alone but also by words. And not always with remarkable efficiency. Strikes, lawsuits, divorces, all sorts of public nuisance and private misery, often come just from the gaggling incompetence with which we express ourselves. Americans and British get at cross-purposes because they use the same words with different meanings. Men have been hanged on a comma in a statute. And in the valley of Balaclava a mere verbal ambiguity, about *which* guns were to be captured, sent the whole Light Brigade to futile annihilation.

Words can be more powerful, and more treacherous, than we sometimes suspect; communication more difficult than we may think. We are all serving life sentences of solitary confinement within our own bodies; like prisoners, we have, as it were, to tap in awkward code to our fellow men in their neighboring cells. Further, when A and B converse, there take part in their dialogue not two characters, as they suppose, but six. For there is A's real self—call it A_1; there is also A's picture of himself—A_2; there is also B's picture of A—A_3. And there are three corresponding personalities of B. With six characters involved even in a simple tête-à-tête, no wonder we fall into muddles and misunderstandings.

Perhaps, then, there are five main reasons for trying to gain some mastery of language:

We have no other way of understanding, informing, misinforming, or persuading one another.

Even alone, we think mainly in words; if our language is muddy, so will our thinking be.

By our handling of words we are often revealed and judged. "Has he written anything?" said Napoleon of a candidate for an appointment. "Let me see his *style*."

Without a feeling for language one remains half-blind and deaf to literature.

Our mother tongue is bettered or worsened by the way each generation uses it. Languages evolve like species. They can degenerate; just as oysters and barnacles have lost their heads. Compare ancient Greek with modern. A heavy responsibility, though often forgotten.

Why and how did I become interested in style? The main answer, I suppose, is that I was born that way. Then I was, till ten, an only child running loose in a house packed with books, and in a world (thank goodness) still undistracted by radio and television. So at three I groaned to my mother, "Oh, I *wish* I could read," and at four I read. Now travel among books is the best travel of all, and the easiest, and the cheapest. (Not that I belittle ordinary travel—which I regard as one of the three main pleasures in life.) One learns to write by reading good books, as one learns to talk by hearing good talkers. And if I have learned anything of writing, it is largely from writers like Montaigne, Dorothy Osborne, Horace Walpole, Johnson, Goldsmith, Montesquieu, Voltaire, Flaubert and Anatole France. Again, I was reared on Greek and Latin, and one can learn much from translating

Homer or the Greek Anthology, Horace or Tacitus, if one is thrilled by the originals and tries, however vainly, to recapture some of that thrill in English.

But at Rugby I could *not* write English essays. I believe it stupid to torment boys to write on topics that they know and care nothing about. I used to rush to the school library and cram the subject, like a python swallowing rabbits; then, still replete as a postprandial python, I would tie myself in clumsy knots to embrace those accursed themes. Bacon was wise in saying that reading makes a full man; talking, a ready one; writing, an exact one. But writing from an empty head is futile anguish.

At Cambridge, my head having grown a little fuller, I suddenly found I *could* write—not with enjoyment (it is always tearing oneself in pieces)—but fairly fluently. Then came the War of 1914–18; and though soldiers have other things than pens to handle, they learn painfully to be clear and brief. Then the late Sir Desmond MacCarthy invited me to review for the *New Statesman;* it was a useful apprenticeship, and he was delightful to work for. But I think it was well after a few years to stop; reviewers remain essential, but there are too many books one *cannot* praise, and only the pugnacious enjoy amassing enemies. By then I was an ink-addict—not because writing is much pleasure, but because not to write is pain; just as some smokers do not so much enjoy tobacco as suffer without it. The positive happiness of writing comes, I think, from work when done—decently, one hopes, and not without use—and from the letters of readers which help to reassure, or delude, one that so it is.

But one of my most vivid lessons came, I think, from service in a war department during the Second War. Then, if the matter one sent out was too wordy, the communication channels might choke; yet if it was not absolutely clear, the results might be serious. So I emerged, after six years of it, with more passion than ever for clarity and brevity, more loathing than ever for the obscure and the verbose.

For forty years at Cambridge I have tried to teach young men to write well, and have come to think it impossible. To write really well is a gift inborn; those who have it teach themselves; one can only try to help and hasten the process. After all, the uneducated sometimes express themselves far better than their "betters." In language, as in life, it is possible to be perfectly correct—and yet perfectly tedious, or odious. The illiterate last letter of the doomed Vanzetti was more moving than most professional orators; 18th Century ladies, who should have been spanked for their spelling, could yet write far better letters than most professors of English; and the talk of Synge's Irish peasants seems to me vastly more vivid than the later style of Henry James. Yet Synge averred that his characters owed far less of their eloquence to what he invented for them than to what he had overheard in the cottages of Wicklow and Kerry:

Christy. "It's little you'll think if my love's a poacher's, or an earl's itself, when you'll feel my two hands stretched around you, and I squeezing kisses on your puckered lips, till I'd feel a kind of pity for the Lord God is all ages sitting lonesome in His golden chair."

Pegeen. "That's be right fun, Christy Mahon, and any girl would walk her heart out before she'd meet a young man was your like for eloquence, or talk at all."

Well she might! It's not like that they talk in universities—more's the pity.

But though one cannot teach people to write well, one can sometimes teach them to write rather better. One can give a certain number of hints, which often seem boringly obvious—only experience shows they are not.

One can say: Beware of pronouns—they are devils. Look at even Addison, describing the type of pedant who chatters of style without having any:

Upon enquiry I found my learned friend had dined that day with Mr. Swan, the famous punster; and desiring *him* to give me some account of Mr. Swan's conversation, *he* told me that *he* generally talked in the Paronomasia, that *he* sometimes gave in to the Plocé, but that in *his* humble opinion *he* shone most in the Antanaclasis.

What a sluttish muddle of *he* and *him* and *his!* It all needs rewording. Far better repeat a noun, or a name, than puzzle the reader, even for a moment, with ambiguous pronouns. Thou shalt not puzzle thy reader.

Or one can say: Avoid jingles. The B.B.C. news bulletins seem compiled by earless persons, capable of crying round the globe: "The enemy is re-*port*ed to have seized this im*port*ant *port*, and reinforcements are hurrying up in sup*port*." Any fool, once told, can hear such things to be insupportable.

Or one can say: Be sparing with relative clauses. Don't string them together like sausages, or jam them inside one another like Chinese boxes or the receptacles of Buddha's tooth. Or one can say: Don't flaunt jargon, like Addison's Mr. Swan, or the type of modern critic who gurgles more technical terms in a page than Johnson used in all his *Lives* or Sainte-Beuve in thirty volumes. But dozens of such snippety precepts, though they may sometimes save people from writing badly, will help them little toward writing well. Are there no general rules of a more positive kind, and of more positive use?

Perhaps. There *are* certain basic principles which seem to me observed by many authors I admire, which I think have served me and which may serve others. I am not talking of geniuses, who are a law to themselves (and do not always write a very good style, either); nor of poetry, which has different laws from prose; nor of poetic prose, like Sir Thomas Browne's or De Quincey's, which is often more akin to poetry; but of the plain prose of ordinary books and documents, letters and talk.

The writer should respect truth and himself; therefore honesty. He should respect his readers; therefore courtesy. These are two of the cornerstones of style. Confucius saw it, twenty-five centuries ago: "The Master said, The gentleman is courteous, but not pliable: common men are pliable, but not courteous."

First, honesty. In literature, as in life, one of the fundamentals is to find, and be, one's true self. One's true self may indeed be unpleasant (though one can try to better it); but a false self, sooner or later, becomes disgusting—just as a nice plain woman, painted to the eyebrows, can become horrid. In writing, in the long run, pretense does not work. As the police put it, anything you say may be used as evidence against you. If handwriting reveals character, writing reveals it still more. You cannot fool *all* your judges *all* the time.

Most style is not honest enough. Easy to say, but hard to practice. A writer may take to long words, as young men to beards—to impress. But long words, like long beards, are often the badge of charlatans. Or a writer may cultivate the obscure, to seem profound. But even carefully muddied puddles are soon fathomed. Or he may cultivate eccentricity, to seem original. But really original people do not have to think about being original—they can no more help it than they can help breathing. They do not need to dye their hair green. The fame of Meredith, Wilde or Bernard Shaw might now shine brighter, had they struggled less to be brilliant; whereas Johnson remains great, not merely because his gifts were formidable but also because, with all his prejudice and passion, he fought no less passionately to "clear his mind of cant."

Secondly, courtesy—respect for the reader. From this follow several other basic principles of style. Clarity is one. For it is boorish to make your reader rack his brains to understand. One should aim at being impossible to misunderstand—though men's capacity for misunderstanding approaches infinity. Hence Molière and Po Chu-i tried their work on their cooks; and Swift his on his menservants—"which, if they did not comprehend, he would alter and amend, until they understood it perfectly." Our bureaucrats and pundits, unfortunately, are less considerate.

Brevity is another basic principle. For it is boorish, also, to waste your reader's time. People who would not dream of stealing a penny of one's money turn not a hair at stealing hours of one's life. But that does not make them less exasperating. Therefore there is no excuse for the sort of writer who takes as long as a marching army corps to pass a given point. Besides, brevity is often more effective; the half can say more than the whole, and to imply things may strike far deeper than to state them at length. And because one is particularly apt to waste words on preambles before coming to the substance, there was sense in the Scots professor who always asked his pupils— "Did ye remember to tear up that fir-r-st page?"

Here are some instances that would only lose by lengthening:

It is useless to go to bed to save the light, if the result is twins. (Chinese proverb.)

My barn is burnt down—
Nothing hides the moon. (Complete Japanese poem.)

Je me regrette. (Dying words of the gay Vicomtesse d'Houdetot.)

I have seen their backs before. (Wellington, when French marshals turned their backs on him at a reception.)

Continue until the tanks stop, then get out and walk. (Patton to the Twelfth Corps, halted for fuel supplies at St. Dizier, 8/30/44.)

Or there is the most laconic diplomatic note on record: when Philip of Macedon wrote to the Spartans that, if he came within their borders, he would leave not one stone of their city, they wrote back the one word—"If."

Clarity comes before even brevity. But it is a fallacy that wordiness is necessarily clearer. Metternich when he thought something he had written was obscure would simply go through it crossing out everything irrelevant. What remained, he found, often became clear. Wellington, asked to recommend three names for the post of Commander-in-Chief, India, took a piece of paper and wrote three times—"Napier." Pages could not have been clearer —or as forcible. On the other hand the lectures, and the sentences, of Coleridge became at times bewildering because his mind was often "wiggle-waggle"; just as he could not even walk straight on a path.

But clarity and brevity, though a good beginning, are only a beginning. By themselves, they may remain bare and bleak. When Calvin Coolidge, asked by his wife what the preacher had preached on, replied "Sin," and, asked what the preacher had said, replied, "He was against it," he was brief enough. But one hardly envies Mrs. Coolidge.

An attractive style requires, of course, all kinds of further gifts—such as variety, good humor, good sense, vitality, imagination. Variety means avoiding monotony of rhythm, of language, of mood. One needs to vary one's sentence length (this present article has too many short sentences; but so vast a subject grows here as cramped as a djin in a bottle); to amplify one's vocabulary; to diversify one's tone. There are books that petrify one throughout, with the rigidly pompous solemnity of an owl perched on a leafless tree. But ceaseless facetiousness can be as bad; or perpetual irony. Even the smile of Voltaire can seem at times a fixed grin, a disagreeable wrinkle. Constant peevishness is far worse, as often in Swift; even on the stage too much irritable dialogue may irritate an audience, without its knowing why.

Still more are vitality, energy, imagination gifts that must be inborn before they can be cultivated. But under the head of imagination two common devices may be mentioned that have been the making of many a style—metaphor and simile. Why such magic power should reside in simply saying, or implying, that A is like B remains a little mysterious. But even our unconscious seems to love symbols; again, language often tends to lose itself in clouds of vaporous abstraction, and simile or metaphor can bring it back to concrete solidity; and, again, such imagery can gild the gray flats of prose with sudden sun-glints of poetry.

If a foreigner may for a moment be impertinent, I admire the native gift of Americans for imagery as much as I wince at their fondness for slang. (Slang seems to me a kind of linguistic fungus; as poisonous, and as short-lived, as toadstools.) When Matthew Arnold lectured in the United States, he was likened by one newspaper to "an elderly macaw pecking at a trellis of grapes"; he observed, very justly, "How lively journalistic fancy is among the Americans!" General Grant, again, unable to hear him, remarked: "Well, wife, we've paid to see the British lion, but as we can't hear him roar, we'd better go home." By simile and metaphor, these two quotations bring before us the slightly pompous, fastidious, inaudible Arnold as no direct description could have done.

Or consider how language comes alive in the Chinese saying that lending to the feckless is "like pelting a stray dog with dumplings," or in the Arab proverb: "They came to shoe the pasha's horse, and the beetle stretched forth his leg"; in the Greek phrase for a perilous cape—"step-mother of ships"; or the Hebrew adage that "as the climbing up a sandy way is to the feet of the aged, so is a wife full of words to a quiet man"; in Shakespeare's phrase for a little England lost in the world's vastness—"in a great Poole, a Swan's-nest"; or Fuller's libel on tall men—"Ofttimes such who are built four stories high are observed to have little in their cockloft"; in Chateaubriand's "I go yawning my life"; or in Jules Renard's portrait of a cat, "well buttoned in her fur." Or, to take a modern instance, there is Churchill on dealings with Russia: "Trying to maintain good relations with a Communist is like wooing a crocodile. You do not know whether to tickle it under the chin or beat it over the head. When it opens its mouth, you cannot tell whether it is trying to smile or preparing to eat you up." What a miracle human speech can be, and how dull is most that one hears! Would one hold one's hearers, it is far less help, I suspect, to read manuals on style than to cultivate one's own imagination and imagery.

I will end with two remarks by two wise old women of the civilized 18th Century.

The first is from the blind Mme. du Deffand (the friend of Horace Walpole) to that Mlle. de Lespinasse with whom, alas, she was to quarrel so unwisely: "You must make up your mind, my queen, to live with me in the greatest truth and sincerity. You will be charming so long as you let yourself be natural, and remain without pretension and without artifice." The second is from Mme. de Charrière, the Zélide whom Boswell had once loved at Utrecht in vain, to a Swiss girl friend: "Lucinde, my clever Lucinde, while you wait for the Romeos to arrive, you have nothing better to do than become perfect. Have ideas that are clear, and expressions that are simple." (*"Ayez des idées nettes et des expressions simples."*) More than half the bad writing in the world, I believe, comes from neglecting those two very simple pieces of advice.

In many ways, no doubt, our world grows more and more complex; sputniks cannot be simple; yet how many of our complexities remain futile, how many of our artificialities false. Simplicity too can be subtle—as the straight lines of a Greek temple, like the Parthenon at Athens, are delicately curved, in order to look straighter still.

COMPREHENSION QUIZ

1. Which of the following statements is a reason for trying to gain some mastery of language?
    a. We have no other way of understanding, informing, misinforming, or persuading one another.
    b. Even alone, we think mainly in words; if our language is muddy, so will our thinking be.
    c. By our handling of words we are often revealed and judged.
    d. All of the above.
2. Lucas believes that
    a. languages evolve like species.
    b. it is possible to teach young men to write well.
    c. it is wise to encourage students to write on topics that they care nothing about.
    d. languages do not degenerate; only their users.
3. The author cites a passage from Addison as an example of
    a. clarity.
    b. faulty use of pronouns.
    c. brevity.
    d. skillful use of paradox.
4. Which of the following kinds of writing is Lucas concerned with in this essay?
    a. Poetry.
    b. Poetic prose.
    c. Public oratory.
    d. Plain prose.
5. The first requirement for developing a good style is
    a. a classical education.
    b. honesty.
    c. long practice.
    d. a sense of humor.

DISCUSSION QUESTIONS

1. A famous epigram asserts that style is the man. Does Lucas' essay support this notion?
2. How can we improve our style? Is it merely a matter of ransacking the dictionary and rhetoric handbooks?
3. Lucas says that it is impossible to teach young men to write well. Do you agree? Has your writing improved as a result of suggestions given in English classes?
4. How would you describe your own writing style?
5. Lucas suggests that most men are more concerned with improving their golf handicap than with improving their talk. Do you agree? If he is correct, what does this suggest about their values?

WRITING SUGGESTIONS

1. Develop the following topic: "Advice to a Freshman English Student."
2. Defend American slang against Lucas' charge that it is "linguistic fungus."
3. Analyze the prose style of a distinguished American or English writer, showing how he fulfills the requirements for a good style as set forth by Lucas.

Recommended Readings to Part IX

Cannon, Garland. "Linguistics and Literature," *College English, 21* (1960), 255–260.

Hill, Archibald A. "An Analysis of *The Windhover*: An Experiment in Structural Method," *PMLA, 70* (1955), 969–978.

Hymes, Dell. *Language in Culture and Society*. New York: Harper & Row, 1964.

Landor, Herbert. *Language and Culture*. New York: Oxford University Press, 1966.

Langer, Susanne K. *Philosophy in a New Key*. Cambridge: Harvard University Press, 1942.

Rosenthal, M. L., and A. J. M. Smith. *Exploring Poetry*. New York: Macmillan, 1955.

Schlauch, Margaret. *The Gift of Language*. New York: Dover, 1955.

Spitzer, Leo. "Language—The Basis of Science, Philosophy and Poetry," in *Studies in Intellectual History*, George Boas et al. (eds.), Baltimore: Johns Hopkins Press, 1953.

Wellek, René, and Austin Warren. *Theory of Literature*. New York: Harcourt, Brace & World, 1949.

The Question of Usage

X

Usage

by MARGARET M. BRYANT

Language Always Changing

To many educated persons, grammar appears to be one of the few remaining eternal verities. They know that the meanings of words change, that slang is ephemeral (yesteryear's "23 skidoo" has given way to "Scram," "Take a powder," "Hit the road," or "Get lost"), and that to a certain extent styles alter with regard to spelling and even punctuation, but they have the comforting belief that syntax in the language, like the multiplication table in arithmetic, is fixed and immutable. But just as the meanings, spelling, and sounds of words change with the years, so does syntax. What is good English today will not with any certainty be good English tomorrow. This fact may be observed from reading the literature of past centuries. Old English seems practically a foreign language, and a modern reader needs a great many notes even for understanding a play by Shakespeare. Shakespeare, for example, omitted articles where we include them, as in *creeping like snail* and *in table of my heart,* and included them where we omit them, as in *at the least* and *at the last.* Likewise the negative occupied a different position in the sentence, as in *I not think* and *it not appears to me.* The double and sometimes triple use of the negative for emphasis, common in Old English, still survived in Shakespeare as in *say nothing neither* and *Nor this is not my nose neither.* This intensive use of the negatives can still be heard among the illiterate. These examples are sufficient to show that language is in a constant state of flux.

Usage, the Sole Arbiter

As changes gradually come about in language, the only arbiter to be considered in linguistic matters is usage. The purist may like to hold on to the expression he learned in his early days, but he will find that his wishes are disregarded. Language change is a democratic process, and the few invariably make way for the many. Horace, the great Latin poet, recognized that "use is the sole arbiter and norm of speech," a tenet upheld by John Hughes in his essay *Of Style* (1698) when he wrote "general acceptation . . . is the only standard of speech." Dr. Johnson in the *Plan* for his dictionary stated that he would "endeavour to discover and promulgate the decrees of custom." He was too intelligent a student of language not to know the power of usage. So did Lord Chesterfield, who said "Every language has its peculiarities; they are established by usage, and whether right or wrong, they must be complied with." In the eighteenth century, however, the chief exponent of this doctrine was the philosopher, theologian, and chemist, Joseph Priestley, who stressed the significance of usage in his *Rudiments of English Grammar* (1761) and in his *Theory of Language* (1762), a point of view promoted by George Campbell in his *Philosophy of Rhetoric* (1776). Thus one can see that throughout the centuries students of language have recognized the fact that usage is the most important criterion of language.

It Is Me

The history of the phrase *It is me* well illustrates the change in syntax and the force of usage. In Old English we find *Ic hit eom (I it am)*, which changed in Middle English to *(H)it am I*. Since *it* was felt to be the subject *am* was changed to *is,* resulting in *It is I. It is I* has now shifted to *It is me,* the *me* being used, no doubt, because of its position after the verb, for the accusative case generally follows the verb. *Me* was competing with *I* for supremacy as early as the sixteenth century, and one can find instances of it in the work of such writers as Sir Richard Steele, Jane Austen, Joseph Conrad, as well as in more modern books.[1] William Ellery Leonard termed *It is I* "suburban English,"[2] suggesting that the phrase is overcorrect. *It is me* or *It's me* is now the phrase employed in informal colloquial speech and writing and *It is I* is reserved for formal, literary style.

•   •   •

Who and Whom

After discussing the personal pronouns, one immediately thinks of the interrogative pronouns *who* and *whom.* Just as the objective case is used after the verb, so there is a strong tendency to use the nominative before

[1] See George H. McKnight, *Modern English in the Making* (New York, D. Appleton and Company, 1930), pp. 532–533.
[2] W. E. Leonard, "Concerning the Leonard Study," *American Speech* (Vol. VIII, No. 3, October, 1933), p. 58. See also Wallace Rice, "Who's There?—Me," *ibid.,* pp. 58–63.

the verb. *Who,* therefore, is often found instead of *whom* in sentences like *Who did you call? Who is the letter from?* In both instances word order dictates the case. There is, however, more involved here than word order; that is, the tendency to substitute the nominative *who* for *whom* in every position. A note under *whom* in the *OED* reads "no longer current in natural colloquial speech." Jespersen likewise says that "the form *who* is generalized, so that it is now practically the only form used in colloquial speech."[3] He continues by showing that this has been true for at least three centuries, citing examples from Shakespeare, Marlowe, Addison, Sheridan, and George Eliot. He also points out that many people have become so conscious of the *who* and *whom* controversy that they feel proud at remembering to use *whom,*[4] a symptom of the decadence of the form. Kemp Malone, however, considers the use of *who* and *whom* a matter of style. That is, in unstudied style one will use *who* in sentences like "*Who* will you choose?" and "*Who* will you speak to?" but in a studied style *whom* will be substituted for *who.*[5]

The Relative Who and Whom

There is at present a state of confusion also in regard to the form of the relative pronoun to be employed in sentences like *We hire persons whom we think are good.* Here the form *whom* is used as the subject of *are.* This use, no doubt, occurs as a result of an attempt to be "correct," and is one of the best evidences of the disappearance of the form, for it is a use against the tendency of the language—the caseless use of *who.* Collections of this use have been made by various students of the English language, among them Weekley, Jespersen, Fowler, and Robertson,[6] to show what is happening to one of the few remaining case forms in Modern English.

Other Confusion of Who and Whom

Another place where *whom* is often used as the subject of a verb is in a clause introduced by a preposition such as *There was considerable doubt as to whom should be elected.* Here *whom* is used as the subject of

[3] Otto Jespersen, *Essentials of English Grammar* (New York, Henry Holt and Company, 1933), p. 136.

[4] *Ibid.,* p. 137.

[5] "Whom," *College English* (Vol. X, October, 1948), pp. 37–38. See also discussion by James B. McMillan, " 'Who' and 'Whom'," *College English* (Vol. VII, November, 1945), pp. 104–105.

[6] See Weekley, *Cruelty to Words* (New York, E. P. Dutton & Co., 1931) , pp. 23–27; Jespersen, *Essentials of English Grammar, op. cit.,* p. 137; H. W. Fowler, *A Dictionary of Modern English Usage* (Oxford, Clarendon Press, 1926), pp. 724–725; Stuart Robertson, *The Development of Modern English* (New York, Prentice-Hall, Inc., 1934), pp. 502–503.

should be elected. The whole clause, and not *whom,* is object of the preposition *to.* There must be a consciousness of the different forms *who* and *whom* in the mind of the speaker or writer who employs *whom* in this construction. The use is not so natural that there is no confusion, one of the first indications of the departure of a form. The same confusion exists in the use of *whomever,* as in *Write this to whomever asks for a book.*

Only

In discussing the cases of the pronouns we have seen the importance of word order, one of the chief syntactical devices of Modern English, often determining the appearance of a particular construction. To avoid grammatical anarchy English has developed a system of standardized sentence order, and in Modern English the modifying words generally come immediately before the words they modify. One of the most familiar sentence patterns is made up of the subject, adverbial modifier, verb, and object, as *He carefully did the work.* This pattern tends to be followed even when the adverb does not logically refer to the verb as in *We only had one left,* an order objected to by purists but found by Leonard to be established in Modern English.[7] Palmer and Blandford in their *Grammar of Spoken English* state: "In spoken English it [*only*] generally occupies the pre-verbal position. . . ."[8] The great majority of speakers place *only* before the verb and even in literature one can find instances of it. Matthew Arnold's *Dover Beach* will serve as an example:

> But now I only hear
> Its melancholy, long, withdrawing roar.[9]

Marckwardt and Walcott call this usage literary English.[10]

Split Infinitive

The pattern of putting the adverb before the verb has produced a strong tendency to place the adverbial modifier of an infinitive immediately before the infinitive and after the *to,* the sign of the infinitive, which was originally a preposition meaning "toward" and governing the dative case, and not properly a part of the infinitive. The prepositional force of *to* ceased to be felt as early as the fourteenth century, and then by analogy

---

[7] S. A. Leonard, *Current English Usage,* published for the National Council of Teachers of English (Chicago, Inland Press, 1935), pp. 136–137.

[8] P. 186.

[9] Ll. 24–25.

[10] A. H. Marckwardt and F. Walcott, *Facts About Current English Usage,* NCTE Monograph, No. 7 (New York, D. Appleton-Century Company, 1938), p. 35.

the adverb began to take its place after the *to* and before the infinitive and has been employed by good writers for several centuries. In Modern English, however, the split infinitive has been the subject of a great deal of controversy because of the authoritarian grammarians of the eighteenth and nineteenth centuries, who selected it as something to be avoided under all circumstances. The persons who have come under the sway of those authoritarians are not aware of the changes that have gone on in the English language since the death of Dryden and are willing to run the risk of ambiguity and awkwardness rather than split an infinitive. Those same persons do not object to verb phrases being divided by an adverb as in *He does not write to me,* or *She is always working for others;* or to subjects and predicates being separated as in *He always writes, He generally reads at night;* or to the separation of the preposition from its object in a verbid phrase such as *of successfully writing* in *He told of successfully writing the book.* Then *to always write* is not very different from *he always writes.* Despite the authoritarian hold, good writers and speakers have continued to split the infinitive where avoiding it would have caused ambiguity or patent artificiality, and at last students of English usage have shown that the split infinitive is established.[11] The more recent handbooks and grammars are willing to acknowledge it. One even goes so far as to say that it is "no longer considered one of the seven deadly sins of college composition."[12] The literary precedent for it has been pointed out by many students of language.[13] With all the evidence that has been piled up in the last half century, it would seem that even the "die-hard purist" would be willing to accept a few split infinitives in preference to awkwardness and ambiguity. In the long run the great forces of analogy, clarity, and word order win against the authoritarian.

One

Another pronoun about which there has been a great deal of discussion is the indefinite *one,* used impersonally. It is not quite parallel to the French *on* or the German *man* in the phrases *on dit* and *man sagt,* but handbooks once insisted that the form should be consistently employed throughout a sentence, as in *One rarely enjoys one's luncheon when one is tired.*

---

11 S. A. Leonard, *Current English Usage, op. cit.,* pp. 122–124.

12 John M. Kierzek and Walter Gibson, *The Macmillan Handbook of English,* 4th edit. (New York, The Macmillan Company, 1960), p. 390.

13 T. R. Lounsbury, *The Standard of Usage in English* (New York, Harper & Row, 1908), pp. 240–268; Fowler, *op. cit.,* pp. 558–561; G. O. Curme, *Syntax* (Boston, D. C. Heath & Company, 1931), pp. 458–467 and "Origin and Force of the Split-Infinitive," *Modern Language Notes,* Vol. XXIX, No. 2, pp. 41–45 (February 1914); Otto Jespersen, *A Modern English Grammar,* Part V, *Syntax,* Vol. IV (Copenhagen, Ejnar Munksgaard, 1940), p. 330; H. Poutsma, *A Grammar of Late Modern English,* Part I, *The Sentence,* 2nd edit. (Groningen, P. Nordhoff, 1928), p. 462.

This is called the established form in *Current English Usage*. The comments on this sentence, however, implied that even though it was correct, it was somewhat stilted. One linguist wrote: "*One* followed by one or more *one's* never wholly excluded *one* followed by one or more *he's*. A series of *one's* strikes many (including me) as a kind of pedantry. As a matter of fact, probably most people who stick rigidly to *one* have acquired it by effort."[14] More recent handbooks with the up-to-date viewpoint accept *he* after *one*. Marckwardt and Cassidy say: "Writers today do not hesitate to insert forms of the pronoun *he*."[15] Perrin and Dykema make a distinction between formal English where *one* may be used and informal English where it is not. They then add: "American usage stands firmly by older English usage in referring back to *one* by *he, his, him* (or *she, her*),"[16] giving as an example: *One is warned to be cautious if he would avoid offending his friends and bringing their displeasure down upon his head.* This statement may be further substantiated by a sentence from Professor Fries' *American English Grammar,* in which he writes: "If one could conjure up Shakspere or Spenser or Milton, he would find their English strange to his ears not only in pronunciation but in vocabulary and grammar as well."[17] In early Modern English *one* was followed by *his, him,* and *himself* and today everyone prefers to carry on the tradition. Sentences are usually recast to avoid the excessive use of *one,* but the problem arises because the English language does not possess a generalized pronoun that does duty for *he, she,* and *it.*

None

There has also been a great deal of discussion as to whether *none* is singular or plural. Those who insist that *none* is properly a singular use the argument that it is equivalent to *no one. No one* and *not one* are now used when we wish to emphasize the singular, but *none* may be singular or plural, and its use in the plural is more common. *None* with the plural verb can be traced back to the Middle English period. It was not, however, until the end of the period and the beginning of the early Modern English period that *none* came to be followed or preceded immediately by a plural verb form. The idea uppermost in the speaker's mind determines the use of a plural or a singular verb. Professor Fries found in his investigation of this usage that with but one exception *none* was used with the plural verb as

[14] S. A. Leonard, *Current English Usage, op. cit.,* p. 106.

[15] A. H. Marckwardt and F. G. Cassidy, *Scribner Handbook of English,* 3rd edit. (New York, Charles Scribner's Sons, 1960), p. 348.

[16] P. G. Perrin and K. W. Dykema, *Writer's Guide and Index to English* (Chicago, Scott, Foresman & Company, 1959), p. 612.

[17] C. C. Fries, *American English Grammar* (New York, Appleton-Century-Crofts, 1940), p. 6.

were *any* and the disjunctive pronouns *neither* and *either*.[18] S. A. Leonard in *Current English Usage* shows that *None of them are here* is established usage.[19] He quotes an author saying, "It is pure priggishness to pretend that *none* is always singular." Recent dictionaries point out that it is generally used with a plural verb. An example of the plural usage is: "*None* of these people would be doing what *they were* doing if *they* knew what was in store."[20]

• • •

Adjective or Adverb

There are other expressions in English with divided usage, such as *I feel bad* or *I feel badly*. The question concerns the use of the adjective or the adverb. The theory behind the use of the adjective is that *feel* is a copula or a linking verb, joining the subject *I* with the predicate adjective *bad*. The person who employs *badly* has a feeling that an adverb is more "correct." The adverb is identified to him by an *-ly* suffix and so by analogy he uses *badly* instead of *bad*. S. A. Leonard found that *badly* is established in good colloquial English in sentences like *I felt badly about his death*, and some of the judges approved the expression as appropriate to formal literary English.[21] There are numbers of similar expressions in current English, such as "to rest easy," "easy come, easy go," "to sit quiet," "to shine bright," "to stand firm," in which the adjective is preferable. Curme numbers about sixty linking verbs in present-day English which have the adjective after them and says, "Their wide and varied use is the most prominent feature of our language."[22] Among them are *appear, become, taste, sound, look, grow,* and *act*.

Slow or Slowly

Another question of usage arises with *slow* and *slowly*. The choice is not between adjective and adverb as with *bad* and *badly*, but between adverb and adverb. *Slow* is an old adverb, going back to the Old English adverbs that ended in *-e* instead of to those that ended in *-lice*. The latter has given us the modern ending *-ly*, but the former has disappeared, leaving a number of adverbs with the same forms as adjectives, among them *hard*,

[18] *Ibid.*, pp. 50, 56.
[19] *Op. cit.*, pp. 103–104.
[20] *Saturday Review* (April 9, 1955), p. 20/3.
[21] *Current English Usage, op. cit.*, pp. xv, 136.
[22] G. O. Curme, *Parts of Speech and Accidence* (Boston, D. C. Heath and Company, 1935), p. 67.

fast, first, much, loud, low, and *slow.* The purist may object to *Go slow,* but history and universal usage sanction it. *Go slow* is a more vigorous expression than *Go slowly;* however, in making the choice rhythm and euphony generally determine the decision. Note both forms in one poetic line from Arthur Hugh Clough: "In front the sun climbs slow, how slowly" ("Say Not the Struggle Naught Availeth").

Shall and Will

There may be a question concerning *slow* and *slowly,* or *bad* and *badly,* or *these kind* and *those kind,* but when one looks up *shall* and *will,* he is completely bewildered. The literary uses of *shall* and *will* provide one of the most vexatious—and ludicrous—situations in the study of English. The rules are so intricate, and so artificial, that H. W. and F. G. Fowler took more than twenty pages of their book *The King's English*[23] to expound the exact procedures prescribed by grammarians for various circumstances. For more than a hundred years there have been many vigorous discussions and much written on this subject. Professor Fries, who has devoted a great deal of time to this question, writes:[24] "In all this mass of material there is hardly a general statement . . . for which a direct contradiction cannot be found coming from a source that merits careful consideration. Thus, after a century . . . there are no accepted views of what the actual usage of these two words is, of the meaning and trend of the development of that usage, and of the causes that gave rise to it." Editors and writers in formal English generally use *shall* in the first person and *will* in the second and third for the simple future, following the rules laid down in most handbooks, and reverse the process for the emphatic future. However, in speech and informal writing in America one generally finds *will* in all persons. In the emphatic future there is a tendency to use *shall* in all persons. In speech, however, determination is shown by stress rather than by the word. Either *shall* or *will* may be heard. The use of the contractions *I'll, you'll, he'll,* etc. has undoubtedly helped in establishing will. The speaker may think he is avoiding the issue when he employs the contraction, but he is really establishing the usage of *will,* for *I'll* is a contraction, phonetically, of *I will,* not of *I shall.* No one follows the rules laid down in most grammars and handbooks. The users of the language have for the most part ignored the many fine-spun distinctions, even in writing. For instance, who uses *shall* with *you* in questions, such as *Shall you be in your office this morning?* This construction has no place in present-day grammars. *Shall,* however, is often

---

[23] H. W. and F. G. Fowler, *The King's English* (Oxford, Clarendon Press, 1924), pp. 133–154.

[24] Fries, *American English Grammar, op. cit.,* p. 151.

employed in the first person in questions, as *Shall I open the door? Shall we get the food?*[25]

•   •   •

Like as a Conjunction

The purist opposes converting *like* into a conjunction; that is, using it in place of *as* and *as if* in introducing clauses, as in *It looks like it will rain. Like,* however, is accepted in Standard English when the verb is omitted from the clause, as *It looks like rain, It fits him like a shoe.* The grammarian explains *like* here as a preposition, overlooking the fact that *like* as a preposition was converted from *like* as an adjective. The *OED* comments concerning the substitution of *like* for *as*: "Now generally condemned as vulgar or slovenly, though examples may be found in many recent writers of standing." In spoken English *like* is increasing in usage. One hears it daily, even on the lips of cultivated speakers, as evidenced by a study of the Linguistic Atlas records of the Upper Midwest and North Central States.[26] It must be said, however, that it occurs more frequently in the West and South than in the East. Were it not for the editors and publishers who follow stylebooks, *like* would probably become established in standard literary English. Professors Perrin and Dykema say, "Historically both forms are good, since both are parts of the older *like as* ('Like as a father pitieth his children . . .'). Some speakers have taken *as,* others *like. Like* is preferable from the standpoint of meaning, because *as* has several different meanings and several functions in the language and so is relatively weak. *Like* is more exact and more emphatic in a comparison than as can be."[27]

Observation Necessary

The examples of divided usage cited in this chapter serve to show that in the study of the English language more observation is necessary and less prohibition. We need grammars based on what is true of the language we use rather than on some person's idea of what it should be. Some progress

[25] For the discussion of *shall* and *will,* see Charles C. Fries, "The Periphrastic Future with *Shall* and *Will* in Modern English," *PMLA* (Vol. 40, 1925), pp. 963–1024; "The Expression of the Future," *Language* (Vol. 3, 1927), pp. 87–95; *American English Grammar, op. cit.,* pp. 150–168. For a fairly good picture of present-day usage, see Perrin and Dykema, *op. cit.,* pp. 693–695, and Paul Roberts, *Understanding Grammar* [New York, Harper & Row, 1954], pp. 147–153.

[26] Jean Malmstrom, *A Study of the Validity of Textbook Statements About Certain Controversial Grammatical Items in the Light of Evidence from the Linguistic Atlas* (a dissertation at the University of Minnesota, 1958), Microfilm 58-7012. Pp. 40–42, 266–268.

[27] *Op. cit.,* pp. 582–583.

has been made in this direction by recent studies, but we need more. In fact we should have a comprehensive survey of syntactical usage in present-day English. Each person must also learn to observe the language he uses and hears in order to know what is good current English.

Each person must also decide for himself what grammatical and word forms he will accept for his own writing and speaking. The choice is not so easy as it may seem, because in some circumstances it cannot be made on the basis of one's own knowledge or taste, however superior or informed. If for instance, one is writing for a periodical that adheres to the eighteenth- and nineteenth-century grammatical taboos, the splitting of infinitives is almost certainly going to provoke the wrath of the powers that be. Even if one is an independent author, the splitting of infinitives and the use of "like" as a conjunction will cause large segments of the public to regard the writer as careless or ignorant of the niceties of the language. In conversation, too, the choice is sometimes difficult. One may feel perfectly justified in saying "like I did," but the listener may draw the inference that the speaker "doesn't know any better." The purist is always around, and it is not easy to make him admit that usage is the "sole arbiter and norm of speech."

COMPREHENSION QUIZ

1. The use of the phrase "It is me" can be traced as far back as
   a. 1900.
   b. the Revolutionary War.
   c. the 16th century.
   d. the 19th century.
2. As far as using "who" and "whom," the word "who" has been practically the only form used in colloquial speech for at least how many centuries?
   a. one.
   b. two.
   c. two and one-half.
   d. three.
3. Good writers and speakers have made a practice of splitting infinitives
   a. whenever they want.
   b. never.
   c. only to show the effects of bad grammar.
   d. where avoiding it would have caused ambiguity.
4. To say "*One* rarely enjoy's *one's* luncheon when *one* is tired,"
   a. used to be the established form but has now given way to the use of "he" after the first "one."
   b. has always been incorrect.
   c. is considered the up-to-date viewpoint on the correct use of *one*.
   d. none of these.

5. The most prominent feature of our language, according to this essay, is
   a. the acceptance and use of the split infinitive.
   b. the wide and varied use of linking verbs followed by adjectives.
   c. the use of indefinite pronouns both singularly and plurally.
   d. the use of the world "like" as a conjunction.
6. Which of the following usages would the purist shun?
   a. "Go slowly."
   b. "It looks like it will rain."
   c. "It is I."
   d. "One cannot always choose one's friends."
7. Providing one of the most vexatious and ludicrous situations in the study of English is the literary uses of
   a. "who" and "whom."
   b. "slow" and "slowly."
   c. "bad" and "badly."
   d. "shall" and "will."
8. Contributing to the establishment of "will" in common usage in America has been
   a. emphasis by grammarians.
   b. common use of contractions such as "I'll," "You'll," and "He'll."
   c. a more definite need for "shall" in the emphatic future form.
   d. a clear agreement upon its usage by all principal authorities.

DISCUSSION QUESTIONS

1. Have you had trouble with the use of "who" and "whom"? What arguments would you have for eliminating completely the word "whom"? What arguments against?
2. Bryant says that in the sentence, "We only had one left," the adverb "only" does not logically refer to the verb "had." Do you agree? If so, to what does the word "only" refer?
3. Cite two examples of where not splitting an infinitive results in awkwardness or ambiguity.
4. Demonstrate an ability to use "good" and "well" correctly, according to current usage.
5. Probably the most common questionable use of "like" in recent times is the statement by a tobacco company that "_____ tastes good *like* a cigarette should." Cite other examples of questionable usage of words.
6. How does one go about following Bryant's admonition to "learn to observe the language he uses and hears"?
7. Comment on the closing sentence of the essay.
8. In your experience, would you say that college English professors of today are purists?
9. What liberties do you feel you can take in employing the kinds of usages identified in this essay, without jeopardizing your grade on themes, term papers, etc.?

10. If usage is the most important criterion of language, what are some other important criteria of language?

WRITING SUGGESTIONS

1. Write a paper affirming or challenging Bryant's statement that "We need grammars based on what is true of the language we use rather than on some person's idea of what it should be."
2. Explain and justify your feelings about the statement that "Usage is the most important criterion of language."
3. Write an eyewitness account of an automobile accident, making full use of today's slang. Rewrite the account using a "more educated" kind of grammar.

Grammar
for Today

by BERGEN EVANS

In 1747 Samuel Johnson issued a plan for a new dictionary of the English language. It was supported by the most distinguished printers of the day and was dedicated to the model of all correctness, Philip Dormer Stanhope, Fourth Earl of Chesterfield. Such a book, it was felt, was urgently needed to "fix" the language, to arrest its "corruption" and "decay," a degenerative process which, then as now, was attributed to the influence of "the vulgar" and which, then as now, it was a mark of superiority and elegance to decry. And Mr. Johnson seemed the man to write it. He had an enormous knowledge of Latin, deep piety, and dogmatic convictions. He was also honest and intelligent, but the effect of these lesser qualifications was not to show until later.

Oblig'd by hunger and request of friends, Mr. Johnson was willing to assume the role of linguistic dictator. He was prepared to "fix" the pronunciation of the language, "preserve the purity" of its idiom, brand "impure" words with a "note of infamy," and secure the whole "from being overrun by . . . low terms."

There were, however, a few reservations. Mr. Johnson felt it necessary to warn the oversanguine that "Language is the work of man, a being from whom permanence and stability cannot be derived." English "was not formed from heaven . . . but was produced by necessity and enlarged by accident." It had, indeed, been merely "thrown together by negligence" and was in such a state of confusion that its very syntax could no longer "be taught by general rules, but [only] by special precedents."

In 1755 the *Dictionary* appeared. The noble patron had been given a great deal more immortality than he had bargained for by the vigor of the kick Johnson had applied to his backside as he booted him overboard. And

From Bergen Evans, "Grammar for Today," *The Atlantic Monthly*, March, 1950. Reprinted by permission of the author.

the *Plan* had been replaced by the *Preface,* a sadder but very much wiser document.

Eight years of "sluggishly treading the track of the alphabet" had taught Johnson that the hopes of "fixing" the language and preserving its "purity" were but "the dreams of a poet doomed at last to wake a lexicographer." In "the boundless chaos of living speech," so copious and energetic in its disorder, he had found no guides except "experience and analogy." Irregularities were "inherent in the tongue" and could not be "dismissed or reformed" but must be permitted "to remain untouched." "Uniformity must be sacrified to custom . . . in compliance with a numberless majority" and "general agreement." One of the pet projects of the age had been the establishment of an academy to regulate and improve style. "I hope," Johnson wrote in the *Preface,* that if "it should be established . . . the spirit of English liberty will hinder or destroy (it)."

At the outset of the work he had flattered himself, he confessed, that he would reform abuses and put a stop to alterations. But he had soon discovered that "sounds are too volatile and subtle for legal restraints" and that "to enchain syllables and to lash the wind are equally undertakings of pride unwilling to measure its desires by its strength." For "the causes of change in language are as much superior to human resistance as the revolutions of the sky or the intumescence of the tide."

There had been an even more profound discovery: that grammarians and lexicographers "do not form, but register the language; do not teach men how they should think, but relate how they have hitherto expressed their thoughts." And with this statement Johnson ushered in the rational study of linguistics. He had entered on his task a medieval pedant. He emerged from it a modern scientist.

Of course his discoveries were not strikingly original. Horace had observed that use was the sole arbiter and norm of speech and Montaigne had said that he who would fight custom with grammar was a fool. Doubtless thousands of other people had at one time or another perceived and said the same thing. But Johnson introduced a new principle. Finding that he could not lay down rules, he gave actual examples to show meaning and form. He offered as authority illustrative quotations, and in so doing established that language is what usage makes it and that custom, in the long run, is the ultimate and only court of appeal in linguistic matters.

This principle, axiomatic today in grammar and lexicography, seems to exasperate a great many laymen who, apparently, find two hundred and five years too short a period in which to grasp a basic idea. They insist that there are absolute standards of correctness in speech and that these standards may be set forth in a few simple rules. To a man, they believe, of course, that they speak and write "correctly" and they are loud in their insistence that others imitate them.

It is useless to argue with such people because they are not, really, interested in language at all. They are interested solely in demonstrating their own superiority. Point out to them—as has been done hundreds of times —that forms which they regard as "corrupt," "incorrect," and "vulgar" have been used by Shakespeare, Milton, and the Bible and are used daily by 180 million Americans and accepted by the best linguists and lexicographers, and they will coolly say, "Well, if they differ from me, they're wrong."

But if usage is not the final determinant of speech, what is? Do the inhabitants of Italy, for example, speak corrupt Latin or good Italian? Is Spanish superior to French? Would the Breton fisherman speak better if he spoke Parisian French? Can one be more fluent in Outer Mongolian than in Inner Mongolian? One has only to ask such questions in relation to languages other than one's own, language within which our particular snobberies and struggles for prestige have no stake, to see the absurdity of them.

The language that we do speak, if we are to accept the idea of "corruption" and "decay" in language, is a horribly decayed Anglo-Saxon, grotesquely corrupted by Norman French. Furthermore, since Standard English is a development of the London dialect of the fourteenth century, our speech, by true aristocratic standards, is woefully middle-class, commercial, and vulgar. And American speech is lower middle-class, reeking of counter and till. Where else on earth, for instance, would one find crime condemned because it didn't *pay!*

In more innocent days a great deal of time was spent in wondering what was the "original" language of mankind, the one spoken in Eden, the language of which all modern tongues were merely degenerate remnants. Hector Boethius tells us that James I of Scotland was so interested in this problem that he had two children reared with a deaf and dumb nurse on an island in order to see what language they would "naturally" speak. James thought it would be Hebrew, and in time, to his great satisfaction, it was reported that the children were speaking Hebrew!

Despite this experiment, however, few people today regard English as a corruption of Hebrew. But many seem to think it is a corruption of Latin and labor mightily to make it conform to this illusion. It is they and their confused followers who tell us that we can't say "I am mistaken" because translated into Latin this would mean "I am misunderstood," and we can't say "I have enjoyed myself" unless we are egotistical or worse.

It is largely to this group—most of whom couldn't read a line of Latin at sight if their lives depended on it—that we owe our widespread bewilderment concerning *who* and *whom*. In Latin the accusative or dative form would always be used, regardless of the words' position in the sentence, when the pronoun was the object of a verb or a preposition. But in English, for at least four hundred years, this simply hasn't been so. When the pronoun occurs at the beginning of a question, people who speak natural,

fluent, literary English use the nominative, regardless. They say "Who did
you give it to?" not "Whom did you give it to?" But the semiliterate, in-
timidated and bewildered, are mouthing such ghastly utterances as a recent
headline in a Chicago newspaper: WHOM'S HE KIDDING?

Another group seems to think that in its pure state English was a Lapu-
tan tongue, with logic as its guiding principle. Early members of this sect
insisted that *unloose* could only mean "to tie up," and present members
have compelled the gasoline industry to label its trucks *Flammable* under
the disastrous insistence, apparently, that the old *Inflammable* could only
mean "not burnable."

It is to them, in league with the Latinists, that we owe the bogy of the
double negative. In all Teutonic languages a doubling of the negative
merely emphasizes the negation. But we have been told for a century now
that two negatives make a positive, though if they do and it's merely a matter of logic, then three negatives should make a negative again. So that
if "It doesn't make no difference" is wrong merely because it includes two
negatives, then "It doesn't never make no difference" ought to be right
again.

Both of these groups, in their theories at least, ignore our idiom. Yet
idiom—those expressions which defy all logic but are the very essence of
a tongue—plays a large part in English. We go to school and college, but
we go to *the* university. We buy two dozen eggs but a couple *of* dozen.
Good and can mean *very* ("I am good and mad!") and "a hot cup of coffee"
means that the coffee, not the cup, is to be hot. It makes a world of difference to a condemned man whether his reprieve is *upheld* or *held up*.

There are thousands of such expressions in English. They are the "irregularities" which Johnson found "inherent in the tongue" and which
his wisdom perceived could not and should not be removed. Indeed, it is
in the recognition and use of these idioms that skillful use of English lies.

Many words in the form that is now mandatory were originally just
mistakes, and many of these mistakes were forced into the language by
eager ignoramuses determined to make it conform to some notion of their
own. The *s* was put in *island*, for instance, in sheer pedantic ignorance.
The second *r* doesn't belong in *trousers*, nor the *g* in *arraign*, nor the *t* in
deviltry, nor the *n* in *passenger* and *messenger*. Nor, so far as English is
concerned, does that first *c* in *arctic* which so many people twist their mouths
so strenuously to pronounce.

And grammar is as "corrupted" as spelling or pronunciation. "You
are" is as gross a solecism as "me am." It's recent, too; you won't find it in
the Authorized Version of the Bible. *Lesser, nearer,* and *more* are grammatically on a par with *gooder*. *Crowed* is the equivalent of *knowed* or
growed, and *caught* and *dug* (for *catched* and *digged*) are as "corrupt" as
squoze or *snoze* for *sneezed*.

Fortunately for our peace of mind most people are quite content to let English conform to English, and they are supported in their sanity by modern grammarians and linguists.

Scholars agree with Puttenham (1589) that a language is simply speech "fashioned to the common understanding and accepted by consent." They believe that the only "rules" that can be stated for a language are codified observations. They hold, that is, that language is the basis of grammar, not the other way round. They do not believe that any language can become "corrupted" by the linguistic habits of those who speak it. They do not believe that anyone who is a native speaker of a standard language will get into any linguistic trouble unless he is misled by snobbishness or timidity or vanity.

He may, of course, if his native language is English, speak a form of English that marks him as coming from a rural or an unread group. But if he doesn't mind being so marked, there's no reason why he should change. Johnson retained a Staffordshire burr in his speech all his life. And surely no one will deny that Robert Burns' rustic dialect was just as good a form of speech as, and in his mouth infinitely better as a means of expression than, the "correct" English spoken by ten million of his southern contemporaries.

The trouble is that people are no longer willing to be rustic or provincial. They all want to speak like educated people, though they don't want to go to the trouble of becoming truly educated. They want to believe that a special form of socially acceptable and financially valuable speech can be mastered by following a few simple rules. And there is no lack of little books that offer to supply the rules and promise "correctness" if the rules are adhered to. But, of course, these offers are specious because you don't speak like an educated person unless you are an educated person, and the little books, if taken seriously, will not only leave the lack of education showing but will expose the pitiful yearning and the basic vulgarity as well, in such sentences as "Whom are you talking about?"

As a matter of fact, the educated man uses at least three languages. With his family and his close friends, on the ordinary, unimportant occasions of daily life, he speaks, much of the time, a monosyllabic sort of shorthand. On more important occasions and when dealing with strangers in his official or business relations, he has a more formal speech, more complete, less allusive, politely qualified, wisely reserved. In addition he has some acquaintance with the literary speech of his language. He understands this when he reads it, and often enjoys it, but he hesitates to use it. In times of emotional stress hot fragments of it may come out of him like lava, and in times of feigned emotion, as when giving a commencement address, cold, greasy gobbets of it will ooze forth.

The linguist differs from the amateur grammarian in recognizing all of these variations and gradations in the language. And he differs from the snob in doubting that the speech of any one small group among the languages' more than 300 million daily users constitutes a model for all the rest to imitate.

The methods of the modern linguist can be illustrated by the question of the grammatical number of *none*. Is it singular or plural? Should one say "None of them is ready" or "None of them are ready"?

The prescriptive grammarians are emphatic that it should be singular. The Latinists point out that *nemo,* the Latin equivalent, is singular. The logicians triumphantly point out that *none* can't be more than one and hence can't be plural.

The linguist knows that he hears "None of them are ready" every day, from people of all social positions, geographical areas, and degrees of education. He also hears "None is." Furthermore, literature informs him that both forms were used in the past. From Malory (1450) to Milton (1650) he finds that *none* was treated as a singular three times for every once that it was treated as a plural. That is, up to three hundred years ago men usually said *None is.* From Milton to 1917, *none* was used as a plural seven times for every four times it was used as a singular. That is, in the past three hundred years men often said *None is,* but they said *None are* almost twice as often. Since 1917, however, there has been a noticeable increase in the use of the plural, so much so that today *None are* is the preferred form.

The descriptive grammarian, therefore, says that while *None is* may still be used, it is becoming increasingly peculiar. This, of course, will not be as useful to one who wants to be cultured in a hurry as a short, emphatic permission or prohibition. But it has the advantage of describing English as it is spoken and written here and now and not as it ought to be spoken in some Cloud-Cuckoo-Land.

The descriptive grammarian believes that a child should be taught English, but he would like to see the child taught the English actually used by his educated contemporaries, not some pedantic, theoretical English designed chiefly to mark the imagined superiority of the designer.

He believes that a child should be taught the parts of speech, for example. But the child should be told the truth—that these are functions of use, not some quality immutably inherent in this or that word. Anyone, for instance, who tells a child—or anyone else—that *like* is used in English only as a preposition has grossly misinformed him. And anyone who complains that its use as a conjunction is a corruption introduced by Winston cigarettes ought, in all fairness, to explain how Shakespeare, Keats, and the translators of the Authorized Version of the Bible came to be in the employ of the R. J. Reynolds Tobacco Company.

Whether formal grammar can be taught to advantage before the senior year of high school is doubtful; most studies—and many have been made— indicate that it can't. But when it is taught, it should be the grammar of today's English, not the obsolete grammar of yesterday's prescriptive grammarians. By that grammar, for instance, *please* in the sentence "Please reply" is the verb and *reply* its object. But by modern meaning *reply* is the verb, in the imperative, and *please* is merely a qualifying word meaning "no discourtesy intended," a mollifying or de-imperatival adverb, or whatever you will, but not the verb.

This is a long way from saying "Anything goes," which is the charge that, with all the idiot repetition of a needle stuck in a groove, the uninformed ceaselessly chant against modern grammarians. But to assert that usage is the sole determinant in grammar, pronunciation, and meaning is *not* to say that anything goes. Custom is illogical and unreasonable, but it is also tyrannical. The latest deviation from its dictates is usually punished with severity. And because this is so, children should be taught what the current and local customs in English are. They should not be taught that we speak a bastard Latin or a vocalized logic. And they should certainly be disabused of the stultifying illusion that after God had given Moses the Commandments He called him back and pressed on him a copy of Woolley's *Handbook of English Grammar.*

The grammarian does not see it as his function to "raise the standards" set by Franklin, Lincoln, Melville, Mark Twain, and hundreds of millions of other Americans. He is content to record what they said and say.

Insofar as he serves as a teacher, it is his business to point out the limits of the permissible, to indicate the confines within which the writer may exercise his choice, to report that which custom and practice have made acceptable. It is certainly not the business of the grammarian to impose his personal taste as the only norm of good English, to set forth his prejudices as the ideal standard which everyone should copy. That would be fatal. No one person's standards are broad enough for that.

COMPREHENSION QUIZ

1. Prior to working on his Dictionary, Samuel Johnson announced his intention of
   a. "fixing" the pronunciation of the language.
   b. preserving the purity of its idiom.
   c. arresting the corruption and decay of English.
   d. all of the above.
2. After completing his Dictionary, Johnson
   a. announced his satisfaction at having fulfilled his intentions.
   b. emerged a modern linguist.
   c. recommended the formation of a national academy of English.
   d. recorded his gratitude to his patron.
3. Evans believes that the final determinant of speech is
   a. usage.
   b. "correctness."

    c.   tradition based on the classics.

    d.   etymology.

4.   The skillful use of English, according to Evans, lies

    a.   in the master of the parts of speech.

    b.   in the possession of a large vocabulary.

    c.   in the ability to diagram sentences.

    d.   in the recognition and use of idioms.

5.   Evans doubts whether formal grammar can be taught to advantage before

    a.   the third grade.

    b.   the first year of high school.

    c.   the senior year of high school.

    d.   the senior year of college.

6.   Which of the following is *not* the business of the language teacher?

    a.   To point out the limits of the permissible.

    b.   To indicate the confines within which the writer may exercise his choice.

    c.   To report that which custom and practice have made acceptable.

    d.   To set forth his personal taste as the ideal standard which everyone should copy.

DISCUSSION QUESTIONS

1.   What observations about the English language did Samuel Johnson make in his *Preface?* How do they contrast with those expressed in his *Plan?* In what sense is Johnson the first modern linguist?

2.   According to Johnson, what is the duty of the lexicographer and grammarian?

3.   What are the "rules" of English based on?

4.   Why are many people dogmatic about their concepts of "correct" English?

5.   According to Evans, what are the three languages used by the educated man? Does this classification system correspond to yours?

WRITING SUGGESTIONS

1.   Define "correct English."

2.   Compare Evans' comments about "who" and "whom" with those in an English handbook of grammar. Which seems to make more sense?

3.   In a theme, explain why educated speakers of English are more given to experimentation, and why the uneducated are often more conservative in their attitudes toward language.

4.   Write a theme defending (or attacking) the teaching of formal grammar before the senior year of high school.

Fast
as an Elephant,
Strong
as an Ant

by BIL GILBERT

One day recently I was reading a story about the San Diego Chargers when I came across the following sentence describing Mr. Ernie Ladd, a tackle who is said to be 6 feet 9 inches tall and to weigh 300 pounds. Ladd, the report stated, has "a body that a grizzly bear could be proud of." Now, this is an example of the falsely anthropomorphic and the factually inaccurate natural-history metaphor, a literary device widely used by sportswriters and one that I have long thought should be reported to authorities and stamped out.

The description of Ernie Ladd is objectionable on two counts. First, there is no evidence that bears take pride in their personal appearance, physical prowess or muscular development. Among animals, only men seem susceptible to narcissism. And even if grizzlies did have the emotions of a beach boy and sat about the woods admiring their physiques, no bear would be proud of having a body like that of Mr. Ladd.

According to my copy of *Mammals of the World* (Ernest P. Walker, The Johns Hopkins Press, 1964, page 1173), "Grizzlies 2.5 meters [about 8 feet] in length and 360 kg. [800 pounds] in weight have been recorded. . . ." In brief, Mr. Ladd is simply too puny to impress a grizzly even if grizzlies were impressionable in these matters.

I have never been one to criticize without offering constructive alternatives. Additional reading of *Mammals of the World* has uncovered some statistics that may prove useful in the future. Should the need arise, one might accurately (though still anthropomorphically) write that Mr. Ernie Ladd has a body that a female gray seal (150 kg., 2 meters) or a pygmy hippopotamus (160 kg., 1.9 meters, counting tail) might be proud of.

It is not my purpose to embarrass or harass the man who wrote the story. Rather, it is to point out that he is the inheritor, the victim, of a bad journalistic tradition. Sportswriters have been comparing such and such an athlete to this or that animal since the dawn of sports. Many of these long-standing figures, metaphors, similes and tropes are even more wildly inaccurate and ridiculous than the comparison of Mr. Ladd to a grizzly bear.

An example that comes quickly to mind is the expression "wild as a hawk," used to describe either erratic performance (a baseball pitcher who cannot throw the ball across the plate) or untamable behavior (a fractious horse). In both senses the phrase is misleading. As far as control goes, the birds of prey are the antithesis of wildness (in the baseball use of the word). A duck hawk, for example, flying a mile high in the sky, can suddenly turn, dive earthward at 175 mph and strike a tiny sandpiper flying just a few feet above the ground. Sandy Koufax should be so accurate. As to being untamable, I, as a falconer, have often captured a feral adult hawk and in a month had the bird flying free, returning to my hand in response to a whistled command.

My own suggestion is that "wild as a heron" would better suggest the kind of behavior that wild as a hawk is supposed to describe. In many situations herons appear uncoordinated, almost spastic. Seeing a long-legged, gangly heron trying to land or take off from the ground is an experience. Furthermore, herons are far wilder (in the ferocious sense) than hawks. The most painful injury I ever received from an animal was given me by an American bittern (a heron type), who gouged a large hole in my wrist as I was attempting to free him from a fish trap.

"Loose as a goose" is an avian simile, supposedly suggesting extreme suppleness. Actually, geese have rigid pinions and are more or less bound like weight lifters by a heavy layer of pectoral muscle. Straight as a goose, stiff as a goose, pompous as a goose would be all right. But loose as a goose? Never. A better expression of the notion would be: "Though Slats Slattern has been a stellar NBA performer for 12 seasons, he remains young in spirit and loose as a mink." The slim-bodied minks, as well as weasels, ferrets and otters, are designed along the lines of a wet noodle. They look, and in fact are, far looser than a goose can possibly be.

Turning to mammals, an agility simile is "quick as a cat," often used in connection with such athletes as shortstops and goalies. It is true that cats are quicker than some things—turtles, mice, goldfish in bowls, for example—but they are much less quick than many other creatures. Any wheezing old dog worth its salt can catch a cat. I once had a crow so quick that it could fly down and deliver three pecks between the eyes of a cat (which the crow despised) before the feline could raise a paw in self-defense. Not long ago I was watching a tame baboon which had the run of a yard in which was caged an ocelot. The baboon, even though working through bars, would reach into the cage and, while the ocelot was trying to get her reflexes in order, grab the cat by both her handsome tail and pointed ears. Baboon-quick is accurate and has a nice exotic ring to it.

Cats may not be the quickest animals, but at least one of the family, the cheetah, is the swiftest mammal as far as straight-ahead sprinting goes. It would seem that "run like a cheetah" would be a natural simile for sports-writers, but what do we have? "Ziggy Zagowski, slashing left half for the Keokuk Kidneys, ran like a rabbit through the defending Sioux City Spleens." Now, for a few jumps a rabbit can move at a rate of 30 or 35 miles an hour, but 20 mph is its pace for a distance as great as 100 yards. This rate is about the same as—or a bit slower than—that of a journeyman human sprinter over the same course. The chances are that if old Zig could not outleg a bunny he would not have even made his high school team. If, how-ever, he could run like a cheetah it would be a different matter, since those cats can do the 440 at 71 mph.

Since an elephant can skip along as fast as 25 mph (a bit faster than Bob Hayes or the average cottontail), it would be highly complimentary to say of an athlete that he runs like an elephant. However, the expression "ele-phantine" is actually used in sports as a term of derision, to twit a ponderous, slow-moving, clumsy performer. Actually, elephants are not only swift beasts but graceful ones. Despite their size, they are almost as quick as a baboon or as loose as a mink. They can slip quietly through the jungle, stand on a barrel or a ballerina at the behest of a ringmaster. "Horsine" would be a better term to designate a stumblebum. Horses are forever falling over small pebbles, ropes and their own feet. When a horse and rider start down even a gradual incline or up a path slightly narrower than the Pennsylvania Turn-pike, the rider must dismount, and it is he who must lead, guide and, in general, prop up the horse.

Great strength has its place in sports, and it is traditional to describe the athlete who possesses it as being "strong as an ox." As in the case of quick cats and fast rabbits, the simile is not completely false, only inadequate. In proportion to their bulk, oxen are relatively strong but not overpoweringly so. A team of oxen weighing 3,400 pounds can move a dead weight, say a block of granite, equal to about three times its own weight. This is a fair feat when compared to a 150-pound weight lifter who can dead-lift 300 pounds. However, it is a feeble effort when one considers the ant, which can pick up a load 50 times heavier than itself. To speak of a fullback as being strong as an ant would be high praise indeed, since it would signify that the player could, without undue strain, carry the entire opposing team not only across the goal line, but right up into Row E.

Held in high regard by coaches, reporters and fans is the athlete who works incessantly at mastering the fundamentals of his game. Often such persevering types are admired as "beavers." This, of course, is a contraction of the folksy expressions "to work like a beaver" or "to be as busy as a beaver," both of which are based upon a misunderstanding of the beaver's nature and misobservation of the animal's customary behavior. Unlike some animals that must travel many miles a day just to rustle up a square meal, beavers seldom forage more than a hundred yards from their home. Beavers construct their well-publicized dams and lodges only when it is absolutely impossible to find a suitable natural waterscape. The lowly mole, on the other hand, may dig several hundred yards of tunnel in a day in an incessant effort to keep body and soul together. "I like that boy, all spring long he's been moling away," would be an apt way for a coach to describe and praise industriousness.

Canines have a strong attraction for scribes looking for a vivid, if fallacious, phrase. There is, for example, the veteran who is a "sly, foxy" competitor. (If foxes are so sly, how come they never run down the hounds? Who ever heard of a hunt catching a skunk?) Then there is the prizefighter about to addle the brains of his opponent or the fast-ball pitcher poised to stick one in a batter's ear. These violent men, we are often told, have a "wolfish grin" on their faces.

One of the few naturalists who have been close enough long enough to *au naturel* wolves to observe their facial expressions is Farley Mowat, who spent a summer camped virtually on the den step of a family of Arctic wolves. Mowat in his delightful book, *Never Cry Wolf,* claims that *his* wolves were kindly, affectionate, tolerant animals who looked and acted more like diplomats than thugs. This stands to reason. Many creatures besides man are predatory, but hardly any species except man tries to do real violence to its own kind in play while contemplating the prospect with a grin. If such a premayhem facial expression as a "wolfish grin" actually exists, it is probably unique to man. If this peculiar look of violence must be compared to that of some other animal, I recommend the short-tailed shrew.

The short-tailed shrew is one of the commonest animals of North America and one of the most perpetually predatory. Ounce for ounce (which is what a large shrew weighs), there is no busier killer in the world. Awake, the shrew is almost always preparing to kill, is killing or has just killed, and its victims include rodents, reptiles, birds and mammals several times its own size. The shrew, like almost all other mammals, does not kill out of capriciousness or playfulness, but rather because it has an extraordinarily high metabolic rate. It must daily consume the equivalent of its own body weight in order to keep the inner fires burning. (Eat like a shrew, rather than eat like a horse, would better describe the habits of a first baseman who is such a formidable trencherman that he can no longer bend down to scoop up low throws.) When a shrew closes in to kill something, say a white-footed mouse, it wears a really dreadful expression. A shrew is chinless, and its long mouth slashes across the underpart of its muzzle in a cruel, sharklike line. As the tiny killer closes in, its eyes glitter with excitement and two long brown fangs (which, incidentally, drip with a venomous saliva) are exposed. If Sonny Liston looked only half as wicked as a short-tailed shrew he might still be heavyweight champion of the world.

I fully realize that many of the criticisms and suggestions offered here do violence to some of the most cherished traditions of sports journalism, but there is no holding back literary and scientific progress. Consider, for example, the manner in which the style I advocate, high-fidelity zoological metaphor, injects color as well as accuracy into the following interview with Sig Schock of the Pardy Pumas:

"Sig Schock, a big horsine man, grizzled as a Norway rat, leaned back against the plywood bench, taking up a position so that the hot sun beat down on his ant-like shoulders. The eyes, old but still sharp as a barn owl's, flicked over the practice field, where the young Pumas cavorted as quick as so many baboons. 'I'll tell you,' Sig confided in his disconcertingly high, spring-peeperlike voice. 'These kids has got it. The most of them can run like elephants, a couple like cheetahs. And size. We finally got some. We got six boys with builds like a female gray seal's. Course, they're still young, some of them are wild as herons—that's O.K., they got the old desire. Every one of them is a snapping turtle or a raccoon. And I'll tell you something,' the sly, skunky veteran added, lowering his squeaky voice. 'We'll chew 'em up and lay 'em out this season.' A shrewish grin spread across the battered old face."

Leaving you with that, I remain pretty as a peacock, sassy as a jaybird, happy as a clam.

COMPREHENSION QUIZ

1. Gilbert claims that the expressions commonly used by sportswriters
   a. are generally more accurate than those used by poets.
   b. are inaccurate and ridiculous.
   c. demonstrate a knowledge of animals.
   d. are particularly colorful and effective when describing pole-vaulters.
2. The most painful injury Gilbert ever received from an animal was from
   a. an American bittern.
   b. an Alaskan bear.
   c. a disgruntled baboon.
   d. a nervous horse.
3. Gilbert says it would be high praise indeed to speak of a fullback as being strong as
   a. a crow.
   b. a sandpiper.

    c.   a Texas horned toad.

    d.   an ant.

4.   Instead of a "wolfish grin," Gilbert recommends the fearsome expression of the

    a.   hyena.

    b.   elephant.

    c.   cobra.

    d.   short-tailed shrew.

5.   Gilbert believes that an accurate comparison for an athlete who perseveres would be the

    a.   beaver.

    b.   gnu.

    c.   mole.

    d.   kangaroo.

DISCUSSION QUESTIONS

1.   What other inaccurate or far-fetched comparisons can you add to Gilbert's collection?

2.   Why is there a tendency for sports writers to lapse into clichés? Do they really help us to grasp more clearly the ideas presented?

WRITING SUGGESTIONS

1.   Examine carefully today's sports page of your newspaper. List some of the clichés that Gilbert would probably object to; rewrite them to reflect his suggestions.

2.   Gilbert's essay is restricted to clichés from the sports world. Using his technique, write an essay examing clichés from some other area or subject. In your essay, supply "improved" comparisons.

A Defense
of Conventional Usage

by HARRY H. CROSBY and GEORGE F. ESTEY

There is evidence today that we are living in a world of "anything goes." We are exposed to permissive education and nondirective guidance, to a God who is reputedly dead, and to a "situational" morality. Because the so-called revolution in language studies has disseminated the doctrine of usage and laid prescriptive grammar to rest, we might think that, insofar as language is concerned, this is also a time of linguistic chaos and grammatical freedom. This is not true. This is not a time of complete language laxity. Anyone who thinks so is ignorant of the nature of the American psyche and of the function of grammar.

Modern language research shows us that language is an arbitrary system of symbols set up by society. Research also shows us that within any given language there are dialects and jargons so specialized that dwellers in one apartment house or on one mountain top may not be able to communicate with their neighbors in the next street or valley. Nevertheless, a dialect must be used by a sizable number of people to be meaningful, for no one person can make up his own set of symbols and expect to communicate with his fellow men. Studies also show that languages change markedly and dramatically, though there is no indication that such change is, in and of itself, good. The ideal language would be one that would grow when necessary, but would mean tomorrow what it means today and be understood by all people.

Although it is not a perfect language, the spoken dialect that is most widely used in America is called Standard American, or General American. This dialect is thought of as the language of the Middle West, but it is used as far east as New York, Pennsylvania, and rural Connecticut; west of Iowa the area where it is used fans out to the southwest. It skirts southern influences in West Virginia, Arkansas, and southern Missouri. On the north, the region extends into Canada. Travelers in Quebec and the Maritime Provinces find English-speaking Canadians who sound more like Iowans than they do like nearby New Englanders or the British.

We have learned that languages follow the character of their users, and Standard American (Spoken) does indeed reflect the American character. It is easy-going, relatively informal, quick to change, and forceful. It is not, however, the language of "anything goes"; it is not linguistically chaotic. In its title, the operative word is "Standard." In Africa, Europe, and Asia it is rare indeed when every person living within any two-hundred-mile area can communicate with every other person in that area. In the United States and Canada, an area of language similarity almost 4,000 miles wide and 5,000 miles deep, a native of any point in this area can communicate readily with a native of any other, with the exception of some French Canadians. There is no other linguistic area as large anywhere in the world. Even minor differences are disappearing. The spread of education in America, the relative lack of social structure, the mobility of the American people, the proliferation of national publications, and radio and television all have worked to eliminate dialect distinctions.

Besides Standard American, there are two other spoken dialects. Southern American and what has been called "Yankee talk," but their use is diminishing, perhaps regrettably. When an aspirant for stage or television takes elocution lessons, he is taught Standard or General American; Tallulah Bankhead, the daughter of an Alabama congressman, spoke her version of General American on Broadway and in Hollywood. When foreigners are taught English by Americans they are usually taught General American. When the pronunciation of Bronx and Brooklyn children is corrected, they are given General American substitutes. Americans smile gently at ethnic jokes told with an appropriate Jewish or Italian accent, at a Boston twang, at a Southern drawl. They find amusing any deviation from General American.

The differences between Standard American and the other two dialects are colloquial, that is, they are found in informal spoken communication. A college freshman or a college professor from Georgia might say, "You-all come see us, y'heah?" but he would not use such an expression in a freshman theme or in an article for a professional journal. There are a very few dissimilarities in word choice: a southerner might refer to a "poke" of groceries, a midwesterner to a "sack," and a New Englander to a "bag." The Bostonian drinks "tonic," not "pop" or a "soft drink" as in other areas. Their spelling, grammar, and punctuation, however, show few dialect differences. It is almost impossible to detect any regional influence on the nonfiction prose of southerner Robert Penn Warren, midwesterner Adlai Stevenson, Bostonian Edward Kennedy, or southwesterner Barry Goldwater. In spite of some beliefs to the contrary, spoken dialect differences have had very little effect on

American written grammar. Similarly, the influences that have made the American spoken language breezy and casual have had little effect on the construction of written American sentences. There have been many effects on word choice and idioms, but very little on grammar. For that reason it is important to keep in mind the fact that there are two pervasive American dialects: besides Standard American (Spoken) there is Standard American (Written), and in America written English is decidedly not a language of "anything goes."

An inflexible grammar may seem contradictory to the American character, but it has for many years been a characteristic of Americans. Americans, whether they be schoolteachers, writers, politicians, or what have you, have tended to be stricter with grammar than their English peers. So-called grammatical errors are easy to find in English literature:

Nobody will miss her like I shall.　CHARLES DICKENS, *Letters.*

If it don't take, I will leave it off where it is.　GEORGE GORDON, LORD BYRON, *Letters.*

Who has he come for?　GEORGE MEREDITH, *The Ordeal of Richard Feverel.*

Who are they likely to send down to examine us?　RUDYARD KIPLING, *Debits and Credits.*

She did not know whom this strange young man might be.　HUGH WALPOLE, *Fortitude.*

He can't write like he used to.　GEORGE BERNARD SHAW, *Saint Joan.*

Hello, America, this is me.　WINSTON CHURCHILL, 1946.

Having no calendars, their only way of keeping track of the season was to notice and to remember which star-clusters rose just before dawn.　LANCELOT HOGBEN, *Wonderful World of Communication.*

Customarily when an "error" is called to the attention of a well-educated Englishman, he very likely indicates great tolerance. John Dryden spoke cavalierly about grammar. It should be handled, he said, "with well-bred ease." In 1761, Joseph Priestley commented that he knew of no surer way to indicate narrowness of mind than to exercise concern for grammar. "We have," he snorted, "infinitely greater things before us." Winston Churchill summed up the opinion of the cultured Englishman when he stated that he never let the rules of grammar get in the way of communication.

In contrast, American writers have almost invariably insisted on precise, parsable grammar. Benjamin Franklin forced himself to avoid questionable locutions. No one speaks better grammar than the noble savages in James Fenimore Cooper's novels. The prose of Washington Irving, Edgar Allan Poe, Ralph Waldo Emerson, Henry Wadsworth Longfellow, Nathaniel Hawthorne, Herman Melville, and William Cullen Bryant is grammatically immaculate; even the characters in their fiction tend to speak schoolteacher English. The early characters of Henry James speak grammatically; when he moved to England, his characters began to speak more colloquially. Huck Finn was almost the first character in significant American literature to use such constructions as "They was fetching a very nice-looking old gentleman along," and "So him and the dummy started off."

The stereotypes of the American as free, breezy, and informal and the Englishman as reserved, "correct," and formal are contradicted by comparing the language of the London *Times* and *The New York Times;* the grammar in the English paper is vastly more relaxed. The same impression results from a study of almost any equivalent British and American periodical. Likewise, B.B.C. broadcast speech is less grammatical than that of N.B.C. A contrast of British and American humor reveals that there are relatively few English pokes based on language; in America, "howlers," errors in grammar or diction, are frequently published, for they are found highly amusing in the United States. When the British object to American English they object to neologisms that duplicate already existing words, especially if they are longer or pretentious, such as *transportation* instead of *transport* and *motivations* instead of *motives,* or that are based on unsound historical principles, as when Americans use *hospitalize* to mean "send to a hospital," when etymologically the word should mean "convert into a hospital." It is small wonder that the British conceived a dictionary based on historical principles almost a hundred years before there was a similar project in the United States.

When an American deviates in any respect of his language, society whips him with its scorn. In 1928, voters had great difficulty taking Al Smith seriously as a Presidential candidate, in part because of his pronunciation, "*Tidday* I speak to you on the *raddio.*" In 1940, they were amused by Wendell Willkie, the "barefoot boy from Wall Street," who spoke to "Mah fella Amurr-kins." When the mistakes are in grammar, the offender gets real abuse heaped upon him, as did Vice-Presidential candidate John Sparkman, who said, "Well, we run a good race." Sparkman was a Phi Beta Kappa from the University of Alabama, but many northerners considered him a country bumpkin because of his English.

Precise grammar has become in America the instant identification mark of educational, economic, and social status. College admissions officers . . . admit that an application replete with grammar errors or misspellings gets almost no attention, the thought being that such errors reflect an absence of concern, teachability, and self-discipline. In a controlled experiment a group of college teachers was given a set of themes to grade. Unknown to the teachers, there were actually two sets, identical except that in one of the sets there were several grammatical and spelling errors. As might be expected, the second set received much lower grades—but, surprisingly—the papers with the errors were marked lower in content, organization, and style, in the apparently subconscious belief that an ungrammatical writer who can't spell can't organize or develop a thought either. Probably no other quality can so quickly undermine others' confidence in a person than for him to use such expressions as "he don't" or "they was."

[Our] attempt to help students clear up difficulties with grammar, spelling, and punctuation is based on principles that accept these mechanics as a product of logic and convention. These principles are:

1.   If a deviation from conventions in grammar, spelling, or punctuation causes confusion, it should be corrected. The sentence, "John told Bill he had to go home" is indefensible, for the reader is left unsure whether it was Bill or John himself who had to go home. Prose must be clear. The reaction desired from the reader is "I understand," not "What's that again?"

2.   Any deviation identified with the uneducated or the slovenly is rejected. Nothing is gained by "He swum to shore," "You was robbed," "He flang the ball." The reaction desired from the reader is "I understand," not a raised eyebrow or a snigger.

Admittedly these two principles may lead a writer to adopt an essentially conservative posture about punctuation, spelling, and grammar. Lord Chesterfield once advised his son that a gentleman is never the first nor the last to adopt a fad. The desired posture need not be one of conservatism, but it should be one of discrimination. A writer must develop a "feel" for the mechanics of writing; he must acquire "taste." About spelling, he has very little choice. There are almost no acceptable variations. He can use *centre* and *theatre* as proper nouns; a resident of Newton, Massachusetts, for instance, might walk down the *center* of *Centre* Street. He may use phonetic spellings in trade names or highway signs, such as "Nu-Lite," "Thru Street," or "Hi-Way 101," and he may take his choice about some words about which there is as yet little agreement; for instance, "programmed learning" or "programed learning." About punctuation, he has a great deal of choice, so much so that he depends as much upon the sound of his communication as he does upon arbitrary rules.

When he confronts a problem of grammar, however, his choices are limited. When two possible constructions occur to him and one is as clear as the other—and both are acceptable to popular usage—he may, quite frankly, turn to the one that is the more "proper." He will run into such problems rarely, but they do occur. Take these sentences, for instance:

1.   All the students are here, but none of them are very happy.
2.   I must say that he did good.
3.   You will go!
4.   The policeman said I should drive slow.
5.   Ask him who he wants.
6.   You are the person that I want.
7.   I feel badly about this matter.
8.   The document, hopefully, will provide the answer.

If we were to enter the mind of a writer confronted with these sentences, we might encounter responses such as these:

About #1.   Hm-m-m! Bergen Evans says that a majority of writers use *none* as a plural. There is a perverse kind of logic in their defense: after all *zero* is neither singular nor plural, and the sentence does have a plural ring, as though we are saying "All are unhappy," but instead say "None are happy." I guess either *is* or *are* would be satisfactory.

About #2.   This one has a kind of logic too. Strictly speaking, an adverb should be used, "He did well," but "He did good" is more forceful, as though we were saying "He went about doing good." However, even though I am attracted by the force, it does not sound right to me. Apparently "He did well" is more familiar, so I will stick to the strictly grammatical usage.

About #3.   Almost no one knows the distinctions between *shall* and *will*. Whether it is grammatically correct or not, I will use *will*.

About #4.   If I were quoting the policeman directly I would use quotation marks. Whether *slow* is proper is another question. Ironically, the policeman has history on his side. At one time "Walk slow" was as accepted as "Walk fast." Certainly there has never been a "fastly." Through the years, however, strict usage has favored "Drive slowly," one of the occasions where polite usage has been stricter than historical development. Okay, I will use the stricter form, "Drive slowly."

About #5 and #6.   The *who* and *whom* dilemma! *Whom* often sounds prissy, even when it is correct. Some "correct" uses of *whom* sound downright silly—for instance, "Whom's he seeking?" Even "For whom is he calling?" sounds a bit stilted. Settling the matter by using *that* is not very good, because it often makes a split construction necessary: you cannot say "You are the person for that I am looking": you must say, "You are the person that I am looking for." In this dilemma I guess I will stick to *whom* when it is appropriate; when I think *that* is better, I may be able to cross it out entirely.

Ask him whom he wants.

You are the person I want.

About #7 and #8.   Hm-m-m! There comes a time when a person has to draw the line. Ironically, "I feel badly" is used often by the semi-educated, rarely by the uneducated. Half-knowledge tells us that we should use an adverb after a verb, and adverbs have -ly endings. Ergo: shouldn't I use *badly?* But there is also some rule about verbs of sense (*taste, smell, hear, feel*) taking adjective forms. If a fish smells badly, it means something is wrong with his nose. If he smells bad, he stinks. If I taste badly, there is something wrong with my tasting apparatus. I should use adjective forms, as I do when I use forms of the verb *be*.

The fish smells bad.
The fish is bad.

I feel bad.
I am bad.

The meat tastes bad.
The meat is bad.

Thus, "I feel badly" is a ridiculous affectation. I do not care who uses it. *I* won't.

About #8. There are some expressions that irritate me. If I use "hopefully" I should indicate who is doing the hoping. A document can't hope, as the construction seems to suggest. I will write, "We hope that the document will provide the answer we need so badly."

A student often comes to a kind of reluctant truce in the battle with grammar. He says to himself, "Okay, I will be pragmatic and go along. I will wear a tie at dinner. I will not pick my teeth in a café. I will try to write grammatically correct prose. My reader will think of me as an educated, stable, mannerly person, and I am more likely to convince him than if I violate the conventions of grammar." An experienced writer, on the other hand, more often has his respect for grammar based on real admiration. He knows that although his style may be the mark of his own personality, grammar is something invented and refined by society to make the best possible representation of a thought. He does not look at grammar as a discipline, but as part of freedom. Freedom, he reflects, is really only the privilege of exercising one's self-discipline. He concludes that the discipline of grammar is what makes it possible for him to exercise real freedom in thought and style.

COMPREHENSION QUIZ

1. According to Crosby and Estey, which of the following is *not* happening:
   a. Permissive education.
   b. Nondirective guidance.
   c. Linguistic chaos and grammatical freedom.
   d. "Situational" morality.
2. Which of the following dialects is most widely used in this country?
   a. Southern American.
   b. Standard American (spoken).
   c. "Yankee talk."
   d. Western American.
3. When an "error" is called to the attention of a well-educated Englishman, he very likely
   a. indicates great tolerance.

    b.   becomes highly enraged.

    c.   refutes the critic by alluding to Greek and Latin analogies.

    d.   accepts the correction begrudgingly.

4. The instant identification mark of educational, economic, and social status in America has become

    a.   a luxurious home and car.

    b.   precise grammar.

    c.   a permissive and relaxed attitude toward grammar.

    d.   the ability to speak several languages.

5. An experienced writer believes in all of the following *except*:

    a.   style may be the mark of his own personality.

    b.   grammar is something invented and refined by society to make the best possible representation of a thought.

    c.   grammar is a hampering discipline.

    d.   real freedom in thought and style stems from exercising one's self-discipline.

DISCUSSION QUESTIONS

1. According to Crosby and Estey, what are some of the results of modern language research? Do these results support a policy of "anything goes"?

2. In what ways does Standard American reflect the American character?

3. What forces are working to eliminate dialect distinctions?

4. Why have Americans tended to be stricter with grammar than their English peers?

5. How is grammar a part of freedom, rather than a discipline?

WRITING SUGGESTIONS

1. Develop the following statement into a theme: "Modern language research shows that language is an arbitrary system of symbols set up by society."

2. Read the chapters on usage in several high school or college freshman texts. Summarize their advice; does it contrast or compare with that given by Crosby and Estey?

3. Write a theme that illustrates the importance of grammar as a means to educational, economic, and social status.

Recommended Readings to Part X

Bryant, Margaret M. *Current American Usage*. New York: Funk and Wagnalls, 1962.

Evans, Bergen, and Cornelia Evans. *Dictionary of Contemporary Usage*. New York: Random House, 1957.

Follett, Wilson. *Modern American Usage*. New York: Hill & Wang, 1966.

Hall, Robert A., Jr. *Leave Your Language Alone!* New York: Linguistica, 1950.

Hook, J. N., and E. G. Mathews. *Modern American Grammar and Usage*. New York: Ronald Press, 1956.

Quirk, Randolph. *The Use of English*. New York: St. Martin's Press, 1962.